Malaysian Cinema in the New Millennium

Crossings: Asian Cinema and Media Culture

Editors: Po-shek Fu (University of Illinois, Urbana-Champaign) and Man-Fung Yip (University of Oklahoma)

The series "Crossings" publishes books in English and Chinese that investigate Asian cinema and media from cross-disciplinary and cross-methodological perspectives. It situates Asian cinema and media within a global or regional framework and explores different dimensions of transnationality in relation to production, distribution, and reception. It also entails trans-medial interrogations of past and present media culture, looking into the complex interactions of media forms and how they have shaped aesthetic and social practices. Wide-ranging in scope and method, the series places special emphasis on cutting-edge scholarship that draws on careful archival research or derives from vigorous, insightful theoretical study.

Also in the series:

Chinese Cinema: Identity, Power, and Globalization
Edited by Jeff Kyong-McClain, Russell Meeuf, and Jing Jing Chang

Screening Communities: Negotiating Narratives of Empire, Nation, and the Cold War in Hong Kong Cinema
Jing Jing Chang

Remapping the Sinophone: The Cultural Production of Chinese-Language Cinema in Singapore and Malaya before and during the Cold War
Wai-Siam Hee

Malaysian Cinema in the New Millennium

Transcendence beyond Multiculturalism

Adrian Yuen Beng Lee

Hong Kong University Press
The University of Hong Kong
Pokfulam Road
Hong Kong
https://hkupress.hku.hk

© 2022 Hong Kong University Press

ISBN 978-988-8528-52-3 (*Hardback*)

All rights reserved. No portion of this publication may be reproduced or transmitted in any form or by any means, electronic or mechanical, including photocopying, recording, or any information storage or retrieval system, without prior permission in writing from the publisher.

British Library Cataloguing-in-Publication Data
A catalogue record for this book is available from the British Library.

Digitally printed

For my mother
Evelyn Kua Eng Choo
without you, this book would not have been possible

Thank you for
reminding me to study as hard as possible because
"education never goes to waste"
Thank you for telling me to always
"aim for the moon and if you fail you would still land amongst the stars"
and for believing that I would be a doctor, somewhat, despite being a
"slow starter who always caught up and zoomed ahead"
and for admitting that you
"never expected me to be a lecturer, never in your wildest dreams"
Thank you, Ma

Contents

List of Figures	viii
Acknowledgements	x
Introduction: The Malaysian Digital Indies and a Cinema beyond Multiculturalism: New Forms, Aesthetics, and Genres in post-2000 Malaysian Cinema	1
1. The Malaysian Digital Indies (MDI): Transnational Malaysian Cinema, Problematising the National	24
2. The Malaysian Digital Indies: A Digital Independent Transnational Cinema	58
3. 'Beyond Multiculturalism': The Malaysian Postethnic Cosmopolitan Cinema	100
4. 'The Malaysian Decade of Horror': The Malaysian Horror Renaissance	158
5. Conclusion: Towards the Fourth Phase of Malaysian Cinema	190
Filmography: Malaysian Films	199
Filmography: Non-Malaysian Films	213
Appendix I: Database for the Malaysian Digital Indies, 2000–2011	219
Appendix II: Database for Commercial Mainstream Films in Post-2000 Malaysian Cinema, 2000–2011	229
Appendix III: Database for Horror Films in Post-2000 Malaysian Cinema, 2000–2011	246
References	250
Index	272

Figures

Figure 0.1:	Film poster from New Capitol Theatre	2
Figure 0.2:	Plaza Cinema Seremban circa 1945	3
Figure 0.3:	Film poster of *Jagat*	9
Figure 0.4:	Shanjey Kumar Perumal at the New York Asian Film Festival (NYAFF) 2016	10
Figure 0.5:	Film poster of *Lelaki Harapan Dunia*	11
Figure 0.6:	A scene from *Lelaki Harapan Dunia*	12
Figure 1.1:	Film poster of *Sepet*	26
Figure 1.2:	P. Ramlee and music composer Ooi Eow Jin going into the forest to provide emotional support for the soldiers who were defending Malaya from the Communists circa 1960s	48
Figure 2.1:	Liew Seng Tat receiving the VPRO Tiger Award at the International Film Festival Rotterdam 2008	62
Figure 2.2:	Film poster of *Flower in the Pocket*	81
Figure 3.1:	Film poster of *Gadoh*	121
Figure 3.2:	The student cast of *Gadoh*	122
Figure 3.3:	Lee Ah Seng appears on television	128
Figure 3.4:	A scene from *Welcome to Kampong Radioaktif*	130
Figure 3.5:	Orked, Pak Inom, and Mak Atan during a birthday celebration	137
Figure 3.6:	Yasmin Ahmad in her office	140
Figure 3.7:	Yasmin Ahmad during the *Talentime* premiere in Kuala Lumpur, Malaysia	149
Figure 3.8:	Yasmin Ahmad on set for *Mukhsin* 2006	151
Figure 3.9:	On the film set of *Sepet*	156
Figure 3.10:	Yasmin Ahmad taking a break during the production of *Sepet*	157

Figures

Figure 4.1:	Film poster of *Zombitopia*	160
Figure 4.2:	Behind the scenes of *Zombitopia*	160
Figure 5.1:	Film poster of *Barbarian Invasion*	194
Figure 5.2:	Behind the scenes of *Barbarian Invasion*	194
Figure 5.3:	Film screening of the Freedom Film Festival Georgetown Penang 2018	195

Acknowledgements

The journey in the writing of this book has been difficult but doable. It would have been even more difficult, trying, and lonely if I had not been blessed with individuals who are truly generous, sincere, and patiently accompanying me along this journey and making a rocky road smooth. Thank you to all who have helped me along the way. God; Mama Mary; my wife Cynthia Lai Uin Rue; my parents John Lee Fok Chong and Evelyn Kua Eng Choo; Ket Meng Cheong and Bee Eng Cheong; Kua Tai Heng; Lee Yee Ping; Audrey Yue; Fran Martin; Mahyuddin Ahmad; Candida Jau Emang; Frizki Yulianti Nurnisya; Anna Agustina; Emily Yapp; Santi Indra Astuti; Jerry Tan; Yeni Rosilawati; Abdullah Ahmad Badawi; The Ministry of Higher Education Malaysia; Universiti Sains Malaysia; the RAKYAT Malaysia; Ismail Hashim; Gopalan Ravindran; N. V. Prasad; Hassan Abdul Muthalib; Siti Suhada Ahmad Fauzi; Wong Tuck Cheong; Yasmin Ahmad; Orked Ahmad; Liew Seng Tat; Ho Yuhang; Nam Ron; Amir Muhammad; Shanjey Kumar Perumal; Woo Ming Jin; Xhian Way; David Yanez; James Lee; Adibah Noor; Brenda Danker; Odeng Hj. Latif; Ujang Hj. Latif; RosKassim; Izzuddin Ramli; Shaktivel Pathmanathan; Azmyl Yunor; Yap Xhian Way; Sarata Balaya; Mayco Santaella; Dusan Petkovic; Elaine Khaw; Ooi Eow Jin; Wong Jinkei, Alina; Sheldon Chong; Adibah Noor; Thinh Nguyen; Delma Lamb; Kenneth Yung and to all individuals who have helped and encouraged me along the way.

Thank you. Terima kasih. 谢谢. நன்றி

Introduction: The Malaysian Digital Indies and a Cinema beyond Multiculturalism: New Forms, Aesthetics, and Genres in Post-2000 Malaysian Cinema

'Malaysia got cinema wan meh?' 'Oh, you mean go to the cinema to watch films?' 'Malaysian cinema . . . all Malay films wan right?' 'What is there to study about Malaysian cinema?' 'Why are you studying about Malaysian cinema in Australia?' 'Malay films mostly are about ghosts, love and gangsters, right?' 'You mean P. Ramlee films?' 'Are Malaysian films . . . worth watching?' 'If we don't study about Malaysian cinema, who would study it then?' 'Yeah, I only remember *Sepet* made by Yasmin Ahmad, right?' 'Malaysian films got nice films to watch?' 'Malaysian films are Malay films what . . .' 'Ya, I know Yasmin, she made all the television commercials that made me think back of the good old days.' 'Pontianak films?'

The above responses were among some honest opinions that I received when friends, family members, and academics asked me what the content for this book was about. Malaysian cinema. Is there a sustainable cinematic industry that can appeal to the multiethnic and multicultural population, or does this multiethnic and multicultural population feel a sense of attachment towards being represented by the cinematic representations of this cinema in a nation of 33 million?

The journey in writing this book did begin with my own sense of curiosity that led towards an exploration into what Malaysian cinema is truly all about. Growing up in Malaysia, I had a sense of attachment to Hollywood films. I must admit that I also had a curiosity in browsing through the local dailies just to find out the titles of the latest releases in the local cinemas. This was, of course, before the time of the invention of cineplexes and when cinema halls in Malaysia were standalone buildings such as Odeon, Capitol, Rex, Lido, Ruby, and Cathay that eventually replaced the 'wayang pacak' set up at the various *kampungs* (villages).

These cinema halls that were built in the towns were commonly referred to as 'theatres' or 'pictures' and are the legacies of the cinema chains of the Shaw Brothers and Cathay-Keris that experienced their heyday in the 1950s to the 1990s. These cinema halls eventually closed, and the buildings made into little shops selling items that were sold at warehouse prices. The audiences that visited these cinemas were indeed from various ethnic backgrounds, and the experience of watching a film in them was one that moved beyond multiculturalism.

Figure 0.1: Film poster from New Capitol Theatre. Source: Izzuddin Ramli.

I have vivid memories of visiting these cinemas, the first being an invite by my late uncle who worked as a caretaker/projectionist at a cinema in Malacca. He presented me with my first literal peek into the cinema world when he opened a little window at the back of the cinema to give me a glimpse into the film being shown. As I was not tall enough, I remember being lifted so that I could look through the small window. While I have no memory of the on-screen images, I do recall hearing the grinding projector. Little did I know that this was possibly the start of my journey into the cinema world.

I did not have the opportunity to watch films in these cinemas during the 1950s to the 1980s and missed out on experiencing classics such as *Ben Hur* (1959), *The Sound of Music* (1965), *The Terminator* (1984), and *Back to the Future* (1985). The films I watched growing up were screened on the three local terrestrial channels and were limited to the weekend cigarette company sponsored featured films on television known as the 'Dunhill Double' or 'Perilly's Action Movies', or there were the options of watching Hong Kong or Bollywood films. On the other hand, there were the options of watching films on the VHS (and laser disc), which was a rare treat at home. The viewing of films on the VHS was a challenge for the magnetic tape would often dislodge or 'come out' or be ruined by fungus. These tapes also need to be rewound to the beginning after watching. As there was no remote control then,

Introduction

Figure 0.2: Plaza Cinema Seremban circa 1945. Source: Sakthivel Pathmanathan.

I became the human remote control. I could well predict the plot of many films, which led to my mum asking, did you direct this? You should be a film director (which was and is not the number one choice of occupation for the child of Asian parents), leading me to wanting to experience my first film at a cinema. Most people who grew up in Seremban before the 2000s would be familiar with the 'naughtier' posters put up at a local cinema that infamously screened 'not suitable for kids' and adult-themed films.

To experience my first film in a cinema, in 1993, I had to take a bus to the Rex cinema in Seremban and wait almost an hour before the gates opened, so that I could purchase a ticket to *Jurassic Park*. When the caretakers attempted to open the shutters to the ticket booth, I was standing at the front of the line and was constantly pushed into the shutters, due to the unruly crowd. This was when there was no internet purchasing of tickets. When the shutters did open, I had no idea what to do or where to go, and it appeared that the other cinemagoers, who were from all ethnic backgrounds, had no idea what queuing up meant. Noticing the mad dash to purchase tickets for the film, I soon realized that I had to purchase the ticket from a ticket booth. I was fortunate enough to get one, as they quickly sold out.

Malaysians who had the opportunity to visit these standalone cinema halls can vividly share some of the memories of watching a film in them. The first memory is the entrance to the cinema, mostly a stairway. At the entrance were huge glass casings that contained film posters of 'now showing' or 'next change' films. The purchasing of the ticket was done through a ticket booth via a little glass opening. Next was the snack counter that did not sell popcorn but rather a variety of snacks such as *kuaci* (pumpkin seeds), *kacang putih* (local nuts), and *murukku* (Indian snacks), cuttlefish, fruits, and crisps sold in a cone-shaped wrapper. The staff at these cinemas did not wear matching uniforms but were mostly politely and respectfully greeted as 'uncle'. The entrance to the cinema hall was closed by a heavy curtain, and cinemagoers had to present their tickets to the uncle, who either ushered them to their seats or used a torchlight as a guide towards the area where the seats were located.

The journey to the seat itself was memorable, as cinemagoers had to walk onto *kuaci* seed shells, chewing gum, wrappers; and at times, an 'unknown creature', suspected to be a mouse, could run over their feet. Woe to those who chose to wear slippers instead of shoes. Over time, the seats changed from a foldable wooden seat to one that had a worn-out cushion. As smoking was permitted at that time, I remember the beam from the projector being clouded by the grey cigarette smoke that floated upwards, accompanied by the grinding sound of the projector. Pity the projectionist should the sound suddenly go off or should he be unable to replace the reel in time, as he missed the 'cigarette burn', for this would be greeted by loud jeers and booing. Air-conditioning was eventually introduced, so cinemagoers had the opportunity of experiencing watching films from a higher floor (or the balcony) and paying a higher price. Little did we know that hot air moves upwards, and eventually the entire cinema hall became air-conditioned.

Growing up, I had only heard the term 'Malay films' and was never exposed to the term Malaysian cinema until the 2000s. The term Malay films was simply an accepted term to describe Malaysian cinema, as Malaysian films mostly portrayed Malay actors, speaking in the Malay language, and highlighting issues faced by the Malay community. The films also commonly revolved around the melodramatic elements of melodramatic elements of *suka* (love), *duka* (tragedy), and *jenaka* (humour). The titles were also in Malay, and I hardly recall a non-Malay name in the opening and end credits in Malaysian films. Like so many other Malaysians, I am accustomed to preferring Hollywood-, Hong Kong-, and Bollywood-made films. Such trends continue, as Malaysian cinemagoers still prefer watching Hollywood, Hong Kong, and Bollywood films over Malaysian-made films in cineplexes.

And like so many other Malaysians who, when asked what their favourite Malaysian film is, or who is their favourite Malaysian filmmaker, would either locate and point to Malaysian cinema in the 1960s to the films of P. Ramlee or to the 2000s to the films of Yasmin Ahmad. I too found myself similarly guilty of this, probably due to the lack of exposure or even interest in Malaysian cinema. Even as a university student who majored in film, I do not recall watching Malaysian-made films, other than *Amok* (1995), nor were there many discussions about Malaysian films or about their rich history. This situation remains unchanged despite Malaysian films and filmmakers winning numerous accolades in film festivals and competitions abroad. The exposure about the importance of preserving the rich cultural heritage of Malaysian cinema remains wanting. The study of Malaysian cinema within the public and private institutions of higher education that offer film studies or communication programmes still do not place much importance on the study of Malaysian cinema. Ironically, it was in Australia where I found my interest in

Introduction

examining Malaysian cinema, and it was in Singapore where I managed to watch many Malaysian films that were unavailable in Malaysia at that time.

Through my study of Malaysian cinema, I truly understood how cinema exists as a capitalist venture. This is for these cultural products that exist as a form of capitalist products to generate maximum revenue located within the production modes of a capitalist system (Garnham 1992). The films that exist as cultural products within a capitalist system would therefore disseminate dominant ideas as envisioned by the State, for its production, distribution, and exhibition processes are controlled by the State. By understanding that a cinema industry exists within a certain context within a certain society, I also understood how cinema cannot exist within a vacuum (Hayward 1996). Alongside the mainstream commercial Malaysian cinema, there existed a cinema movement on the periphery as an alternative or independent cinema. The cultural artefacts made within this independent industry also existed as a site for contesting ideas, theories, and issues and became a platform for the contestation of state policies that went against official State imaginings and control. In other words, Malaysian cinema was in fact a vibrant industry that went beyond elements of artistic practices, aesthetics and mise-en-scène, and its films were not exactly a mirror of society but became a site of contestation of ideologies and issues. Later, would I learn and come to understand that cinema exists as an economic industry based on the relations of production or on the political economy in which films are produced (Hill, 1986). I would also understand how films should not be simply viewed as a product but that it is necessary to examine and understand films as products that are highly ideological, using Althusser's (1972) notion of ideology. This understanding is also in line with cinema's ideological role in involving how spectators see images that are displayed on the screen (Rodowick 1988).

Although Malaysian cinema remains a commercial enterprise, its cinematic output has been merely mediocre at best. After the closure of the studios and the departure of their Chinese owners, most Malaysian cinematic outlets tended to screen Hollywood films, as these were deemed more profitable. Despite the departure of these studios and the closure of the standalone cinemas, cinema operators in Malaysia were mostly jointly owned or established by Malaysian and foreign companies. The largest cineplex chains in Malaysia, Golden Screen Cinemas (GSC) and Tanjung Golden Village (TGV), were once jointly owned by Hong Kong's Golden Harvest. Singapore's mm2 Asian owns mmCineplexes that purchased Cathay Cineplexes and Lotus Five Star (LFS) cinemas.[1] In the 1980s to the 1990s, most of the films screened in these cinema halls were from Hollywood. In total, approximately

---

1. In total, GSC, TGV, and LFS own approximately 600 screens in Malaysia. In 2017, LFS opened the first cinema halls in the east coast state of Kuala Terengganu, which used digital presentation facilities and Dolby Surround 7.1. In line with the guidelines on entertainment, cultural performance, tourism, and sports activities according to Syariah law, cinema patrons are required to sit in separate zones according to male and female, but families are exempted from this regulation. The east coast state Kelantan remains the only Malaysian state without a cinema after Lido Cinema closed in 1990.

123 Malaysian-made films were released from 1980 to 1989, and 129 Malaysian-made films were released from 1990 to 1999. Among the notable Malaysian-made films screened in Malaysian cinema halls during this period were *Abang* (Elder Brother, 1981), *Ali Setan* (1985), *Mr. Os* (1987), *Abang 92* (Elder Brother 92, 1993), *Sembilu* (Heartache, 1994), *Sayang Salmah* (Loving Salmah, 1995), *Maria Mariana* (1996), and *Senario The Movie* (1999).

Since 2000, Malaysian cinema has experienced a surge in cinematic output. During this time, commercial Malaysian mainstream cinema and the independent film movement, the Malaysian Digital Indies (MDI), which operated from 2000 to 2011, produced more than 350 films. From 2000 to 2021, more than 600 films of various genres such as horror, comedy, action, martial arts, animation, biopics, and shorts were produced. The new millennium also witnessed the (re)emergence of several new genres in Malaysian cinema, in particular: documentaries [*R.A.H.M.A.N.*, 2004, and *Subak*, 2008]; martial arts [*Kinta 1881*, 2008]; superhero [*Cicakman* (Lizardman), 2006]; animation [*Putih*, 2001, and *Budak Lapok* (Broke Kids), 2007]; 3D animation [*Nien Resurrection*, 2000, and *Geng: Pengembaraan Bermula* (Gang: The Adventure Begins), 2009]; and the (re)popularisation of horror [*Visits: Hungry Ghost Anthology*, 2004, and *Jangan Pandang Belakang* (Don't Look Behind), 2007].[2] The (re)popularisation of the horror genre has made it the most popular genre. *Munafik 2* (Hypocrite 2, 2018), which was made with a budget of MYR2.5 million/US$625 000, remains the highest-grossing Malaysian film at MYR48 million/US$12 million. Horror films also remain the highest-grossing genre with films such as *Munafik 2* (2018, MYR48 million/US$12 million); *Hantu Kak Limah* (Ghost of Kak Limah, 2018, MYR36 million/US$9 million); and *Munafik* (Hypocrite, 2016, MYR19.04 million/US$4.76 million) topping the box

---

2. Malaysia's first animated feature is *Silat Lagenda* (Legendary Silat, 1998). In my conversation with Hassan Muthalib on 28 July 2010, in Kuala Lumpur, he mentioned that animation has a distinct history in Malaysia due to the popularity of the *Hikayat Sang Kancil* (The Sang Kancil Chronicles) series broadcast on Malaysian television during the 1980s. He also expressed his regret at the failure of *Silat Lagenda* and *Putih* at the box office due to a lack of audiences. The perception is that animation caters to children, and the adult market for Malaysian animation feature films is non-existent. In my search for the first Malaysian 3D animation feature film, I found conflicting answers in the Malaysian newspapers and the internet. *Utusan Malaysia* stated *Geng: Pengembaraan Bermula* as the first. The *New Straits Times* stated *Nien Resurrection*. An email response from Hassan Muthalib on 7 September 2011 mentioned *Nien Resurrection* as the first Malaysian 3D animation feature, which helped clarify this matter. However, this Cantonese-speaking feature was only released in VCD format and marketed in Hong Kong, as Malaysia was not known for 3D animation back then. *Geng: Pengembaraan Bermula* became the second 3D animated feature but the first to be commercially released in Malaysian cinemas. Malaysia is also set to become the first country in South-east Asia to release a 3D feature film titled *The Hunter 3D*. The film narrates the tale of documentary filmmakers stalked by an unknown force in a rainforest in the Borneo state of Sarawak. The film is directed by Bjarne Wong and produced on a budget of MYR6 million (US$1.5 million) and utilises 3D technology from South Korean and Hong Kong martial arts techniques. *The Hunter 3D* is also multilingual (Bahasa Malaysia, English, Mandarin, and Cantonese). It involves a cast from China (Rocky Lou Qi, Cindy Chen, and Soo Wincci), Taiwan (Tavani Hu), South Korea (Harisu), and Malaysia (Isaac Ong, Carmen Soo, Koe Yeet, and Sharifah Amani and Smith Wong). At time of writing, *Mat Kilau* (2022) directed by Syamsul Yusof, became the highest grossing Malaysian film with a local box-office return of MYR96 million (USD24 million).

Introduction

office. Notably, the film *Dukun* (Shaman, 2018), which was initially banned in 2006, was released in 2018 after the ban was rescinded. The film went on to make MYR10 million/US$2.5 million. The popularity of the horror genre is followed by films from the animation genre, *Ejen Ali: The Movie* (Agent Ali: The Movie, MYR30.5 million/ US$7.6 million); *BoBoiBoy Movie 2* (MYR29.57 million/US$7.39 million); and *Upin & Ipin: Keris Siamang Tunggal* (Upin & Ipin: The Lone Gibbon Keris, MYR26.2 million/US$ 6.55million) topping the box office. Both the horror and animation genres located within the top ten highest-grossing Malaysian films had a combined box office total of MYR189.31 million/US$47.33. Among the biggest production companies that controlled the production of films are Skop Productions, Astro Shaw, MIG Productions, Grand Brilliance, and KRU Studios.

This surge in cinematic output in post-2000 Malaysian cinema is mostly attributed to the vibrant cinematic environment created by the MDI filmmakers. Beginning in 2000, the MDI filmmakers utilised transnational networks to secure sources of funding, co-production, and exhibition. Due to the availability of transnational networks and digital video (DV) technology, the films of the MDI have won numerous accolades at film festivals all over the world. Malaysian cinema of the post-2000s has been a time when Malaysian MDI filmmakers and eventually a number of commercial Malaysian mainstream cinema filmmakers have attempted to go 'beyond multiculturalism' by making films that transcended race, ethnicity creed, and colour. During this time, a number of films were no longer mono-ethnic in nature but were made by a production crew from different ethnic backgrounds and featured casts and characters from various backgrounds. The dialogue in films and film titles was also in various Malaysian languages and dialects. One name that stands out among these filmmakers is Yasmin Ahmad, who transitioned from advertising into filmmaking. Her career, though short-lived, made a significant impact on the styles, aesthetics, and themes of future filmmakers, who emulated her as a filmmaker or were inspired by her films.

Anthony Tham, a Sarawakian-born filmmaker, is one example. Tham's directorial debut, *One Day* (2020), which is available on Vimeo, features scenic locations throughout the East Malaysian states of Sabah and Sarawak through the narrative of forbidden love and tragic romance between two individuals. An engineer by training, Anthony Tham is inspired by the works of Yasmin Ahmad, as he continues to learn and be inspired by continuously watching her films (Wong, 2020). It is thus not uncommon to hear of audiences mentioning that films made by her predecessors 'have a Yasmin Ahmad feel' or are films influenced by 'Yasmin Ahmad-ism'. To commemorate the works of Yasmin Ahmad, the Yasmin Ahmad at Kong Heng Newseum houses artefacts from her filmmaking career, television commercials, as well as poetry and photographs. Set in the town of Ipoh and founded by Yasmin Ahmad's late mother, Mak Inom, and sister Orked, the Yasmin Ahmad at Kong Heng Newseum was built not only to commemorate the legacy and cultural artefacts of Yasmin Ahmad but to also inspire the next generation of filmmakers. In

2014, Yasmin Ahmad was featured as a Google Doodle to commemorate her fifty-sixth birthday. P. Ramlee was also featured in 2017 to commemorate his eighty-eighth birthday.

In essence, films made by MDI filmmakers and a number of films by commercial Malaysian mainstream cinema have attempted to move 'beyond multiculturalism'. Films such as *The Journey* (2014), *Jagat* (2015), and *Ola Bola* (2016) that were made later eventually became a platform for discussing cosmopolitan and humanitarian issues rather than focusing on issues of race, ethnicity, and religion. The usage of the theme of sports as a factor that unites beyond race and ethnicity, besides *Ola Bola*, which was inspired by the Malaysian football team qualifications for the 1980s Moscow Olympics, biopics featuring sporting figures such as Lee Chong Wei through *Lee Chong Wei* (2018) and Nicol David through the to-be-released *I Am Nicol David* have been made. Ace Pictures, which is producing *I Am Nicol David*, won the 22nd World Media Festival award in Hamburg, Germany, through its first of a three-part short series featuring mixed martial arts (MMA) fighter Agilan Thani.[3]

In other examples of Malaysian films moving beyond elements of multiculturalism, in January 2021, *Miss Andy*, which narrates the trials faced by a transgender woman living in Kuala Lumpur and discusses issues about illegal immigration, premiered in Taiwan. In 2018 and 2019, *Guang* and *Redha* narrated stories about the struggles and relationships of individuals with autism who had different learning abilities with their family members. Even the animated Upin & Ipin animated series feature film, *Geng The Adventure Begins* (2009), moves 'beyond multiculturalism' in its multi-ethnic set-up.[4] The films went 'beyond multiculturalism' by highlighting everyday issues faced by everyday people, ones that were not openly discussed in society. The main characters faced racism, poverty, inter-ethnic love, unity, and segregation, without overtly focusing on elements of race and ethnicity. The films were also screened at commercial mainstream cinemas throughout the country.

This move of going 'beyond multiculturalism' also put to question what constitutes and defines Malaysian cinema, as more Malaysian films using various languages, characters, and issues were made by Malaysians from various backgrounds. Earlier MDI films that won accolades at overseas film festivals under the Malaysian flag were, however, not recognized as Malaysian films but as a 'foreign movie' at home. These films were deemed 'foreign' and not 'Malaysian', for they did not have a 70 per cent Bahasa Malaysia dialogue. During the initial stages, a few MDI films failed to qualify for tax exemption. In 2011, Malaysian films produced with non-Bahasa Malaysia dialogues but containing Bahasa Malaysia subtitles were recognised as 'local' films.

---

3. The second short in the series will feature GT race car driver Zen Low, and the third drone-race Amir Haziq.
4. In 2014, the production company of Upin & Ipin Les' Copaque Production was bought by The Walt Disney Company (Barker and Lee 2017).

Introduction

Figure 0.3: Film poster of *Jagat*. Source: Shanjey Kumar Perumal.

The issue of what constitutes a film as 'Malaysian' was again brought to the forefront during the 28th Malaysian Film Festival. Shanjhey Kumar Perumal's Tamil language film, *Jagat* (2015), was disqualified from competing for the Best Malaysian Film. *Jagat* was instead nominated for the Best Picture in the non-Bahasa Malaysia category for national language. This disqualification was done based on the technicality that the film did not fulfil the 70 per cent requirement of a film containing dialogue in Bahasa Malaysia. The disqualification of *Jagat* led to several protests both online and offline from Malaysians and those from the film industry, who questioned if a film in the Tamil language must instead be in the Bahasa Malaysia language to be categorised or termed Malaysian. Despite calls from others to withdraw his film from and to boycott the Malaysian Film Festival, Shanjhey Kumar Perumal was resilient for he had the support of many Malaysians. This compelled the then-Multimedia and Communications Minister Salleh Said Keruak to discard those categories. Shanjey Kumar Perumal eventually won the Best Malaysian Film award for *Jagat*. The film eventually went on to win the Best Film award at the Majlis Pengkritik Filem KL (MPFKL 2016) and was also screened at the New York Asian Film Festival (NYAFF 2016).

Figure 0.4: Shanjey Kumar Perumal at the New York Asian Film Festival (NYAFF) 2016. Source: Shanjey Kumar Perumal.

Since the Golden Age of Malaysian cinema in the 1950s to the 1960s, post-2000 cinema has become another vibrant era of Malaysian filmmaking as the Digital Golden Era of Malaysian cinema. Further efforts at raising the standards of Malaysian filmmaking were made through the opening of the Pinewood-Iskandar Studios in the state of Johor, which opened in 2013. The project cost over MYR680 million/US$170 million to build and contains film stages, television studios, sound stages, dubbing and grading theatres, a forest back lot, and one of South-east Asia's largest paddock tank and deep-water tanks for under water production works. The building of this studio marks the intentions of Malaysia to establish itself as an international location for significant production to take place (Barker and Lee 2017, 2018).

During the Digital Golden Era of Malaysian cinema, Malaysian films were submitted to the Academy Awards for nominations. In total, six Malaysian made films were sent, but none made the nominations. Malaysian films were sent in 2004 (*Puteri Gunung Lendang*/Princess of Mount Ledang), 2012 (*Buhonan*/Bunohan: Return to Murder), 2015 (*Lelaki Harapan Dunia*/Men Who Save the World), 2016 (*Redha*/Beautiful Pain), 2019 (*M for Malaysia*), 2020 (*Roh*/Soul) and in 2021 (*Prebet Sapu*/Hail, Driver!). To a certain extent, Malaysia has already experienced success

Introduction   11

at the Academy Awards. *Life of Pi* (2012), which won the award for Best Visual Effects at the 2013 Academy Awards, included works from a Malaysian team at the Cyberjaya-based subsidiary company of the Californian special effects company Rhythm and Hues. The Malaysian team had worked on the texturing of the tiger's fur (Barker and Lee 2017). When *Parasite* won the award for Best Picture at the 2019 Academy Awards, Minister of Communications and Multimedia Saifuddin Abdullah launched a plan for a Malaysian film to win an Academy Award. Dubbed 'Project Oscar', the target was to eventually work on a long-term plan and strategy of landing an Academy Award for a Malaysian film. This plan, launched in 2020, seemed to be put on hold, as that year was not sympathetic to the film industry in Malaysia.

Figure 0.5: Film poster of *Lelaki Harapan Dunia*. Source: Liew Seng Tat.

Figure 0.6: A scene from *Lelaki Harapan Dunia*. Source: Liew Seng Tat.

In 2020, cities around the world were placed under lockdown as part of efforts to contain the spread of the novel coronavirus, COVID-19. These lockdowns were efforts by governments across the world to contain the spread of the virus by preventing people from moving around, to break the chain of infections. In the early days of the pandemic, the media was abuzz with images and scenes of empty cities and streets. These scenes were eerily like those from a post-apocalyptic film, as city streets around the world became void of vehicular or human presence. In Malaysia, efforts to contain the spread of the virus were made through the various lockdown phases known as the Movement Control Order (MCO). During the MCO, activities that involved large gatherings of people were not allowed. As such, film activities such as watching films in cinemas and film productions were initially not allowed, causing film production and film premieres to be halted. In addition, cinema halls were momentarily closed every now and then, according to the various MCO periods. Film shoots were also limited to strict standard operating procedures (SOPs) that severely hampered the output of films. These situations caused cinematic output and attendance to be at its lowest in the post-2000 Malaysian cinema era.

Kerana Korona (Because of Corona, 2021) by Khabir Bakthiar became the first Malaysian film to narrate the experiences of Malaysians living their lives under the MCO. Produced by Astro Shaw, *Kerana Korona* was the first film to be released by the company in 2021. As cinema halls were not permitted to operate during

Introduction

the MCO, the film premiered on Astro First, a movie-on-demand service exclusive for Malaysian films in Malaysian homes. The film brings together three storylines that intertwine between a couple who grow increasingly distant despite spending more time at home and their son who breaches the MCO lockdown; a medical doctor who faces a workplace dilemma; and an elderly man who ignores the SOPs during the lockdown, causing unnecessary worry to his neighbour. The storylines in *Kerana Korona* are based on true stories and are aimed at creating messages of hope and unity amidst a time of despair and uncertainty during a pandemic.

In 2020, Malaysia also witnessed a political crisis that resulted in a change of the Malaysian government. In February 2020, Tun Dr Mahathir Mohamad announced his resignation as the seventh Malaysian prime minister and subsequently the collapse of his Pakatan Harapan (PH) government. The PH government, which was elected to power in the 2018 general election, was founded on 22 September 2015 and formed by a coalition of the Malaysian United Indigenous Party (Parti Pribumi Bersatu Malaysia, PPBM/BERSATU), the Democratic Action Party (DAP), People's Justice Party (Parti Keadilan Rakyat/KeAdilan), and National Trust Party (Parti Amanah Negara/AMANAH). The main allied political parties of PH are Sabah Heritage Party (Parti Warisan Sabah/WARISAN), United Progressive Kinabalu Organisation (Pertubuhan Kinabalu Progresif Bersatu/UPKO), and United Sarawak Party (Parti Sarawak Bersatu/PSB). The PH government came into power in 2018, after it ousted the ruling Barisan Nasional, which had been in power since the nation's independence. The journey of the PH coalition during the 2018 general election was documented through *M for Malaysia* (2019). Co-directed by Dian Lee and Ineza Rousille, the ninety-two-minute-long documentary captures how the ninety-two-year-old Mahathir Mohamad led the PH coalition to effectively win the general election and become the world's oldest prime minister. The film was screened at the CAAM Festival in San Francisco (2019), DocEdge Film Festival in New Zealand (2019), and Busan International Film Festival (BIFF).

The 2020 Malaysian political crisis, infamously dubbed the 'Sheraton Move', witnessed several members of parliament from the ruling PH government defecting to form a coalition with opposition parties United Malays National Organisation (UMNO) and Parti Islam SeMalaysia (PAS) to form the Perikatan Nasional government. This political defection was aimed at forming a full Malay and Muslim unity government. Among the reasons that led to the downfall of the PH government were ideological differences, infighting between the political parties about the handover date of the position of prime minister from Mahathir Mohamad to opposition leader and former prime minister Anwar Ibrahim, the defection of BERSATU and KeAdilan members of parliament from the PH coalition, and the eventual withdrawal of BERSATU from the PH coalition. This state of uncertainty eventually led to the Yang DiPertuan Agong (the Malaysian King) calling for an individual meeting with every member of parliament to enquire about their preferred candidate for the next prime minister. The Yang DiPertuan Agong eventually appointed Muhyiddin Yassin, president of BERSATU, as the eighth Malaysian prime minister.

The political and health crises were certainly not in line with Mahathir Mohamad's Vision 2020. When Vision 2020 was introduced in 1990, it envisioned a nation that would be fully developed politically, economically, and culturally. In 2020, Malaysians were foreseen to be travelling around in flying cars, living in high-rises, in high-end condominiums, and earning wages equalling those of an industrialised nation. The nation and its people would be prosperous, living high-quality and high-standard lives, and governed by a democratic and stable government. Malaysians would also be a developed nation that is united and equal under the *Bangsa* Malaysia concept. The *Bangsa* Malaysia concept mooted by Vision 2020 had envisioned a 'postethnic' nation, of a united Malaysian nation that looked beyond race, ethnicity, and religion. This Malaysian nation as envisioned by former Prime Minister Mahathir Mohamad also would have fostered and developed a mature democratic political system and a prosperous and just economy that is competitive, dynamic, robust, and resilient, where the wealth of the nation is equally distributed. Malaysia would also be a world leader in science and technology, a fully industrialised nation established in scientific progression. In short, Vision 2020 outlined nine challenges to developing a nation that is united and prosperous, free-spirited, democratised, liberal, scientific, progressive, loving, and has a fair economic system.

As Malaysia continues to cope with the COVID-19 pandemic, the Digital Golden Era of Malaysian cinema, which witnessed the output of more than 600 films, ended the decade with only fourteen films released in 2020. In 2021, only three Malaysian films have been released thus far, a far cry from the cinematic output of the previous two decades. Malaysian cinema halls remain closed, have merged, or ceased operations. The post-2000 era of Malaysian cinema has however, elevated the status of Malaysian cinema from a relatively dormant cinematic industry to one that has witnessed Malaysian films being screened at all film festivals and competitions on all continents. In essence, this vibrant filmmaking atmosphere was made possible with the advent of DV technology, the internet, independent filmmaking, and transnational networks that provided opportunities for co-production, funding, exhibition, and distribution. These factors have contributed to the emergence of the independent film movement dubbed the 'Malaysian Digital Indies' (MDI), and the vibrant filmmaking environment that it functioned in from 2000 to 2011, which is the focus of this book.

A study of this independent cinema will offer a new critical and updated approach to understanding the socio-cultural context and political economy of Malaysian cinema by examining the rise of the MDI, an informal film movement within the context of post-2000 Malaysian cinema. This book discusses how the MDI consists of a new generation of urban-based and cine-literate Malaysian filmmakers who have created a new kind of cinema in Malaysia by choosing to bypass local cinematic regulations and conventions. These filmmakers have a preference for transnational filmmaking methods and DV technology and do not rely on state support. Emerging from national developments and policies, the MDI speaks for and against these policies, using transnational aesthetics, themes, and methods of production, exhibition, and distribution. Being independent and free from state regulations and censorship has allowed them to champion a culturally diverse cinema using cosmopolitan themes and new aesthetic forms. These themes and forms have enabled them to make transnational films, deconstruct the stereotypes of race and ethnicity established in Malaysian cinema, question national policies, and propound a new national identity. Their emergence and presence within local and international cinematic circuits have alleviated the formerly dismal state of Malaysian cinema.

This book intends to be part of the studies of Malaysian cinema, representations of multiculturalism in cinema, and independent cinema in Malaysia. In many ways, it focuses on a new inquiry of Malaysian cinema by examining how the MDI has from 2000 to 2011 repositioned Malaysian cinema within the global arena by achieving significant international acclaim. The MDI situates itself as a film movement among the burgeoning fields of transnational Asian cinema as a result of new critical approaches to state governance and nation-building policies in the region caused by the democratisation of social space. While these factors have significantly had an impact on Malaysian cinema, it is also essential to explore how Malaysian cinema responds to forces of globalisation and neoliberalism. The MDI emerged in an age of (post-) fin-de-sièclisme, as a whole series of questions regarding national identity and nationalism are being raised (Hayward 1993, 5).

This book will therefore explore the political economy and new forms and genres of the MDI and its relation to mainstream commercial cinema through the genres of horror and social realist film. As transnational flows mediate many aspects of contemporary culture, the MDI positions itself as a transnational cinema by displacing and deterritorialising itself from the context of the national. Spurred on by the uncontainable waves of globalisation, repressive cinematic regulations, and the advent of multimedia, the MDI negotiates and contests race and ethnicity, national identity, and culture, through a framework of transnational cinema. A theoretical approach combining transnational and postcolonial studies, and critiques of neoliberalism in Asian cultural studies, will be attempted to illustrate how MDI functions as a site for questioning and proposing a new national identity in the era of advanced global capitalism.

This book offers a new approach to the study of multiculturalism in cinema by examining how the MDI, as an informal film culture, champions cultural diversity using cosmopolitan themes. It is these cosmopolitan themes that enable the MDI to be transnational, as it actively cultivates issues of interracial relationships, cultural and ethnic diversity, humanistic philosophies and universalism, and ideals of global justice to emerge as a 'postethnic cosmopolitan cinema'.[5] This postethnic cosmopolitan cinema envisions a Malaysian nation coexisting harmoniously through cultural diversity, racial, ethnic and religious tolerance, which challenges the backdrop of Malaysian cinema commonly built on ethnic exclusivity.

This book provides a new account of independent cinema in Malaysia. It is also timely, as the MDI emerged alongside current cinematic developments in other regional cinemas that are amid massive transformations blending local culture, European art cinema, independent filmmaking methods, and using transnational connections. I refer to such films as Hong Kong's Fruit Chan- directed *Durian Durian* (2000) and *Public Toilet* (2002), Singapore's Eric Khoo-directed *Be with Me* (2005) and *No Day Off* (2006), The Philippines' Raymond Red-directed *Manila Skies* (2009), Thailand's Apichatpong Weerasethakul-directed *Uncle Boonmee Who Can Recall His Past Lives* (2010), and Australia's Kriv Stender-directed *Boxing Day* (2007). These films have been extensively exhibited, winning accolades at overseas film festivals.

As MDI films have achieved similar accomplishments, this book adopts a new approach and new scholarship to the existing journal articles, newspapers, and online reviews about the MDI. The reason is that independent cinemas such as the Chinese Sixth Generation cinema (Lau 2003; Mo and Xiao 2006; Pickowicz and Zhang 2006), Hong Kong's digital independent cinema (Yau 2001; Morris 2004; Cheung, Marchetti, and Tan 2011), and Thailand's new independent 'New Wave' (Chaiworaporn and Knee 2006; Hunt 2005; Harrison 2005) have been extensively studied, yet these are only modest accounts of the MDI. This book will therefore comprehensively study how the MDI, like its cinematic counterparts, has produced independent films that challenge state regulations and censorship and has secured alternative methods of funding, production, distribution, and exhibition.

The inspiration for this book is derived from the experience I gained as a full-time academic, teaching in private and public universities in Malaysia, and as a "free-time filmmaker", making films when I have the free-time to do so. I wanted to personally experience the process of independent filmmaking and to better understand this process from the research, production, post-production, and exhibition stages, as I personally believe that there is nothing more practical than theories by putting theories into practice. As I teach film production and film theory, I have been heavily involved in working alongside my students to produce shorts for film competitions and festivals. I decided to utilise my knowledge and experience of being involved in the production of television commercials, corporate, training, and event videos into directing my own short films. I then ventured into documenting dying arts and crafts, by making short documentaries through Adrian Lee's Reel Heritage Series. My notable short documentaries are *Barber Kubur* (2017) and

---

5. This concept will be dealt with in Chapter 3.

Introduction 17

The Little Dhoby of Penang (2018), which have been screened in film festivals in Malaysia and abroad.

During the early 2000s, I noticed the rise of the MDI and got to know the key filmmakers of this movement. I employed the approach of Asian cultural studies and interdisciplinary studies. This approach used methodologies such as archival studies of film databases, policy research about films, and fieldwork, which was undertaken during three trips to Malaysia from 2009 to 2010 when I was studying for my PhD in Melbourne. I also analysed over 300 films made by directors of post-2000 Malaysian cinema, over one hundred films from the 1940s to the 1990s, and over one hundred films made by directors from Asia, Europe, and the United States. This required me to spend more than 750 hours of non-continuous viewing of Malaysian films such as *The Elephant and the Sea* (2007) and *Gadoh* (Fight, 2009), and non-Malaysian films such as *Mee Pok Man* (1996) and *The Blair Witch Project* (1999). To further comprehend the cinematic styles and themes of Malaysian cinema, I viewed more than one hundred films from every decade of the 1950s until the 1990s. Films such as *Nujum Pak Belalang* (Pak Belalang the Astrologer, 1959), *Hang Jebat* (1961), *Menanti Hari Esok* (Waiting for Tomorrow, 1977), *Mekanik* (Mechanic, 1983), and *Kaki Bakar* (The Arsonist, 1995) provided me with a clearer understanding of the socio-cultural and political conditions of the nation and its cinema at a given moment. I also studied unattainable films such as *Pontianak* (1957), *Min* (2003), and *Chemman Chaalai* using reviews and analyses written on online blogs and websites such as Variety.com, The Internet Movie Database (IMDb), Criticine.com; Malaysian and international magazines, newspaper articles in publications such as *The Star*, *The Jakarta Post*, *Utusan Malaysia*, and *The New York Times;* and academic literature from journals and conferences such as *Inter-Asia Cultural Studies*, *Journal of Southeast Asian Studies*, and *The Journal of Cultural Studies.*[6]

I then categorised these films into databases which are attached as appendices to this book. These databases provide an outline of Malaysian cinema and the MDI within the context of post-2000 Malaysian cinema. They separate filmmakers and their films into the categories of MDI (Appendix I), mainstream (Appendix II), and horror films (Appendix III), list and classify information such as filmmakers, film titles, languages used, and genres.

I also conducted fieldwork in Malaysia to get a clearer understanding of the organisation of Malaysian cinema. This fieldwork allowed me to better comprehend the values and ideology of filmmakers and their social signification in their

---

6. Although I managed to correspond with Yasmin Ahmad through email on 6 May 2009, before she passed away on 25 July 2009, I used her online blog entries, Yasmin the Storyteller and Yasmin the Filmmaker, to search for details and information about her films, thoughts, and personal life. Online social networking sites such as Facebook, Twitter, and malaysian-cinema@yahoogroups.com have kept me posted with the latest in Malaysian cinema and allowed me to correspond with filmmakers such as Woo Ming Jin, Ng Tian Hann, and Zan Azlee.

film narratives. During this fieldwork, I organised visits to The National Film Development Corporation (FINAS), production houses such as Da Huang Pictures, and informal film clubs, screenings, and film festivals held at Kelab Seni Filem (Malaysian Film Club). They provided me with an understanding of the political economy of Malaysian cinema. During my visit to FINAS, Siti Suhada Ahmad Fauzi (Deputy Director 2 from the Promotion Unit) explained in detail the film policies, licence requirements, and censorship regulations in Malaysia.[7] I was also permitted to gain access to the resource centre and library and to tour the vicinity to get a clearer understanding of the facilities available. I also visited the National Archives Singapore to watch Malaysian films that were made available due to proper archiving.

I then visited prominent key players in Malaysian cinema such as independent filmmakers James Lee, director of *The Beautiful Washing Machine*; Amir Muhammad, director of *Malaysian Gods* (2009); and Nam Ron, director of *Gedebe* (Gangster, 2003); filmmaker and academician Hassan Muthalib (who has been involved in Malaysian cinema since the Golden Age of Malaysian cinema); and Kelab Seni Filem founder Wong Tuck Cheong.[8]

Speaking to representatives from state, mainstream, and independent filmmaking provided me with a critical understanding of the political economy of Malaysian cinema. As a result of these approaches, in-depth data and information regarding the political economy, genres, and aesthetics of the MDI and Malaysian cinema were collected. By critically offering an in-depth examination of the MDI and their articulations to the regional genres and global industrial developments, this approach has also allowed an understanding of the socio-cultural context and political economy contexts of Malaysia and its cinema. The MDI, therefore, emerged alongside a series of state policies and national events.

Before publication, some materials from this book were rewritten and published as articles in academic journals such as *Wacana Seni: Journal of Arts Discourse*, *Pertanika: Journal of Social Sciences*, and *Kemanusiaan: The Asian Journal of Humanities*, and in an academic booklet at the Busan International Film Festival Forum BIFF 2019. Some materials from this book have also been published as book chapters in *Transnational Chinese Cinemas: Corporeality, Desire, and Ethics* and *Antologi Esei Komunikasi Vol. 1*; and presented at various conferences and forums in Malaysia, the United Kingdom, Singapore, South Korea, Australia, Japan,

---

7. In a conversation in Kuala Lumpur with Siti Suhada Ahmad Fauzi on 22 July 2011, she mentioned that filmmakers are required to obtain a permit from FINAS before production is allowed to begin. Once production is completed, a licence from Lembaga Penapisan Filem (LPF) or Malaysian Censorship Board is required for films to be screened at local mainstream exhibition circuits.

8. Nam Ron (loosely translated as 'hot water' in Thai) was a former student and part-time lecturer at the Akademi Seni Budaya dan Warisan Kebangsaan (ASWARA). Trained as an auto-mechanic, he studied the arts of theatre at Akademi Seni Kebangsaan (ASK) in 1994. His feature *Gedebe* is an experimental film inspired by Shakespeare's *Julius Ceasar* that satirically narrates the political relationship between Mahathir Mohammad and Anwar Ibrahim.

Introduction   19

and Indonesia. I have also written articles about Malaysian cinema in my media columns at MalayMail.com and Aliran.com.

Chapter Outline

Chapter 1 discusses how Malaysian cinema has been subjected to the forces of capital and state control. Malaysian cinema has always been a transnational cinema, as each phase of Malaysian cinema has been built on transnational forces and utilised to contest various issues. The rise of the MDI makes Malaysian cinema transnational in new ways in the post-2000 era. This chapter also discusses how, according to state imaginings, cinema has been utilised as a site for contesting exclusion and inclusion. Issues of race, ethnicity, and class are often manipulated within the general production of Malaysian cinema. In line with state policies of creating an ideal middle-class Malay society from the 1970s, this process had sidelined other ethnic minorities. These marginalised communities experienced a form of social and cultural negation and potentially longed for the shared space of cultural identity from which they were excluded. It is crucial to examine the importance of capital and policy control in determining the nature of culture, class, and consumption. Malaysian cinema is not exclusive of politics, mainly when race and ethnicity is a fault line within that cinema. The chapter also discusses a detailed history of how Malaysian cinema has always been a transnational cinema. This begins with how cinema's formation during the era of colonisation and decolonisation using the transnational framework resulted in a heterogeneous multicultural cinema and how modernisation and the neoliberal policies of the 1980s and the 1990s have pushed for creating the ideal middle-class Malay society.

Chapter 2 identifies, defines, and examines this new independent cinema; it also examines the political economy of the MDI and how it came into existence through the different socio-cultural and political changes within an era of intensified modernisation and globalisation. The chapter then outlines the modus operandi of the MDI by examining the transnational production, exhibition, and distribution methods employed. Although this film movement is not entirely a 'radical' cinema, nor does it amount to being anti-establishment, it provides a space for the critical discourse in the socio-cultural and political representations of contemporary Malaysia. This chapter also examines how the MDI has elevated the status of a relatively unknown Malaysian cinema. Using digital technology and the internet, the MDI contests and renegotiates national policies and ethnic and national identities. These transnational methods have allowed the MDI to bypass repressive cinematic regulations while breaking and ignoring habituated cinematic conventions and traditions. This ideology, which discusses taboo subject matter and themes such as politics, ethnicity, sexuality, marginalisation, and gender, depicts a more positive construction and more even-handed representation of society. While not formally belonging to an established organisation or movement, MDI filmmakers have established a distinctively new set of filmmaking elements. These new elements are created through new transnational production methods and funding, distribution and exhibition, and a new audience that relates to the subject matter and themes.

Chapter 3 locates the works of the MDI within the framework of a 'postethnic cosmopolitan cinema'. This framework continues the book's argument that the MDI is a transnational cinema by combining the terms 'postethnicity', 'cosmopolitanism', and 'cinema'. Chapter 3 also analyses how the themes of a postethnic cosmopolitan cinema distinguish the MDI from the ethnocentricity of mainstream cinema. The MDI uses cosmopolitan themes 'beyond multiculturalism' to examine the changing Malaysian socio-political and cultural environment. Rather than focusing on elements of race and ethnicity, the MDI envisions a nation that is both postethnic and cosmopolitan. The usage of cosmopolitan themes has enabled the MDI to deconstruct the stereotypes of race and ethnicity while focusing on contesting issues of interracial relationships, cultural and ethnic diversity, humanistic philosophies and universalism, and ideals of global justice, sovereignty, and multiple and coinciding modernities. The discussion of the envisioning of a postethnic nation asserts that Malaysia's national identity and ethnicity are still undergoing contestation and renegotiation. The MDI contests the accepted construction of 'race' and 'ethnic' communities by proposing coexistence, tolerance, and diversity to create equality through the universality of humanism. This construction allows the MDI to challenge the ethnocentricity of Malay hegemony in Malaysian cinema. The chapter then discusses how the MDI shifted Malaysian cinema from hidebound representations of ethnoracial communities composed of discrete ethnic and racial identities toward envisioning a utopian Malaysian society. The films challenge the disagreeable ethnic history of Malaysian cinema by using the humanistic themes of engaging and embracing the Other.

Chapter 4 examines the (re)popularisation of horror in Malaysian cinema through the key characteristics of the Malaysian horror film or *filem seram*. This chapter also explores how 'The Malaysian Horror Renaissance' and *filem seram* are used as a conscious attempt at reclaiming a positive view of Islam. The chapter also discusses how the boundaries between MDI and commercial filmmaking practices are blurred. This is achieved by analysing the characteristics of contemporary Malaysian horror cinema, which are to some extent common across MDI and commercially produced films. The chapter discusses how the Malaysian horror film is a reflection of the social, cultural, and political anxieties of its time. To examine the Malaysian horror genre from a cinematic, socio-cultural, political, and religious perspective, the historical and cultural functions of the monster in these horror narratives is analysed. This study of the monster is essential in explaining the social-cultural and political anxieties reflected at particular moments. The chapter then discusses how the commercial horror films produced by MDI filmmakers diverge from the works of mainstream horror filmmakers based on different representations

Introduction

of religion, its resistance to cinematic regulations regarding horror films, and the MDI inclination towards pan-Asian themes. The two, however, diverge through their different representations of religion, and the horror films of MDI filmmakers have an inclination towards pan-Asian horror films. MDI filmmakers continue their preference for transnational filmmaking methods, as their horror films are embedded with pan-Asian aesthetics, subject matter, and themes, and are distributed and exhibited beyond Malaysia. Because their popularity led them to be paradoxically reincorporated into the traditional national film culture by producing mainstream films, they continue their preference of using the transnational to contest national issues.

Chapter 5 provides a conclusion to the book and examines the Fourth Phase of Malaysian cinema by looking at the way Malaysian society and its cinema attempt to further move 'beyond multiculturalism'. The chapter begins with a summary of how the historical outline of Malaysian cinema discussed Malaysian cinema as consistently influenced by transnational forces and how it has progressed from a cinema built for capitalist purposes from the 1940s to the 1960s, 1970s to the 1990s, and in the post-2000 period. The chapter then summarises how the MDI has revived a lacklustre Malaysian cinema through the employment of transnational platforms and networks and the employment of postethnic and cosmopolitan issues. This approach has allowed the MDI to intervene in debates about interracial relationships, cultural and ethnic diversity, humanistic philosophies and universalism, and ideals of global justice, without the need to focus on race and ethnicity. The chapter summarises how MDI filmmakers entering mainstream commercial filmmaking could be seen as an acceptance of mainstream filmmaking methods and themes, as well as the acceptance of dominant discourses of race and ethnicity in Malaysian cinema. The chapter then examines the possibilities for prospective research within the fourth phase of Malaysian cinema. Firstly, the chapter proposes that further research be made about production collaborations with China in a search for more funding, co-productions, and distribution and exhibition opportunities. Secondly, research could be done in mapping out the growing interest in filmmaking as well as the various sites of gathering for filmmakers and film lovers that have increased in Malaysia, alongside the festivals and competition circuits that are available in Malaysia. Third, this chapter suggests how research in the fourth phase should examine the rise of filmmakers and filmmaking efforts in the east Malaysian states of Sabah and Sarawak as a recognition towards the prominent names making prominent films about the socio-cultural and political narratives that need to be equally examined. Lastly, this chapter proposes how research into the emergence of more Chinese- and Tamil language-films in the fourth phase of Malaysian cinema and a supposed 'postethnic nation' can actually be recognised as efforts to move 'beyond multiculturalism'. Or, could this phenomenon be studied as a return towards the establishment of ethno-centric cinemas that would segregate Malaysian cinema into a Malay, Chinese, Indian, and a Sabah and Sarawak-centric film industry?

Book Research Questions

As the introduction to my book, this chapter has demonstrated how Malaysian cinema has been subjected to the forces of capital and state control. Throughout this chapter, I have noted and outlined the changing phases based on the networks of power that summarise the ownership and control of Malaysian cinema. I have divided these changes according to three phases: the era of colonisation and decolonisation, the era of government intervention, and post-2000 Malaysian cinema. The key argument of this chapter is that Malaysian cinema has always been a transnational cinema, as each phase of Malaysian cinema has been built on transnational forces and utilised as a site of contesting various issues; however, the rise of the MDI makes Malaysian cinema transnational in new ways in the post-2000 era.

Cinema has been utilised as a site for contesting the progression of exclusion and inclusion according to state imaginings. Issues of race, ethnicity, and class are often manipulated within the general production of Malaysian cinema. In line with state policies of creating an ideal middle-class Malay society from the 1970s, this process sidelined the existence of other ethnic minorities and marginalised non-Malay communities. These marginalised communities experienced a form of social and cultural negation and potentially longed for the shared space of cultural identity from which they were excluded. I examine the importance of capital and policy control in determining the nature of culture, class, and consumption.

My study of the formation of cinema during the era of colonisation and decolonisation using the transnational framework has illustrated the favourable existence of a heterogeneous multicultural cinema. Modernisation and neoliberal policies within the 1980s and 1990s have pushed for the creation of the ideal middle-class Malay society. State intervention and involvement have created a homogeneous national cinema through the practice of exclusion. While the mainstream cinema of this era failed to capitalise on the benefits of globalisation, the MDI has emerged as a transnational cinema. Lacking support in state funding, locations for exhibition, and oppressive laws barring its creativity, it moved beyond the Malaysian borders and was widely accepted by the audiences of international film festivals. The deterritorialisation of this transnational and cosmopolitan cinema then problematises the accepted notion of Malaysian national cinema constructed on elements of race and ethnicity, influenced and determined through the control of capital and policies. It offers a site for contesting hegemonic ideologies by providing a voice for the marginalised subaltern community untouched by mainstream cinema.

This introduction has established the hypothesis and background for my research questions while underlining the importance in the study of contemporary Malaysian cinema. Using the framework of transnational cinema, I review the elements that constitute Malaysian cinema and search for changes, if any, that can be found in post-2000 Malaysian cinema. How can Malaysian cinema be theorised as transnational cinema? How does the MDI help construct the national identity of postcolonial Malaysia? What changes, if any, can be found in the representation of the marginalised in society? What are the new genres and new forms emerging in post-2000 Malaysian cinema and through the MDI? How does the MDI advance the growth and development of interethnic relationships in a multi-ethnic community such as Malaysia? What are the best methods for studying the financing, production, distribution, and reception of the MDI when its 'nationality' is questioned due to its movement across Malaysian borders? How does the framework of transnational cinema help us to critically examine the specificity of the national cinema against the overwhelming force of transnational capital? This book analyses how the MDI is constituted as a site for contesting these state policies and ideologies in a postcolonial nation undergoing socio-cultural and political transitions.

1

The Malaysian Digital Indies (MDI): Transnational Malaysian Cinema, Problematising the National

The new millennium marked the revival of Malaysian cinema. From 2000 to 2011, more than 300 films were produced. The increased number of films signified the radical transformation and turnaround of a sluggish industry. This figure is comparatively superior to the number produced in the previous two decades, a combined total of slightly over 200 films. Central to these transformations was the emergence of a new independent digital cinema operating from the 'outside' or 'margins' of commercial mainstream cinema. This radical transformation into a culturally vibrant and technologically innovative industry has also repositioned Malaysian cinema globally. This phenomenon started with the unexpected recognition and acceptance of the new digital independent cinema by audiences and critics at overseas film festivals. Located in the local and global interstices, this new cinema is termed the 'Malaysian Digital Indies' (MDI). The MDI contests hegemonic representations of preceding cinema by exploring complex themes and subject matter that question contemporary Malaysia's fundamentals.[1]

This new generation of filmmakers emerged in the era of advanced global capitalism and growing transnationalism and when mainstream cinematic output was at its lowest. These filmmakers emerged in the cultural environment of post-2000 in Malaysia and were compelled to move across national boundaries in search of capital, a sympathetic audience, and foreign co-production opportunities. As a result, they have made their presence felt in local and international cinematic circuits and within the burgeoning field of regional Asian cinema. Their films have also drawn praise, criticism, and serious discussion in academic circles, the press, and the internet. The MDI was created through technological advancement from transnational flows of capital, knowledge, and technology. It also presents new generic orders, aesthetics and narrative styles, and production methods that deconstruct culture, religion, identity, and representation issues. MDI successfully initiated its cinematic gaze by employing cosmopolitan themes in denouncing and correcting

---

1. The term 'Indies' rather than 'Indie' is used in this book to partly describe this film movement because the singular noun of 'Indie' cannot refer comfortably to a film movement. For example, the Italian neo-realist film belongs to a movement. It is a (collective) type of film that typifies the movement called Italian neo-realism.

distorted stereotyped ideologies and representations of Malaysian society. In short, the MDI adopted transnational modes of filmmaking to contest national issues and the extant political economy of Malaysian cinema through new genres, narratives, and aesthetics.

Rooted within the context of a multicultural Malaysia in an increasingly borderless world, transnationalism has continued to transform Malaysian cinema into a more socially, culturally, and politically insightful cinema. Its progressive transition from the national to transnational modes allowed the MDI to emerge as a platform to deconstruct race and ethnicity stereotypes established in an ethno-centric Malaysian cinema, question national policies, renegotiate race and ethnicity, and propound a new national identity.[2] Being transnational disengaged the MDI from established cinematic conventions to contest national issues.

By transcending geographical and cultural borders, contestations occurred through the (re)introduction of supernatural and horror genres in *Susuk* (Charm Needles, 2008) and *Histeria* (Hysteria, 2008); class-contestations and social realism in *Bukak Api* (Open Fire, 2000) and *The Beautiful Washing Machine* (2004), and the taboo inter-religious and inter-ethnic discourse through *Sepet* (Chinese Eyes, 2005) and *S'kali* (Altogether, 2006).[3] These developments also led the MDI away from being a racially exclusive ethno-centric cinema. Non-Malay directors introduced non-Malay-language films such as *Spinning Gasing* (2000), *Woman on Fire Looks for Water* (2009), *At the End of Daybreak* (2009), and *Chemman Chaalai* (The Gravel Road, 2005). These changes have subsequently allowed post-2000 Malaysian cinema, the MDI in particular, to evolve into a cinema embedded in localised themes and subject matter defined by transnational, global, and neoliberal forces.

The primary focus of this book is the MDI, which is situated within the context of early post-2000 Malaysian cinema. The book is the first sustained enquiry of this media and cultural form. The theoretical argument which frames this query is itself unprecedented. The MDI transitions from the local to the global. This transnational cinematic movement was fundamentally led by increasing globalisation and dependence on dispersed transnational networks, which include foreign co-production, funding, production, exhibition, and distribution. These elements

---

2. The terms ethnic (*bangsa*) and race (*kaum*) are used interchangeably in this book due to Malaysia's multicultural setting. For example, the Chinese can be categorised as either an ethnic or a racial community. Religion also becomes a critical marker of ethnic boundaries and a symbol of differentiation caused by political overtones rather than by the fundamentals of the religion.

3. In Malaysia, discussions about race, ethnicity, and religion are considered taboo, inflammatory, and seditious. Anyone caught inciting others on these issues is deemed threatening the country's security and can be punished under the Internal Security Act (ISA) (1960). Under the ISA, the police under the Ministry of Home Affairs (Kementerian Dalam Negeri) can detain a suspected individual merely based on suspicion, without an arrest warrant or evidence. An individual can be detained for an initial maximum sixty-day period. Thereafter, the individual can be held without trial for a two-year renewable period, to be approved by the Home Affairs Minister, and permits an indefinite detention period without trial. Due to ISA objections, a new act known as the Security Offences (Special Measures) Act 2012 (SOSMA) was introduced to replace it. The act was gazetted on 22 June 2012.

Figure 1.1: Film poster of *Sepet*. Source: MHz Film.

merge as a platform that contests and negotiates national issues such as hegemonic state-led policies, race and ethnicity, culture, and national identity.

The MDI represents the growing transnationality of Malaysian cinema. Therefore, this book explores how transnationalism has allowed the MDI to serve as a position to negotiate and redefine national policies, multiculturalism, and national identity. The MDI employed transnational methods that provided a voice for the politically oppressed, socially marginalised, and economically disadvantaged through the contestation of ideas related to socio-politics, multiculturalism, and class conflict. Anderson's (1991) stress on the importance of mediated communication in print capitalism is employed to argue how this transnational cinema's growing popularity compels both nationalist awareness and global cosmopolitanism.[4] While the MDI operates at the margins of the mainstream margins, it displaces mainstream cinema's restrictedness caused by the lack of a fair cultural policy that promotes cultural diversity. As transnationalism allows for the emergence of new representations, existing and nominal understandings of race and ethnicity, culture, and national identity in Malaysian cinema have become increasingly redundant. This was also made possible through the formulation of state policies and national events that took place since the nation's independence in 1957. The next section discusses how the MDI found its niche and thrives in Malaysia due to several factors.

---

4. Print capitalism precipitated this search and made it more fruitful and possible for more people to think above themselves and relate themselves to others in profoundly new ways (Anderson 1991, 36).

National Policies and Events

Various state policies and national events influenced the rise of the MDI. They have allowed the MDI to challenge and create new media and cinematic practices that have brought about new cultural pathways. Five national policies have indirectly shaped the MDI: the New Economic Policy (NEP) (1971), National Culture Policy (NCP) (1971), Vision 2020 (1991), National Development Policy (NDP) (1991), and the Multimedia Super Corridor (MSC) (1996). The three national events are: film censorship and piracy, the awakening of civil society, and the emergence of the Malaysian New Wave filmmakers.[5]

The New Economic Policy and the National Culture Policy

The NEP was aimed at equal wealth distribution to reduce poverty and inter-ethnic income disparity.[6] This increase was achieved by restructuring the economic composition of national wealth. Economically disadvantaged ethnic communities were awarded benefits such as skills training, land for development, and financial aid. The main target ethnic community was the Malay/*Bumiputera* and the creation of Malay/*Bumiputera* middle-class capitalists capable of competing beyond national borders. Introduced in the 1950s, the term *Bumiputera* can be translated as 'sons of the soil'. Originating from a Sanskrit word, the categorisation of the term *Bumiputeras* include the Malay majority and the indigenous communities of Sabah and Sarawak (Daniels 2005, 40–41). The *Melayu Baru* (New Malays) are entrepreneurial middle-class subjects moulded within Islam's principles rather than capitalism and are engineered according to state imaginings of Malay parity with non-Malays in a capitalist economy (Ong 1999, 204). They are self-made and accomplished individuals who are competent, learned and knowledgeable, sophisticated, honest, disciplined, trustworthy, competent, and capable of self-achievement (Khoo 1995, 336–338). This change in socio-economic status was to be realised by reducing their dependence on agriculture and absorbing them into the corporate sector (Cheah 2002, 140).[7]

---

5. The Malaysian New Wave filmmakers will be discussed in detail in Chapter 2.
6. The NEP was to restructure national wealth's economic composition from a 4:33:63 ratio of *Bumiputera*, other Malaysians, and foreign ownership to a 30:40:30 ratio.
7. The distribution of wealth among ethnic communities was unequal when based on principles of primordial racial incompatibility introduced by the British divide-and-rule policy. The Chinese controlled the financial capitals of tin mines, ports, and financial institutions. The Malays remained in the rural villages as fishers, paddy planters, or lowly ranked civil servants while the Indians worked the plantations. The creation of racially segregated trades had masked the actual purpose of limiting interactions to hinder any great deal of interaction among the three central ethnic communities. This segregation reduced the possibilities of a united nationalistic consensus which could lead to a rebellion. The delineation of economic roles based on the lines of ethnicity created a racially segregated plural society. The inequality in sharing the nation's wealth ultimately caused a rift that created feelings of disparity and distrust (Brown 1996, 217). For a detailed discussion about how the British colonial legacies have immensely affected ethnic relations through five political legacies, see Brown 1997, 525–530.

28   *Malaysian Cinema in the New Millennium*

To achieve this, the NEP developed preferential treatment courses to elevate the Malay social and economic standings. Political and economic spaces occurring within a space of 'graduated sovereignty' were readjusted to redirect global capital flow into creating a commercial and industrial community of Malay entrepreneurs, industrialists, and professionals (Ong 1999).[8] This amalgamation of politics with ethnic community importance has resulted in the country's political system effectively paralysing civil and political freedom (Verma 2004, 54).[9] Many Malays lacking entrepreneurial skills or capital were invited into entrepreneurship merely based on their political connections (Khoo 1995, 104–105). These privileges led to a crisis of the unexpected outcome of the Malays expecting prosperity as their birthright (127).[10] This situation occurred as certain Malay groups viewed the NEP's assistance as protectionism elements due to their historical experiences of exclusion from the economy's modern sectors (104). As courses of affirmative action strengthened the Malay polity, the future growth of multicultural rights became thwarted.

The efforts of producing a more comprehensive range of middle-class capitalist Malays resulted in a common perception that the non-Malays/non-*Bumiputeras* are of 'second-class' status (Gatsiounis 2005; Montlake 2008). The 'graduated sovereignty' system of the NEP allowed for more significant investment in the Malay biopolitical development, effectively constructing the world's first ethnically based form of affirmative action (Ong 1999, 218). This system that fundamentally denied the awarding of rights and benefits to the other ethnic communities encouraged a structure of ethnic and class-based government that naturalised racial differences in the country (218). In effect, the NEP enhanced the political and economic capital share of the disadvantaged Malays.

The NEP has been criticised for its shortcomings in reducing the poverty rate, inter-ethnic income disparity, and creating equal wealth distribution. While the NEP was interfered with by politicians and technocrats who controlled and decided the receivers of benefits, neoliberalist policies further restructured the remuneration of capital, presenting a significant disadvantage and inequality when wealth is shifted from the bottom of society to the top (Embong 2007).[11] This situation led to further marginalisation among the Malays, as only 'preferred Malays' were provided

---

8. Ong defines 'graduate sovereignty' as a series of zones subjected to different kinds of governmentality and varies in the mix of disciplinary and civilising regimes. These zones, which do not necessarily follow political borders, often contain ethnically marked class groupings, which in practice are subjected to regimes of rights and obligations that are different from those in other zones (1999, 7).

9. The four areas in which Malays enjoy a unique position are: reservations of land designated as Malay land, quotas to the public services, quotas in respect of the issuing of licenses or permits for operating business, and preferential treatment in the granting of scholarships, bursaries, and state aid (Verma 2004, 58–59).

10. Under Article 153, only the *Bumiputeras* are entitled to receive preferential treatment (Lee 2005, 212).

11. This increased politicisation of the rural areas' delivery mechanism resulted in intra-ethnic divisions within and along party lines. Both UMNO and non-UMNO members viewed NEP as UMNO's property. Due to structural constraints and political connections, many of the rural poor were excluded from the development process under the NEP (Embong 2007, 120–121).

The social and economic readjustments of the NEP occurred from 1971 to superior access to rights, benefits, and claims in a privileged environment created by corporate, social, and political networks with special privileges that unevenly favoured the upper-middle classes (Ong 1999, 218).[12] The ordinary and working-class Malays were conversely subjected to enormous social and psychological stresses when plucked out of rural life patterns (Khoo 1995, 336–337). This push for increased Malay participation in an industrialised economy meant the progressive urbanisation of rural Malays carried out through rural-to-urban migrations (Verma 2004, 101).[13]

The social and economic readjustments of the NEP occurred from 1971 to 1990. In 1991, the NDP was introduced, to focus on economic development towards nation-building formation. The NDP was a more 'balanced' economic development policy serving society as a whole while allowing Malay modernisation assistance (Zakaria and Suzaina 2005). The NDP contained ideologies of an evolving nationalism, freer capitalism, a universalising Islam, and a scripted populism. These ideologies shifted the economic dependence on an industrialised economy towards post-industrial conditions under one united rubric Malaysian nation (B. T. Khoo 2003, 328–329). Under the NDP, the main objectives of the NEP, poverty eradication and restructuring within the context of economic growth, were maintained. Simultaneously, a greater focus on the qualitative aspects of Malay participation through cooperation between Malay and non-Malay companies was encouraged. As the NDP was criticised as a continuation of incomplete NEP policies (Gomez 2008), the New Economic Model (NEM) was introduced by former Prime Minister Najib Razak as part of a selective series of economic liberalisation measures to revamp the shortcomings of the NEP gradually.

Launched 30 March 2010, the NEM is an economic policy to make the country more competitive. Economic reforms will embrace more market-friendly, merit-based, and competitive economic policies that aim to transform the country into a high-income nation with three goals: creating a high-income nation, economic sustainability, and economic inclusiveness. Formulated by the National Economic Advisory Council, the NEM focuses on inclusiveness so that all Malaysians will benefit and share in the country's wealth, irrespective of race and ethnic community. It targets six National Key Economic Activities to be the engines of growth to generate high growth rates, including oil and gas, electronic and electrical, tourism, agriculture, and financial services. It remains unclear if the NEM will achieve the objective of abolishing ethic-based affirmative action. While acknowledging the need to reform the rent-seeking, ethic-based, and patronage system, it

---

12. Poverty eradication programmes were formulated and implemented to benefit primarily the Malay poor in rural areas (Embong 2007, 130).
13. Islamic resurgence was also linked to urbanisation following the implementation of the NEP. It drew the Malay masses from their secure rural environments to what were mostly non-Malay, non-Muslim cities where economic disparities were stark (Verma 2004, 101).

30   *Malaysian Cinema in the New Millennium*

still emphasises the design of practical measures that strike a balance between the unique position of the *Bumiputera* and the others.[14]

In addition to the NEP, the NCP emphasised Malay culture's supremacy and dominance in shaping the Malaysian national identity. The NCP introduced three principles that served as guidelines for building the Malaysian national culture: 1. The National Culture must be based on the indigenous [Malay] culture; 2. Suitable elements from the other cultures may be accepted as part of the national culture; and 3. Islam is an essential component in the moulding of the National Culture. While the NCP encouraged a common culture among its diverse citizenry (Hefner 2001), this official attempt at regulating multiculturalism was criticised as being too essentialist and centred on the idealised civilisation of Malay culture (Zawawi 2004, 133). This drive at enhancing the Malay social standing and influence was led by the public prestige and pageantry of employing the Malay language, personalities, and cultural symbols (Ong 1999, 141), intentionally directed towards a homogenous Malaysian nation built on the fundamentals of the Malay culture and Islam. The MDI contests this dichotomisation of *Bumiputera*/non-*Bumiputera*, the self/others, Malay/non-Malay, and Malay language/non-Malay language. The book will discuss how the MDI contests these 'binary oppositions' used in spheres of economic, social, political, and language disparities.

Vision 2020 (Wawasan 2020)

In 1991, Mahathir launched Vision 2020 (*Wawasan* 2020). Thus far, Malaysia's achievement has been perceived as one-sided, heavily economic, and not matched by a similar political sphere achievement. The political challenge of creating 'a united Malaysian nation', or a *Bangsa* Malaysia, is more significant and critical than is the economic challenge of sustaining the current economic growth level in Malaysia's effort to become modern (Mohamad 1991). Vision 2020 focused on economic development towards the formation of nation-building. It envisions a modernised Malaysia in the economic, political, cultural, and spiritual dimensions (Goh 2001, 163).[15] Based on Prime Minister Mahathir Mohamad's blueprint for economic growth, wealth-accumulation, and nation-building, Malaysia was to

---

14. For more detailed information on the NEM, see National Economic Advisory Council (2010).

15. Mahathir Mohamad served as Malaysia's fourth prime minister from 1981 to 2003. Malaysia's prime ministers are Tunku Abdul Rahman (1957–1970), Abdul Razak (1970–1976), Hussein Onn (1976–1981), Mahathir Mohamad, Abdullah Ahmad Badawi (2003–2009), Najib Razak (2009–2018), Mahathir Mohamad (2018–2020), Muhyiddin Yassin (2020–2021) and Ismail Sabri Yaacob (2020–present). According to Cheah, the Malaysian prime ministers are described as: Tunku Abdul Rahman 'Bapa Kemerdekaan' (Father of Independence), Abdul Razak Hussein 'Bapa Pembangunan' (Father of Development), Hussein Onn 'Bapa Perpaduan' (Father of Solidarity) and Mahathir Mohamad 'Bapa Pemodenan' (Father of Modernisation) (2002, 113).

The Malaysian Digital Indies: Transnational Malaysian Cinema   31

achieve Newly Industrialised Nation status by 2020.[16] Mahathir sought to galvanise the public imagination through ideas of a shared vision of prosperity, a concept captured in the idea of a *Bangsa* Malaysia (Hilley 2001, 4).[17] By incorporating camaraderie, and full and fair partnership, *Bangsa* Malaysia envisions projecting Malaysian nationalism on the global economy to compete as a universal reckoning force (Khoo 2003, 330–331).[18] For Malaysia to become a nation fully developed economically, politically, socially, spiritually, psychologically, and culturally, nine central and strategic challenges have to be overcome (Mahathir 1991).[19] It is thought that if *Bangsa* Malaysia is a nation with political allegiance and commitment to the country, the nation will be living in harmony and at peace with itself, territorially and ethnically integrated through full and fair partnership (Mahathir 1991, 2–3). The need to create a 'united Malaysian nation' under the *Bangsa* Malaysia concept has become more imperative than has the need to sustain the current economic growth in Malaysia's modernisation efforts. In a broad economic sense, this need indicates that Malaysia's state being 'one state with several nations' is a coherent variant of a capitalist entity. However, it is still searching for a parallel coherence in the political and ideological sense because there exist strong competing nations-of-intent (Shamsul 1996, 327–330). Vision 2020 is an effort to mobilise nationalist pride by corroborating Malaysia's global standing as a newly industrialised country (Goh 2001, 163).[20]

Vision 2020 and *Bangsa* Malaysia were met with mixed responses and con-flicting views.[21] While the vision of a *Bangsa* Malaysia allowed many Malaysians to imagine a nation's formation in supra-ethnic terms, official details on achieving this remained indefinable (Williamson 2002, 411). Some viewed the establishment of

---

16. As Malaysia's longest-serving Prime Minister of twenty-two years, Mahathir introduced various policies to launch Malaysia as a global brand name. Among the policies introduced were the Look East Policy, Privatisation Policy, and Malaysia Incorporated. This economic reshuffle heavily based on the Reaganomics and Thatcherism neoliberal economic ideals of privatisation, free markets, and commoditisation of essential services marked a significant change in the socio-cultural and political structure. For more information on Mahathir's modernisation policies, see Hilley 2001; Khoo 1995, 2002; and Ooi 2006.

17. The term *bangsa* can be directly translated as either ethnicity or race in the Malay language. In short, the term *bangsa* Malaysia loosely put together is defined as the Malaysian race. According to Mahathir, *Bangsa* Malaysia is a united Malaysian nation that does not recognise ethnicity and is not about being Malay, Chinese, India, Iban, or Kadazan. However, people that identify with the country speak Bahasa Malaysia and accept the constitution. He further adds that creating a *Bahasa* Malaysia would lead to the eventual removal of special privileges for the *Bumiputeras*. This statement was commended by politicians and former opposition leader Lim Kit Siang as 'the most enlightened' on nation-building in recent years (Asiaweek 1995).

18. *Bangsa* Malaysia has often been alleged to bear similarities with the 'Malaysian Malaysia' slogan proposed by Lee Kuan Yew in 1963. However, individual scholars have denied these similarities by stating that there are qualitative differences between these two concepts. Lee Kuan Yew's concept suggests a nation of equal status irrespective of race and ethnicity, colour, and creed. However, Mahathir's *Bangsa* Malaysia suggests the accepted continued constitutional recognition of the Bumiputera position to retain their political dominance (Shamsul 1996, 330).

19. For a detailed discussion of the nine central and strategic challenges of Vision 2020, see Cheah 2002, 65–66; Hilley 2001, 5–6; and Shamsul 1996, 327.

20. For a detailed script of Mahathir's speech on Vision 2020, see Mahathir 1991.

21. For a theoretical analysis of how *Bangsa* Malaysia is interpreted differently, see Ooi 2006, 53–56.

Bangsa Malaysia as a united people by recognising non-Malay cultural and religious uniqueness. Others believed this term simply meant a Malaysia united under Malay rule (Ibrahim 2008). The non-Malays felt that Vision 2020 was an enlightened aim by Mahathir at ending Malay nationalism. They expected a shift when *bangsa*, understood as 'race', was being abandoned for the more republican understanding of *bangsa* as 'nation', as in nation-state (Ooi 2006, 57). The non-Malays envisioned an 'imagined community' of Malaysians with equal rights regardless of ethnicity (Cheah 2002, 66).

Vision 2020 could also be perceived as reconstructing Malaysia as a 'nation-less' state (Ibrahim 1998). Seen as an effort in resolving Malaysia's nation-building dilemma, Vision 2020 will unite 'one state with several nations' or 'nations-of-intent' towards one distinctively Malaysian nation (Shamsul 1996, 327). This 'nation-of-intent' would depend on assimilation and integration, regardless of ethnicity. Malaysians will identify themselves as *Bangsa* Malaysia and not as Malay, Chinese, Indian, Iban, or Kadazan while speaking the national language of Bahasa Malaysia and accepting the Malaysian Federal Constitution (Ooi 2006, 51–53).[22] Thus, Malaysians' nationality should rightfully elude the divisive segregation between *Bumiputeras* and non-*Bumiputeras* or even Malays, Chinese, Indians, and others.[23]

Vision 2020's 'imagined community' of the *Bangsa* Malaysia contributed to a growing consciousness for a new Malaysian national identity.[24] The MDI works that deconstruct class and ethnic representations focus on cultivating a national identity beyond race and ethnicity; in other words, a new 'Malaysian cinematic imagined community'.[25]

The Multimedia Super Corridor (MSC)

The launch of the Multimedia Super Corridor (MSC) marked Malaysia's entry into the digital age. This cybercity is based on the need to create an 'information and

---

22. The term Bahasa Malaysia was first introduced by Malaysia's first prime minister, Tunku Abdul Rahman (Joseph 2014). In 1986, the term was switched to Bahasa Melayu. In 2007, to infuse Malaysians with a sense of belonging that transcends ethnicity, the term Bahasa Malaysia was reintroduced. Article 152 of the Malaysian Federal Constitution 152 stipulates Bahasa Malaysia as the Malaysian national language. However, while the national language is termed Bahasa Malaysia, its English translation remains the Malay language and not the Malaysian language.
23. According to ethnic communities, this management based on non-voluntary affiliations is carried out by official state forms such as applications for passports, identification cards, and birth certificates requiring a mandatory declaration of one's ethnicity. The Malaysian population currently stands at 32.73 million people. The official ethnic demographic makeup is Malays and *Bumiputeras* (69.6 per cent), Chinese (22.6 per cent), Indians (6.8 per cent), and Others (1 per cent) (Department of Statistics 2020). Malaysians are required to declare if they are Malay, Chinese, Indian, or 'Lain-lain' (Others, or other ethnic minorities), or as *Bumiputera* or non-*Bumiputera*.
24. Benedict Anderson has claimed that 'it is imagined because the members of even the smallest nation will never know most of their fellow-members, meet them, or even hear of them, yet in the minds of each lives the image of their communion' (1991, 6).
25. For more information on Malaysia's ethnic and cultural diversity, see Andaya and Andaya 2001, 3–4.

knowledge-based' society competent in competing globally. It is projected as a catalyst serving the regional and global markets for multimedia products and services. Stretching fifteen kilometres wide and fifty kilometres long, from the Kuala Lumpur City Centre (KLCC) to the Kuala Lumpur International Airport (KLIA), it houses 'intelligent city' Putrajaya, 'cybercity' Cyberjaya, and the Multimedia University (Ibrahim and Goh 1998, 9). [26] Built on Mahathir's foresight that the FDI-driven export-oriented industrialisation was nearing its end, the MSC would bring Malaysia from the industrial age of the twentieth century into the information age of the twenty-first century.

Backed by the '10-point Multimedia Bill of Guarantees', the MSC will bring together four key elements: the best possible physical infrastructure; new laws, policies, and practices; high-capacity global telecommunications; and logistics infrastructure in a high-powered non-stop shop (Ibrahim and Goh 1998, 25).[27] The economy had to diverge from the industrial age of manufacturing and assembling electronics to attain further foreign investments. This divergence paved the way for an information age of research and development work, technological innovation, software engineering, and developing new IT-based service industries (Khoo 2003, 32–33). The government offered foreign investors who relocate their businesses to this high-powered, one-stop IT centre investment and financial incentives such as tax exemptions, research and development grants, and non-financial incentives such as free ownership and no internet censorship (28–33). While allowing newer media technologies to materialise, the internet also emerged as a site for disseminating information across borders. The internet, as a new paradigm of electronic media, provides resources for self-imaginings. It also becomes a space of contestation or 'imagined space' that transforms mass mediation discourse through new resources and new disciplines to construct imagined selves and worlds (Appadurai 1996, 3).

The MSC has significantly benefitted the MDI. Several MDI filmmakers, such as Tan Chui Mui and Deepak Kumaran, are graduates, tutors, or lecturers from the Multimedia University, which is part of the MSC. The MSC has also been a valuable source of information that has opened up a 'gateway of access' to transnational and independent channels away from state control. Incorporating the internet as a site for exhibition and distribution by the MDI will be discussed in this book.

Film censorship and piracy

In Malaysia, strict film censorship has been in existence since the early 1980s.[28] The 'Four Major Elements of Film's Contents' deemed suitable for filmic content are public security and peace, religion, socio-cultural, and decency and morality. While

---

26. Kuala Lumpur is often abbreviated as KL (pronounced 'Kay Ell').
27. For a detailed explanation of the 10-point Multimedia Bill of Guarantees and a comprehensive explanation of the MSC, see Ibrahim and Goh 1998.
28. For more information on these four significant aspects, refer to Kementerian Dalam Negeri 2010, 11–24.

a film that contains such themes, storylines, parts, or dialogues is permitted, these themes are to be given close attention and scrutiny to avoid creating controversy and uncertainty amongst Malaysians (Kementerian Dalam Negeri 2010, 5). Veteran film producer Hajah Ruhani describes film censorship as 'the worst enemy of our film industry' (Latif and Groves 1994). Film censorship is governed by the Lembaga Penapisan Filem (LPF) or Malaysian Censorship Board, which perceives itself as the 'moral and national guardian' of Malaysian society (Khoo 2006, 108). It is described as 'scissor-happy' for controversially censoring films, causing them to end up with an incoherent narrative (106).[29]

Established under the Film Censorship Act 2002, the LPF lays down the legislation to be followed before films, commercials, filmic trailers, and publicity materials can be released. Once a film is approved, it will receive a certificate that permits the distributor to screen the film. The censors are also given a copy of a set of guidelines, a pink 'Film Censorship Board Manual' that details the board's duties and the censorship process. A certain degree of conservatism and reluctance to accept new ideas by the LPF causes a film to be banned or heavily censored. Film censorship in Malaysia is driven by six standard policies that can be summarised as: to protect the public from negative influences that will cause immoral acts threatening public safety; to protect the country and government from the spread of anti-government films and films that may threaten national sovereignty; to avoid films that uphold cults, fanaticism, criticise and condemn any religion without final remorse or punishment; to maintain the harmonious relationships between ethnic communities; to become a guide that preserves national culture and values; and to prevent individuals or organisations from physical and moral degradation caused by films with hearsay and rumours (Kementerian Dalam Negeri 2010, 6).

Acts of kissing, swearing, and themes of homosexuality, sex, and interracial romances are banned outright (D'Oliviero 2004, 106). Under the pretence of fear of offending in a multi-ethnic and religious society, local censorship guidelines have labelled themes of race, religion, politics, crime, violence, brutality and horror, as 'sensitive and precarious issues' (Lent 1990, 197). Cinematic discussions of racial dominion, diplomatically sensitive issues, disrespect of religion, and glorifying communism have been traditionally banned, repressed, or beyond discussion (197). Independent filmmaker James Lee associates LPF's suppressive methods as akin to a 'cultural Taliban', due to its strict monitoring and control over filmmakers' content and scripts (Krich 2003).

To avoid LPF censorship, filmmakers practise self-censorship by deleting or choosing not to shoot scenes they anticipate will be deleted by the LPF (Khoo 2006, 111–112). Irony and parody are used to criticise state policies, or extra scenes deemed even more sensitive than the intended ones, are shot to distract the censors (111–112). To avoid certain scenes being deleted, before submitting to the LPF for

---

29. For details on films that are not approved for viewing, refer to Kementerian Dalam Negeri 2010, 35.

approval, filmmakers and editors avoid shooting these scenes or delete material that they feel might be deemed controversial. To ensure continuity, editors and filmmakers will consciously remove certain scenes to avoid an incoherent narrative. This cautious culture has led to filmmakers being unwilling to take risks in producing films that are critical, for fear of facing backlash from the authorities. Certain films also carried a 'straightforward' message that subversively yield a social critique of race, class and gender (111–112). Filmmakers are creative in their self-censorship practice but are denied expression, creativity, and criticism. And audiences are denied the opportunity to engage with critical films.

This filmmaking environment can be termed a 'Cinema of Denial', created through a combination of government restrictions, self-censorship, and the lack of critical films for audiences (Khoo 2006, 111–112). 'Serious films' that challenge the status quo or express dissent are seen as risky ventures and extremely difficult to produce or screen (107). This challenge is done at the risk of violating laws such as the (now repealed) Internal Security Act (ISA) 1960 and the Sedition Act. These laws create a repressive atmosphere, causing filmmakers to hold back from being critical of the state or from tackling contemporary social issues deemed sensitive towards national unity (107). This atmosphere causes local filmmakers to continue lobbying for a more 'liberal regime', more freedom, and fewer restrictions to produce movies (Baharudin and Groves 1994).

The call for a more liberal filmmaking atmosphere since the 1980s was met with the release of new censorship guidelines effective 15 March 2010. The new guidelines were based on the input, feedback, and recommendations from Malaysian film practitioners, non-governmental agencies, academics, representatives from the print and electronic media, and relevant governmental organisations. Seventeen years later in 2010, these revamped guidelines promised greater flexibility to ensure that a film's continuity or a filmmaker's creativity is not disrupted by censorship. The changes took into account current trends and lifestyles that do not conflict with Islam or disagree with Malaysia's cultures, religions, and norms. Specifically, the significant changes made are the allowance of previously banned words if used in non-offensive manners and consultation with the LPF to assess a script and storyboard so that offensive content and changes can be made according to guidelines before shooting begins. The censorship process now begins by requiring filmmakers to have their scripts vetted by the LPF before production begins. According to the LPF, the LPF are consulted not for approval but for advice on what is acceptable, so that filmmakers can avoid shooting scenes that might be censored (Koay 2010). MDI filmmakers Liew Seng Tat and Amir Muhammad, however, feel that the film industry is now more restrictive, as the LPF now has control right from the beginning. They feel that censorship is an outdated repression method, as audiences are smarter, more mature, and more liberal (Koay 2010). This cultural and cinematic environment has caused the MDI filmmakers to move across national boundaries in search of capital, a sympathetic audience, and foreign co-production opportunities.

Because of this cultural and political atmosphere set by the LPF, Malaysians have resorted to accessing banned films through unconventional and illegal methods. Such methods include downloading or watching banned films on the internet, crossing the border into Singapore or Thailand, and buying pirated copies of films. While film producers lament the loss of income due to piracy, this illegitimate industry has indirectly allowed for the emergence of the MDI. Piracy has inadvertently exposed Malaysians to banned films. Book publisher Dhojee Roshishan stated that the ease in obtaining pirated copies of films has helped educate and expose Malaysians to more films. Even his aunt, who resides in a village, has been exposed to Akira Kurosawa films (Krich 2003). Malaysia's piracy problem started due to the increased popularity of Hong Kong–based Cantonese serials and movies, which were not available on local television. The introduction of VHS-based tapes in the 1980s, video CD (VCD, also known as compact disc digital video) in the 1990s, and digital versatile discs (DVDs) in the year 2000 have provided Malaysians with cheaper and uncensored options, albeit illegally.

The demand for and supply of pirated films is ongoing. It is not uncommon for these films to be openly sold on street corners and night markets (D'Oliviero 2004, 106). In Yasmin Ahmad's *Sepet*, the main cast members, Jason and Orked, meet when she visits Jason's stall in search of pirated copies of Takeshi Kaneshiro's films. Her act of searching for films from a street vendor selling pirated films rather than from a licenced dealer and without any traces of guilt reflects the acceptance of piracy in Malaysia. Amir Muhammad's online article states that Yasmin Ahmad's films are available for illegal downloading using the torrent software. However, he adds that Yasmin would not have disapproved of this, as she believed that 'piracy is stealing from greedy people' (2010). Piracy and illegal downloading methods have also ironically introduced Kurosawa, Verhoeven, Fellini, and Bergman to Malaysian filmmakers. These bonus film materials have become a referencing source in aiding local filmmakers to understand production methods and approaches (Hassan 2010). With such ease of accessibility, it will be necessary to re-evaluate the need for censorship or the role of the LPF.

The awakening of civil society

The 1990s was a time of economic growth, prosperity, and wealth accumulation in Asia. It was also a time of renewed nationalism and socio-political awakening in Asia. In Malaysia, the Mahathir administration was troubled by financial and political crises such as the 1998 Asian financial crisis and dismissal and prosecution of his former deputy, Anwar Ibrahim. In 1998, Anwar Ibrahim's sacking as deputy prime minister cum finance minister sparked the *Reformasi* movement. It protested against the manner Mahathir had removed Anwar from office. The protestors showed their disapproval by holding large-scale demonstrations in the streets and mosques of the sacking and arrest of Anwar under the ISA. *Reformasi* was also a call

The Malaysian Digital Indies: Transnational Malaysian Cinema 37

for reform against Mahathir's authoritative rule and rampant corruption (Loh and Khoo 2002, 20). The term is borrowed from Indonesia's protests during the Suharto era, which called for reform or *Reformasi*.

In Malaysia, the internet has also been tremendously influential in the awakening of civil society. During the height of the Mahathir-Anwar crisis in 1998, the growing accessibility of the internet and information technology savviness created an alternative platform for the publication and dissemination of information, ideas, and views deemed too sensitive for mainstream media controlled by the state. This growing accessibility led to the internet becoming an alternative site of information, further empowered by the government's 'no censorship' guarantee. Dubbed the 'Fifth Estate', the internet has been manipulated and utilised to facilitate communication and interaction, virtual mobilisation, and participation among individuals and groups in civil society; it also performs checks and balances on the state (Tan 2010).

The internet as the location for rebellion, the subject of insurgent agency, and a site of cultural hybridity (Bhabha 2004, 294–295) helped broaden and locate a platform for public discussion and social action (Naughton 2001, 147). Mass rallies were primarily organised and spread using the internet, leading to the birth of *Reformasi* politics (Johan 2001).[30] Therefore, the internet was utilised by *Reformasi* activists as a platform to circulate alternative voices, communicate, and discuss social and political criticisms. This utilisation led to an immense loss in the ruling government's hegemony over civil society (B. T. Khoo 2003, 99–107). The internet was used as an alternative channel to the government media for information, analysis, and commentary in websites such as *freemalaysia, sangkancil, adilnet, and saksi* that featured spirited, critical, and alternative report commentaries. The popularity of the internet as alternative media is reflected through visits to *Reformasi* sites such as *Laman Reformasi*, registering over five million hits while approximately thirty *Reformasi*-related sites existed (Johan 2001, 105–106). The *Reformasi* movement was also supported by 'international links' by countries such as Japan (*Anwar Support*), Thailand (*Reformasi Anwar Ibrahim*), and Australia (*Australia Reform Web*) (Tan 2010, 279). The MSC, which was initialised as the state's project to prepare the nation for an increasingly globalised world in the information age, had instead been usurped as a popular alternative method of disseminating information, exchanging ideas, and discussing socio-political issues across space and time.[31]

These *Reformasi* rallies witnessed Malaysians, irrespective of race and ethnicity, creed or religion, pouring onto Kuala Lumpur's streets demanding a fairer and

---

30. For a discussion on how the internet has contributed to and enhanced the struggle and development of the *Reformasi* movement and civil society in Malaysia, see Tan 2010.

31. The accessibility of the internet and freedom from censorship has led to the emergence of news portals and blogs that provide alternative news and critical views. Popular websites such as Malaysiakini and Free Malaysia Today have provided a platform for alternative news and views to be discussed openly. Opposition political parties have established websites such as PAS's Harakah Daily, PKR's Suara-Keadilan, and DAP's DAP roketkini, without requiring a printing permit under the Printing Presses and Publication Act (1984).

just government.[32] Regardless of ethnicity and class, it sparked the socio-political awakening that led to a reignition of Malaysian nationalism and political awareness. This situation occurred through a heightened consciousness of the government's power, a suppressive legislative and judicial power that can so quickly be brought to bear down on political dissent (Johan 2001, 105).[33] Silent voices also surfaced from within the Malay community, both sceptical and critical of state policies (Lee 2005, 212). These voices also emerged from the ruling coalition's Barisan Nasional (BN) dominant Malay-Mulsim political party, the United Malays National Organisation (UMNO), and raised doubts and anxieties regarding the unconstructive outcomes of affirmative action on the Malay communities (106).[34] The *Reformasi* movement was primarily an uprising that inspired new forms of expression that changed the Malaysian socio-cultural and political environment. This awakening of civil society also led to the significance of multi-ethnicity in Malaysia.[35]

The awakening of civil society and the contesting of socio-cultural and political policies in Malaysia is the thematic focus of the MDI. The MDI focuses on the contestations of issues based on class, politics, ethnicity, and intellectual dynamics. These issues concerning class, politics, ethnicity, and intellectual dynamics occurred in a decade that witnessed the transition of power between three Prime Ministers: Mahathir Mohamad to Abdullah Ahmad Badawi, then to Najib Razak.[36]

---

32. The 1998 *Reformasi* movement has been the catalyst that allowed for the coalescing of individuals from different ethnic backgrounds and has led to greater awareness regarding ethnic equality. Since the *Reformasi* protests, the nation has witnessed at least four major street rallies participated in by individuals from differing ethnic communities calling for electoral reforms (Bersih 2007; Bersih 2011), the abolition of the ISA (Anti-ISA 2009), and the educational reforms (anti-PPSMI/*Pengajaran dan Pembelajaran Sains dan Matematik dalam Bahasa Inggeris*/movement against the teaching of mathematics and science in English, 2009). The HINDRAF (Hindu Rights Action Force) street rally in November 2007 was not included. It was a movement that solely championed the social, economic, and political rights of the ethnic Indian community in Malaysia. However, the movement has been highly influential in Malaysia's changing political scenario and has a global following. For more information regarding the marginalisation of the Indian ethnic community in Malaysia, see Nagarajan (2009) and Lim (2009).

33. For more information regarding the sacking of Anwar Ibrahim and the *Reformasi* movement, see Verma 2004, 109–113.

34. The United Malays National Organisation (UMNO) is the dominant Malay-Muslim political party in the fourteen-party Barisan Nasional (BN) coalition. Onn Jaafar founded UMNO in 1948 to oppose the formation of the Malayan Union. UMNO cooperated with the Malayan Chinese Association (MCA) and the Malayan Indian Congress (MIC) to form the Alliance Party (Parti Perikatan) to contest in the first general election on 27 July 1955. After the 13 May 1969 race riots, the Alliance Party's concept of cooperation between various and multiple parties was reinstitutionalised as Barisan Nasional on 1 July 1974 (Brown 1996).

35. Anwar Ibrahim's supporters launched the new multi-ethnic Parti KeADILan Nasional (now known as Parti KeADILan Rakyat/PKR) as their chosen vehicle contesting the upcoming elections and for bringing about change. Moreover, it is noteworthy that PKR then joined hands with the other opposition parties. This coalition includes the Chinese-based Democratic Action Party (DAP) and the Malay-Muslim based Parti Islam to forge a multi-ethnic opposition known as the Barisan Alternatif (B.A.) (a loosely based unregistered now defunct coalition known as the Pakatan Rakyat (P.R.)). These developments suggest that ethnicism discourse might indeed have been overtaken by a discourse of developmentalism (Loh 2002, 21). PR has been dismantled due to irreconcilable ideological conflict primarily between DAP and PAS.

36. On 31 October 2003, Mahathir stepped down as prime minister to be succeeded by his deputy, Abdullah Ahmad Badawi. On 3 April 2009, another transfer of power occurred when Najib Razak succeeded Abdullah as the fifth prime minister of Malaysia.

The MDI was a new informal film culture that has created a new political economy of Malaysian cinema. The transnational networks created through the MSC have opened up a 'gateway of access' away from state control and towards a democratic space. This space of awareness has allowed for discourses about ethnic and racial equality that champions Vision 2020 while aiding the rise and awakening of civil society. Therefore, the MDI is a cinema movement that emerged from national developments and policies that ironically challenge the suppressive political and cultural environments caused by film censorship, the NEP, and NCP.

To further understand the MDI, it will be necessary to examine the history of Malaysian cinema. In the last six decades, state intervention has contextualised the changing nature of Malaysian cinema. Built on transnational forces from the 1940s to the 1960s, the NEP and NCP turned Malaysian cinema into a Malay-centric national cinema in the 1970s. In the 1990s, changes in the Malaysian socio-political landscape inadvertently altered Malaysian cinema's social and political-economic settings. This amalgamation of race- and ethnic-based policies, the 'nationalising' of cinema, strict cinematic regulations, and the awakening of civil society eventually led to the emergence of the MDI.

Transnationalism

Before exploring the history of cinema in Malaysia, it is crucial to understand transnationalism and its impact on the chronological journey of filmmaking in Malaysia. While different scholars offer differing definitions of the term 'transnationalism' (Basch, Schiller, and Blanc 1994; Hannerz 1996; Kearney 1995; Lionnet and Shih 2005; Morris 2004; Portes, Guarnizo, and Landolt 1999; Vertovec 1999), the term is widely accepted as the creation of an increasingly globalised and borderless world, where culture and capital flow across deterritorialised and eroded national borders. The prefix 'trans-' signifies changing conditions, situations or environments, and movements beyond, across, or through space and boundaries. The term 'nation' refers to many people living within a territory, with shared social and cultural aspects, united and administered by a sovereign government. Put together, 'transnational' denotes movements across and beyond the borders of a nation.

Transnationalism suggests the mobility to transfer globalised images, information, people, and capital across borders and space. This phenomenon has created a condition of cultural interconnectedness and mobility, which affects the varying relationship between the nation-state, capitalism, and capital movement (Ong 1999, 4). This creation of subjects, technologies, and ethical practices as linked and dominant concepts through various international, transnational, networks and connections creates forms of 'transnational connectivities' (Grewal 2005, 3). These connectivities cause the political and economic functions of nation-states to be influenced by present global capital accumulation structures and connected alterations (Schiller, Basch, and Blanc 1995, 52). Thus, transnationalism has allowed for capitalist expansion, technological advancement, and labour movements to flow across borders through migration.

This 'border crossing' method has created networks of long-distance relationships that override national borders and space. Such movements across borders achieved through social movements and networks eventually influence the sovereignty of a nation (Vertovec 1999, 2). This situation stemmed from scholarly arguments about whether this globalised world has evolved from the 'global village' and transitioned into a more refined form of 'global pillage' (Hunt and Leung 2008, 2–3). Therefore, transnationalism negates the nation's significance and autonomy when transnational flows erode and deterritorialise national borders. This negation occurs as transnational labour migration movements involve people's movement, capital flows and products, and ideologies (Nonini 2002, 8). And this negation of national sovereignty requires an understanding of 'transnational perspectives', representing a new angle on understanding the nation, the international community, and nationalism and internationalism (Gearhart 2005, 35–36). These transnational networks span great distances globally and ignore the existence of international borders.

National borders become increasingly irrelevant when transnational flows affect countries' political practices, policies, and economic activities. The nation-state that is occurring as part of a broader project of globalisation gives way to world cities that function as central hubs of flexible capital accumulation, communication, and control (Schiller, Basch, and Blanc 1995, 49). This situation occurs as transnational spaces exist as contestation sites for the negotiation of identities, gender, ethnicity, race, class, and nationality (Yeoh et al. 2003, 2–3) and is possible for transnational spaces located beyond national autonomy borders. Transnational spaces exist as a site for transnational flows to constitute a liberal global market, cultural hybridisation, and development of democracies and human rights (Lionnet and Shih 2005, 5–6).

Transnational spaces create transnational networks that exist as a site of political engagement and avenue of capital while reproducing culture and reconstructing places and localities (Vertovec 1999, 1–2). These spaces allow for cultures, policies, and issues to be negotiated without interference. Transnational flows could also paradoxically lead toward the possible strengthening of the nation-state. Nationalism and identity politics are possibly increased when large numbers of deterritorialised people revitalise, recreate, or reinvent their traditions and political claims to territory and histories (Schiller, Basch, and Blanc 1995, 52). This transnational global system of ties, interactions, exchanges, and mobility represents a growing occurrence that continuously affects the nation-state.

There also exist what some have described as 'good' and 'bad' transnationalisms. 'Good' transnationalism is liberal, open to, and tolerant of other nations and cultures; 'bad' transnationalism exploits and manipulates a nation's vulnerability to better export workers and markets or even carry out acts of aggression (Gearhart

2005, 39). While 'good' and 'bad' transnationalism often work in concert, an examination of migratory movements or 'transnational migration' is required to better comprehend 'good' and 'bad' transnationalism. Transnational migration occurs when immigrants build and maintain simultaneous multi-stranded social relations, which bond their societies of origin and settlement by creating and reconstituting their simultaneous embeddedness in multiple countries (Schiller, Basch, and Blanc 1995, 48). As the pursuit of capital becomes the primary rationale for immigrants to migrate, this is usually performed by 'transmigrants'.

Transmigrants are immigrants who develop and sustain several cross-boundary familial, economic, social, organisational, religious, and political associations in the home and host nations (Basch, Schiller, and Blanc 1994, 7). Despite maintaining multiple ties, transmigrants are not sojourners because they continue to influence their host country's economics and politics while maintaining and sustaining involvement, influences, and connections with their sending countries (Schiller, Basch, and Blanc 1995, 48). Transmigrants living transborder lives experience the predicament of participating in the nation-building processes of multiple nation-states. These predicaments occur when identities and practices configured by hegemonic categories, race, and ethnicity, become profoundly rooted in the nation-building practices of these nation-states (Basch, Schiller, and Blanc 1994, 22). Transmigrants are also influenced by 'push/pull plus networks' (Nonini 2002). These networks set the conditions that 'push' or force individuals to leave their home country, or 'pull' or attract migrants to resettle in host countries (8–9). Such migration forms can be understood as economic, cultural, and political resistance towards their home countries. Their movements within transnational networks generate productive relationships.

The existence of immigrants as minorities has created 'minor transnationalism'. Minor transnationalism amasses transnationalised communities and identities, minority movements, and dispersed groups to construct a global civil society to challenge the immense forces of major transnationalism (Koshy 2005, 116). This challenge occurs by circulating global cultures, ideas, and capital within growing international integration spaces created by globalising forces in communication, migration, and capital movements (Lionnet and Shih 2005, 6–7). This challenge also struggles to position cultural practices and communication networks from the margin to the centre (Lionnet and Shih 2005, 6–7), conditions which have created resistant 'minor' transnational networks that flow from 'below'.

Transnational forces led the MDI filmmakers to acquire flexible positions within transnational networks and space, offering countless possibilities for production, distribution, and exhibition. Therefore, MDI filmmakers are no longer rigorously confined to time, distance, and space restrictions. Their pursuit of capital across multiple borders entitles them to the status of 'flexible citizenship' (Ong 1999). As 'multiple-passport holders', their displacement from the confines of the national displaces and problematises frameworks on what constitutes the Malaysian national cinema. The MDI transnational cinema presents a new cinematic framework of production, distribution, exhibition, and consumption. The discussions above have established how the different Malaysian cinema phases have been affected by different forms of transnationalism. This discussion establishes that Malaysian cinema has been transnational since its inception. The following section will examine this by reviewing the literature on Malaysian cinema, providing a framework that locates Malaysian cinema within the global context. This study of Malaysian cinema's history will examine its financing, production, distribution, and reception.

The History of Malaysian Cinema

The three phases of Malaysian cinema

The history of Malaysian cinema can be divided into three distinct phases. The first phase was influenced by network flows of capital, knowledge, labour, and capitalism; the second phase was influenced by state policies and Islamisation, and the third phase by globalisation. Within each phase, transnational forces have been heavily present due to transborder migratory movements, nation-building policies, and technological advancement. The three phases of Malaysian cinema were then influenced by the different forms of cinematic transnationalism employed: globalising transnationalism, cosmopolitan transnationalism, opportunistic transnationalism, milieu-building transnationalism, affinitive transnationalism, epiphanic transnationalism, auteurist transnationalism, modernising transnationalism, and experimental transnationalism (Hjort 2009).

The first phase occurred during the colonisation and de-colonisation period centred on the nation's independence in 1957.[37] Cinema was built on opportunistic transnationalism elements that presented an opportunity for interim monetary gains without the need to create lasting networks or valuable social bonds (Hjort 2009, 19–20). This phase witnessed Malaysian (Malayan) cinema's birth on the transnational forces of Malay actors, Chinese capital and labour control, and Indian creativity in search of capital gains. This transnational production method echoes the late filmmaker, historian, and critic Hamzah Hussin's description of how the Malaysian film industry was founded on Chinese money, Indian imagination, and Malay labour (van der Heide 2002, 105). The production, exhibition, and distribution of films during this phase were a duopoly between the Shaw Brothers' Malay Film Productions (MFP) and Cathay-Keris Films. Importance was given to economic issues in search of wealth that brought together three different nations. This phase also witnessed the Golden Age of Malaysian cinema and the eminence of P. Ramlee as Malaysia's most forceful entertainer. The majority of his films employed

---

37. During its independence from the British on 31 August 1957, Malaysia was known as Malaya. The incorporation of Singapore and the Borneo states of Sabah and Sarawak on 16 September 1963 led to Malaysia's official formation (Andaya and Andaya 2001, 274–277).

The Malaysian Digital Indies: Transnational Malaysian Cinema   43

a mixture of satire, melodrama, and comedy. Films such as *Miskin* (Poverty, 1952), *Antara Dua Darjat* (Between Two Classes, 1960) and the four *Bujang Lapok* films reminded audiences about the duties and struggles that lay ahead in the nation-building process of this newly independent nation. The *Bujang Lapok* comedies revolve around the lives of three broke bachelors, Ramli, Sudin, and Aziz, in search of love, fortune, and fame. The films *Bujang Lapok* (Broke Bachelors, 1957), *Pendekar Bujang Lapok* (Broke Bachelor Warriors, 1959), *Ali Baba Bujang Lapok* (Ali Baba and the Broke Bachelors, 1961), and *Seniman Bujang Lapok* (Broke Bachelor Artists, 1961) serve as criticisms and satires on the issues of poverty, illiteracy, and materialism.

The second phase occurred after 13 May 1969, which saw race riots.[38] During this time, cinema was used as a medium to help support NEP and NCP growth in line with Mahatir's modernisation era in the 1980s. Modernising transnationalism forges transnational networks to develop regulative ideals in society. It disseminates modernisation mechanisms through decisions designed to nurture a film culture that looks beyond the national (Hjort 2009, 24). During this phase, efforts to nationalise cinema meant the phasing out of Chinese and Indian influences and the emergence of *Bumiputera* independent companies and *Bumiputera* filmmakers. Films were almost entirely built around the *Melayu Baru*'s cinematic projection. An independent Malaysian New Wave movement also emerged to discuss Malay problems in a modernising nation. The Malaysian New Wave incorporated transnational influences through the lingering Indian cinematic styles, Islamic themes from the Iranian revolution, and foreign influences from Malay filmmakers sent for overseas training. During this phase, Malaysian cinema was divided into commercial mainstream cinema with filmmakers such as A. R. Badul [(*Mr. Os*), 1987], Z. Lokman [*Cikgu Romantik* (Romantic Teacher), 1993], and Zulkeflie M. Osman [*Suci Dalam Debu* (Pure in Dust), 1992]; and Malaysian New Wave directors such as Rahim Razali [*Abang* (Elder Brother), 1981], Mansor Puteh [(*Seman*), 1986], Shuhaimi Baba [*Ringgit Kasorrga* (High Society), 1995], and U-Wei Saari [*Jogho* (Champion), 1999]. The Malaysian New Wave produced films that discussed 'serious' issues faced by society, such as corruption, marginalisation, and poverty.

Since 2000, Malaysian cinema has been experiencing its third phase as it re-emerges internationally within the era of globalisation. This re-emergence is firstly aided by the increased porousness of national borders, the internet, the advent of cheaper filmmaking digital technology, and the lack of local governmental support.

---

38. One of the rationales provided by academics behind the riots was growing fear and suspicion of one ethnic community's probable ascendancy over the other. The Chinese were defending their language and cultural identity from Malay domination. At the same time, the Malays felt the community's ascending support towards the primarily based Chinese opposition parties as a threat to their political superiority (Brown 1996, 230–231). The worsening unrest and fighting had led to the Yang di-Pertuan Agong declaring a State of Emergency and suspended the constitution and parliament on 14 May. All executive powers were transferred to the National Operations Council (NOC), which operated as the temporary government headed by Deputy Prime Minister Abdul Razak (Andaya and Andaya 2001, 268).

Influenced by globalising transnationalism, inadequate local sources have forced these filmmakers to search for transnational funding to recover filmmaking costs (Hjort 2009, 21). Secondly, most MDI filmmakers are driven by 'push/pull plus networks' (Nonini 2002). These filmmakers are deterritorialised by local 'push' factors such as repressive cinematic regulations, which regulations deny them recognition as Malaysian films, and overseas 'pull' factors that attract them to utilise available funding, incentives, and exhibition circuits.

This phase is also the most dynamic era of Malaysian cinema. These films, critical of state policies, inequalities, and injustice in society, employ milieu-building transnationalism elements. While milieu-building transnationalism develops an artistically innovative and economical response to Hollywood, the MDI uses artistic undertakings as an alternative to commercial Malaysian mainstream cinema. Milieu-building transnationalism aims to transfer certain positive features, where comprehensive cultural policies significantly develop a viable film milieu (Hjort 2009, 18). The era of globalisation characterises this current growth of Malaysian cinema and its utilisation of transnational networks to create new approaches, production methods, exhibition, and distribution. In recognition of this, a further examination of these three phases will provide a framework for analysing how Malaysian cinema has always been a transnational cinema.

The first phase: The early beginnings (the 1890s to the 1960s)

Early Malaysian cinema began as a form of collective cinema between Malaysia (Malaya) and Singapore. Both countries often share a lot historically and culturally, as a result of British colonial rule. The birth of Malaysian (Malayan) cinema in Singapore led to both countries having similar cinematic histories. For both countries, the element of multi-ethnicity was also the most prominent. This element resulted from the mass migration of Chinese and Indian nationals to fill the vast job opportunities created by the British colonialists. This mass migration indirectly led to the birth of Malaysian cinema. An account of the origins of cinema in Malaysia would best illustrate the ethnic composition.

Malaysian cinema was pioneered by the three largest ethnic communities in Malaysia: Malay, Chinese, and Indian. This multicultural element, however, was not efficiently exploited on screen. Therefore, the first phase of Malaysian cinema was in line with 'opportunistic transnationalism', when cinema was financially exploited without any long-term obligations (Hjort 2009). Since the Malaysian cinema industry is essentially a commercial trade, the emphasis was placed on producing profitable films to recuperate their heavy investments. Malaysian cinema was therefore catered primarily for Malay audiences. Cinematic narratives often centred on the Malay culture using Malay casts. Non-Malays were customarily cast in intermittent roles as extras or were significant in 'concealed' roles of directing, producing, and technical support. Early films such as B. S. Rajhan's *Seruan Merdeka* (Call of

Freedom, 1946), L. Krishnan's *Selamat Tinggal Kekasihku* (Farewell My Lover, 1955), and P. Ramlee's *Gerimis* (Drizzle, 1968) portrayed some non-Malays as lead characters. In brief, Malaysian cinema has been transnational since its inception and was founded on the division along ethnic lines. This cinema was built by the transnational forces of Chinese capital and labour control, Indian creativity, and Malay actors.

Cinema arrived in Malaya during the early part of the twentieth century. However, scholars have offered conflicting opinions on the time, making it difficult to ascertain the exact arrival date of cinema in Malaya. The very first account was at the end of the nineteenth century. In 1897, a screening of scenes of the royal procession of the golden jubilee of Queen Victoria in Singapore using a Cinématographe by a Mr. Paul (Muthalib 2017). Other scholars claim that newspapers reported the public viewing in Kuala Lumpur of a film showing the golden jubilee of Queen Victoria but due to this event's prestige, only members of the royal elite and those closest to them were invited to witness this occasion (Lent 1990; Latif 2001). Others however claim that the first film screened in Malaya was in 1902 (Hassan and Wong 2002; Latif 2001). That the arrival of cinema happened in 1907, when an Englishman named Willis built the very first cinema in Singapore, but this point has been contested (Hatta 1997, 52). At that point, the screening of films merely exhibited the new medium, was not a commercial enterprise, and was restricted to upper-class echelons of society.

Scholars, however, attribute the beginning of Malaysian commercial cinema with *Laila Majnun* (1933) (Hatta 1997; van der Heide 2002; Hassan and Wong 2002; Hamzah 2004; Khoo 2006; Latif 2001). *Laila Majnun* was adapted from a famous Sanskrit love story predating Shakespeare's *Romeo and Juliet*. Produced as the first indigenous film in Malay, it was directed by B. S. Rajhans and financed by S. M. Chisty of Bombay Chemical Company (Latif 2001, 165–166). According to Hassan, 'No one living today has seen the film'. Suki Nordin, the lead actor, had not seen the film, as he was away on tour with a *bangsawan* troupe when it was screened. The film's acting mode was heavily inflected with the *bangsawan* style and came complete with the ubiquitous 'song and dance' (2006, 44). In less than fifteen years, commercial cinema became readily established in Malaya. Chinese entrepreneurs built cinema halls in significant towns in Malaya or brought portable screening equipment to the *kampongs* (Lent 1990, 186). In 1937, two brothers from Shanghai, Run Run Shaw and Runme Shaw, attempted to produce locally made films adapted from Chinese stories, directed by Chinese directors, and local *bangsawan* actors (a form of traditional Malay opera and known to have been influenced by Indian theatre during the nineteenth century by visiting Indian travellers) (Latif 2001, 168).[39] The Shaw Brothers established a film unit in Singapore and produced nine films within

---

39. For more information on the *bangsawan* influence on early Malaysian cinema, see Hatta (1997, 53–57) and Latif (2001, 165–167).

three years, but they were not well received by local audiences (Kahn 2006, 126). The inability of local audiences to identify with Chinese stories and themes, and the advent of the Japanese Occupation, brought the Shaw Brothers' cinematic venture to a quick end (Hassan and Wong 2002, 301–302).

The studio era

In 1949, the Shaw Brothers returned and resumed production under the company MFP. Based in Singapore, at no. 8 Jalan Ampas, MFP's studio system emulated the highly successful Hollywood production and star system (Latif 2001, 168–171). The closest rival to MFP was Cathay-Keris. Formed from the partnership of Ho Ah Loke and Loke Wan Tho in 1953, Cathay-Keris Films marked the beginning of the duopoly of the production, distribution, and exhibition of Malay films. The two Chinese studios practically dominated every phase of production, exhibition, and distribution. From thirty-five cinemas in 1929, the number increased to 368 in 1975 (Armes 1987, 149). The initial ownership and control of early Malaysian cinema was concentrated in Chinese hands. They owned the rights to production, distribution, and exhibition circuits. Their resources led to creating a transnational cinema, which blended Chinese capital, a Malay workforce, and Indian creativity. MFP brought in notable Indian directors such as B. S. Rajhans, L. Krishnan, and B. N. Rao. Malays were employed as crossover actors from the *bangsawan* troupes. This transnational flow of resources produced a network of institutions, commodities, capital, and human resources no longer strictly restrained by time, distance, and space. It created a unique hybridity of style, identification, and ideology to become the foundation of Malaysian cinema.

In 1955, the prominence of transnational foreign influence was expanded to the Philippines. MFP engaged the services of Filipino directors, due to their cultural and language resemblance. The similarities between Tagalog and Bahasa Malaysia and the lifestyle resemblance between southern Filipino Muslims and Malays helped alleviate cultural differences. Filipino directors introduced efficient American-influenced shooting and lighting techniques (van der Heide 2002, 136). The filmmakers engaged were prominent and critically acclaimed: Ramon Estella, Rolf Bayer, and Lamberto V. Avellana. Their achievements were mirrored by recognition and accolades from various international film festivals. While these directors were among the best in Asia and had directed numerous films in Malaya (Hatta 1997, 85), only *Sergeant Hassan* (1958) by Avellana became well known. Nonetheless, a benchmark had ultimately been set during the short stint that these directors were working. This phenomenon justifies the argument that transnational cinema emerges in the interstices between the local and the global.

The Indian filmmakers' cinematic style greatly influenced Malaysian cinema, as the Indians and Malays had many cultural similarities.[40] Besides being culturally connected, the Indians were better versed in English and were paid less (van der Heide 2002, 133). Most of them merely reproduced locally successful Tamil, Hindi, or Bengali film scripts in Malay (Latif 2001, 166). The employment of melodramatic methods, laden with overacting elements, song, and dance, was progressively well-accepted as the outline of early Malay cinema (Hassan and Wong 2002, 301). Building and constructing a national identity and culture was not significantly prominent, for these films were Indian. The only prominently Malay feature was the Malays casts speaking Malay (Hatta 1997, 68).

Nonetheless, these films had not hindered local audiences from accepting the styles adopted by the Indian directors, for Indian cinema was already popularly accepted (van der Heide 2002, 141). To some extent, Indian cinema and culture will be continually relevant to the Malaysian film culture (van der Heide 2002, 11). Malay film has a preference for the Indian film and narrative style that still exist subconsciously in present-day cinema (Latif 2001, 166–167). The employment of Indian directors was heavily influenced by specific institutional demands and cinema's geopolitics and economics.

While cultural similarities between the Malays and Indians have benefitted the Indian directors, they occasionally erred in their cinematic representation of Malay lifestyles. These directors were unaware of Malay etiquette and manners when Malay women were portrayed as unrefined, alluring, immodest, and not appropriately dressed (Hatta 1997, 80). Furthermore, there was the expurgation of the Malay cultural identity, for the style and techniques of song and dance were Indian in essence (80). These cultural problems led to calls for a Malay director who could better identify with the Malay socio-cultural existence. One of the main difference separating the two studios was that, although Cathay-Keris emulated the system of using Indian directors, Malay individuals were eventually given opportunities by Cathay-Keris to establish themselves as directors (71). As Malay nationalistic sentiments grew, literary activists expressed their unhappiness about Malay status in cinema. They lamented the production of Malay films in foreign hands and called for a deeper understanding of the Malay customs and traditions (87). In line with mounting nationalistic sentiments about the advent of the nation's independence in 1957 was the call for a Malay director well versed in the Malay culture. This call was met by P. Ramlee.

---

40. The cultural similarities between the Indians and the Malays can be seen through the influences of Indian cultural heritage in the Malay way of life, art forms, and popular entertainment. Examples are the adaptation of stories from the Hindu epics of *Mahabharata* and *Ramayana* in the famous traditional Malay art forms of *Wayang Kulit* and *Makyong*. The Malays found it easy to understand the plots and characters of Indian films, as they were presented along with the same linear structure as that of the Indian epic stories (Hatta 1997, 79).

P. Ramlee and the Golden Age of Malaysian cinema

The years 1955 to 1965 are often dubbed the Golden Age of Malaysian cinema (Hatta 1997; Khoo 2006; Latif 2001). This period witnessed the intense rivalry between MFP and Cathay-Keris that led to the pinnacle of cinematic output and a vast improvement in cinematic qualities (Hassan and Wong 2002, 303–304). While Malaysian cinema remained transnational, this period also corresponded with calls for greater Malay involvement at the industry's helm. These calls were met with P. Ramlee's directorial debut as Malaysia's first transnational actor and director. As MFP introduced P. Ramlee, in return Cathay-Keris introduced S. Roomai Noor as its first Malay director in 1956, which ultimately paved the way for Malay directors' domination (Hatta 1997, 88).

Ramlee's films existed as transnational products. His films were heavily influenced by the filmmaking techniques of Akira Kurosawa, John Ford, Alfred Hitchcock, and Satyajit Ray (Latif 2001, 182–183) and diversely influenced by Indian and Japanese predecessors. They also adopted historical dramas, contemporary melodramas, romance, and Middle-Eastern type fantasies (Kahn 2006, 128).[41] Born Amar Teuku Zakaria bin Teuku Nyak Puteh, P. Ramlee is recognised as Malaysia's most prominent cinematic figure. His talents ranged from acting, directing, and scriptwriting, to singing and composing. P. Ramlee was hailed as the first superstar of Malaysian cinema. Local and international audiences recognised his talents as a filmmaker, songwriter, and actor. Numerous awards from Asia-Pacific Film Festivals bore testament to his talents, and his films are often studied as a reflection of the culture and changing society during postcolonial times.

His debut film, *Penarik Becha* (Trishaw Puller, 1955), was hailed as the best Malay film in 1955. The confidence of MFP in Ramlee's capabilities was rewarded with immense success. After *Penarik Becha*, Ramlee directed over thirty films for

Figure 1.2: P. Ramlee and music composer Ooi Eow Jin going into the forest to provide emotional support for the soldiers who were defending Malaya from the Communists circa 1960s. Source: Elaine Khaw.

---

41. In 1973, he died and was posthumously awarded the title of Tan Sri. He remains a national icon. His films continue to be rerun on local television, and his works are continuously studied. For a detailed account of Ramlee's life, see Harding and Ahmad (2002) and Awang and Khor (2005).

them. His flexibility in crossing over different genres and amalgamating various musical styles from different cultures led him to become a lucrative asset (Kahn 2006, 128). His movies were popular with Malays and screened in cinemas across Malaya, Singapore, and Indonesia (129). The tremendous popularity of Ramlee also extended to Hollywood. Hollywood was keen on developing the Malayan film market, as the Malayan filmgoing public then earned the most money per head of population (129). This figure disproved the theory that Malays were incapable of handling directorial roles.

The success of Ramlee as a Malay director lay in his ability to interact closely with the audience. Although the Indian filmic approaches lingered in Malay films, Ramlee blended the storylines with local colour and values (Hatta 1997, 92). His portrayal of Malay class struggles and ultimate rise enabled him to empathise with audiences and, likewise, his audiences with him. His use of comedy and satire to critique religion, racial tolerance, and social class served as reminders to the Malays to amend their weaknesses and shortcomings (Hassan and Wong 2002, 306). It is through these constructions that new expressions of politics, culture, and economics in line with state institutions and apparatuses were created (Mahyuddin and Lee, 2015). The themes depicted in his films bear a closer resemblance to the period's social reality than do the fantasised tales of the Indian world.

The establishment of a Malay cinema culture was a strenuous effort to instil a sense of pride and belonging by creating a national film character representing the people's traditions and cultures (Hatta 1997, 88–93). The popularity of Malay films can thus be attributed to their realistic and unpretentious themes. Ramlee's films also continuously attracted multi-ethnic audiences and created an incorporative sense of 'Malaysianness' (van der Heide 2002, 141). This attraction occurred because Malaysians' social and cultural backgrounds were similar to the struggles due to social and cultural backgrounds to those faced by the newly independent society coping with modernity. It was a crucial uniting element required in a newly independent nation searching for its national identity.

The decline of the cinema industry

The cinema industry suffered a decline and faced a severe financial crisis from the late 1960s. Among the reasons was the increase in production costs, union problems, the introduction of television, and intense transposition of films from Hong Kong, India, and Indonesia. Audiences had also become intolerant of local films with shallow storylines using outdated and recycled themes (Hassan and Wong 2002, 307–308).[42]

---

42. In 1963, the Department of Broadcasting/Radio Televisyen Malaysia (RTM) was launched. RTM is currently under the Ministry of Information, Communications and Culture.

In 1967, MFP ceased production, and in 1973, Cathay-Keris. The critical factor that led to the closure of these studios was Singapore's secession from Malaysia in 1963.[43] This event led to the emigration of talents from Singapore to Kuala Lumpur's Merdeka Studios (Hatta 1997). Opened by the Shaw Brothers in 1964, the studios were seen as a dichotomisation of the industry. Eventually, Merdeka Studios encountered the same insubstantial economic and technological troubles that primarily caused the audience to abjure Malay films. Their eventual closure in 1980 marked the end of Malaysia's studio system (Hassan and Wong 2002, 307–309).

The second phase: The nationalisation of cinema (the 1970s to the 1990s)

The second phase was of modernising the transnationalism (Hjort 2009) of nationalising cinema. In 1972, the film industry hit its lowest point. Hundreds of filmmakers were made jobless when studios faced difficulties in hiring foreign or local talents and properly qualified personnel. At the same time, filmmaking facilities and equipment became insufficient and obsolete (Lent 1990, 190). Audiences had the displeasure of watching washed-up actors lined with archaic themes when studios could not recruit new talents or hire overseas actors (191). This situation resulted in many films being heavily criticised for having unrealistic and uninspiring storylines which lacked a social conscience (190).

The cinematic content of Malaysian cinema continued to be Malay-centric. Although cinema occasionally highlighted issues of socio-cultural criticism through the films of Ramlee, it was dismissed as pure entertainment (Kahn 2006, 107–133). Films contained melodramatised and romanticised themes related to Malay culture, customs, and traditions (*adat*), class, 'blood', Islam's virtues, qualities of leaders, and romantic love (128). The cinema industry chose to stay away from being embroiled in the current political and social struggles of that moment, for fear of offending the colonial masters (193). This failure to propagate Malay nationalism and capitalise on the cinema's popularity was that the Chinese owned Malaysian cinema. This failure led to more significant government intervention calls to transfer cinema ownership and control to the *Bumiputera* community.

Malaysian cinema had always been a privately owned enterprise, and ownership and control lay in the hands of Chinese entrepreneurs. Simultaneously, non-existent governmental support, financing, and facilities did not hinder the industry's growth.

---

43. Issues relating to ethnicity, the unique positioning of Malays, parliamentary and cabinet representation, national security and parliamentary elections were questioned by Singapore's People's Action Party (PAP). This situation led to distrust between the (then) Alliance Party (now BN) and PAP in policymaking relating to politics and economics. It was made worse when PAP questioned the affirmative action for Malays as discrimination against the Chinese. The ideological differences were evident when PAP called for fairness and equality among all race and ethnic communities. The UMNO elites and MCA did not accept Lee Kuan Yew's 'Malaysian Malaysia' campaign well. They saw his questioning of Malay rights as a seditious and plausible cause for ethnic violence (Cheah 2002, 54). In 1965, PAP unwillingly agreed to the Alliance Party's decision to secede Singapore from Malaysia.

The state was never actively involved in developing policies for Malaysian cinema's growth, which was commonly accepted as popular entertainment. Its focal idea as a commercial enterprise would be the aim of wealth accumulation. However, the industry's decline led to calls by several filmmakers for state intervention to revive the industry and nationalise Malaysian cinema (Hatta 1997). In 1975, the then-Minister of Trade and Industry proposed forming a National Film Corporation to end the reliance on foreign films and monopolisation of production, distribution, and exhibition in a few corporations (Hassan and Wong 2002). Government intervention aimed to place the Chinese-owned cinema industry under national control. These policies were designed to significantly exploit cinema by diffusing the Malay cultural identity as the new subject matter. Although this practice of cinema relocation was generally the transfer of capital control from foreign dominance to Malaysian ownership, it had inadvertently excluded the participation of other ethnic communities.

Criticisms of the domination of production, distribution, and exhibition by specific organisations and heavy reliance on foreign films were indirect allusions to the end of Chinese control. FINAS was formed through the National Film Corporation Act (1981) and placed under the Ministry of Trade and Industry.[44] In line with ensuring the continued sustainability of Malaysian films, its objectives were to promote, nurture, and facilitate its development. FINAS was launched to support the film industry financially through funding and loans, technical assistance, and budding filmmakers' training, and policies to help alleviate the industry. Its main complex at the former Merdeka Studios houses production, post-production, and film exhibition, including a film training institute. FINAS also intended to promote Malaysian national identity internationally by publicising Malaysian culture through its films (Narayasamy 2005, 13). FINAS was established to protect the local film producers and stimulate the growth of local films to accommodate local consumption. To avoid competing with the local producers, to ensure a healthy business environment, FINAS is not directly involved in the film trade. The move to insist on compulsory Bahasa Malaysia subtitles for all imported films was a positive shift towards national unity and nation-building efforts (Hassan and Wong 2002, 313–314). The Anti-Trust Bill limits participation to production or distribution, distribution and exhibition, or production and exhibition. Additional measures to boost and build a Malaysian film industry of international standard were encouraging more film productions.[45] FINAS introduced schemes such as lifting film stock duties and introducing the Entertainment Tax Scheme and the *Skim Wajib Tayang* (Compulsory Screening Scheme). The Entertainment Tax Scheme collects 25 per cent of the domestic box office to be refunded to certified local films.

---

44. In 1986, FINAS was placed under the Ministry of Information. It was then placed under the Ministry of Culture, Arts and Heritage on 27 March 2004.

45. For the objectives, vision, and mission of FINAS, see http://www.finas.gov.my/.

The Compulsory Screening Scheme states that a local film must be screened for a minimum mandatory period of fourteen consecutive days in local cinemas. Only one local film is allowed for release every two weeks, to avoid competition among local producers. On 23 February 2011, the Malaysian cabinet introduced the Films Return Incentive Scheme to replace the Entertainment Tax Scheme. The new incentive scheme was based on ticket sales returns and box-office collections.[46]

A closer examination of these policies and guidelines shows the state's approach to assisting *Bumiputera* filmmakers through the need for capital enlargement, ownership, and participation in the more attractive and lucrative occupations (Jomo 2004, 19). The representations of the nation in Malay films did not reflect the nation-state's construction or celebrate Malaysia's cultural diversity and hybridity. Further efforts to 'Malayanise' the film industry leaned towards 'anti-Chinese' efforts to minimise the ownership and control of Chinese-owned film companies to de-emphasise several national or cultural identity ideas in post-1969 Malaysia (Raju 2008, 70).

Government intervention in ending Chinese participation in Malaysian cinema can be divided into two phases. The first phase was the proposed establishment of a third chain of cinemas to compete directly with the Shaw Brothers and Cathay-Keris or through a buyout of company shares. The influential role of cinema in Malaysia shows that films screened in Malaysia have a cumulative effect on the psyche or national mentality by quietly influencing the audience's thoughts, behaviours, and receptivity (Baharudin 1983, 2). The second phase required the takeover of all independent cinemas by FINAS (6–8). FINAS aimed to correct the disparity between the *Bumiputera* and non-*Bumiputera* companies by assisting the *Bumiputera* community in obtaining a minimum of 30 per cent involvement in the production, distribution, and exhibition of a film (117). FINAS thus acts as a 'catalyst' to revitalise the film industry with effective *Bumiputera* involvement (13). A detailed understanding of an exclusively *Bumiputera* cinema industry's effects to create nation-building, national identity, and national unity is essential.

The independent *Bumiputera* era

The collapse of the Chinese-owned studio system altered Malaysian cinema's landscape when ownership and capital control shifted from foreign to local ownership. Despite Malaysian films being nationalised, their focus remained Malay-centric. The NEP's affirmative action helped establish independent *Bumiputera* production companies. The NEP, also dubbed the '*Bumiputera* policy' (Shamsul 1998), was well

---

46. For example, MYR200,000 (US$50,000) would be returned to a film with a box-office collection or ticket sales between MYR2 million (US$500,000) and MYR4 million (US$1 million), 10 per cent returned to a film which collects between MYR4 million (US$1 million) and MYR6 million (US$1.5 million), and 5 per cent returned to a film which collects MYR6 million (US$1.5 million). Films that collect more than MYR6 million (US$1.5 million) will not be given any incentives.

The Malaysian Digital Indies: Transnational Malaysian Cinema

reflected through the *Bumiputera* era's cinema. This interplay between state-legalised discriminatory policies which benefitted *Bumiputera* capitalist profiteering is examined.

In 1967, the first independent *Bumiputera* production company, Gabungan Artis Filem Company (GAFICO), was formed (Hatta 1997, 123). In 1972, the government attempted to fill the void of an almost absent film industry through the establishment of Fleet Communications (a subsidiary of Fleet Group, the investment arm of the ruling party, UMNO) as an effort to produce a new genre of Malay films (Zawawi 2007, 514–515). Founded by then-Finance Minister Tengku Razaleigh, it was direct involvement of the state in the film industry through direct investment and co-production. In 1975, the full-colour box-office hit *Keluarga Si Comat* (Comat's Family, 1975) led prospective investors to believe that quick returns could be made in the film industry. Directed by Aziz Sattar and produced by Deddy M. Borhan leading an all-Malay crew, its success was seen as the dawn of the Malay film revival (Hassan and Wong 2002, 314). The film revolved around the Malay lifestyle and featured an entire Malay cast, while pioneering the way for full-colour features although the first full-colour feature, *Buloh Perindu* (The Magical Bamboo, 1953), was produced by Cathay-Keris. MFP produced its first colour film, *Hang Tuah* (The Legend of Hang Tuah), in 1956. This venture proved too costly for processing because it had to be done abroad due to the lack of a local film processing lab. Although films continued to be made in black and white until 1975, notable colour features such as *Raja Bersiong* (Fanged King, 1968) were occasionally made.

In 1976, Perfirma Film Production successfully produced *Menanti Hari Esok* by overseas-trained Jins Shamsuddin (Hatta 1997, 123). However, the inadequate grasp of filmic concepts of production, marketing, and distribution led to their eventual closure (Hassan and Wong 2002, 314).

The need to enhance the social standing of the *Bumiputeras* created a new group of overseas-trained filmmakers. These individuals were sent abroad through government sponsorship to receive formal education in arts or film. Notable directors who have emerged from this sponsorship are Hafsham, Jins Shamsuddin, Rahim Razali, and Mansor Puteh, who pioneered the Malaysian New Wave film movement (Hassan and Wong 2002, 316).

The Malaysian New Wave

Despite efforts at nationalising cinema, transnational influences continued to inspire Malaysian cinema through a new group of filmmakers who were trained abroad. These overseas-trained filmmakers sponsored by the government created the Malaysian New Wave film movement that challenged various social issues and state policies. Profoundly influenced by elements of realism and artistic cinematic styles of European cinema, the Malaysian New Wave directors often produced thought-provoking 'artsy' films.

54   *Malaysian Cinema in the New Millennium*

The Malaysian New Wave filmmakers reintroduced transnational influences of foreign-based filmmaking techniques, skills, and themes. The continued transnationalism of Malaysian cinema (albeit an almost one-way flow) focuses on the flows of cultural hybridity that construct the national, the international, and the transnational, without concern for geographical locations and physical boundaries. This flow problematises the currently accepted notions of a pre-existing national identity being negotiated through national cinema. These thought-provoking films provided a new platform that challenged and discussed various social issues, mainly about the Malays being caught in the threshold of upholding their traditional values and struggling in a modernising Malaysia.

In the 1970s, the cultural flows and influences from the Middle East *dakwah* movement heavily influenced Malaysian cinema.[47] The call for a rebranded appearance of Islam and the conflict between the 'new' Islam and the Hindu-influenced Malay tradition was often critiqued by Malaysian New Wave directors (G. C. Khoo 2003, 230–231).[48] This situation created a dilemma for urban Malay women and men caught between traditionalism and modernity based upon Islamic faith (Khoo 2006, 109). Malay women and men were constructed through the obligation of language and modern Islam's practices as defined by the constitution and the customary practice of Malay *adat* (customs and traditions). As the practice of *adat* heavily influenced by Hinduism and mystical elements is prohibited in film, its incorporation into Malaysian New Wave films such as *Selubung* (Veil of Life, 1992) and *Perempuan, Isteri dan . . . ?* (Woman, Wife, and Whore, 1993) meant that it challenged state-given definitions of *adat* and Islam (109). For the sake of national unity and pride, these filmmakers practised self-censorship to continuously prove their obedience to Islam's superiority in Malaysia and challenged seeking an identity balancing between Islam, *adat*, and modernity (108–109).

---

47. Led by Anwar Ibrahim, Angkatan Belia Islam Malaysia (ABIM), a radical student movement, called for the mobilisation and transformation of Islamic youth. It upheld Islamic values, principles, and law by establishing an Islamic state. In the 1970s, Malay students sent abroad under the NEP came in contact with Middle Eastern students influenced by the Iranian Islamic revolution and their ideas of a revivalist Islam. Upon return, they began a populist political Islamic youth movement calling for missionary work, social welfare, proselytisation, and Islamisation. Heavily critical of the government's stand on power abuse, corruption, and Westernisation, the movement's holistic Islamic view of social, economic, and spiritual growth was shared with the opposition PAS. In response to declining government support and growing civil unrest, the government responded by appointing Anwar Ibrahim to the government (Esposito and Voll 2001, 183–190). For a detailed examination of the *dakwah* movement, see Khoo 1995, 159–162. For a detailed examination of the government's response to the Malaysian *dakwah* movement (see Chong 2006, 27–31).

48. According to Shamsul, the motivation for the *dakwah* movement was: an attempt to overcome the pressures of modernisation or to construct a reply to it; a type of anti-imperialist, anti-hegemonical movement; an expression of spiritual renewal generated from within a given religion, such as the move to 're-Islamise knowledge'; a counter-movement to rationalisation; an attempt to resolve how to live in a world of radical doubt; an expression of modernity through reformulation of cultural gestalt; a reinterpretation of traditional symbols and systems of meaning; and an attempt to reinvent and reconstruct tradition, thus allowing a redefinition and assertion of ethnoreligious identities in a plural society (1995, 112).

Women directors became prominent in the 1980s, probably due to the influence of the simultaneous global rise of feminist movements. An examination of Malaysian cinema history shows that Malaysian filmmakers have been predominantly men, and the first attempt to introduce a female director, in 1962, failed. Siput Sarawak's proposed directorial debut through the film *Mata Syaitan* (Satan Eyes, 1962) was met with objections from the Cathay-Keris workers' union. Among the objections were her lack of directing experience and inept writing and reading skills. Ultimately, she agreed to have Hussein Haniff direct the film instead (Hamzah 2004, 102–103).

Nonetheless, Saadiah became the first female Malaysian film director through her directorial debut, *Ceritaku Ceritamu* (My Story, Your Story, 1979) (Jamil Sulong 1990). While her works were not screened beyond the Malaysian shores, her contribution paved the way for other successful women filmmakers such as Shuhaimi Baba, Erma Fatimah, and Yasmin Ahmad. During this era, female empowerment and feminist themes were highlighted through *Femina* (1993) and *Layar Lara* (The Sad Screen, 1997). However, these films hardly discussed the proper cinematic representation of female subjects from a critical viewpoint (Hassan and Wong 2002).

Film genres and themes successfully matured with Aziz M. Osman's sci-fi film *XX Ray* (1992) and *Perempuan, Isteri dan . . . ?*. Overseas-trained Malaysian New Wave filmmakers such as Rahim Razali, U-Wei Haji Saari, and Shuhaimi Baba were heavily influenced by Western classical cinema. They were more artistic, daring, radical, and bold, They highlighted corruption, tensions, and frustrations resulting from the Malays' marginalisation and modernisation (Hassan and Wong 2002). Filmmakers such as Adman Saleh, who produced *Amok* (1995), employed heavy elements of realism to depict the Malay struggles with modernisation and were critical of society and class (Zawawi 2007). Another specific accomplishment of the Malaysian New Wave filmmakers was the emergence of Malay films achieving international acclaim at international film festivals. U-Wei Saari's *Kaki Bakar* was the first Malaysian film screened at the Cannes Film Festival (Hassan and Wong 2002, 320–324). Made in 1995 and inspired by William Faulkner's *Barn Burning*, *Kaki Bakar* was originally shot on video to be slotted as one of the many locally made TV dramas televised on the government-owned television network RTM. It was denied airtime, reportedly due to its relatively strong social commentaries (Koay 2001, 6).

This achievement of screening films at an international film festival was to be emulated by the MDI filmmakers whose works are influenced by the *Bangsa Malaysia*, the advent of inexpensive DV equipment, the democratisation of social space through the internet, and increased political and social awareness through the *Reformasi* movement.

2000–2012: The third phase, post-2000 Malaysian cinema, and the Malaysian Digital Indies

The growing forces of globalising transnationalism continue to influence Malaysian cinema. In an increasingly globalised world, filmmakers have begun to rely heavily on transnational methods of funding, production, distribution, and exhibition to compensate for the inadequacy of local resources (Hjort 2009). Therefore, it has become increasingly complex to locate a Malaysian cinema as a purely national effort, for its films continue to be transnational.

A new generation of Malaysian filmmakers constitutes the MDI. These filmmakers emerged in the era of advanced global capitalism and neo-Islamisation in Malaysia. During their emergence, mainstream cinematic output was also at its lowest. This film movement has made its presence felt in the local and international cinematic circuits and within the burgeoning field of regional Asian cinemas. The MDI, as a transnational cinema, problematises the identity of the national cinema. It is problematised when the MDI operates on transnational networks of production, distribution, exhibition, and consumption and fails to fit appropriately within the Malaysian borders. This progressive transition from national to transnational context has allowed this cinema to emerge as a platform to deconstruct stereotypes established in Malaysian cinema. This cinema also questions national policies and contests hegemony, renegotiates race and ethnicity, and constructs a new national identity.

The MDI's subject matter and themes also problematise the state's customary ideologies by emerging as a site for contesting hegemonic and accepted state ideologies. By working around state film regulations, MDI filmmakers have been undaunted in tackling issues long ignored by mainstream Malaysian commercial cinema. While these policies and events have facilitated the emergence of the MDI, these films move beyond superficial multiculturalism through cosmopolitan themes. Without belonging to any particular ethnic community, the MDI renegotiates multiculturalism and adopts a postethnic approach. The postethnic approach, which refers to the study of ethnicity 'beyond multiculturalism' using cosmopolitan themes (Hollinger 1995), challenges the hegemonic exclusivism and mainstream negation of a culturally diverse Malaysia. The postethnic approach imagines a postethnic nation that moves beyond the indoctrination of race and ethnicity. Ultimately, how does this move by the transnational MDI problematise and contest national cinema's accepted notions and national identity?

The emergence of the MDI as a transnational cinema rightfully deconstructs Malaysian cinema as problematic. It has been built on the ageing of particular discourses of race and ethnicity. The current artistic visual cinema expressed through the MDI is generally perceived as the coming of a new artistic cinematic movement. In this book, the MDI is viewed as an 'offspring' of the movement of committed arthouse films that emerged in the 1980s under the Malaysian New Wave framework.

While the mainstream cinema of this era failed to capitalise on globalisation's benefits, the MDI has emerged as a transnational cinema. Lacking the support in state funding and locations for exhibition, and having oppressive laws barring its creativity, it moved beyond the Malaysian borders. Audiences of international film festivals widely accepted it. The deterritorialisation of this transnational and cosmopolitan cinema problematises the accepted notion of Malaysian national cinema constructed on race and ethnicity elements, influenced and determined by controlling capital and policies.

This book will further discuss the elements that constitute Malaysian cinema and search for changes presented by the MDI in the post-2000 Malaysian cinema era. How can Malaysian cinema be theorised as a transnational cinema? How does the MDI help construct the national identity of postcolonial Malaysia? What changes, if any, can be found in the representation of the marginalised in society? What are the new genres and new forms emerging in post-2000 Malaysian cinema and through the MDI? How does the MDI advance the growth and development of inter-ethnic relationships in a multi-ethnic community such as Malaysia? What are the best methods for studying the financing, production, distribution, and reception of the MDI when its 'nationality' is questioned due to its movement across Malaysian borders? How does transnational cinema's framework help us critically examine the national cinema's specificity against the overwhelming force of transnational capital? This book analyses how the MDI is constituted as a site for contesting these state policies and ideologies in a postcolonial nation undergoing socio-cultural and political transitions.

2

The Malaysian Digital Indies: A Digital Independent Transnational Cinema

'It was a little surprising that an international magazine picked up on a low profile Malaysian art film such as this. But all credit to it for doing so. I often find that foreigners give Malaysian artists more respect and support than Malaysians themselves. I think we have to try harder to win over our own people in the future. As said, we're some ways from being able to do that consistently, but hopefully we can someday'

—Pete Teo, *15Malaysia* Project Producer in reference to *Time Magazine's* article on James Lee's DV feature, *Call If You Need Me* (2009) (Logeswary 2009).[1]

This chapter discusses how the MDI has created a new informal film culture and cinema's political economy through its independence in production, exhibition, and distribution methods. It focuses on how transnational methods employed by the MDI have enabled this cinema movement to contest national issues while challenging the backdrop of Malay hegemonic cinema. The rise of the MDI is concurrent with the present technological craze and industrial boom in Asia. The introduction of the cheaper and more affordable DV format and foreign co-productions has revived the film industry in many parts of Asia. Its transnational digital filmmaking is inexpensive and has helped many filmmakers overcome the problem of budget constraints.

---

1. Premiering at the 14th BIFF in South Korea, *15Malaysia* is a project consisting of fifteen short films about Malaysia. Led by project producer and multiple award-winning singer and songwriter Pete Teo, *15Malaysia* features some of the country's more prominent independent film directors, actors, musicians, and politicians. The projects highlight socio-political, cultural, and religious issues in Malaysia and were done using a mixture of comedy, melodrama, black humour, and semi-documentaries. The videos can be viewed online at http://15malaysia.com/films/. They have been downloaded more than half a million times from the website and have 105,947 fans on the popular social networking website Facebook. Teo described the response to *15Malaysia* as 'pretty phenomenal' when the *15Malaysia* websites achieved fourteen million visits within its first sixty days. Among the more popular films are *Potong Saga* (2009) and *Meter* (2009), which Teo describes as having achieved the status of 'popular cultural icons'. According to him, the reasons for the success of this project were that *15Malaysia* provided a channel to discuss these issues and Malaysians were starving for social-politically informed dialogue beyond the normal sycophantic whitewash from official sources (Logeswary 2009). The success of this project premiering in film festivals around Asia and Europe has surprisingly received much media coverage from local mainstream media such as English dailies *The Star* and the *New Straits Times*.

The Malaysian Digital Indies: A Digital Independent Transnational Cinema 59

This situation has led many young filmmakers on shoestring budgets to embrace the DV format due to its affordability, versatility, and efficiency. This form of technological accessibility has lowered the entry barrier for many aspects of filmmaking. Before making its way to Asia, the DV format was used by filmmakers in the US and Europe. The advent of the consumer camcorder in the 1980s and the usage of DV technology with ultra-low budgets in the 1990s led to the production of notable independent digital films such as Michael Almereyda's *Another Girl Another Planet* (1992), Daniel Myrick and Edwardo Sanchez's *The Blair Witch Project* (1999), and René Besson's *Boxes* (2000). Digital technology also revived Peru's Grupo Chaski's career through *Sueños lejanos* (2007). In Europe, the Danish Dogme 95 utilised digital filmmaking technology to produce avant-garde films. Notable features include Thomas Vinterberg's *The Celebration* (1998), Lars von Trier's *The Idiots* (1999), and Kristian Levring's *The King is Alive* (2000). In Asia, the Sixth Generation Chinese cinema is almost synonymous with digital filmmaking (Hageman 2009, 74). It has inspired Jia Zhang Ke's *In Public* (2001), *Unknown Pleasures* (2002), and *Still Life* (2006).

In Southeast Asia, the DV format inspired Thai filmmaker Thunska Pansittivorakul to produce *Voodoo Girls* (2003), Michael Shaowanasai and Apichatpong Weerasethakul to produce *The Adventures of Iron Pussy* (2003), and Aditya Assarat to produce *Wonderful Town* (2007). In Singapore, Djinn produced *Return to Pontianak* (2001), while James Toh, Abdul Nizam, and Cheah Chee Kong produced *The Music Teacher, Haura*, and *Click Stories About Love* (2000) compilation. In Indonesia, Rizal Mantovani and José Purnomo produced *Jelankung* (2001), and Riri Riza produced *Eliana, Eliana* (2002). In the Philippines, Khavn de la Cruz produced *The Twelve* (2000), John Torres produced *Todo Todo Teros* (2006) and *Auraeus Solito's Ang Pagdadalaga ni Maximo Oliveros* (2005). These films were made using the DV format and meagre budgets.

Similarly, the DV format revived the Malaysian film industry. Since 2000, a new generation of Malaysian filmmakers has been making its presence felt within the local and international cinematic landscape. This new independent cinematic movement emerged when cinematic output in the Malaysian cinema industry was at its lowest and experiencing an unprecedented decline. Since the emergence of the MDI, this phenomenon has been reversed. Malaysian daily the *New Straits Times* describes the MDI as a group of 'young, high-spirited and enthusiastic filmmakers' with 'bold and fresh minds' who have elevated the status of Malaysian cinema (Hafidah and Faridul 2004, 11).

In post-2000 Malaysian cinema, the number of Malaysian-made films has increased more than 600 per cent, from just six films made in 2000 to a record-breaking forty-one in 2011.[2] This chapter discusses how the MDI deconstructs the current Malaysian social-cultural and political landscape within the era of

---

2. Information obtained from the FINAS website.

post-nationalism, globalisation, and neoliberalism, both thematically (on an ideological level) and through its means of production.

As explained, the MDI is a new generation of Malaysian filmmakers emerging in the era of advanced global capitalism. Pioneering the MDI is a new generation of cine-literate independent filmmakers. MDI filmmakers such as Amir Muhammad, Tan Chui Mui, Deepak Kumaran Menon, Yasmin Ahmad, and Ho Yuhang mostly come from middle-class urban backgrounds, are well educated, or educated overseas. The MDI comprises filmmakers with formal filmmaking training (Tan Chui Mui, Deepak Kumaran, and Liew Seng Tat studied filmmaking at Multimedia University), who are media practitioners (James Lee has a background in theatre productions, and Yasmin Ahmad was an advertising executive), or self-taught filmmakers (Ho Yuhang and Khoo Eng Yow are engineers by profession). Based in Malaysia's capital city, Kuala Lumpur, these filmmakers mostly employ DV equipment due to budget restrictions and their knowledge and proficiency with technology.

Their urban backgrounds and overseas education have exposed them to Western notions of liberalism, free speech, and democracy. Such forms of exposure have led them to comprehend better the current political and cultural suppression in their own country. Functioning in the increasingly suppressive cultural environment of the post-2000 era in Malaysia has compelled these filmmakers to move across national boundaries in search of capital, a sympathetic audience, and foreign co-production opportunities. This progressive transition has allowed the cinema to emerge as a platform to deconstruct the stereotypes of race and ethnicity established in Malaysian cinema, question national policies, contest hegemony, renegotiate race and ethnicity, and constitute a new national identity. By working around state film regulations, MDI filmmakers have been undaunted in tackling issues long ignored by mainstream Malaysian commercial cinema. As a result, the MDI has made its presence felt in local and international cinematic circuits and within the burgeoning field of regional Asian cinemas.

The MDI employs transnational methods to contest national issues. It serves as a platform for contesting or negotiating national policies, race and ethnicity, and national identity. The MDI also problematises the established notions of national cinema constructed on race and ethnicity elements influenced and determined by the control of capital and policies. The MDI challenges this hegemonic representation by resisting existing theorisations of race, culture, politics, and national identity in Malaysia. The MDI achieves this by boldly discussing 'taboo' and 'untouchable' issues relating to sexuality, race and ethnicity, gender relations, and politics. This preference for highlighting unconventional topics has led to them being conveniently ignored by the state and has forced them to seek support from abroad. For that reason, this new cinema has emerged as a transnational cinematic movement that is being deterritorialised and marginalised by both the state and commercial mainstream cinema.

The term 'Malaysian Digital Indies' is employed as an all-encompassing term to identify this movement. Firstly, these films are produced by Malaysian filmmakers who try to characterise Malaysia's different side in attempting to create multicultural Malaysian films representing the nation's diverse background. These filmmakers are attempting to create films that justly reflect the socio-cultural and political backgrounds of the country. Secondly, as a result of globalisation and transnational forces, the MDI utilises the DV format and the internet, which has been growing in popularity and acceptance as a new form of filmmaking and has now liberalised many film movements within the Asian continent. Finally, the term 'Indies' demonstrates independence and resistance. This movement employs and refuses to succumb to state support, influence or pressure, and commercialisation. For example, Amir Muhammad, who is referred to as the 'godfather of new Malaysian filmmaking' (Stephens 2011), aptly describes the low-budget *Lips to Lips* (2000) as an independent film that is 'independent in all the important senses of the word' (Diani 2008a).[3] *Lips to Lips* was made using DV technology, without any professional actors or public funding. Bypassing the LPF ensured its theme of exploring sexuality was maintained.

In deconstructing the current local socio-cultural and political landscape, the MDI has ignored cinematic conventions and traditions long practised by mainstream commercial cinema in Malaysia. This sense of freedom has allowed these filmmakers to significantly have more of an impact on Malaysian cinema and international film festivals than their mainstream compatriots have had. Films such as Amir Muhammad's *The Big Durian* (2003), James Lee's *Room to Let* (2002), Deepak Kumaran Menon's *Chalanggai* (Dancing Bells, 2007), and Ho Yuhang's *Rain Dogs* (2006) have figured prominently and won awards at local and international film festivals. Examples of such achievements can be illustrated by Malaysia's first entry in the Sundance Film Festival through Amir Muhammad's *The Big Durian* in 2004. Yasmin Ahmad's *Sepet* (2005) won the Best Asian Film Award at the 2005 Tokyo International Film Festival. Ho Yuhang won the Best Director Award at the Nantes Three Continents Festival for *Rain Dogs*. Tan Chui Mui took the Fipresci Award and New Currents Award at the 11th BIFF and the VPRO Tiger Award at the 36th International Film Festival Rotterdam for *Love Conquers All* (2006). James Lee's *Call If You Need Me* received the Silver DV Award at the 2009 Hong Kong International Film Festival. Malaysia's second film at the Cannes Film Festival was Chris Chong's *Caméra d'Or* contender, *Karaoke* (2009). Liew Seng Tat won the VPRO Tiger Award and Prince Claus Fund for *Flower In The Pocket* at the International Film Festival Rotterdam 2008, the 'Le Regard d'Or' (Golden Gaze) Award at the 22nd Fribourg International Film Festival 2008, and the Jury Prize (Lotus du Jury) at the 10th Deauville Asian Film Festival 2008. Woo Ming Jin became the first Malaysian

---

3. The first Malaysian digital feature film has the same name as Vladimir Nabokov's short story published in 1956.

Figure 2.1: Liew Seng Tat receiving the VPRO Tiger Award at the International Film Festival Rotterdam 2008. Source: Liew Seng Tat.

filmmaker to have his films featured at the 'big three film festivals': *Monday Morning Glory* (2005) at the 2006 Berlin Film Festival, *Woman on Fire Looks for Water* (2009) at the 2009 Venice Film Festival, and *The Tiger Factory* (2010) at the Cannes Film Festival 2010.

The relationship between commercial mainstream cinema in Malaysia and the MDI can be described using the centre-periphery relation. This relationship stems from opposing principles and filmmaking methods, purposes of existence, and different forms of representation. This state of difference is maintained on the condition that hegemonic control, dominance, and myth-making is decisively dominated by the cinema in the centre (Hayward 1993). This places mainstream cinema in Malaysia at the centre while the MDI is pushed to the periphery. This relation in an economic reality determined by global forces requires a new study of contemporary Malaysian cinema.

Malaysian cinema needs to be studied from the inseparable effects of globalisation, transnationalism, and capital and policy control. While the MDI narratives are infused with an assortment of localised characteristics and issues, its films are produced mainly using transnational elements and funding. They are mostly screened at overseas film festivals. The transnationality of the MDI, therefore, problematises the significance of a national cinema. This problematisation occurs as the MDI, while existing as a platform to contest the national, is heavily influenced by

The Malaysian Digital Indies: A Digital Independent Transnational Cinema 63

transnational forces. Should the MDI then be recognised as a national cinema, or displaced as a form of national cinema due to its transnational elements?

It is crucial to examine further the reasons the urban-born and -bred MDI filmmakers have, unlike their predecessors, drawn both praise and criticism that called for severe discussions in academic circles, in the press, and on the internet. This book is directly concerned with the radical contemporaneity and innovation presented by the MDI. Hence, there is a need first to identify and define this new independent cinema concerning the restructuring of Malaysian cinema within the contexts of its urban and social experiences. It is also necessary to outline the MDI's political economy, which has intricately sustained this cinema's growth by presenting both opportunities and challenges. The MDI's ability to produce cross-border films and secure foreign funding while exhibiting and distributing beyond Malaysian borders is also worth exploring.

As a result of working around the system without adhering to the proper cinematic regulations, these filmmakers have successfully secured networks for international marketing, distribution and exhibition, funding, audiences, and co-productions in the Asian region and worldwide, a feat previously unachievable by their predecessors, at least not within the past two to three decades. These factors combined have inevitably repositioned the MDI as a transnational cinema. These films are made using mostly local talents, resources, and locations. They are spurred on by the uncontainable waves of globalisation, oppressive local cinematic regulations, the advent of multimedia, and the internet.

These films become transnational when they contain the trans-border elements of being funded by overseas sources, being produced through collaborative productions with overseas production houses, or featuring foreign talents and circulating predominantly within overseas film festivals. Justin Ong's *Subak* (2008) is one of the best examples of an MDI film employing transnational qualities. *Subak* documents the archaic irrigation system (*subak*) used by paddy farmers in Bali. It was shot without a script, entirely in digital high definition (HD), and with post-production work completed partly in Australia. Before its Cannes Mipdoc screening, *Subak* was chosen for The Asian Pitch project (a competition co-organised by Japan's NHK, South Korea's KBS, and Singapore's MediaCorp) that provided funding of MYR320,000 (US$80,000). *Subak* was also on display in Taiwan's National Museum of Fine Arts during the Asian Art Biennial.[4]

This chapter essentially comprises two sections. The first section will examine the characteristics and traits of an 'independent cinema' in general and Malaysia.

---

4. Justin Ong received his tertiary education and film training from the US with degrees from Marquette University in Milwaukee and the New York Film Academy. His stint in the US has allowed him to work on the CBS television game show *Hollywood Squares*. In 2007, Justin Ong released his first documentary, *Thaipusam*, and had since produced and written works for the National Geographic Channel, The Discovery Channel, NHK, BBC Worldwide, and Channel News Asia. His documentary *Fight Masters — Silat* (2009) was awarded Best Direction at the 15th Asian Television Awards (2010) and Best Cultural Documentary at the Malaysian Documentary Awards (2010).

This examination establishes the cinematic codes, forms and styles, subject matter, and production methods of an independent cinema. It will explore the independent cinema's position as an 'outsider' cinema operating at the margins and its functions as an alternative to the Hollywood studio system.

The second section of this chapter will examine the significant similarities between the MDI and the Chinese Sixth Generation cinema, which similarly operates on transnational resources and capital. The Chinese Sixth Generation cinema is a new generation of filmmakers created after the Tiananmen Square Massacre in 1989. This cinema movement has been labelled as 'dissident', 'underground', 'independent', 'cinema of the urban generation', and 'revolutionary'.[5] Unlike its predecessors, the Sixth Generation focuses on urban and contemporary issues by documenting China's painful transformation from a socialist-style state into a new global capitalist state and its destructive impact on Chinese individuals.

The state previously ostracised this group of filmmakers because of its resolute political and social aversion to their film art. Consequently, its films were initially locally banned from being exhibited.[6] For that reason, circulation and distribution methods have mainly been transnational, and films have been widely circulating within the circuits of overseas film festivals.[7] Like its Chinese counterparts, the MDI documents the impacts of urbanisation and modernisation in Malaysia, exists as an independent cinema, does not receive any form of state support, utilises DV equipment, resists state cinema regulations, and features more prominently at overseas film festivals. The Chinese Sixth Generation's traits, such as its production and funding, themes and styles, exhibition, distribution, and consumption, are similarly shared with the MDI. The MDI also functions as an alternative to its local mainstream cinema.

As the MDI is a relatively new cinematic movement, it would be ideal for studying and defining using more established independent cinema movements. An examination of the traits and characteristics of the independent cinema and the Chinese Sixth Generation cinema serves to establish a theoretical framework to understand better and comprehend the functions and operations of the MDI.

---

5. The filmmakers' negation of the state, their non-commercial approaches, and claim to artistic purity have led their films to be dubbed as 'individualistic film' (*geren dianying*), 'art film' (*yishu dianying*), 'avant-garde film' (*xianfeng dianying*), 'auteur film' (*zuo-zhe dianying*), or 'new wave film' (*xinchao dianying*) (Mo and Xiao 2006, 145).

6. According to Mo and Xiao, many Sixth Generation filmmakers later incorporated into the mainstream film industry have done well within the conventional film establishment. These filmmakers can be categorised into four groups. Filmmakers such as Hu Xueyang, Guan Hu, Lou Ye, Wang Rui, Jiang Ge, and Lu Xuechang have jobs inside the state film industry. The second group, Zhang Yuan, He Jianjun (He Yi), Wu Di, and Wang Xiaoshuai, are not associated with the state-operated studio system. The third group are filmmakers constantly shifting between underground and mainstream filmmaking. The fourth are filmmakers on the state studio payroll, such as Li Jun, who moonlight and take on independent film projects (2006, 144–145).

7. In recent years, most Sixth Generation filmmakers, with Jia Zhangke and Wang Xiaoshuai, have begun making mainstream films by progressing from the periphery to the public domain. Their works have been openly made available in commercial mainstream cinemas across China with uneven box-office returns but also in the form of bootlegged DVD copies (Lu 2010, 105).

The Malaysian Digital Indies: A Digital Independent Transnational Cinema

Although China and Malaysia are vastly different in scale, local concerns, racial and ethnic diversity, and maturity of the national film industry, this book refers to the Chinese Sixth Generation cinema due to it being a more established independent cinema movement as compared to its independent filmmaking counterparts in the Philippines or other Southeast Asian nations.

Existing and established literature has been written on American independent cinema (Hillier 2001, 2006; Holmlund 2005; Levy 1999; O'Pray 2006; Tzioumakis 2006). The Chinese Sixth Generation cinema (Cornelius and Smith 2002; Lin 2002; Lu 1997; Zhang 1997) will be used to examine the similarities, traits and characteristics, themes and subject matter shared with the MDI. This examination will help to conclude if this new cinema falls within the framework of an independent cinema. This framework will help us better understand the MDI's resistance and negotiation against mainstream cinema, commercialisation, state policies, and cinematic regulations. It would be fitting to examine the independent cinema's traits and characteristics to define and characterise the MDI.

Defining Independent Cinema

Digital filmmaking has opened up a whole new dimension of filmmaking. The world of filmmaking has been revolutionised with the arrival of a large volume of affordable and consumer-friendly yet high-end digital filmmaking equipment. This phenomenon has led to the rise of accessible filmmaking, since it often requires high budgets due to expensive technology. At the same time, non-linear editing software for home computers has also been optimised. The new digital filmmaking method has been embraced by production companies with a small start-up capital or individual filmmakers. This method has led to filmmakers identifying themselves as 'independent' since they no longer rely on major studios or corporations for funding and equipment.

The term 'independent' commonly refers to a cinematic project's non-reliance on the state of studio systems. Its unconventional production, distribution, and exhibition methods and funding from the private sector and foreign investment create an 'in dependence' through joint or co-productions (Pickowicz and Zhang 2006, ix). This form of independence is not a new phenomenon. Historically, it mostly emerged in Europe and the US in the 1920s, often associated with resistance against the studio system or Hollywood (Hillier 2001; Levy 1999; Tzioumakis 2006).

The independent cinema constructs 'alternative', non-Western cinema movements that differ in both format and content, rather than perpetuating a cinema of Hollywood aesthetics (Chapman 2003, 37–38). For example, European cinema is often described as a cinema of art or culture, funded or subsidised by the state, and a cinema that relies on 'pain and effort'. Simultaneously, Hollywood is a cinema of mass entertainment or popular culture, based on a box-office system relying on pleasure and thrills (de Valck 2007, 14). Since the early twentieth century, films produced by independent filmmakers are defined as 'different' from the dominant or mainstream and operate at the margins or sidelines (Levy 1999). This situation allowed for the emergence of European avant-garde and alternative movements which deconstructed the tabooed political and sexual content through: 'foreign cinema' with expressive camera mobility and revolutionary montage theories (German Expressionism, Soviet montage, and French Surrealism) in the 1920s (Sarris 1968); 'art house' and 'new wave' cinemas from the late 1950s; and the 1960s Latin American radical political 'Third Cinema' (Cuban revolutionary cinema and Brazilian Cinema Novo movement) (Chapman 2003).

These films show a contempt for the conventional subject matter and modes of representation popularised by Hollywood (Tzioumakis 2006, 1–2). While these cinemas differ economically, aesthetically, and stylistically, they contain less powerful narratives by being character- rather than plot-driven (Hillier 2001, ix–xiv). Alternative viewpoints are expressed using experimental approaches that employ a form of radical, auteur-driven, and youthful cinema, often carrying the mark, signature, or trademark of a particular director (Holmlund 2005, 3). This form of independence in filmmaking allows filmmakers to command greater control while preserving their artistic and aesthetic qualities.

In aesthetic qualities, independent films differ from the mainstream by offering slightly less conventional and dramatic stories. Both critics and audiences often see independent films as a form of social engagement or aesthetic experimentation presented using a distinctive visual look, unconventional narrative patterns, and a self-reflexive style (Holmlund 2005, 3). Independent films deconstruct or subvert classical Hollywood narratives by using narrative intransitivity, estrangement rather than identification, and unpleasure instead of pleasure (Chapman 2003, 36–37). Such challenging filmmaking methods have led independent films to be known as intellectual, evocative, and high-spirited (Tzioumakis 2006, 13). Film stars and special effects are also absent in independent films. Actors and crew members consist of friends, family members, or strangers met on the street; locations can be anywhere except film studios; and films are sometimes shot without scripts (Hillier 2006, 248).

The independent film is also marked by distinctive camera work styles such as long takes using minimal camera movements and single takes. Such lengthy shots create a lethargic pace that allows for a minimalist and melancholic effect to highlight cinematic rawness and realism to expose social experiences' emotional charge (Hillier 2006, 248). Silence and still moments are used to allow an emotional engagement to present itself and to non-verbally inform the audience about the harshness and cruelty faced in a materialistic world (Chapman 2003, 36–37). The majority of independent films are unconventional, non-conservative, and non-formulaic, without the production qualities of Hollywood.

An independent film is not financed by major entertainment companies, from business-related sources, or the state. Independent films are mostly produced using low budgets by a young generation of filmmakers resisting the influence and pressures of significant companies controlling the film industry (Tzioumakis 2006, 1–2). This form of financial independence is one of resistance against commercialisation. *15Malaysia* project producer Pete Teo defines filmmaking independence as the production of low-budget films not funded within commercial cinema's infrastructure (Logeswary 2009). Rather than turning over to work commercially for prestige and money, established independent filmmakers choose to remain independent, to exercise greater control over their work (Tioseco 2006). The funding for films is, therefore, procured through alternative means.

International film festivals have become a crucial platform for the procurement of funding. These festivals have become the alternative cinema marketplace to search for funding from attending notable film professionals and government officials with business agendas and political purposes (de Valck 2007, 14).[8] Transnational connections are an essential factor in the sustenance of independent cinema and inadvertently expose independent filmmakers to funding sources through their affiliations with foreign filmmakers, administrators, film scholars, and critics (Lau 2003).[9] Film festivals, therefore, exist as a strategic site allowing visitors to meet, works to be promoted, and deals to be conferred.

Independent films are also funded using cash awards won at international film festivals. Film festivals have become a source of securing global funding through the resources provided by institutions such as the Hubert Bals Foundation and the Balkan Fund. These funds focus on assisting aspiring filmmakers from Third World countries through monetary support. For example, the Hubert Bals Fund from the Rotterdam International Film Festival, a cinephile's festival (and not a celebrity-driven one), has discovered new talents in Asian cinema and has introduced many new Asian works in Europe (Chan 2011, 254). In 1988, the Hubert Bals Fund helped almost 900 independent filmmakers from Asia, the Middle East, Eastern Europe, Africa, and Latin America.[10] The fund has approximately €1.2 million (US$1.59 million) annually with the support of the Dutch Ministry of Foreign Affairs, Dutch non-governmental development organisations Hivos-NCDO Culture Foundation, the DOEN Foundation, Dioraphte Foundation, and Dutch public broadcasting network NPS. This amount is capable of awarding individual grants of approximately €10,000 (US$13,200) for script and project development, €20,000 (US$26,400) for digital production, €30,000 (US$39,600) for post-production, €10,000 (US$13,200)

---

8. For a detailed discussion regarding the historical development of film festivals, see de Valck 2007.
9. The importance of film festivals has led to the growing importance of research in the area. In 2008, Marijke de Valck and Skadi Loist started the online-based Film Festival Research Network to facilitate studies on the phenomenon of film festivals. The research features an annotated bibliography, academic resources, festival listings, and current news related to film festivals and research. For more information regarding the Film Festival Research Network, see http://www.filmfestivalresearch.org/.
10. Besides being a location for funding, film festivals as key institutions support cinematic development by increasing and inspiring the creativity of local talent and industry infrastructure by offering budding filmmakers stints and residencies at the Berlinale Talent Campus, *Cinéfondation*, and *Résidence du Festival*.

for workshops, or €15,000 (US$19,800) towards distribution costs, funded films being screened at film festivals such as Cannes, Venice, Locarno, Toronto, and Busan.[11]

International film festivals are also alternative distribution and exhibition networks. Approximately 501,000 film festivals are held every year (Chan 2011, 253). Thus, international film festivals are increasingly recognised as necessary points of passage, providing gateways for the production, distribution, and consumption of films (de Valck 2007). Since most independent films are not distributed due to high reproduction and advertising costs, these 'sites of passage' crucially determine the success or failure of a film or filmmaker (de Valck 2007.). Independent films are mostly targeted at 'niche' audiences drawn from all ages, places, and ethnic communities (Hillier 2006, 248). Therefore, film festivals gauge a film's popularity, as the festivals congregate film critics, filmmakers, producers, media reporters, film distribution representatives, film fans, and celebrities.[12]

The accumulation of higher added value, both economically and culturally, is garnered through positive criticisms and praise from film critics and audiences rather than through red carpet premieres and symbolic acts of award ceremonies (de Valck 2007). Film festivals were once used as alternative distribution and exhibition circuits for European films that oppose Hollywood cinema. Now they form part of a marketing strategy through their increased use as platforms to create a media hype to help a film achieve a box office release (de Valck and Loist 2009). Attaining higher cultural values would allow a film to be more likely accepted for exhibition at other festivals and sold to cinema circuits. This acceptance is attained through the 'dogma of discovery', which exploits the ideas of 'auteur' and 'new wave' ingeniously suited for marketing purposes (de Valck 2007). The primacy of film festivals as alternative distribution and exhibition sites is also exemplified through irregular and occasional events held at diverse venues (Iordanova 2009). Therefore, international film festivals are becoming more commercialised and are fulfilling their purpose as an alternative distribution and exhibition site.

Film festivals function as the exhibition and distribution sites for lesser-known independent films to bypass state legislation and censorship. Film festivals internationally appeal as a secure zone that allows for films banned in their prospective countries to receive recognition for aesthetic achievements, cultural specificity, or social relevance (de Valck 2007). This situation has created a culture of access that delegitimises the oppressive forces of censorship and state control in many national film cultures (Ezra and Rowden 2006, 6). Therefore, international film festivals provide filmmakers with the opportunity to express individual and personal ideas to an interested overseas audience. The notion of bypassing official state regulations

---

11. This information was obtained from the Hubert Bals Fund website; see http://www.filmfestivalrotterdam.com/en/about/hubert_bals_fund/.

12. Ho Yuhang states that many are not familiar with this film movement; he understands that it will generate a different audience following from that of Malaysian commercial films (Diani 2008b).

The Malaysian Digital Indies: A Digital Independent Transnational Cinema 69

adds to a film's allure (Chan 2011, 259). In effect, an increasing number of films either prohibited or subjected to strict cinematic, cultural, or political controls are being made available at international film festivals.

In Malaysian cinema, the term 'independent filmmaking' has been making headlines. Malaysian cinema has been functioning as an independent cinema since the departure of the Shaw Brothers. The withdrawal of Chinese capital and the collapse of the studio system in 1980 meant non-adherence to the studio system's production methods, as discussed in Chapter 1. This withdrawal caused a shift in Malaysian cinema. The term 'independent cinema' is often associated with resistance to the influence of the studio system.

However, the *Bumiputera* filmmakers established independent production companies to fill the Malaysian film industry's void. The films produced by the *Bumiputera* filmmakers abandoned studio system's mass production, and filming was no longer done at indoor studios. Distribution and exhibition was no longer controlled or monopolised by the studios. Funding and financing were often secured from local *Bumiputera* businesspeople, and these entrepreneurs placed importance on recovering their investments. Despite being 'independent', these films remained profit-oriented and commercialised. Therefore, Malaysian cinema can be best described as a commercially independent but ideologically dependent cinema industry that has detached itself from the studio system's workings.

Besides the independent Malaysian New Wave filmmakers of the 1980s and 1990s (as discussed in Chapter 1), independent filmmakers employing DV technology have existed before the current MDI phenomenon. Individual filmmakers such as Bernice Chauly, Farouk Al-Joffrey, Mansor Puteh, Stephen Teo, and Julian Cheah have been making experimental films, short films, commercial features, and documentaries without being attached to any movement or the mainstream commercial industry (Khoo 2008). These filmmakers often employed themes of social injustice, political situations, and the depiction of culture. For example, Chauly's *Bakun* (The Dam, 1995) highlighted the indigenous Kayan community's plight of being forced to evacuate their land, seized to construct the Bakun Hydroelectric Corporation dam (Khoo 2008.).[13]

Osman Ali is another individual often credited with the growth of independent digital cinema. His idea, *Odisi*, screened fifty-minute video segments on a local television channel. *Odisi* effectively launched the careers of once unknown filmmakers Yasmin Ahmad, Ho Yuhang, and Bernard Chauly (Hassan 2009).[14] The MDI was pioneered by Amir Muhammad and James Lee. The beginning of the MDI is attributed to Amir's digital feature *Lips to Lips*. This duo is often regarded as the leaders of independent digital filmmaking in Malaysia. They have been instrumental in

---

13. For more information regarding Chauly's *Bakun* and the issues about the hydroelectric dam construction, see Stavropoulos and Phillips 2000.
14. *Odisi* was screened by the local television network NTV7 (Natseven TV). NTV7 was launched on 7 April 1998, as Malaysia's third private free-to-air television station.

providing opportunities for more filmmakers trained in DV technology. The introduction of the MDI has re-established and reworked the accepted milieu of filmmaking in Malaysia.

Malaysian cinema has remained 'independent' since 1980. Thus, the MDI can be defined as being independently produced without state funding, not adhering to the state methods of production, distribution, exhibition and ideology, and cinematic regulations. This cinema became independent through its transnational funding, overseas co-productions, and distributing and exhibiting works abroad without help from the state.

The MDI: Filem Kita Wajah Kita? (Our Films, Our Image?)

The academic study of the MDI's meteoric rise (as defined above) has yielded only modest results (van der Heide 2006; Khoo 2006, 2007; Raju 2008; Mahyuddin 2008). These studies have been limited to journal articles, small-scale studies, and online through online forums, cinema review websites, and blogs. Scholars and journalists alike have termed this new cinema movement 'The Digital Filmmakers' (Hassan 2005b), 'Just-Do-It-(Yourself) filmmaking' (Khoo 2007), 'Non-Malaysian Films' (Amir 2007), the 'New Millennium Indies' (Mahyuddin 2008), 'Mahua Cinema' (Raju 2008), 'The Little Cinema of Malaysia' (Hassan 2007), and 'Camcorder Capers' (Krich 2009). These writings define and characterise the MDI as a cinema of 'outsiders', 'Others', 'underground' or 'revolutionary' because of its valour and boldness in openly addressing social-cultural, political-economic, religious, and sexual issues while highlighting the plights the marginalised. The MDI is considered bold, for these issues are considered taboo for open discussion.[15] These terms describe the MDI as a forward-looking and promising cinema movement that is fresh, vibrant, bold, and unafraid of discussing and resisting existing theorisations of race, culture, politics, and national identity in Malaysia.

Khoo characterises the MDI as an underground movement (shooting without the necessary permits and not applying for an exhibition or distribution licence), low-budgeted, not-for-profit, employing guerrilla filmmaking methods (making use of any location), produced without the thought of screening in commercial cinemas, and bypassing the approval of the LPF (Khoo 2007, 228). She further adds that these films are independent when the filmmakers willingly disregard the multiple inclusion barriers into Malay cinema and prefer to be independent in production and funding to produce low-budget, avant-garde, and artistic films (Khoo 2006, 123). Mahyuddin (2008) stresses the importance of differences between the Malaysian New Wave 'mainstream' independent film industry and the 'New Millennium Indies'. He states that using digital technology, the New Millennium

---

15. As mentioned in Chapter 1, open discussion of race, ethnicity, and religion are considered sensitive and can be punishable under the (now repealed) ISA or Sedition Act.

The Malaysian Digital Indies: A Digital Independent Transnational Cinema

Indies began by producing short films. Their feature films are comparatively 'different' from mainstream productions. The New Millennium Indies follow a bolder and unconventional generic order, aesthetic, and narrative style that allows more freedom in discussing matters of sexuality, race and ethnicity, gender relations, and politics. Mahyuddin further states that the term 'indies' is more socially, culturally, and politically crucial by highlighting localised subject matter (2008, 10).

Hassan Muthalib describes the current cinematic movement as a 'cinematic revolution past due'. Vernon Emuang, producer of *Lips to Lips*, states that these urban and overseas-educated filmmakers push the limits of the Malaysian cultural landscape through a handful of overtly radical works highlighting the problems of the multi-ethnic middle-class society while successfully giving a voice to marginalised communities such as the LGBTQ community, feminists, and ethnic minorities (Krich 2003).

MDI filmmaker Ho Yuhang describes the propelling spirit of independent filmmakers as hopeful, chaotic, muddled, and disorganised (Agusta 2004). He adds that, as filmmakers, they enjoy their work and make films for films' sake without being bothered about analysing or cultivating trends (Agusta 2004.).[16] While admitting that it was still too early to judge this movement's sustainability, Ho adds that although many are still unfamiliar with this movement, he anticipates that it will generate a different audience from that of mainstream Malaysian cinema (Diani 2008b).

The MDI: Crossing intra-national boundaries

During the Festival Filem Malaysia 18 (18th Malaysian Film Festival), the MDI announced its arrival and coming of age. *Sepet*, the only film representing the MDI, swept six awards during this event, including the much-coveted Best Film award. The other awards were Best Picture, Best Director, Best Supporting Actress, Most Promising Actor, Most Promising Actress, and Best Original Story (Mumtaj 2005).[17] *Sepet*'s win was deemed controversial when it defeated Saw Teong Hin's multi-million-dollar production, *Puteri Gunung Ledang* (Princess of Mount Ledang, 2004). *Sepet*'s win was seen as placing itself outside the mainstream by offering an alternative narrative from the representations propagated by commercial Malaysian mainstream cinema. *Sepet*'s win over *Puteri Gunung Ledang* inadvertently challenged the establishment of the Malay cinematic identity, as the latter was seen as *the* epic Malay film due to its storyline (the exaltation of the Malacca Sultanate and

---

16. Amir Muhammad echoed this statement during my conversation with him on 25 July 2010. I asked him, 'Why do you make films?' In response, he said, 'for fun'.

17. In other local and international film festivals, *Sepet* won the Ninth Malaysian Video Award, the 27th Creteil International Women Directors Festival in France, the Golden Chinese Arts Awards and the Anugerah Era 2005, and the Best Asian Film Award in the Winds of Asia section of the 18th Tokyo International Film Festival (Koay 2005).

Malay culture) and costly budget (MYR15 million/US$4.5 million). *Sepet's* victory counteracted Malaysian cinema's notion as a site of exclusion and inclusion built on race, ethnicity, and class. This aesthetic articulation in the Malaysian cinematic space also deconstructed and challenged stereotyped representations in commercial Malaysian mainstream cinema.

This transformation in Malaysian cinema was only made possible by breaking away from old cinematic conventions. The transformation was realised by challenging the hegemony of Malaysian cinema on two levels. Firstly, the MDI consciously departs from the glossier representation of mainstream Malaysian cinema. Breaking away from these restrictions created an innovative and fresh form of aesthetic articulation in the Malaysian cinematic space. This breakaway deconstructs and challenges the stereotyped representations of Malaysian mainstream cinema. While employing transnational filmmaking methods, the themes and subject matter are heavily national and document the present-day Malaysia changes.

By crossing demographic lines, the MDI challenges the myopic portrayal of Malaysian life in Malaysian mainstream cinema. The MDI provides a platform for the contestation and criticism of society by capably transcending class, gender, age, or ethnicity. It resists the works of Malaysian mainstream cinema, commonly perceived as an ethno-centric cinema that focuses on the problems and lifestyles of the Malay community. The typical Malaysian film builds a stereotypical storyline that revolves around the tiresome, 'tried and tested', monotonous entertainment that contains melodramatic elements of *suka* (love), *duka* (tragedy), and *jenaka* (humour). Popularly known as 'Malay cinema', it provides its audiences with a false perception that Malaysia is merely made up of the Malay community or that only problems of the Malay community are highlighted. At the same time, other ethnic communities are sidelined. Malay cinema employs melodramatic storylines, Malay actors, highlights issues of the Malay community, and uses the Malay language. It does not highlight the other ethnic communities of Chinese, Indians, and other indigenous populations that constitute 30 per cent of the Malaysian population. Portraying racial integration in cinema should be a positive way for the various ethnic communities to rid themselves of any prejudice or hostility.

Second, hegemony in Malaysian cinema is challenged through the introduction of moving beyond the multiculturalism of the MDI. At the start, this informal film culture prominently consisted of mostly ethnic Chinese Malaysian youths aged below thirty-five. Raju (2008) uses the term 'Mahua Cinema' to categorise their films that embody most MDI films. The films of Ho Yuhang, James Lee, Tan Chui Mui, Ng Tian Hann, and Khoo Eng Yow are almost similar in narratives, themes and subject matter, languages, and modus operandi. Their films are similar representations of Chinese characters that only intermingle with other Chinese characters; they are located within the Chinese community and only speak Mandarin or amalgamating Chinese dialects such as Cantonese, Hokkien, and Hakka. This collective usage of 'Chinese-ness' goes beyond its cinematic representation. It is accidental by

The Malaysian Digital Indies: A Digital Independent Transnational Cinema 73

no means, but it is a direct challenge to and criticism of Malaysia's political economy and mainstream cinema.

The filmic narratives highlight the difficulties and predicaments the Chinese communities face in Malaysia, by employing themes of loneliness, heartache, poverty, and betrayal. For example, the narratives in James Lee's *Call If You Need Me*, Tan Chui Mui's *Love Conquers All*, and Ho Yuhang's *At the End of Daybreak* (2009) are similar tales of self-discovery. The characters are predominantly from the ethnic Chinese community; even Tung's aunt (played by Yasmin Ahmad) in *Rain Dogs* and the Indian thugs in *Love Conquers All* and *Call If You Need Me* speak fluent Cantonese. In these films, the protagonists in their journeys of self-discovery learn about the 'real world' through simultaneous experiences of camaraderie and love, as well as betrayal, violence, and neglect. These tales represent Chinese communities who view Malaysia as their homeland but are being sidelined, as they are not provided with any forms of preferential treatment. It also speaks of how these filmmakers have been compelled to employ transnational funding and production methods when their films are not recognised by the state as 'Malaysian' despite the films being made by Malaysians in Malaysia and using Chinese dialects spoken throughout Malaysia.

In the narratives, the characters journey from one location to another in search of an unfulfilled sense of belonging in Malaysia's cinematic space unrepresented in mainstream Malaysian films. These narratives are captured using long takes and long shorts, and the narratives develop at a deliberately unhurried pace. These journeys of self-discovery and cinematic styles represent the ongoing search and longing for a Malaysian national identity that equally recognises everyone regardless of ethnicity. The collective presence of MDI Chinese films, which contested the homogeneity of ethnocentrism in cinema, not only forced their presence to be felt, but their filmic narratives are also indirect criticisms of state and cultural policies that have sidelined them. The success of the MDI ethnic Chinese filmmakers has prompted the emergence of mainstream films produced in Mandarin. Earlier attempts at producing Chinese-language films were Brjarne Wong's *Possessed* (2006), Michael Chuah's *Seed of Darkness* (2006), and C L Hor's *Kinta 1881* (2008). These films emulated the MDI transnational production methods by being co-produced with Hong Kong, Singapore, and China. However, they failed miserably at the box office. In 2011, Chiu Keng Guan's *Great Day* (2011) emulated the success of his earlier film *Tiger Woohoo* (2010). Both films were produced by Astro Shaw and made MYR6 million (US$1.5 million) and MYR4 million (US$1 million), respectively. The singer turned filmmaker Ah Niu then produced *Ice Kacang Puppy Love* (2010). The film similarly made a high return of MYR4 million (US$1 million), and in 2011, rapper Namewee's directorial feature-length debut, *Nasi Lemak 2.0* (2011), made MYR7 million (US$1.75 million). While these films were made in Malaysia and were financially successfully, the language content, which was not 70 per cent in Bahasa Malaysia, classified them as 'foreign movies'.

The Chinese MDI films challenge the ideological framework of mainstream Malaysian cinema by going beyond the nation-state. After being denied access to local filmmaking resources, they focused their attention on the foreign resources of transnational networks. Such networks have been made available through China's dominance as a global political and economic superpower. At the same time, its opening market offers broad access to filmmaking resources and opportunities.

While the Chinese MDI filmmakers are, in essence, Malaysians, this nonetheless renews their cultural and economic realignment with China as Malaysian-born Chinese diasporic filmmakers in Asia. The rise of China and the Chinese-ness in the MDI has led towards a regional and global alignment, as the MDI has been predominantly influenced by East Asian cinema networks from Hong Kong, Taiwan, and China. These Sino-nation states have provided the ethnic Chinese MDI filmmakers with transnational links such as co-production opportunities through Andy Lau's Focus Films from Hong Kong; through cinematic aesthetics of the Taiwan New Wave filmmakers, especially the styles of Malaysian-born Tsai Ming-Liang; the shared characteristics of the MDI and the Sixth Generation Chinese cinema; and the relocation of Da Huang Pictures to Beijing in search of co-production opportunities to tap the vast Chinese market. These Sinophone (Shih 2007) articulations in the MDI can therefore be read as a challenge to the political economy of China's cinema and the cinema of their respective homeland: Malaysia.

The MDI, therefore, appears more significant than Malaysian mainstream cinema, which refuses to reflect on Malaysia's cultural diversity. This representation of other ethnic communities and marginalised communities is a form of cultural and political resistance by the MDI in challenging racial and ethnic portrayal in Malaysian cinema. To paint a clearer picture of Malaysian society and depict a more positive construction of an even-handed representation of society, filmmaker James Lee calls for fairer contributions from all ethnic communities. He says that as a multi-religious, multicultural, and multi-ethnic society, the country should reject dichotomisations of East vs West, Islam vs non-Islam, and needs ten perspectives on everything for ethnic communities to rid themselves of prejudice or hostility (Krich 2003). While Lee's previous work mostly highlights the urban Chinese's predicaments, it represents the emergence of a sidelined ethnic community.

His struggle is supported by Ho Yuhang, whose works employ critical realism and social realism in depicting a side of Malaysia that is often hidden from view or marginalised, a side thought to be non-existent or chosen not to be seen (Hassan 2005a). His films, such as *Min* (2003) and *Sanctuary* (2004), force audiences to make the separation between what is real and what is fictional by showing us a side of Malaysia unknown to many. In contrast, Deepak Kumaran highlights the plight of the Malaysian Indian ethnic community through *Chemman Chaalai* (2005) and *Chalanggai*, while Osman Ali's *Bukak Api* (2000) explores the subject matter of sexual and HIV/AIDS awareness among transgender sex workers in Kuala

Lumpur.[18] The film is produced by PT Foundation, a non-profit organisation that provides education on HIV/AIDS prevention, care and support programmes, sexuality awareness, and empowerment programmes for vulnerable communities. The film employs social and critical realism elements to expose Malaysia's 'unseen side' and provide a sympathetic light on marginalised communities rather than existing as comedic relief in supporting roles in the Malay films (Khoo 2006). These changes have led to the production of a diversity of films, ideas, issues, and narratives providing a voice for marginalised communities.

The non-derogatory English, Mandarin, Tamil, and various Chinese dialects present a more credible view of Malaysia's multicultural environment. The filmmakers have adopted the usage of English, Mandarin, and Tamil while often subtitling their films. Film titles in English, Mandarin, and Tamil were also almost unheard of before the emergence of the MDI. This situation represents a more inclusive cinema accommodating previously unseen ethnic communities. In their efforts to establish a more Malaysian cinema, the MDI convincingly forces their voices and thoughts to be heard to reclaim their position within the core of the multi-racial, multicultural, and multi-ethnic Malaysian society. This effort puts forth a sense of cosmopolitanism that appeals significantly to Malaysian and overseas audiences.

The MDI represents the longing for a more socially inclusive form of Malaysian cinema. For local films to be more truly Malaysian in nature, other ethnic communities must be equally represented or at least represented. The MDI problematises the notions of Malaysian cinema being constructed on elements of race and ethnicity. It introduces a new perspective of constructing Malaysia's national identity through a 'postethnic cosmopolitan cinema'. As a postethnic cosmopolitan cinema, the MDI envisions a postethnic Malaysian nation beyond race and ethnicity. Amir Muhammad's *Lips to Lips* and Teck Tan's *Spinning Gasing* (2000) are postethnic cosmopolitan films that move beyond multiculturalism elements.[19] Both films are black-humoured attempts at depicting a pragmatist's view of Malaysia's modernisation. Consisting of an English-speaking multi-racial cast, these films are direct and bold criticisms against issues of racial and religious tolerance, stereotyping, and sensitivity. Both films critically examine these issues, which are often undisclosed and deemed too sensitive for open discussion. The concept of the 'postethnic cosmopolitan cinema' will be discussed in detail in Chapter 3.

Spinning Gasing, however, has certain similarities to L. Krishnan's *Selamat Tinggal Kekasihku* (1955). In both films, the characters are similarly burdened by the demands of culture, values, and religion, caught between tradition and modernisation. However, set against a backdrop of a rapidly modernising society almost

---

18. The term 'bukak api' is street lingo that means 'to have sex with a client'.
19. Previous attempts at producing films 'Malaysian' using multi-ethnic casts were attempted through L. Krishnan's *Selamat Tinggal Kekasihku*, P. Ramlee's *Sesudah Subuh* (After Dawn, 1967) and *Gerimis* (1968), Othman Hafsam's *Mekanik* (1983), and Shuhaimi Baba's *Mimpi Moon* (Moon's Dream, 2000).

fifty years later.[20] *Spinning Gasing* demonstrated that the social and language hybridity of this multi-ethnic society, and open discussions of inter-racial relationships and homosexuality, could be a successful formula. The film lifted the dismal state of Malaysian cinema. It was deemed a 'landmark achievement' and a 'remarkably intelligent piece of filmmaking' (Johan 2002) by boldly highlighting issues commonly faced by the post-13 May 1969 generation, a characteristic shared by the MDI filmmakers themselves.[21] *Spinning Gasing*'s innovative ideas of tackling and contesting tabooed issues in Malaysia led it to face an initial ban by the LPF. Subsequently, a heavily censored version was granted permission to screen in Malaysia. It was nonetheless disqualified from competing in the Festival Filem 16 (16th Malaysian Film Festival) for reasons cited as 'technical'. *Spinning Gasing* was, however, a success at international film festivals by garnering numerous accolades.

Sepet, like *Spinning Gasing* and *Selamat Tinggal Kekasihku*, deals with an inter-ethnic relationship, inter-ethnic assimilation, and Malaysia's search for its national identity. While the film was popularly acclaimed abroad, the film's straightforward manner on how Yasmin Ahmad discussed issues about the Malay community drew controversy in Malaysia. Although praised for being fresh and innovative, it was also harshly publicly condemned. Public condemnations included debates and arguments in the mainstream press, academic circles, and parliament (Chok et al. 2005). The pinnacle of these criticisms came from a forum entitled *Sepet dan Gubra Pencemar Budaya* (*Sepet* and *Gubra*, Corrupters of Malay Culture).[22] In a forum held in a locally televised national programme, *Fenomena Seni*, the film was attacked, and the potential negative consequences of *Sepet* and *Gubra* (Anxiety, 2006) on the Malay community were questioned. The programme, aired on 23 April 2006, included on the panel film critic and journalist Akmal Abdullah and local film producer Raja Azmi Raja Sulaiman. They questioned the depiction of an inter-ethnic relationship in Yasmin Ahmad's films that might corrupt the Malay culture. Also criticised was the film's female protagonist of firm Islamic religious upbringing in a courtship with a Chinese male with a problematic background. Such forms of

---

20. L. Krishnan's *Selamat Tinggal Kekasihku* made the first attempt at portraying racial integration. The film speaks of forbidden love between ethnic communities. This subject was relatively new and taboo due to the ethnic tensions and differences during the Japanese Occupation and Communist Insurgence. In general, *Selamat Tinggal Kekasihku* was well accepted by most Malayan audiences but faced fierce protests in the town of Kota Bharu. The two reasons given for these protests were the notion of a Malay boy dying for a Chinese girl and the image of a dog continually appearing in the film. Hamzah argues that in the former reason, the honour and dignity of the Malay community were tarnished when the Malay boy had to die for the Chinese girl. In the latter, in Islam, dogs are seen as *haram* (unclean) (2004).

21. See Chapter 1 for discussions about the 13 May 1969 race riots.

22. *Gubra* was released as the sequel to *Sepet*. Similar to *Sepet*, *Gubra* deals with the issues of inter-ethnic love relationships. Its main character, Orked, is made to come to terms with Jason's death when she meets his brother, Alan. In *Gubra*, Yasmin once again attempted to test the boundaries of religious tolerance and the LPF. In the movie, a Muslim *Bilal* is seen patting a crippled dog and befriends sex-workers. According to Yasmin, it is more important to be compassionate and non-judgmental towards the less fortunate than to allow ourselves to be blinded by religious hypocrisy (Bissme 2006).

open criticism in Malaysia demonstrate that race and ethnicity remain at the core of Malaysian society.

As a cinema of outsiders that operates on transnational methods, capital and resources, the MDI bears a certain resemblance to the Chinese Sixth Generation cinema. MDI filmmakers are similarly an urban generation who employ transnational methods to contest and negotiate national issues and policies. It would be fitting to compare the MDI traits and characteristics with those of the Chinese Sixth Generation cinema.

The MDI and the Chinese Sixth Generation Cinema

It is crucial to analyse the MDI characteristics by establishing a comparative perspective analysing its shared characteristics with the Chinese Sixth Generation cinema. As mentioned, comparing the MDI with an established film movement will establish a theoretical framework to understand better how the MDI functions and operates. This framework engages existing literature written on the Chinese Sixth Generation cinema (Pickowicz and Zhang 2006; Pickowicz 2006; Lu 1997; Corliss 2001; Cornelius and Smith 2002; Lin 2002; Lau 2003; Mo and Xiao 2006; Zhang 2007). This framework establishes how the MDI shares characteristics in being a movement of urban filmmakers who employ critical subject matter. Themes that contest the national have an aversion to local film censorship and regulations and employ transnational modes of exhibition, distribution, and consumption at international film festivals.

The MDI can be compared to the Chinese Sixth Generation cinema in the 1990s, distinguishing itself from the preceding Fifth Generation. The Sixth Generation departs from the obsession of the Fifth Generation with national and historical allegories. Instead, the filmmakers focus on issues related to their immediate surroundings, social realities, and humanity while being more technically innovative and defiant and more oppositional and politically subversive (Mo and Xiao 2006, 149–153). In contrast, the MDI departs from the approaches, styles, subject matter, and themes of the Malaysian New Wave independent movement of the 1990s (as discussed in Chapter 1). The Sixth Generation Cinema and the MDI were similarly created through various factors: the introduction of digital filmmaking technology, a repressive filmmaking environment, and strict censorship laws (Hageman 2009).

This framework will identify and analyse the MDI characteristics from and those it shares with the Chinese Sixth Generation cinema in establishing itself as a digital independent transnational cinema.

The urban generations

The MDI filmmakers' environments are largely urban based, focusing on issues, subject matter, and themes against urban backdrops. Based in Kuala Lumpur, this independent cinema movement has evolved from a small-scale phenomenon into a vibrant and diverse form of film practice that has gained popularity both locally and internationally. This movement comprises a generation born after the 13 May 1969 race riots. MDI filmmakers possess a deep sense of political and social consciousness, stemming from their exposure to the socio-cultural and political conditions arising from nation-building policies such as the NEP and NCP (as discussed in Chapter 1).

The Chinese Sixth Generation filmmakers or 'Urban Generation' are similarly urban based and are graduates of the Beijing Film Academy (BFA) or the Central Drama Academy, mostly individuals born in the early 1960s. These filmmakers started making small-scale, experimental films and documentaries that focus on the experience of the urbanisation of the filmmakers (Zhang 2007). They also belong in the twenties to thirties age group. They have been exposed mainly to the Cultural Revolution (Mo and Xiao 2006, 144). Chinese filmmakers such as Zhang Yuan, Hu Xueyang, and Wang Xiaoshuai are urban-based filmmakers previously living and working within an environment that is obscure, hostile to, and ignorant of their film art (Lin 2002, 261–263). The MDI works similarly represent the politicisation of urban landscapes to provide a space for challenging current representations of ethnicity, race, and sexuality, and promoting creative expression and creative thinking.

The MDI is an informal network of amateur filmmakers and audiences. The majority of these filmmakers started making short films before eventually producing feature films. Many were self-taught, with little or no training in the field of filmmaking, crossing over from the fields of law and engineering, or were already active in the fields of media and communications. For example, Amir Muhammad was a lawyer by training and an active columnist in a local daily before studying film in New York. This group of young, energetic, and enthusiastic filmmakers, such as James Lee, Amir Muhammad, and Ho Yuhang, are from urban backgrounds and were educated overseas. Films are shot and produced at real locations, on the streets, or in borrowed apartments, using material entities in contemporary urban geography. This characteristic is shared by Sixth Generation filmmakers who make films using material entities in contemporary urban geography (Zhang 2007).

MDI films mostly focus on the unprecedented large-scale urbanisation of Malaysians in large cities such as Kuala Lumpur and Johor Bahru. As the most developed Malaysian city, Kuala Lumpur provides the backdrop of an urban landscape and has become the central focal and meeting point for the emergence of the MDI.[23] As the centre for both arts and cinema in Malaysia, Kuala Lumpur has also become the site for talented individuals, academics, journalists, producers, and filmmakers to congregate and share ideas, thoughts, and opinions. The city has therefore presented the MDI with both opportunities and challenges.

---

23. As discussed in Chapter 1, the film industry moved to Kuala Lumpur when Merdeka Studios was opened in 1964.

The films underline filmmaking as a spatial issue that captures the alternative imagery and socio-cultural mappings of big cities such as Kuala Lumpur through the filmmaker's critical gaze (Khoo 2008).[24] MDI filmmakers capture the problems and issues the residents face in an urbanised society as the subject matter of their films. For example, James Lee's *Room to Let* discusses how its filmic characters experience urbanisation in cities and the problems caused by socio-economic inequality, psychological anxiety, and moral confusion.[25] These issues in MDI films are shared by the Chinese Sixth Generation filmmakers, whose films mostly focus on the unprecedented large-scale urbanisation and globalisation of a Chinese community facing vast changes rooted in socio-economic inequality, psychological anxiety, and moral confusion (Zhang 2007). The characters in MDI and Sixth Generation films similarly long for love and recognition while experiencing alienation, solitariness, and the superficiality of urban society. Tales of society's limitations, alienation of urban youth, a marginalised working class, and mindless capitalist consumption are presented through non-pretentious themes in a non-melodramatic way. This method allows the public to empathise with the characters and stories in the films, for it is, in general, a story about and for them.

Like their Chinese counterparts, MDI filmmakers are urban based, have been exposed to repressive socio-cultural and political policies, and have experienced urbanisation's effects on a personal level. These real-life experiences are reflected through their filmic characters. They have been utilised as the themes and subject matter for their films. Having an overseas education has also exposed MDI filmmakers to notions of democracy, equality, and freedom of speech, enabling them to be bold in contesting national issues.

Employment of themes, styles, and subject matter that contest the national

MDI films employ realism elements in their critique of society and can be a powerful tool for disseminating positive nation-building and inter-ethnic elements. MDI films are a platform for contesting and negotiating race and ethnicity, national identity, and state policies. The themes and subject matter in MDI films contest the nation, nationality and nationalism, symbolise the longing for a unified national identity.

The MDI consolidates itself internationally by creatively and passionately employing cosmopolitan themes. It displaces the ethnocentric elements of mainstream cinema in Malaysia by providing a voice for the politically oppressed,

---

24. As Malaysia's capital city, Kuala Lumpur contains modern infrastructure, telecommunication facilities, skyscrapers, and bustling shopping malls and complexes, which profoundly resemble the infrastructure of modern cities such as New York. Like New York, Kuala Lumpur is where dreams and aspirations are met, visions and riches are made, and achievements and ambitions are achieved.

25. I draw similarities between Berg and the mysterious figure in Pier Paolo Pasolini's *Teorema* (1968). Both characters are mysterious figures who wander through a household. Tsai Ming-Liang also inspired the cinematography in *Room to Let*.

socially marginalised, and economically disadvantaged. MDI films incorporate local cultures blended with contemporary issues by contesting and negotiating ideas relating to socio-politics, race and ethnicity, and class conflict. The Sixth Generation filmmakers similarly criticise national issues. This group explores the characters' psychological depth and unendorsed social and political views as unconventional subject matter, using difference, innovation, avant-garde, and formulistic narrative structures (Mo and Xiao 2006, 148). Their films are more contemporary and urgent in portraying China's current development by mainly concentrating on personal accounts of young people's lives, and symbolise a cultural product which emerged from the social change reflective of China's modernisation (Lau 2003). Both MDI and Sixth Generation films appear to cross demographic boundaries by employing cosmopolitan themes understood by many viewers. These films satisfy the audiences' needs to see more of their culture, problems, and aspirations being discussed on screen.

The MDI's serious films lack entertainment and amusement qualities to engage their audiences to reflect on their daily lives. The anti-romantic feeling and mood renouncing glamour are similarly shared by Sixth Generation films that discuss ordinary people's lives through stories with a humanistic thrust (Mo and Xiao 2006, 149–152). The employment of minimalist and generic titles such as *The Days* (1994), *Postman* (1995), and *Platform* (2000) and the usage of documentary footage create an impression of 'simply living' (Lau 2003). Documentary-styled shooting allows for a sense of *xianchang* (being on the scene) that captures *xiandaixing* (the contemporary spirit) or sense of an amateur cinema that allows for the documentation and witness of the immediacy of contemporary events and an enhanced cinéma vérité-style through video. In contrast, long takes symbolise the unity of the event (Zhang 2007). This technique of using long takes creates a strong 'on the spot' experience, the camera functioning as witness to ongoing events in accentuating immediacy and objectivity (Mo and Xiao 2006, 152).

MDI films are similarly pragmatic and down to earth. Amir Muhammad's films, such as *The Big Durian* and *Malaysian Gods* (2009), have popularised the usage of documentary-styled shooting in creating a sense of being on the scene. *Malaysian Gods* is an example of the MDI's continually discussing and highlighting Malaysia's social and political injustice issues. *Malaysian Gods* was made to celebrate the democratic process by commemorating the *Reformasi* street protest caused by Anwar Ibrahim's sacking.

In *Malaysian Gods*, Amir mobilises the camera as the 'witness' in retracing the protest march's steps and locations. This method creates a strong on-the-spot experience and sense of immediacy, as observers, eyewitnesses, and individuals express their opinions about the event and the socio-political changes the country had endured over the previous ten years. His unorthodox Tamil usage (instead of Bahasa Malaysia or English) in conducting interviews demonstrates the filmmaker's

The Malaysian Digital Indies: A Digital Independent Transnational Cinema   81

Figure 2.2: Film poster of *Flower in the Pocket*. Source: Liew Seng Tat.

diversity of other languages used in Malaysia.[26] Due to the nature of the content, audiences would naturally be anticipating the documentary and archival footage of the *Reformasi* marches. The absence of this footage would leave audiences with a sense of anti-climactic shock and a greater sense of curiosity in exploring the issue of *Reformasi* in more detail. Such banal approaches also expose socio-political issues experienced through the everyday lives of ordinary people.

This sense of contemporaneity, achieved through the use of long takes in Azharr Rudin's *Punggok Rindukan Bulan* (This Longing, 2008) and Liew Seng Tat's *Flower in the Pocket* (2007), has allowed for a sense of unity and immediacy in dealing with issues of absence, loneliness, and longing for a parent. This sense of loneliness in the characters rejects the romantic feelings and glamour often associated with commercial mainstream cinema. For example, *Gadoh* (2009) aims to expose the racial and religious fissures often repressed by commercial mainstream

---

26. Of the three largest ethnic communities, the Indian is the smallest. This community uses Tamil as the primary language of communication in their community.

cinema, by highlighting mundane and pragmatic topics of day-to-day life struggles, loneliness, and critical political views that transgress ethnic and gender borders. The film challenges the hegemonic representation of *Bumiputera*/non-*Bumiputera*, the self/others, Malay/non-Malay, Malay language/non-Malay language dichotomy. The film adopts a bolder and unconventional generic order, aesthetic, and narrative style that allows for more freedom in discussing matters relating to race relations and politics. *Gadoh* becomes more socially, culturally, and politically significant through its employment of a wide range of more localised subject matter relating to Malaysia's multiculturalism. The film achieves this by directly criticising the national education system for its failure to inculcate education and values. Students are taught not to question or think critically, for fear of reprimand, but have been infused with a sense of fear that limits critical thinking and freedom of speech. *Gadoh* also criticises the increased polarisation and sectarian misrepresentation of society.

In filmmaking style, MDI films, like Sixth Generation films, suffer technically from poor techniques (Mo and Xiao 2006, 148–155). The small budgets and lack of high-end technology have caused MDI films to suffer from technical problems, low audio quality, inability to sustain prolonged dramatic tension, and fragmented and non-cohesive narratives. To create a sense of immediacy and be contemporary, the MDI employs children and ordinary Malaysians as non-professional actors. This preference rejects the star quality popularised by mainstream cinema in Malaysia, which employs popular actors, singers, and models.

Sixth Generation films also reject Hollywood's star quality by employing non-professional everyday folk as actors and actresses. These characters offer little facial or verbal inflexion and few dramatic gestures (Corliss 2001). The main characters in *Punggok Rindukan Bulan* and *Flower in the Pocket* are children who display strong affection and emotional stability while offering little facial or verbal inflexion or few dramatic gestures. MDI filmmakers such as Ho Yuhang, Yasmin Ahmad, and James Lee often employ non-professional actors in their films such as *Sanctuary*, *Rabun* (My Failing Eyesight, 2002) and *Snipers* (2001).

The MDI and Sixth Generation have similarities in their employment of themes, subject matter, and filmmaking styles.[27] The MDI's rejection of romanticism and glamour allow for discussions of 'serious' and contemporary issues using realism elements. As the MDI functioned in a repressive political and cultural environment, their films that criticised the state and its policies and many MDI films did not seek for the production and screening approvals from the LPF or FINAS.

---

27. This characteristic will be further discussed in Chapter 3 in analysing how these characteristics, which employ cosmopolitan narratives, allow MDI films to go beyond the elements of race and ethnicity.

Avoidance of film censorship and regulations

MDI filmmakers have preferred to remain independent and would not need to apply for a state permit for production or require their works to be approved by the LPF or risk their works being censored. Due to their preference for highlighting marginalised people's lives and dealing with politically sensitive subject matter (Mo and Xiao 2006, 148), MDI films, like Sixth Generation films, are conceptually and thematically rooted in individualistic and political values departing from state-sanctioned ideological lines (Mo and Xiao, 148–155).[28] As discussed, MDI films which contest and negotiate state policies, race and ethnicity, and national identity are unrestricted by ideological constraints set by strict censorship. To avoid their works being targeted for censorship, they do not apply for state permits, as their works are intended to be exhibited and distributed overseas.

However, MDI filmmaker Amir Muhammad became the first Malaysian filmmaker to have his films *Lelaki Komunis Terakhir* (2006) and *Apa Khabar Orang Kampung* (Village People Radio Show, 2007) banned by the LPF.[29] While Amir's other films that criticise injustice in society caused by political situations and question state policies and hegemony escaped censorship, the word 'communist' in the title led to *Lelaki Komunis Terakhir* being banned. Set to be the first locally produced documentary screened in commercial cinemas, this semi-musical documentary based on the life of former Malayan Communist Party (MCP) leader Chin Peng (real name Ong Boon Hua) cannot even be screened privately.[30] Filming initially faced protests from the UMNO youth group (*Utusan Malaysia* 2005), but it received a 'U' rating without any cuts by the LPF. Documenting the birthplace of Chin Peng and chronologically mapping his life through his travels, this 'road movie' was made without a single piece of footage of Chin Peng himself, and his name is only mentioned once.[31] Locals were interviewed about their daily routines,

---

28. Since the early twenty-first century, Chinese censors have abandoned the regulation of the film market using heavy-handed approaches towards the remaining underground filmmakers. This situation can be attributed to several factors. Politically, censors have taken a different approach partly due to the change in party ruling by a new generation of leaders then led by Hu Jintao. Economically, the audiences following the works of these filmmakers belong to a minority group. In contrast, many former underground filmmakers have begun to move on with the times by combining and compromising between art-house aspirations and economic needs (Lu 2010, 108).

29. According to Yasmin Ahmad, *Lelaki Komunis Terakhir* premiered at the 56th Berlin International Film Festival in 2006 and delighted the audience (2006). The film was partly funded by the Jan Vrijman Fund of Amsterdam and produced on a budget of MYR80,000. *Lelaki Komunis Terakhir* was paradoxically allowed to be screened in Singapore cinemas, albeit with an NC16 rating, when Singapore suffered the same threat from the MCP during the Emergency in 1948–1960. The title of the film *Apa Khabar Orang Kampung* is based on the title of a song by a popular Malaysian singer, the late Sudirman, and was played at the beginning and end credits.

30. For more information regarding the Malayan Emergency, see to Andaya and Andaya 2001, 269–274.

31. The film was described as intelligent and ambitious, as a 'journey into the porous borders between fact and fiction, the past and the present, myth and memory and people and place' and celebrates the continuities and the changes that afflict ordinary people's lives and gives them a voice within their understanding of Malaysia (McKay 2006).

juxtaposed with the occasional breaking into dance and tongue-in-cheek song interludes that parodied the former British ruler's propagandist lyrics in combating communism. The only scenes that would have been deemed controversial were the interview segments featuring exiled former communist fighters living in southern Thailand. These individuals lamented the British colonists' broken promises and the Malaysian government's refusal to allow them to return to Malaysia despite having received pardons (further discussed in *Apa Khabar Orang Kampung*).[32] These scenes were, however, initially passed without any cuts.

In another example of defying state permits and censorship, *Gadoh*, co-directed by Brenda Danker and Nam Ron, was filmed over almost twelve months and premiered at HELP University in Kuala Lumpur and has been screened at various public screenings and fundraisers. The screenings of the film were, however, twice blocked by the police. While *Gadoh* has been widely exhibited and distributed for over a year without proper licenses, the film was stopped from being exhibited because it was deemed a possible threat to public order (Chan 2010). On 27 July 2009, the first incident occurred when the police deemed the screening an illegal gathering and prevented the organisers from screening the film at an open-air location in Penang. The second incident occurred in Malacca on 31 August 2010, as the police prevented organisers from screening the film to commemorate the Malaysian national day (Merdeka day).

Lelaki Komunis Terakhir, *Apa Khabar Orang Kampung*, and *Gadoh* openly bypassed censorship and cinematic regulations, and the filmmakers did not face the quandary of producing documentaries and feature films in secret (Corliss 2001). The subject matter and themes in both films are deemed sensitive. However, the filmmakers did not face the harshness of their Chinese Sixth Generation counterparts when the Chinese government issued a blacklist of eight filmmakers and collectives from producing films in China and prosecuting anyone found providing with them assistance (Cornelius and Smith 2002, 107–111). While film censorship and strict cinematic regulations continue to affect the MDI, they did not have to smuggle their films out of the country like their Chinese counterparts did (Corliss 2001). This bypassing of FINAS and the LPF allows for artistic and financial freedom in dealing with issues considered taboo in mainstream cinema, such as sex, race, politics, and religion. To avoid unnecessary objections and protests for artistic freedom and a guarantee against censorship, MDI filmmakers have chosen transnational networks, spaces, and methods to produce, finance, exhibit, and distribute their films.

---

32. In 1989, the MCP ended its armed struggle to overthrow the Malaysian government. The signing of the peace treaty ended the forty-one-year armed struggle on 2 December, in Haadyai, Thailand. It was signed by the Malaysian government representatives Wan Sidek Wan Abdul Rahman (Secretary-General of the Ministry of Home Affairs), Hashim Mohd Ali (Chief of Defence Forces), and Mohd Haniff bin Omar (Inspector General, Royal Malaysia Police). Representing the MCP were Chin Peng (Secretary-General), Abdullah C. D. (Chairman) and Rashid Maidin (Central Committee Member). For more information regarding the 1989 peace treaty, see Ratanachaya 1996.

Transnational production methods and funding

Like the Sixth Generation Filmmakers who operate on small budgets with funds secured from local and overseas private sources (Lu 1997, 9), MDI funding and production capital are mostly sourced outside Malaysia. This preference occurs because MDI filmmakers have either received little or no support from FINAS. Like their Chinese counterparts, these filmmakers have preferred to raise their own funds rather than depending on state funding (Corliss 2001). For example, Ho Yuhang was unsuccessful in securing funding from FINAS for *Sanctuary* because his film was deemed as not being a multicultural representation of Malaysia and not up to filmmaking standards. Lina Tan, the producer of *Gol dan Gincu* (Goal and Lipstick, 2005), was told that funding has been suspended and to reapply with a recurring MYR600 (US$150) script review fee (Surin 2005). This situation led MDI filmmakers to secure alternative methods in raising funds. Ng Tian Hann's *First Take, Final Cut* (2004) was financed using a credit card cash advance. Deepak Kumaran chose to independently raise the MYR150,000 (US$45,000) needed to produce *Chemman Chaalai*. He also received funds from the Hubert Bals Script Development Fund and the National Geographic Society's Seed Grant, All Roads Film Project. Yasmin Ahmad used her savings, and her producer and art director sold their cars to raise funds for *Sepet* while waiting for loan approval from FINAS (Surin 2005). The possibility of low-budget filmmaking meant MDI filmmakers no longer entirely relied on state funding, which would restrict film productions to state control forces.

Films are often produced on low budgets, transnational funding, and co-productions supporting their works. Funds are obtained from foreign sources such as film festivals, countries, corporations, and foundations. For example, NHK (Japan), Hubert Bals Foundation (Rotterdam), and Jan Vrjiman (Amsterdam) have provided funding and co-production opportunities (as discussed in Chapter 1). Amir Muhammad received the Nippon Foundation Grant (Nippon Foundation's Asian Public Intellectual Fellowship) to carry out research and to fund the films *The Year of Living Vicariously* (2005) and *Tokyo Magic Hour* (2005). For Tan Chui Mui, besides receiving the occasional grants from FINAS for her short films, most of her funding has come from the Netherlands, France, and South Korea. As a former Cinefondatio Residence participant, she received a grant of €10,000 (US$13,200) from the Hubert Bals Fund for script development for her first feature, *Love Conquers All*. Her second feature, *Year Without a Summer* (2010), was funded by the Asian Cinema Fund, Vision Sud Est, ACF Script Development Grant, Hubert Bals Fund, Global Film Initiative, and Digital Production Fund.[33]

---

33. The film was shot using a 35 mm film camera in Tan's hometown, Kampung Sungai Ular, in Kuantan, located on the eastern coast of the Malaysian Peninsular. Written, directed, and edited by Tan, the film stars Nam Ron as the main character. It was produced by Liew Seng Tat; Nyu Ka Jin, James Lee, and Amir Muhammad are executive producers.

The other Malaysian filmmaker whose work has eminently relied on transnational funding and international co-productions is Ho Yuhang. In addition to his first feature, *Min*, which was commissioned by local Malaysian television channel NTV7, his other feature *Sanctuary* was funded by local production company Red Films and produced by James Lee's Doghouse73 Pictures.[34] His next features, *Rain Dogs* and *At the End of Daybreak*, are fitting examples of a Malaysian film made using transnational capital and a transnational workforce. *Rain Dogs* resulted from a co-production between Ho's locally owned production company Paperheart, the Hubert Bals Fund, and Ho's participation in the Papercut film project.[35] He was among six filmmakers from Asia selected to produce a feature film shot using HD technology. This project, sponsored by Andy Lau's Focus Films, produced Chinese language films that featured diasporic Chinese communities across Asia. The other places were Singapore, Hong Kong, Taiwan, and China.

Ho's fourth feature, *At the End of Daybreak*, was co-produced by Paperheart, October Pictures Ltd. (Hong Kong), and M&FC (Music & Film Company, South Korea) and was supported by the Asian Cinema Fund, Hubert Bals Fund, Hong Kong Financing Forum, and Paris Projects. The film was shot entirely in Malaysia and assisted by Taiwanese sound crew 3H. Post-production work for the film was carried out in Malaysia, Taiwan, and South Korea. South Korean Cho Seong-woo composed the soundtrack of the film. The film also employs a cast made up of Malaysian and Hong Kong actors, Tsui Tin Yau and Kara Wai Ying Hung.

Further transnational and transborder assistance occurred when the BIFF Asian programmer Kim Ji-Seok assisted Yasmin Ahmad in completing post-production work for her film *Muallaf* (The Convert, 2008). Liew Seng Tat was awarded the Prince Clause film grant for *In What City Does It Live*. Overseas foundations seemed more encouraging in the building and development of the Malaysian cinema for Tan Chui Mui and Liew Seng Tat, who were offered stints at the Cinefoundation Cannes Residency to learn about scriptwriting and filmmaking, and networking opportunities with other filmmakers, producers, and distributors.

Working under a strict budget restricts the use of high-technology equipment. The DV format is often utilized while groundbreaking editing effects and popular actors are absent, pointing to a lack of commercial value. Amir Muhammad describes this phenomenon as a filmmaking method that permits freedom and

---

34. I have been unsuccessful in obtaining a copy of *Min*. I tried getting it from Ho Yuhang by communicating with him through Facebook. While he mentioned that the film is not sold on DVD, and I would need to obtain it from him, my attempts to do so have failed. We exchanged seven messages from 8 December 2009 until 13 January 2010. In a message on 21 December 2009, he described *Min* as a 'very difficult' and 'stubborn' film and 'you will "pengsan" (pass out)' from watching it.

35. Paperheart is partly owned by Ho Yuhang and Lorna Tee from Hong Kong. Besides producing *Rain Dogs* and *At the End of Daybreak*, the company's most notable achievement is its production support of Malaysian-born Taiwanese filmmaker Tsai Ming-Liang for the film *I Don't Want to Sleep Alone* (2006), which was shot in Malaysia. The film was initially banned in Malaysia, but a censored version with five cuts was eventually released.

The Malaysian Digital Indies: A Digital Independent Transnational Cinema   87

achieves the impossible without being restricted by celluloid film constraints. One such impossibility is *Lips to Lips* being made on a 'cheap but still a lot' budget of MYR60,000 (USD15,000) (Diani 2008a).

This sense of impossibility is achieved through MDI camaraderie, creativity, and passion. The sense of camaraderie among the filmmakers was demonstrated when Tan Chui Mui funded Liew Seng Tat's *Flower in the Pocket* using her prize money from the New Currents Award. In return, Liew agreed to sponsor Tan's next film, should he win an award for *Flower in the Pocket*.[36] MDI filmmakers also often work for a modest salary or, at times, for free, experiences which have provided invaluable for budding filmmakers. Production crews and talents often switch roles, each playing numerous interchangeable roles, thus creating a closely knit group or network. One such example of individual role-switching between productions is James Lee. Lee became prominent as a director of independent films in Malaysia with his feature film debut, *Snipers*, and his trilogy, *Before We Fall in Love Again* (2006), *Things We Do When We Fall in Love* (2007), and *Waiting for Love* (2007). He has also starred in Amir Muhammad's *Lips to Lips* and Liew Seng Tat's *Flower in the Pocket* and was the producer for Amir Muhammad's *The Big Durian* and Ho Yuhang's *Sanctuary*. He was then the cinematographer for Azharr Rudin's *Majidee* (2005) and Tan Chui Mui's *Love Conquers All*.

Despite successfully garnering overseas accolades under the Malaysian flag, MDI films continue to face difficulties locally in securing state funds and censorship approvals. Even though they were made by Malaysians and depict a Malaysian background, these films were earlier not recognized by FINAS as Malaysian films. The FINAS Act and National Film Policy deems a locally produced film as 'foreign' and not 'Malaysian' if its language content is not 70 per cent in Bahasa Malaysia. A film also fails to qualify as 'Malaysian' should it contain scenes shot mainly outside Malaysia. Failure in securing a 'Malaysian' film status results in the inability to qualify for the 25 per cent tax exemption should a film be screened in local cinemas (see Chapter 1). Certain films were given due recognition as 'Malaysian' by former FINAS Director-General Mahyidin Mustakim, who stated, 'The local film industry has somehow recorded several achievements in garnering awards at international film festivals.' For example, *Mukhsin* won the Crystal Bear (Special Mention) Best Feature Film and many others. Films by local filmmakers such as *Flower in the Pocket*, *Love Conquers All*, *As I Lay Dying*, *Chalanggai* have also brought honour to the country at international festivals like Busan International Film Festival (2007) and 4th Independent Film Festival of Portugal (2007). These films were included in the list of Malaysian films at international film festivals.

On 29 January 2011, former Minister of Information, Communication and Culture Rais Yatim announced that all Malaysian-made films using Mandarin, Cantonese, or Tamil, with Bahasa Malaysia subtitles are now recognized as 'local

---

36. This was mentioned during my conversation with Wong Tuck Cheong on 26 July 2010, in Kuala Lumpur.

movies' and no longer 'foreign movies'. The first film to benefit from this reverse in policy was Ah Niu's Mandarin-language film *Ice Kacang Puppy Love*. Similarly, the call for Malaysian films made in the languages of the Borneo states of Sabah and Sarawak and dialects such as Kadazan, or Iban language to be recognized as 'local movies' was put forth by the production company of the digitally produced *Saloi The Movie* (2010) (Bernama 2011).

In 2011, the debut feature length film, *Nasi Lemak 2.0*, by rapper turned film-maker Namewee was denied the 25 per cent tax rebate.[37] Neither did the film receive any funding from FINAS. *Nasi Lemak 2.0*, however, received positive reviews as a film propagating ethnic and racial tolerance reflecting the 1Malaysia policy, but FINAS denied its tax rebate, citing Namewee as a controversial figure.[38] Amir Muhammad spells out the inconsistencies present in the system. For example, *Persona Non Grata* (2006) and *Qaisy dan Laila* (Qaisy and Laila, 2005) did not have a 70 per cent Bahasa Malaysia dialogue, and *Gong* (2006), which was shot entirely in Indonesia, were all successful in obtaining a tax exemption (Amir 2007). This predicament was similarly felt by Sixth Generation filmmakers, who have accused the Film Bureau of 'killing' Chinese cinema, as they were denied local funding (Cornelius and Smith 2002, 107–111).

While the Sixth Generation Cinema depended on foreign funding due to its subversiveness, the MDI has heavily relied on transnational and trans-regional co-productions to help lift the dismal state of Malaysian cinema. Foreign funding and investments were regularly channelled into the country to help fund many works of the MDI filmmakers.

---

37. Namewee (real name: Wee Meng Chee) attracted controversy when he released a song criticizing Malaysia's state of affairs. The song 'Negarakuku', which blended the rhythm from the Malaysian national anthem, 'Negaraku', with his singing and rapping, was made when he studied at Taiwan's Ming Chuan University. The song was deemed controversial for demeaning the national anthem, openly criticizing the NEP, Malays, Islam, and police corruption. Although Namewee removed the clip from YouTube, copies remain on the website. The song was received with positive and negative criticisms from the online community. The media and public outcry were so immense that then-Prime Minster/Home Minister Abdullah Ahmad Badawi issued a gag order on local mainstream media. After Namewee issued a public apology, the Malaysian police announced that Namewee would be investigated under the Sedition Act (1948). He continued his style of open criticisms, blending vulgarity and music and loading the clips on YouTube. His other video clips such as '邱老師 ABC 時間' (ABC Time with Teacher Qiu) (*Qiu Lao Shi ABC Shi Jian*) and 'Namewee fuck TNB 停電了！黄明志大鬧國家能源局' (Namewee's Row with TNB) (Namewee fuck TNB *Ting Dian Le! Huang Ming Zhi Da Nao Guo Jia Neng Yuan Ju*) were received with mixed criticism by the public. Namewee has also starred in the 2009 short films *Potong Saga* and *Meter* and in Pete Teo's public service announcement 'Undilah', which he partly composed.

38. Malaysia's sixth prime minister, Najib Razak, launched the '1Malaysia' (*Satu* Malaysia in Bahasa Malaysia) policy. According to the 1Malaysia website, 1Malaysia stresses national unity and ethnic tolerance cultivated through the values of perseverance, a culture of excellence, acceptance, loyalty, education, humility, integrity, and meritocracy. '1Malaysia', however, has been criticized by various parties for its ambiguity, including former Prime Minister Mahathir Mohammad and current opposition leader, Anwar Ibrahim.

Transnational exhibition and distribution at international film festivals

Since the collapse of the Chinese studio system and up to the year 2000, Malaysian films remained relatively unheard of beyond Malaysia. Locally produced films catered mostly to the domestic market's needs had failed to be distributed and exhibited beyond the country. Despite similarities in culture, language, and lifestyles, Malaysian cinema has not been very popular in Singapore or even Indonesia. The MDI, however, has altered this scenario. Like the Chinese Sixth Generation Cinema, most MDI films seek to attract foreign audiences searching for more excellent cultural value. A film with more excellent cultural value becomes easier to sell to cinema circuits and an ancillary market when the film is selected for a festival program, screened in a competition, or honoured with an award (de Valck 2007, 38).

While the MDI has gained international achievements in exhibiting its works at international film festivals throughout this research, it must be duly noted that, before the establishment of this cinematic movement, international film festivals had already begun screening the cinematic works of Malaysian filmmakers, be it those of commercial mainstream or independent filmmakers. In 1995, U-Wei's *Kaki Bakar* (1995) became the first Malaysian film to be screened at the Cannes Film Festival. Other notable features screened in Europe were Saw Tiong Hin's *Puteri Gunung Ledang* (Venice International Film Festival, 2004), Hishamuddin Rais's *Dari Jemapoh ke Manchestee* (From Jemapoh to Manchester, 1998) (Stockholm International Film Festival, 1998; Rotterdam Film Festival and Berlinbeta International Film Festival, 1999), and Shuhaimi Baba's *Pontianak Harum Sundal Malam* (Pontianak Scent of the Tuber Rose, 2004) (Estepona Fantasy and Terror Film Festival, Spain, 2004).

Like the Sixth Generation filmmakers, MDI filmmakers enjoy greater recognition and more significant influence beyond national borders. International film festivals have become an important exhibition source, as MDI filmmakers have placed greater emphasis on foreign reception of their films that will allow for greater access to foreign funding, production, and distribution networks (Pickowicz 2006, 13). Many filmmakers have adopted the strategy of making a relatively low-budget underground film on a new and sensitive topic for it to be labelled as 'censored'. An agent will 'place' the film in a foreign film festival. When it gets noticed, the film gets picked up by art-house circuits abroad; a critic is 'bribed' into penning it as a 'wonderful but controversial work banned in China' while hoping for broadcast on foreign cable television. With this funding garnered abroad, funding for other underground work is possible, hoping the state makes friendly overtures by offering more lucrative opportunities. The filmmaker would then move between aboveground and underground to address foreign and domestic viewers' different consumer needs and interests (2006, 13).

MDI filmmakers have recognized the importance of international film festivals. Their films have successfully travelled across continents, altering Malaysian cinema's international perception while paving the way for more prospective filmmakers' emergence. These filmmakers have successfully secured networks for international marketing, distribution, and exhibition that have emerged in the Asian region and worldwide. This unconventional mode of distribution and exhibition within film festival circuits allows for the presentation of unique ethnic, national, or identity-based communities. Film festival circuits deterritorialised cinema from its present frameworks and permit it to freely circulate or 'migrate', allowing better accessibility and a broader scope for films to reach more audiences (Ezra and Rowden 2006, 7). International film festival circuits have been highly influential and significant in the growth and development of the MDI.

This form of trans-border connection has also assisted in distribution and exhibition when an increasing number of Malaysian films have successfully been exhibited at international film festivals. Using the Actor-Network Theory, film festivals can be seen as obligatory points of passage, because they are events — actors — that have become so important to the production, distribution, and consumption of many films that, without them, an entire network of practices, places, and people would fall apart. These actors are of vital importance and constitute obligatory stops for the network flows (de Valck 2007, 36).

MDI films exhibited at overseas film festivals since the early 2000s are better known abroad than at home. The growing popularity of film festivals worldwide has helped disseminate and sustain the MDI's viability by being a source for distribution, exhibition, and consumption. International film festivals and a new global ecumenical film culture have been elemental forces in cinema's sustainability (Yoshimoto 2006, 255). For example, Malaysia was again represented at the Cannes Film Festival by Chris Chong's directorial debut, *Karaoke*, after a fourteen-year lapse. The seventy-five-minute Malay-language feature was screened at the 62nd Cannes Film Festival from 14 to 28 May 2009. It was also nominated for the Caméra d'Or (Golden Camera) award. The plot revolves around Malaysia-style karaoke videos and *balik kampung ritual* (returning to one's village) (Subhadra 2009, 22).

Digital technology has also led to the increased transnational circulation of films, conveniently primed in video, DVD, and new digital media formats. For example, James Lee's *The Beautiful Washing Machine* (2004) was the first Malaysian-made film distributed in South Korea, when its distributing rights were purchased by CJ Entertainment for release in art-house cinemas, on DVD, and on television (Hafidah and Faridul 2004). The internet is also utilized as a platform for film exhibition and distribution. This has led to the increased disregard for national borders, which encloses the state's ideology and aesthetics, thus dislocating the hegemony of representative politics over the cinematic community (Ezra and Rowden 2006, 6).

The internet has been utilised as a site for disseminating information relating to the release of new movies by independent filmmakers, details relating to screening time and venues, and forums and blogs. In the early 2000s, blogs such as the malaysian-cinema@yahoogroups.com that transitioned to Facebook groups

The Malaysian Digital Indies: A Digital Independent Transnational Cinema   91

have provided these filmmakers with a platform to discuss, analyse, or disseminate information such as screening sessions, need for talents, fundraising, sale of
equipment, call for entries for film festivals, and need for human resources. Foreign
filmmaking methods and the downloading of foreign films either through legal or
illegal methods have been done online. The internet has helped sustain the MDI
by providing a platform for posting short films, documentaries, and feature films
discussing socio-political issues deemed 'sensitive' that have not obtained permits
for release from the Malaysian authorities. Distributing on the internet, seminars,
film festivals, and workshops has allowed *Gadoh* to escape censorship and reach
wider overseas audiences. While copies of *Gadoh* are directly sold online, a random
search on the internet yielded file-sharing websites offering this film for (illicit)
download.[39]

MDI films have created transborder formations that move across national
boundaries via dispersed networks. Teck Tan's *Spinning Gasing* travelled in search
of an overseas audience due to the resistance it faced from the LPF.[40] As the film
was initially banned in Malaysia, *Spinning Gasing* became transnational when it
premiered at the Hawaii International Film Festival in 2000. It is internationally distributed by Buena Vista Columbia Tristar Films (Malaysia) and has won the Netpac
Special Mention Award at the Hawaiian International Film Festival 2000 (USA),
and Best Actress Award at the Cinemaya Festival of Asian Films India (Cinefan)
2001.

The LPF initially banned *Spinning Gasing* for its unconcealed discussions about
religion, ethnicity, and sexual longing and dissatisfaction. While the film contains
hints of a commercial effort, it effectively exposes and showcases the growing
volatility and complexity of the social realities and divergent voices from different
ethnic communities that make up Malaysian society. Tan uses an urban setting in
drawing out the effects of urbanization and racism experienced by city dwellers, by
highlighting the effects of ethnic identity intricately and delicately bound by race,
religion, and class differences. Co-produced by Niche Film and Spinning Gasing
Films, *Spinning Gasing* was shot using 35 mm film celluloid over almost twelve
months on a budget of MYR2.5 million. At the time of its release, Malaysian audiences' reactions to a film that departs from Malaysian mainstream cinema remained

---

39. A random search on the internet for the film yielded results from YouTube and Vimeo.
40. While *Spinning Gasing* remains Teck Tan's only feature film, his list of achievements includes the ATOM
    Awards Special Prize for *My Tiger's Eyes* (1993), the AWGIE Awards for Best Original Television nomination
    for *The Family Spirit* (1994), Playbox Asialink Playwriting Prize for *Pontianak* (1995), and the Bronze Medal
    for the New York International Film and TV Festival for the documentary *The Chinese Diggers* (1998). An
    expatriate filmmaker, Teck Tan returned to Malaysia in 1997 after working in the Australian film industry.
    Tan cites renowned filmmakers such as Bernardo Bertolucci, Pier Paolo Passolini, Francis Ford Coppola, and
    Sergei Eisenstein as having influenced his work. He was also exposed to the theatrical works of Bertold Brecht
    and Samuel Beckett. He started his film career by making experimental films with the Super 8 movie camera
    and worked on television commercials, telemovies, and mini-series before working on *Spinning Gasing*.
    Besides being trained in film and television in Australia, Teck Tan underwent six months of working in China
    and Italy as John Lone's stand-in in Bernardo Bertolucci's *The Last Emperor* (1987).

92   *Malaysian Cinema in the New Millennium*

uncertain. The heavily censored version with twenty-five cuts, however, failed to make an impression locally, having a gross return of MYR484,000 (approximately US$141,000).

Spinning Gasing only premiered in Malaysia on 18 October 2001. Then-Information Minister Khalil Yaakob launched it in Kuala Lumpur. The film festivals that exhibited *Spinning Gasing* before its Malaysian premiere were the Singapore International Film Festival, Los Angeles Asian Pacific Film Festival, Fukuoka Asian Film Festival in Japan, Sydney Asia Pacific Film Festival, and the San Diego Asian Film Festival. After its Malaysian premiere, the film continued to be exhibited at overseas film festivals. The list includes The Jakarta International Film Festival (2001), Bangkok International Film Festival (2001), Asiatica Film Festival in Italy (2001), Cinemaya Festival of Asian Films (CINEFAN) in India (2001), Slamdunk Film Festival in the US (2002), and the Commonwealth Film Festival in the United Kingdom (2002).

Sepet is another example of an MDI film employing transnational distribution and exhibition. It premiered in 2004 at the inaugural Malaysian Film Festival held in Singapore but only premiered in Malaysian cinemas in 2005 after the LPF removed eight scenes.[41] *Sepet* is distributed by Columbia Tristar Film Distributors International and Lighthouse Pictures Singapore. It has won international accolades for the Best Feature Film in the ASEAN category at the Ninth Malaysian Video Awards (2004), Grand Prix du Jury Award at the Creteil International Festival of Women's Films in France, Best Asian Film at the 18th Tokyo International Film Festival (2005), and Best Film at the Global Chinese Golden Arts Malaysia (2005). *Sepet* was also internationally screened at the Fourth Commonwealth Film Festival (2005), Barcelona Asian Film Festival (2005), and 48th San Francisco International Film Festival (2005).

The MDI's preference for exhibiting and distributing through film festival networks has elevated Malaysian cinema's status. In the next chapter, this characteristic will be further discussed by examining how the employment of cosmopolitan themes by the MDI allows the filmmakers to gain better access to such networks.

Exhibition and distribution in Malaysia

While the MDI as a transnational cinema has achieved more overseas success than local success, the MDI's impact in Malaysia needs to be analysed. A local cinema rejected *The Beautiful Washing Machine* because it was 'too slow-moving and not marketable'. *The Big Durian* was only screened twice in Malaysian cinemas (Santhi 2004). There have, however, been instances of MDI films being exhibited at commercial exhibition circuits. For example, *First Take, Final Cut*; *At the End of Daybreak*;

---

41. The Malaysian Film Festival held in Singapore is organized by Cathay-Keris Films, a Cathay Organisation Holdings Ltd subsidiary.

The Bird House (2007); and *The Pirate and the Emperor's Ship* (2008) were screened at Malaysia's Golden Screen Cinemas (GSC) using the eCinema technology.

The first digital film screened at GSC's eCinema was the independent horror anthology *Visits: Hungry Ghost Anthology* (2004) by Ho Yuhang, James Lee, Ng Tian Hann, and Low Ngai Yuen. *Lelaki Komunis Terakhir* and *Nasi Lemak 2.0* were scheduled to screen at these eCinemas. However, they were cancelled due to the controversies surrounding these films. Films by MDI filmmakers have also been screened on Malaysian television. Besides Osman Ali's *Odisi* series mentioned earlier, Astro's movie-on-demand service Astro First has screened films by MDI filmmakers such as *Nasi Lemak 2.0* and *Petaling Street Warriors* (2011). These sites have allowed individual MDI filmmakers and their films to appear on mainstream commercial exhibition and distribution circuits.

MDI films are mostly independent of the local commercial exhibition circuits. As discussed, the reason is that MDI films such as *Gadoh* and *The Big Durian* were produced without permission from FINAS and the LPF and hence did not qualify for the *Skim Wajib Tayang* (Compulsory Screening Scheme).[42] As MDI films are catering to a niche audience, they are often screened at private locations such as lecture theatres or halls of private colleges and universities.[43] The films are also screened at private 'blink-and-you-miss-it' screenings, non-commercial public screenings and fundraisers, or through events organized by The Actor's Studio and the Kelab Seni Filem, which assists and promotes the talents of budding locals. Local film festivals such as the Freedom Film Festival or those organized by local universities and colleges such as HELP University College, Monash University Malaysia, and Han Chiang University College have provided the MDI with local exhibition circuits. Film screenings have also been held annually at events and locations such as the Malaysia Video Awards, the Selangor Chinese Assembly Hall, the Annexe Gallery Central Market, and the National Art Gallery.

One of the platforms cultivating and supporting the budding filmmakers is Kelab Seni Filem (Malaysian Film Club). Established in 1974 and equivalent to Singapore's Film Society, it provides a platform and meeting point that draws together new and established works by local students, animators, and independent filmmakers. As the oldest-running film club in Malaysia, Kelab Seni Filem is a platform to showcase works that do not make it to commercial cinemas.[44] Screenings are held on Wednesday nights at REXKL (previously at HELP University in Kuala Lumpur), and shorts and foreign feature films are shown to its members during regular screenings.

---

42. See Chapter 1 for my discussion about the *Skim Wajib Tayang*.
43. GSC provides the services of eCinema (electronic cinema), which uses high-end LCD (Liquid Crystal Display) projectors. This technology allows MDI filmmakers to screen their works digitally without needing to convert to 35 mm.
44. See https://www.facebook.com/kelabsenifilemmalaysia/

More than an establishment for filmmakers to exchange ideas and learn from one another, Kelab Seni Filem, as a new informal public film culture, also organized Malaysian Shorts and Malaysian Documentaries, a competition that showcases the works of new and upcoming independent filmmakers. This competition, held three times a year, has previously seen the participation of established MDI filmmakers Tan Chui Mui, James Lee, and Linus Chung. Participants have been students from higher learning institutions such as Multimedia University, Cenfad (Centre for Advanced Design), Limkokwing University of Creative Technology, and Australian and UK universities. These showcases boast an extensive scope of horror, drama, animation, and experimental and music videos. Its founder, Wong Tuck Cheong, has been instrumental in elevating Malaysian cinema's status by establishing overseas networks for securing funding and while travelling abroad to introduce these works to film festival curators. Being a one-time member of Fripesci has enabled Wong to become known by visiting curators and filmmakers that call on him, establishing him as a network link between visiting and local filmmakers (Koay 2009).

Another problem faced by the MDI is the distribution and sales of films locally. These filmmakers are not clustered, as a formal organization reduces the capacity and capability of managing and marketing these films. Copies of the films are also made available through direct sales by the filmmakers who promote them during seminars, film festivals, and workshops. These filmmakers have also used the internet to help distribute and sell their works, reaching a larger audience. As a case in point, Amir Muhammad stated through his blog that his locally banned *Lelaki Komunis Terakhir* has been exhibited in over twenty film festivals overseas, openly sold in stores in Singapore, is distributed online by Red Films and on Da Huang Picture's website, is sold on Amazon.com, and has had television rights bought by South Korean television company EBS (Amir 2006). Websites belonging to local book agents such as Silverfish Books and MPH or production houses Da Huang and Red Films have helped promote local talents by distributing and selling these works in their stores and through virtual stores on the internet. Sales and distribution on the internet allow these films to avoid censorship and reach wider overseas audiences.

The internet also exists as a platform to accommodate and make known the presence of MDI filmmakers. For example, Woo Ming Jin, Amir Muhammad, and Yasmin Ahmad have used the internet to gain publicity and dispense information. Filmmakers post their director notes, screening locations and time for future releases, trailers, interviews, media reports, personal thoughts, and film reviews online through personal blogs and online social networking sites such as Facebook, Friendster, and YouTube.

The production, distribution, and exhibition for Woo Ming Jin's *The Elephant and the Sea* (2007) were documented through his blog of the same name. Amir Muhammad used his blogs 'Komunis & Kampung' and 'Writing by Amir' to create an online social presence. Zan Azlee proficiently utilizes the internet as a platform

The Malaysian Digital Indies: A Digital Independent Transnational Cinema   95

for exhibition and distribution. His website fatbidin.com exhibits his latest documentaries, writings, and travels; it distributes his works and advertises his services as a lecturer and freelance media practitioner. He also exhibits his works on zanazlee's Channel on YouTube and the Fat Bidin Media Facebook page. Zan Azlee also actively communicates with the public through Twitter and Facebook.

The internet is utilized as a site for distribution and promotion using word-of-mouth publicity and e-newsletters. It also accommodates popular file-sharing websites such as Rapidshare, FilesTube, and torrent sites that offer MDI films for download. As discussed earlier, while copies of *Gadoh* are directly sold online, a random search on the internet yielded file-sharing websites offering this film for (illicit) download.[45] Distributing on the internet has also allowed *Gadoh* to avoid censorship and reach wider overseas audiences. Even though music copyright is a deterrent to broader distribution and sales, this has not stopped the filmmakers from distributing the films privately to close friends, and family (Khoo 2004a, 20).

The emergence of the MDI has also led to a surge of interest in the making of short films. Beginning with Malaysia's first film school, the Malaysian Film Academy, film studies have now become a well-accepted course of study offered by institutions of higher learning such as the state-supported ASWARA (National Art Culture and Heritage Academy), local universities such as Universiti Sains Malaysia (USM), Universiti Kebangsaan Malaysia (UKM), and Universiti Teknologi Mara (UiTM), and private institutions of higher learning such as Sunway University, UCSI University, Limkokwing University of Technology, HELP University, Multimedia University (MMU), and the Malaysian Institute of Integrative Media (MIIM). This popularity demonstrates the MDI's acceptance in highlighting the concerns of the marginalised with a previously unknown bluntness and immediacy, which disrupts and challenges hegemonic state policies and forces.

Close-up: Da Huang Pictures and the MDI

Despite the rising popularity of digital filmmaking in Malaysia and the emergence of the MDI, it is difficult to categorise these filmmakers under an officially recognised organisation or movement. To obtain the support of FINAS and guarantee a return on investment, the majority of film production companies and production houses prefer to produce television commercials, television drama series, or big-budget commercial films. Films employing slapstick comedy and love stories generally do not encounter much resistance from the LPF. The two largest production companies, Metrowealth Films and Tayangan Unggul, continue to produce films that do

---

45. A random search on the internet for the film yielded results from more than a dozen file-sharing websites such as RapidShare and FilesTube offering the film for (illegal) download. The search also displayed results of popular video-viewing websites such as YouTube and Vimeo. *Gadoh* has been viewed more than 117,000 times on YouTube.

not question the status quo. These films also generally appeal to mass audiences and are screened in commercial exhibition circuits nationwide.

The establishment of film production companies that focus on independent digital filmmaking can be traced to the establishment of James Lee's Doghouse73 Pictures in 1999.[46] Lee's earlier films utilised the analogue 8 mm video format (Video 8) when DV filmmaking was still in its infancy in Malaysia. His earliest attempts produced a total of four short films under the gangster and experimental genre, such as *Ah Yu's Story* (1998), *Think Positive!* (1999), and *Survivor* (1999), before releasing his first DV feature, *Snipers*, in 2001.[47] Incorporating Lee's experience with theatre, the MDI was formed when Amir Muhammad collaborated with Lee. Lee was hired as the main character in *Lips to Lips*.[48]

Production company Red Films also supports the independent filmmaking industry. Established in 2004, Red Films has produced Bernard Chauly's teen flick *Gol dan Gincu* and distributed Woo Ming Jin's debut film, *Monday Morning Glory*. Red Film's support of independent filmmakers has also allowed for overseas co-productions through *Fang* (2005), a collaboration between Red Films and Ground Glass Images of Singapore. Red Film's efforts in developing independent filmmakers' works have allowed many films to be exhibited at regional and international exhibition circuits. The films are *The Bird House* (19th Tokyo International Film Festival), *Monday Morning Glory* (48th San Francisco International Film Festival and 2006 Bangkok International Film Festival), *Visits*, *Hungry Ghost Anthology* (2004 Tokyo International Film Festival), and Bernard Chauly's *Nenek Unta* (2005) (Produire Au Sud selection at Nantes).

In 2005, Amir Muhammad, James Lee, and Liew Seng Tat collaborated with Tan Chui Mui to establish Da Huang Pictures. Da Huang is a production house that

---

46. Information regarding Doghouse73 Pictures was available on http://doghouse73pictures.posterous.com/. The website's heading sums him up as James Lee, 李添興 (Li Tian Xing), Film & Theater Director, Malaysia. While most work and information are currently updated and focused through the Da Huang Pictures website, information on the Doghouse73 website was occasionally updated on the now defunct website. Updates are now on https://www.facebook.com/doghouse73pictures/

47. Made with MYR15,000 under the production company Artsee.net, *Snipers* was the second Malaysian film to be made digitally. Shot in Kuala Lumpur, *Snipers* incorporates three interweaving short stories that revolve around a mysterious gunman called Paul, a rifle, and assassinations. Other characters in the film are Ah Loong, a professional assassin who is given a chance to redeem his errant past; Steve Tan, a recently retrenched and out-of-work restaurant worker suspicious of his wife's fidelity; and Ismail, a desperate restaurateur. Each independent story has the theme and subject matter of self-centredness in a money-oriented world, thus criticising the difficulty of life in Kuala Lumpur, with its rising cost of living, by using a recession-hit Kuala Lumpur as its backdrop. Besides being made with a modest budget, *Snipers* demonstrated the sense of camaraderie and role switching when its cast and crew consisted of Amir Muhammad and Vernon Adrian Emuang.

48. James Lee (born Lee Thim Heng) ventured into filmmaking as a trained graphic designer. While working odd jobs and without proper training or experience in filmmaking, his enrolment in the Actors Studio Theatre and eventual role as the main actor in Amir Muhammad's *Lips to Lips* launched Lee's reputation as one of the pioneers of independent filmmaking in Malaysia. In 2008, he ventured into the commercial mainstream industry by producing the horror film *Histeria*. This trait of moving from the independent to the mainstream can be attributed to the Sixth Generation's methods discussed earlier. Similarly, Amir Muhammad co-directed a commercial mainstream film titled *Susuk* (2008).

is currently the main force behind independent digital filmmaking in Malaysia.[49] Based in Kuala Lumpur, most of its productions embrace DV technology and are heavily influenced by works of art-house auteurs Tsai Ming-Liang, Chen Kaige, and Wong Kar-Wai. The roots of their success lie in their ability to tap into and absorb international filmmaking styles and methods that have generated interest in regional festivals and markets. This success has motivated other filmmakers such as Woo Ming Jin, Azharr Rudin, and Khoo Eng Yow to present visual narratives about Malaysian stories untouched by mainstream cinema in Malaysia.

Da Huang also exists as a platform for contesting and negotiating state-led policies and the Malaysian ethnic and national identity. This multi-ethnic representation continues to deconstruct and problematise 'taboo' and 'untouchable' issues untouched by mainstream cinema in Malaysia. As such, these filmmakers of diverse ethnic backgrounds continue to attempt to create 'Malaysian' films, discussing and highlighting national issues and policies that continue to shape existing theorisations of race, culture, politics, and national identity.

Exhibition and distribution of Da Huang Pictures

Da Huang has utilised roadshows and film festivals to exhibit and distribute their films. These roadshows are generally held around the country at various locations and at different times. The aim of the roadshows is to introduce works of budding filmmakers, promote and market current films, and enhance the popularity of more established filmmakers. While roadshows provide Da Huang with a method of exhibiting and distributing, they also expose the public to their works. Films are exhibited at theatrettes in universities or colleges, usually loaned for some time without charge or for a small nominal fee.

The audience and event marketing have been provided and sourced by the location owners on the internet through popular online guides such as KLUE, homegrown space, or Time Out Kuala Lumpur. Colleges and universities provide an audience. While no tickets are sold, a small nominal fee for entry is sometimes required, or an advanced booking for tickets is required as a form of invitation. Most screenings are privately held events due to films discussing 'sensitive' themes and subject matter. Question-and-answer sessions are also usually held after each screening. These sessions are a popular method of marketing oneself as a filmmaker and one's film titles. They also create awareness about the current wave of independent digital filmmaking in Malaysia.

The Da Huang website is for the sales and distribution of films while dispensing useful information. Aspiring and established filmmakers alike find information efficiently displayed and categorised under different databases. These databases

---

49. For more information regarding Da Huang Pictures, see http://www.dahuangpictures.com or https://www.facebook.com/DaHuangPictures/

provide information such as filmmaking workshops, overseas filmmaking grants, and the availability of funds, film festivals, film competitions, film reviews, and filmmaking residencies. FINAS does not offer such forms of information to MDI filmmakers. By applying for available funds and grants, interested filmmakers are given the autonomy of bypassing bureaucratic measures of applying for grants and licences from FINAS. Filmmakers are provided with more choices to directly apply for funds, training schemes, and grants from the awarding bodies and foundations. Bypassing state funding also means bypassing state regulations and censorship. This method allows filmmakers to maintain creative control in their work and the freedom to explore themes and subject matter without worrying about self-censorship. Alternative and unconventional sources have been made available for Da Huang filmmakers and other aspiring filmmakers shunned through lack of opportunities.

This form of transnational exchange of information on the Da Huang website or Facebook page works both ways. Firstly, these opportunities and resources offer Malaysian filmmakers opportunities to secure transnational funding, co-productions, and resources. Secondly, the website introduces Malaysian cinema to prospective overseas companies and foundations interested in providing co-production, funding, and collaboration with developing nations. This transnational flow of talents, funding, and expertise also allows Malaysian cinema to have greater access to transnational training, research, writing, styles, funding, and methods. And the network results in the quality of works, and the number of films produced in recent years has significantly improved.

In August 2011, Malaysian news portal *Sin Chew Daily* carried a report about Da Huang Pictures' closure. The newspaper quoted James Lee as having 'mixed emotions', of feeling content about the current situation of the Malaysian cinema industry but feeling discontent about the low-cineliteracy rate of Malaysian audiences regarding MDI films and their failure at recuperating production costs (2011). Within a matter of days, Da Huang Pictures posted an announcement on its website, stating its relocation to Beijing while remaining a registered Malaysian company. The company decided to relocate due to the rising opportunities presented to co-produce Chinese independent films because of Tan Chui Mui's current residence in Beijing. Da Huang also stated that it would continue to support the production of both local and international independent films.[50]

This occurrence is in line with the argument above concerning the regional alignment between China and ethnic Chinese Malaysian filmmakers, the rise of Sinophone cinema (Shih 2007), and the way the MDI is influenced by China's rise and its filmmaking industry regionally and globally. In summary, Da Huang has contributed to the current resurgence of Malaysian cinema by serving as an

---

50. At time of writing, Da Huang Pictures continues to operate in Malaysia. There were also claims that the news was wrongly reported by *Sin Chew Daily*.

alternative site and platform for the production, distribution, and exhibition of Malaysian cinema. This form of independent digital filmmaking has allowed filmmakers greater control of creative content, production quality, and networks for exhibition and distribution using transnational sources.

3

'Beyond Multiculturalism': The Malaysian Postethnic Cosmopolitan Cinema

The MDI works within the framework of a 'postethnic cosmopolitan cinema' to argue that it is a transnational cinema that combines 'postethnicity', 'cosmopolitanism', and 'cinema'. It is crucial to analyse how a postethnic cosmopolitan cinema's themes distinguish the MDI from mainstream cinema. The MDI uses cosmopolitan themes that go 'beyond multiculturalism' to examine the changing Malaysian sociopolitical and cultural environment. The MDI envisions a postethnic and cosmopolitan nation. The usage of cosmopolitan themes has enabled the MDI to deconstruct race and ethnicity stereotypes while focusing on contesting interracial relationships, cultural and ethnic diversity, humanistic philosophies and universalism, and ideals of global justice, sovereignty, and multiple and coinciding modernities.

This chapter discusses how cosmopolitan themes have enabled the MDI to transcend borders. MDI films can move across borders in search of overseas capital and a sympathetic audience because of the universal relevance of cosmopolitan themes, which are broad, humanistic, and universal. Trans-ethnic/trans-racial love, hope, and humanism, easily translate across cultures, appeal to a globally prominent ideology. Because cosmopolitan themes renegotiate multiculturalism and deconstruct the stereotypes of race and ethnicity, MDI films adopt a postethnic approach to challenge mainstream cinema's hegemonic exclusivism and negation of a culturally diverse Malaysia.[1] This postethnic approach is necessary in demonstrating how the nation-building process remains incomplete and suggests that it is better to conceptualise the Malaysian nation as a single yet diverse/heterogeneous community and not a nation of separate ethnicities and absolute races. To achieve this, the MDI employs *Bangsa* Malaysia as a postethnic concept that refigures race and ethnicity, religion, and other cultural differences.[2] *Bangsa* Malaysia projects an egalitarian society with shared fundamental characteristics by incorporating differences and

---

1. As discussed in Chapter 1, ethnic contestation and integration have often been the focal point in the Malaysian nation-building process. Although history states that the struggle for independence was successfully achieved through compromise and cooperation among the ethnic communities, it was ethnicity itself that has been greatly contested.
2. See the discussion of *Bangsa* Malaysia in Chapter 1.

cultivating solidarity. In short, the MDI envisions an imaginary *Bangsa* Malaysia that is both postethnic and cosmopolitan.

How this digital independent cinema, termed the Malaysian Digital Indies (MDI), created a new informal film culture that challenged the hegemony of Malaysian cinema needs to be further examined. The MDI emerged from a repressive political and cultural environment to employ transnational production, exhibition, and distribution methods that challenge Malaysian cinema's current political economy. These transnational networks allowed, even forced, the MDI to move abroad, as they were mostly denied any form of state support. The MDI then used these transnational influences to create new production methods, aesthetics, and cosmopolitan themes to narrate Malaysian nationhood's alternative stories.

Cosmopolitan themes have enabled the MDI to transcend borders. MDI films can move across borders, searching for overseas capital and a sympathetic audience because of the universal relevance of cosmopolitan themes, which are broad, humanistic, and universal. Trans-ethnic/trans-racial love, hope, and humanism easily translate across cultures, appeal to a globally prominent ideology, and go beyond discussions of race and ethnicity without belonging to any particular community or nationality. Because cosmopolitan themes renegotiate multiculturalism and deconstruct race and ethnicity stereotypes, MDI films draw away from the Malay-centric mainstream cinema.

The MDI adopts a postethnic approach to challenge mainstream cinema's hegemonic exclusivism and negation of a culturally diverse Malaysia. This postethnic approach is necessary for demonstrating how the nation-building process remains incomplete and suggests that it is better to conceptualise the Malaysian nation as a single yet diverse/heterogeneous community and not a nation of separate ethnicities. To achieve this, the MDI employs *Bangsa* Malaysia as a postethnic concept that prefigures race and ethnicity, religion, and other cultural differences. *Bangsa* Malaysia projects an egalitarian society with shared fundamental characteristics by incorporating differences and cultivating solidarity. As such, MDI films are about the envisioning of an imaginary *Bangsa* Malaysia that is both postethnic and cosmopolitan.

How the MDI consciously contests these racial and ethnic assumptions and stereotypes by dismissing the need to propagate racial and ethnic ideologies is another element that requires further investigation. This chapter examines the imaginary *Bangsa* Malaysia of the MDI. Because *Bangsa* Malaysia is both postethnic and cosmopolitan, this chapter merges these concepts to suggest the framework of a 'postethnic cosmopolitan cinema'. The 'postethnic cosmopolitan cinema' concept will support this book's argument of the MDI challenging the backdrop of Malay cinema because postethnicity uses cosmopolitan themes to move 'beyond [official] multiculturalism' (Hollinger 1995). This framework is both timely and necessary for examining the changing Malaysian socio-political and cultural scene. Malaysians today have become more aware and increasingly critical of ethnic consciousness.

Since its independence, Malaysia has been one of Asia's most plural and multi-ethnic societies. Malaysia celebrates ethnic tolerance and understanding with an economic blueprint influenced by various social and cultural experiences. During independence, one of the main challenges was to establish a stable economy with equal wealth distribution. From the socio-cultural perspective, one of the governing forces influencing the modern nation is Islam as its religion. Conversely, globalisation has introduced the growing influences of secularism from Western culture. The adoptions of neo-liberal and modernisation policies have altered Malaysia's socio-political and economic environment from an underdeveloped nation fast-tracked into a global economic force. This phenomenon led by the new forces of global, transnational capitalism has caused a renegotiation of the joint production and reproduction characterisations of the nation-state, culture, identity, and modernity (Ong 1999, 22). Over the past few decades, the Malaysian socio-economic and political policies have been primarily dictated and built on former prime minister Mahathir Mohamad's mix of neo-liberalist socio-political-economic interests until the emergence of post-2000 Malaysian cinema. Today's cosmopolitan and internet-savvy generation are exposed to and emancipated by Western notions of democracy, meritocracy, and liberalism. They acknowledge that race and ethnicity are increasingly contested and negotiate the continued state indoctrination of racial and ethnic allegiance (Azly 2009, 429).

While one could acknowledge that race and ethnicity remain inseparable from the daily negotiations in everyday life, in the reading of MDI films, perhaps it is worth imagining a postethnic cosmopolitan nation that moves beyond indoctrination by race and ethnicity. In defining ethnicity's nature, it must be understood that the nature of ethnic relations in Malaysia is uniquely different, as ethnicity has always been deeply embedded in the workplace, schools, and politics. The concepts of race and ethnicity appear difficult to distinguish, for race contains an ethnic dimension. Ethnicity generally seems to be racialised (Gracia 2007), and both concepts are often used interchangeably in Malaysia. Both concepts, however, have negative connotations and labelling that promote prejudice, discrimination, and abuse, for these concepts support the status quo of inferiority imposed on dominated groups by dominant groups to control and oppress (Gracia 2007). This matter is further complicated, as religion becomes the critical marker of ethnic boundaries and a symbol of differentiation (Chee 2010, 99–110). Ethnicity, race, and religion are commonly used in official and non-official discourses. Filing a form for the application of a banking account requires the declaration of ethnicity and religion. The Malaysian identification card (MyKad) categorises Malaysians into 'Islam' and 'non-Islam'. This method of defining an ethnic community through its distinctive physical characteristics, language, religion, customs, institutions, or cultural traits is wrong-ended, has significant consequences for ethnic relations, and cannot be an adequate method of optimistic public administration (Corlett 2007). The country has to therefore move beyond ethnic allegiance and work through the trauma caused by the 13 May 1969 race riots that altered the course of Malaysian history (Khoo 2006) and its ensuing policies supposedly formulated to restore ethnic and race relations. This chapter, therefore, suggests the postethnic cosmopolitan cinema as a new model for examining ethnic and race relations in Malaysia.[3]

The discussion on how the MDI fits within a postethnic cosmopolitan cinema framework will be in two sections. Section one defines the terms 'postethnic' and 'cosmopolitanism' and discusses how they complement each other in creating a 'postethnic cosmopolitan cinema'. It then examines how cosmopolitanism and the postethnic perspective problematise ethnic identity and move beyond discussions of multiculturalism. The postethnic perspective breaks the deadlock within multicultural debates by favouring a cosmopolitan approach over pluralism.

Cosmopolitanism then proposes creating new transnational networks connecting social movements that identify with a moral concern for humanity regardless of borders. This situation allows cosmopolitanism to recognise diversity without categorising it according to nationality, ethnicity, religion, language, and race. In doing so, cosmopolitanism promotes a form of postethnic diversity with a sense of empathy that proposes harmonious coexistence through tolerance and acceptance of different beliefs, culture, religion, and opinions.

The terms 'postethnic' and 'cosmopolitanism' complement each other in creating a 'postethnic cosmopolitan cinema' that problematises ethnic identity and moves beyond multiculturalism discussions. Therefore, it is crucial to establish how they complement each other. To further define the postethnic cosmopolitan cinema, the significant features shared by the postethnic cosmopolitan cinema, Third Cinema, and accented cinema are examined. A theoretical framework will thus be established better to comprehend the functions and operations of the MDI. This framework will explain how the postethnic cosmopolitan cinema has similar features such as the oppositional and revolutionary themes of Third Cinema and issues of belonging and marginalisation of accented cinema.

The second section demonstrates the characteristics of the Malaysian postethnic cosmopolitan cinema. It explores the potential of using the postethnic cosmopolitan framework in reading the MDI works and supplements these characteristics with examples from MDI films. Finally, it offers a close reading of *Sepet* (2005) as a model example of a Malaysian postethnic cosmopolitan film. This section will address the following questions: How can the two concepts of postethnicity and cosmopolitanism be reconfigured to provide an instructive reading of the MDI as a 'postethnic cosmopolitan cinema'? How do MDI films imagine constructing a postethnic Malaysian nation that looks beyond multiculturalism and ethnic allegiance? How do MDI films deconstruct the portrayal of Malaysians in the mainstream cinema in favour of a nation built on mutual respect, protection of cultural diversity, humanity, and universal equality? How do MDI films acknowledge and

---

3. I have briefly outlined the cause and effects of the 13 May 1969 race riots in Chapter 1.

embrace the reality that Malaysians have multiple belongings and divided loyalties and coexist with individuals from other cultures with similarly divided loyalties and complex identities? How do cosmopolitan themes deconstruct representations in Malaysian mainstream cinema favouring the building of new group identities, new individual identities, and new transnational cultural combinations? These questions will be addressed throughout the chapter and be brought together in an analysis of *Sepet*.

Postethnic Cosmopolitan Cinema

It is essential to review the terms 'postethnicity' and 'cosmopolitanism' to define the framework for postethnic cosmopolitan cinema. These terms are then drawn together and applied to cinema to define the 'postethnic cosmopolitan cinema'. Primarily, the term postethnicity suggests a rethinking of multiculturalism. Postethnicity moves 'beyond multiculturalism' by criticising multiculturalism, as its limitations have grown gradually noticeable, and the concept has become obsolete (Hollinger 1995, 2–3). The definition of postethnicity by Hollinger (1995) allows for envisioning a postethnic nation, and it is employed in the book. This is because the postethnic perspective breaks the deadlock within multicultural debates by favouring a cosmopolitan approach. Therefore, the step towards a postethnic perspective begins by rejecting pluralism and privileging cosmopolitanism (3–5). Postethnicity proposes the study of ethnicity 'beyond multiculturalism' through its support and criticisms of multiculturalism elements (2–3). The politics of multiculturalism, as defined by Hollinger and applied to the US, has been highly criticised on two levels. Firstly, multiculturalism has become too much about expressing differences and does not permit the expression of individual ethnic identity (2–3). Secondly, the politics of multiculturalism has become a sensitive and possibly volatile issue through its management of ethnic community relationships. Thirdly, as modern technology of the government managing the modern nation-state, it segregates society into an absolute society with no shared sense of identity, operating without a sense of being a singular imagined community, with no unified cultural nationalism (Ang 2010, 3–5). As multiculturalism has 'outgrown itself', it no longer provides a stable orientation toward cultural diversity to negotiate current conflicts and convergences (Hollinger 1995, 1–2). The postethnic perspective does not discard multiculturalism but moves 'beyond multiculturalism', as multiculturalism's limitations have become gradually noticeable as the concept has become obsolete. In what follows, this book will argue how cosmopolitanism is postethnic in nature, by recognising diversity without the need to categorise it according to nationality, ethnicity, religion, language, and race.

While both cosmopolitanism and pluralism commonly promote elements of coexistence, tolerance, and diversity (Hollinger 1998, 52), the two concepts depart: pluralism stresses the identification of its 'own kind' by respecting established boundaries of ethno-racial communities and refusing offers for solidarity (Dunne 2008; Hollinger 1995, 1998). In Malaysia, conflicts continually exist due to the flowering of pluralism caused by previous successful British manipulations and the exploitation of society (Shamsul 2001, 206). The economic rift introduced through the 'divide and rule' policy (Brown 1996, 217) placed different cultures within the same social or cultural space (Hefner 2001, 4) without positing on diverse paths to the same truth in joining diverse communities with overlapping but distinctive ethnic interests (Banchoff 2007, 4–5). While recognising the equality, tolerance, mutual respect, and peaceful coexistence between the diverse ethnic, language, religious, and culture communities (Boase 2005, 1–2), this pluralistic landscape remains a source of tension and conflict (Embong 2001, 60). The current socio-political and cultural climate is increasingly pluralistic because Malaysia consists of uniform ethnoreligious units and diverse ones capable of highly divergent trajectories and development (Shamsul 2001, 205).

In contrast, cosmopolitanism suggests creating new transnational networks that identify with a moral concern for humanity regardless of borders. Cosmopolitanism achieves this by confronting and recognising diversity without discriminating between nationality, ethnicity, religion, language, race, and identity (van Hooft 2009, 5). Cosmopolitanism, therefore, recognises diversity without categorising it according to nationality, ethnicity, religion, language, and race. This recognition allows cosmopolitanism to protect cultural diversity. Individuals are concurrently positioned as outsiders and insiders, as individuals and group members, as self and the other, as local and global (Rumford 2007, 3). This acknowledgement of solidarity with a multiplicity of others allows for the engagement with the 'Other' as extensively as possible.

In doing so, cosmopolitanism promotes postethnic diversity by accepting different beliefs, cultures, religions, and opinions. This acknowledgement calls for the creation of a worldwide community practically attached to the interests of humanity. It is based on the cosmopolitan creation of a global democracy of shared citizenship (Robbins 1998, 1). This Kantian worldwide community is committed to promoting justice, human rights, and shared values by creating new transnational frameworks connecting social movements and identifying with a concern for humanity regardless of borders (Dunne 2008; Vertovec and Cohen 2002; Appiah 2006).

These frameworks are based on the Stoic idea of upholding the vision of global democracy and world citizenship (Vertovec and Cohen 2002, 1). Belonging to a worldwide community focuses on the fluidity of evolving relationships between the community and the world (Rumford 2007, 2). It is committed to the universal values of democracy and social justice (Vertovec and Cohen, 10). This community is bounded towards each other through new alliances of local and global social movements which challenge conventional ideas of belonging, identity, and citizenship (Hall 2002, 25). This allegiance implies belonging to a universal community that moves beyond the need for ethnic and racial identification by fostering an understanding and connection between all humanity.

The terms 'postethnicity' and 'cosmopolitanism' come together in cinema as the postethnic cosmopolitan cinema. The postethnic cosmopolitan cinema employs cosmopolitan themes to propose postethnic conditions of moving beyond the need for ethnic and racial identification by fostering an understanding and connection between all humanity. This cosmopolitan perspective of global equality renegotiates relationships within the individuals' communities, how individuals are bounded and move between them, and their relationships to others (Rumford 2007, 2–3). Being both postethnic and cosmopolitan, it contests the constructed characters of 'race' and 'ethnic' communities by contesting, renegotiating, and redefining national policies and ethnic and national identities. This reflects the call for equality through 'global humanism', as humanity requires respecting others' rights and needs by understanding religious, racial, nationality, and ethnic divides (van Hooft 2009, 5–6). Therefore, the postethnic cosmopolitan cinema distances itself from the socially constructed character of ethnoracial communities by accepting different beliefs, culture, religion, and opinions. In short, the postethnic cosmopolitan cinema envisions an imaginary of one postethnic society that welcomes difference and diversity.

In the next section, the postethnic cosmopolitan cinema alongside Third Cinema and accented cinema to draw out its common characteristics, ideological perspectives, and anxieties is examined.

Locating the postethnic cosmopolitan cinema: Comparing Third Cinema and accented cinema

This section compares the shared features of the postethnic cosmopolitan cinema and more established cinema movements. This comparative perspective is necessary to establish how the postethnic cosmopolitan cinema borrows from and shares features with these cinemas. Sean Cubitt's cosmopolitan cinema inspires the concept of postethnic cosmopolitan cinema that is established in this chapter. According to Cubbitt, 'cosmopolitan' refers to a cinema aimed at a wide selection of international audiences through its humanistic themes that appeal to a diverse and global population (2004). Cosmopolitan cinema thinks and feels beyond the nation by focusing on a thematic concern of the globe or internationalism, which projects a desire for a worldwide community of human beings through the persistent flow of images about global forces (Schwartz 2007, 160). These images commonly share a philosophical and thematic purpose of seeking for an elusive humanist ethic flowing through borderless networks of production, distribution, and exhibition (Cubitt 2004). Therefore, the postethnic cosmopolitan cinema similarly appeals to global audiences through its employment of cosmopolitan themes beyond discussions of race and ethnicity, such as marginalised groups, interracial relationships, cultural and ethnic diversity, humanistic philosophies and universalism, and ideals of global justice.

The postethnic cosmopolitan cinema also shares characteristics with two movements that emerged from the world cinema, Third cinema, and accented cinema. In theory, world cinema is located as the antithesis of Hollywood, non-English-language and mainly non-Western cultural products and practices from a non-Eurocentric perspective (Dennison and Song 2006). World cinema is a parallel term based on music (world music) or cuisine (fusion cuisine) that signifies the blending and hybridity of national and international, ethnically specific, and globally politicised characteristics (Elsaesser 2005, 496). While categorisation of cinema movements under world cinema's grouping is extensive, the postethnic cosmopolitan cinema shares features with the Third Cinema and accented cinema. World cinema has historically and semantically been recognised as Third Cinema's reworking and situated in 'third' position after Hollywood (First cinema). European art cinema (Second cinema) is also the first cinematic movement that overtly challenged Hollywood and European film productions (Codell 2007). World cinema now refers to the emergent indigenous cinema and film cultures worldwide after Third Cinema discarded nationalist struggles' political agenda. It is no longer made up of the politicised Third Cinema of the 1970s, the Indian art and avant-garde cinema, or African Francophone cinema (Elsaesser 2005, 496–497). In general, the non-ethnocentric perspective of the postethnic cosmopolitan cinema allows it to explore issues of human rights, the underprivileged, and conflicts between tradition and modernity. This perspective locates the postethnic cosmopolitan cinema and world cinema in binary opposition to the commercial mainstream cinema. By suggesting world cinema is sought after beyond producing nations' home markets because of its opposition, it conveniently categorises, confines, and situates world cinema apart from other cinema movements (Dennison and Song 2006). This suggestion negatively endows it with an ethnographic-ethnic label for otherwise unclassifiable film fare (Elsaesser 2005). It inadvertently overlooks cinematic movements such as the politically engaged Latin American Third Cinema (Dennison and Song 2006). Third Cinema has become an alternative to Hollywood's methods of mass entertainment production that espouses a capitalist, middle-class, and Western imperialist ideology; and the 'author's cinema', 'expression cinema', 'Nouvelle Vague', and 'Cinema Novo' that form Second Cinema (Solanas and Getino 1976). While Second Cinema permits the filmmaker freedom of expression through non-standard cinematic language development, it confines the filmmaker to the 'System' permits (1976, 52). However, as these requirements do not fit within the 'elitist' Second Cinema workings, they are fittingly found within Third Cinema characteristics (1976, 52).

Being in opposition to the mainstream means non-reliance on state support. Distribution and exhibition are carried out in private locations such as universities and cultural centres. Global film festivals are utilised in securing capital, resources, co-production deals, and venues. For production resources, portable (DV) cameras, available lighting, and locations are fully utilised due to budget restrictions. This independence enabled these filmmakers to contest and renegotiate state policies and societal taboos. Not to be confused with Third World cinema, Third Cinema was launched in 1969 by Argentine filmmakers Fernando Solanas and Octavio Getino through their manifesto *Towards a Third Cinema*, which actively challenged, opposed, and rejected the hegemony of more conventional forms of cinema. Third cinema struggles against the decolonisation of culture by distinguishing itself as an alternative to First Cinema (Hollywood) and Second Cinema (European cinema).

The postethnic cosmopolitan cinema replicates three features of Third Cinema, first by replicating the oppositional and revolutionary feature of the Third Cinema. Through its research and experimentation, Third Cinema's flexibility allows it to adapt to shifting dynamics within social struggles (Willemen 1989, 10). This feature can be applied to the cinemas of any nation confronting antagonism and oppression. Third Cinema films achieve this by making a call to action, whether in armed struggle or otherwise. By metaphorically using the context of a guerilla war, the camera becomes the unlimited expropriator of image-weapons. Simultaneously, the film projector symbolises a gun capable of discharging twenty-four frames per second (Solanas and Getino 1976, 57). In fighting the System, the filmmaker uses the camera to document ingenuous images through educational films, pamphlet films, didactic films, report films, essay films, and witness-bearing films to reconstruct historical events (1976, 55). The postethnic cosmopolitan cinema similarly confronts political establishments. In Malaysia, filmmakers facing political oppression resist the ideological supremacy of the state. While the MDI does not aggressively confront the current political regime by calling to armed struggle, the films represent a struggle towards change in society and cinema. For example, Andrew Sia's *Kopi O Khau Sikit Kurang Manis* (Unsweetened Coffee, 2006), Fahmi Reza's *10 Tahun Sebelum Merdeka* (Ten Years Before Merdeka, 2007), and Soh Sook Hwa's *Kayuh* (Cycle, 2009) question state ideologies by expressing a new culture of social change.

These documentaries aim at decolonising Malaysian minds to transform society by creating socially and politically conscious audiences in the wake of growing political, cultural, and social repression in Malaysia. This effort is similar to that of Third Cinema, which discusses the logical relationship between social existence and cultural practices (Willemen 1989, 2) to actively create a form of political and radical consciousness aimed at decolonising minds (Gabriel 1982, 3). As an informal film culture unrestricted by censorship laws, the MDI decolonises cinema and culture by highlighting its nation's plights and struggles.

Second, like Third Cinema, the postethnic cosmopolitan cinema opposes mainstream cinema by challenging the accepted filmmaking methods by making films that the mainstream cannot assimilate. The MDI adopts the politics of deconstruction and openly challenges the accepted filmmaking methods of mainstream cinema. While the Third Cinema uses a style resisting Hollywood (Codell 2007) and moves against the System, the MDI similarly makes films that resist Malaysian mainstream cinema's narrative structure. For example, the films of Ho Yuhang and Tan Chui Mui abandon stereotypical storylines of *suka* (love), *duka* (tragedy), and *jenaka* (humour), melodramatic content that were explored in Chapter 2. Their films do not focus on the narrative's goals, do not glorify the protagonists through close-ups, do not resolve problems and dilemmas, do not focus on aesthetic appeal, and do not use music and sound effects. The MDI utilises the documentary technique of Third Cinema, using portable cameras and shooting using available light (Solanas and Getino 1976, 54–60), Marxist aesthetics, Italian neo-realism, and Grierson's notion of the social documentary (Willemen 1989, 4). The MDI favours these cinematic techniques for their potential to present issues in a manner readily identifiable by the ordinary masses (Codell 2007). This experimentation with film form and style allows the MDI, like the Third Cinema, to confront issues neglected by mainstream cinema by expressing a different set of aspirations that form the national cultural space occupied by filmmakers and audiences (1989, 4). It is in this context of expressing a new culture and of social changes that all the themes are taken in the context of class struggles, giving religion or spirituality a special significance (religion), preserving the cultural make-up of society (culture), the struggle for the emancipation of both humanity and women (sex), but without the theme of armed struggle against imperialism and a class enemy on the home front (armed struggle). Issues such as the effects of urbanisation, poverty, sexuality, religion, and the marginalised and oppressed are highlighted to decolonise minds through a radical consciousness leading to a revolutionary transformation of society. Like Third Cinema, the MDI focuses on more urgent, immediate, and cosmopolitan issues than on the filmmaker's ethnicity.

Third, like the Third Cinema, the postethnic cosmopolitan cinema has established new funding, production, distribution, and exhibition systems. As mentioned, international film festivals have been a primary source of capital, production, exhibition, and distribution for non-mainstream films. Third Cinema filmmakers have similarly raised capital from the European film festival circuits (Solanas and Getino 1976, 54–60). The MDI and the Third Cinema as democratised cinemas aim at creating social and politically conscious audiences. The MDI, like the Third Cinema, bypasses the system and the law by producing films without permits and target overseas exhibition and distribution.[4] Therefore, their films have been 'unlawfully' screened without permits at private sessions held at universities and cultural centres, or online to avoid being targeted by raids, restrictions, banning, and censorship by the System. Films such as Brenda Danker and Nam Ron's *Gadoh* (2009) and Lau Kek-Huat and Chen Jin-Lian's *Absent Without Leave*

---

4. A Malaysian film must have a FINAS production permit and be approved by the LPF before being screened in cinemas. See Chapters 1 and 2.

(不即不离) (2016) are two examples of films that were not approved for screening in Malaysia by the LPF but have been widely screened on the Internet and overseas whilst winning awards.[5] While these methods, at times, make the recovery of costs almost impossible due to these restrictions, it allows for the films to reach a wider audience. As such, resources to make such films would need to be easily accessible in making critical films for critically receptive spectators. Therefore, the MDI has successfully secured Asian and global networks to make their films more accessible and make critically receptive spectators and for purposes of funding, distribution, exhibition, and co-productions.

The MDI also replicates specific accented cinema characteristics. The accented cinema (Naficy 2001) consists of diasporic, exiled, and ethnic cinemas of Third World nations. The accented cinema is an 'engaged cinema' of artisanal films critically aware and mindful of history, politics, ethnicities, nationalities, and identities experienced through deterritorialisation by specific individuals experiencing an exiled and diasporic life (30). This situation arises due to their independence from dominant cinema, which positions them in the interstices of social formations and cinematic practices in society and the film industry (10). The filmmaker's liminal position creates a sense of 'border consciousness' characterised by multifocality, multilingualism, asynchronicity, critical distance, fragmented or multiple subjectivities, and transborder amphibolic characters (31). This position similarly allows them to exploit the system by understanding the contradictions, anomalies, and heterogeneity at the local and global levels (46–47), as the multiple determinants of race, class, gender, and membership in divergent, even antagonistic, historical and national identities intersect at the border or the margins of the mainstream (31).

The postethnic cosmopolitan cinema, like the accented cinema, has been sidelined. This accented position allows MDI films to explore issues similarly untouched by other countries' mainstream cinema. This position at the border allows films such as *Bukak Api* (2000) to explore issues of sexuality and transsexuality; *The Bird House* (2007) to explore the tension between modernity and traditionalism; *Monday Morning Glory* (2005) to talk about terrorism; and *Love Conquers All* (2006) to highlight the tale of gullibility, betrayal, and trust. This position at the border allows these films to connect with films globally and regionally from other cinema movements which address similar themes and anxieties; this allows them to create transnational networks with filmmakers working in other languages, dialects, and accents. While MDI films travel overseas, they attempt to preserve the accent in the films. MDI polylingual films capture unadulterated, ethnically pronounced accents of the languages of Bahasa Malaysia, English, Mandarin and Tamil as well as various Chinese dialects. This accent and language authenticity is preserved and retained through the use of titles, subtitles, intertitles, blocks of text, and on-screen

---

5. For a list of Malaysian films that were not approved for screening by the LPF, see https://freedomfilm.my/pesta-tut/filem/

'Beyond Multiculturalism'

typography. Films produced at the mainstream margins connect with overseas audiences, as they are mostly circulated beyond Malaysian borders (Raju 2008, 74).

Second, postethnic cinema is driven by a desire for the homeland. Accented filmmakers in exile, or diasporic, memorialise and fetishise this desire within their film narratives (Naficy 2001, 11). While MDI filmmakers are neither exiled nor living abroad, they desire a homeland through their search for nationhood. Their search for a sense of belonging is similar to that of accented filmmakers driven by a forbidden desire to return to their homeland. Living at abroad places causes the exiled and diasporic filmmakers to be motivated and directed by three forms of journeying: outward journeys of escape, home seeking, home founding; journeys of quest, homelessness, lostness; and inward, homecoming journeys (33). The films express stories of the individual's experience with exile and diaspora and become hybridised in their use of forms that cut across the national, typological, generic, and stylistic boundaries (31). MDI filmmakers become deprived of a sense of nationhood when they become marginalised by race and ethnic-based policies. MDI filmmakers who do not employ Malay-centric themes and subject matter are similarly denied state funding. This negation deterritorialises MDI filmmakers into an 'exiled' state. In their state of exile, MDI filmmakers, in their ineffectual search for equal recognition as Malaysians, are represented by their filmic characters who search for a sanctuary, a place to call home. This search for belonging is similar to that of the characters in the accented cinema. MDI films, like accented cinema, employ alienated characters who display a sense of loss, loneliness, and sadness. The emotions of characters displaying sadness, loneliness, and alienation caught in too claustrophobic urban spaces (27) are captured using long takes, single-frame filming, cathected sounds, images, and chronotopes (11). Audiences also identify with emotions through memories of vision and voice that revolve around themes of journeying, travelling, and nomadic wandering (29). This accented style of the MDI reflects the filmmakers' personal experiences of dealing with separation from the homeland.

Third, both postethnic cosmopolitan cinema and accented cinema employ a collective mode of production. Accented cinema films are low budget, self-funded, sponsored by personal and private companies, and philanthropists (Naficy 2001, 31). In order to lower costs, films are similarly produced using multiplication or accumulation of labour, the director principally performing multiple functions (48). The assemblage of labour from varying nationalities inevitably leads to language problems. While the director often fills the vacant role of a bilingual actor, multilingualism creates a form of complexity that contributes to the appreciation of a particular accent that acts as the self-reflexive agent of narration and identity (50). The MDI similarly practises this mode of production. While films are already made on small budgets and through private funding, individuals often switch numerous roles and work for free or modest salaries to lower costs. The internet and webcasting have significantly developed the distribution and exhibition of the MDI and accented cinema films. The internet has allowed both accented cinema and the MDI to bypass political and commercial forms of censorship. While the accented cinema abandoned its search for an audience through specialised film tours, festivals, college libraries, university courses, and academic conferences and distribution companies (51–52), the MDI continues to search for an audience at such venues and through the internet.

The Malaysian Postethnic Cosmopolitan Cinema

The very idea of a 'postethnic cosmopolitan cinema' remains a flexible construction. The MDI as a postethnic cosmopolitan cinema contests issues relating to interracial relationships, cultural and ethnic diversity, humanistic philosophies and universalism, and global justice ideals in a nation increasingly shaped by transnational and globalising forces. The employment of cosmopolitan and postethnic themes in the narratives and themes of MDI films then enables the creation of transnational production, distribution, and exhibition networks. This globalising dimension allows the MDI to engage with questions of global justice, sovereignty, multiple and coinciding modernities at the local and global levels, and multiple cross-national symbolic languages of belonging and marginalisation.

The transnational production, distribution, and exhibition methods of the MDI and its postethnic and cosmopolitan themes have attached a global appeal of spectatorial identification to its films that transcend racial, ethnic, gender, class, and sexual identities. Identifying the MDI characteristics concerning the socio-political and cultural workings of these cinemas locates it within the framework of a Malaysian postethnic cosmopolitan cinema. This cinema can be recognised through five distinct characteristics: its use of polylingualism, art-house aesthetics and style, direct criticism of state-led policies, targeting of overseas film festivals for exhibition, and organisation through an auteur system.

Polylingualism

The first characteristic of the Malaysian postethnic cosmopolitan cinema is its use of polylingualism. The multiple languages in the MDI make it postethnic and cosmopolitan, as its films refuse to conform to the need of using only Bahasa Malaysia (or the 70 per cent requirement for tax eligibility), the lingua franca of Malaysian cinema since its advent. This linguistic characterisation paves the way for the postethnic cosmopolitan cinema to be placed as dynamic and cosmopolitan. It capably speaks to a broad overseas audience and in multilingual Malaysia along with the act of either maintaining film titles in their original language with the option of translating them into English [for example, *The Beautiful Washing Machine* (2004) is also known as 美麗的洗衣機 (*Mei Li De Xi Yi Ji*)], or calling films by their English language titles as an accepted convention in world cinema (Chapman 2003), [for

'Beyond Multiculturalism'

example, *Flower in the Pocket* (2007) is also known as 口袋裡的花 (*Kou Dai Li De Hua*)], challenging this language homogeneity. It is also a form of acknowledgement that Malaysians do converse in languages besides Bahasa Malaysia.[6]

This polylingual use of Bahasa Malaysia, English, Mandarin, Tamil, and various vernacular dialects challenges the FINAS regulation that requires a film to have 70 per cent Bahasa Malaysia dialogue for it to be recognised as 'Malaysian' and eligible for a tax rebate.[7] This postethnic cosmopolitan cinema then universally appeals across the ethnic divide through the everyday use of Bahasa Malaysia, Mandarin, and English subtitles to compensate for the lack of understanding of a particular language. The MDI also incorporates into its films the conversational 'Malaysian English' or 'Manglish', a hybrid language commonly used by Malaysians. Manglish further provides audiences with a sense of familiarity, as it demonstrates the coexistence and pragmatism in how Malaysians of different cultures converse. The term 'Manglish' is a portmanteau of 'Malaysian English', or 'Mangled English'. It is an informal vocabulary of incorrect grammar that loosely combines a mixture of English, Bahasa Malaysia, Chinese dialects, and Tamil words in a conversation (not all dialects have to be present in the same sentence). Its use is neither derogatory nor demeaning.[8] In Teck Tan's *Spinning Gasing* (2000), using Manglish with various other languages in a sentence suggests a fluidity of switching between languages to provide a slice-of-life depiction of Malaysia's multi-ethnicity. Consider the character Ariff, who states:

'Oh, he's anak Tan Sri, the son. Isn't he just delicious? *Sedap*. I shook hand with him before. The way he held my hand I know what he wants. I can act like such a slut-*kan*?'

and:

'Which market you study Harry? Bananas? London also got *goreng pisang* at night market. *Pasar malam*?'

---

6. In 2002, Mahathir Mohamad spearheaded the drive to improve the standard of English among Malaysians to help improve the employability of local graduates. He acknowledged the status of English as a universal language and a language of the Information Age. To prevent Malaysia from being colonised directly or indirectly with its failure in mastering English, he introduced the teaching of mathematics and science in English to different levels of schoolchildren. This move provoked fierce opposition from linguistic nationalists, ethnic education communities, and from within the government. In 2009, this policy was reversed due to rising pressure from Malay nationalists that claimed the teaching of such subjects in English was neglecting Bahasa Malaysia as the national language. The teaching of mathematics and science reverted to Bahasa Malaysia in 2012. While this move received fierce protests and criticisms from the general public, specifically Mahathir Mohamad, the abandonment of this six-year English policy was caused by the continuous inability to grasp the learning of the subjects, especially by Malay students in rural districts.
7. See Chapters 1 and 2 regarding the tax rebates for Malaysian made films.
8. Manglish is also often referred to as *Bahasa Rojak*, about the mixture of languages. Manglish is often complemented with the term 'lah' at the end of sentences. For example, the sentence 'No thanks. I'm not hungry. You can have my share' would be spoken as 'Dey, I doe-wan to makan lah. You kao tim for me, OK?' The equivalent of Manglish in Singapore is known as Singlish.

Being polylingual creates the opportunity of presenting alternative linguistic practices that confront the status of an imperial language (Miller 2003), in this case, Bahasa Malaysia. In another example, Yeo Joon Han's musical *Sell Out!* (2009) displays the distinction between Manglish and grammatically correct English. Before the characters in the film break into song and dance to the 'Money Song', the scene juxtaposes the differences in English use in a conversation between the protagonist, Eric Tan, and the girl behind the counter in a hardware store. Eric (played by Peter Davis, who is British) points to the padlock he wishes to purchase and says, 'Can I have that padlock please?' The seated girl turns and points to the padlock behind her and asks, 'This one?' He answers, 'The one next to it'. As the girl stands and retrieves it, she turns around and asks him again, 'This one-ah?' (the subtitles display 'This one, right?'). He slightly nods his head. She packs the padlock into a plastic bag and says, 'Thirty Ringgit'. He hands her the money he received from her from an earlier purchase. She stares at him grudgingly and says,

> Girl: 'Sorry tear already, cannot accept.'
> Eric: 'But you just gave it to me a minute ago.'
> Girl: 'Sorry, cannot.'
> Eric: 'But you just gave it to me.'
> Eric: 'Do you accept credit card?'
> Girl: 'Less than fifty Ringgit, cannot.'

While the above scenario portrays a satirical criticism of Manglish and the declining mastery of English among Malaysians, the scene also demonstrates the English language's universality and adaptability. The use of English in MDI films is neither exaggerated nor more pretentious than the way mainstream films in Malaysia use English comically. One example is Saiful excusing himself by saying, 'Sorry I pass away' as he passes his manager in *Lady Boss* (2005). In another example, exaggerated pronunciation and British accents are used in Eddie Pak's *Red Haired Tumbler di Malaya* (Red Haired Tumbler in Malaya, 1994) and Shuhaimi Baba's *Mimpi Moon* (2000) (see discussion in Chapter 2). Although Bahasa Malaysia is the national language, Malaysians, especially the middle class, prefer conversing in English. The reason is that English is a more recognised universal language with a linguistic bond and unifying potential, as it does not belong to any one race in Malaysia. The hybridity of languages in the MDI contests nationalism by amalgamating cultural differences between the different ethnic communities, as the nation is depicted as one great family speaking the same language (Smith 1991, 79).

Although MDI films are produced in Bahasa Malaysia, English, Mandarin, or Tamil (or a combination), they capably move beyond multiculturalism through subtitles. Subtitles allow the audiences to comprehend the dialogue in different languages while lending a valuable literate quality to the experience of watching the film (Kerr 2002). The use of subtitles (rather than dubbing) mediates between

'Beyond Multiculturalism' 115

a spoken source language and a written target text on the screen (Naficy 2001, 122). Subtitles also offer a cosmopolitan appeal. Audiences are connected through English, Bahasa Malaysia, or Mandarin subtitles that retain the language authenticity in its original form and offer a more credible view of Malaysia's multicultural environment. English subtitles are used for international audiences, as the universality of the English language blurs linguistic, ideological, and ethnoracial boundaries. In the opening scene of Khoo Eng Yow's, *The Pirate and the Emperor's Ship* (2008), a community of ethnic Chinese men transport a ship-shaped paper effigy. To avoid an accident, the men shout out directions in the Hokkien dialect and use hand signals. English and Mandarin subtitles allow viewers to understand the documentary's opening scene.

Subtitles also help audiences depart from the imperial normativity of monoculturalism. They permit the audience to wholly listen to another individual's voice while providing full access to their subjectivity, thus acknowledging an individual's language exists as only one of the many languages in the world (Rich 2004, 168). Subtitling in films is nothing new to Malaysians; it has been commonly used in Malaysian television programmes. While television programmes in Malaysia are targeted at specific audiences according to ethnicity and language (Leong and Yap 2007), Hong Kong Cantonese serials, for example, are not merely limited to speakers of the Cantonese dialect. The fixation with Cantonese drama serials began when local television station TV3 started broadcasting Cantonese-dialect entertainment for free in 1984 (Saw and Kesavapany 2006, 83). The television station began airing Cantonese-based entertainment programmes from Taiwan and Hong Kong that mostly targeted Chinese Malaysians (McDaniel 1994, 143). These serials universally appealed to Malaysians across the ethnic divide by using Bahasa Malaysia subtitles to compensate for the lack of understanding of the Cantonese storyline. The MDI can accomplish a similar universal appeal through the use of subtitles.[9] These subtitles represent the hybridity and assimilation of the other ethnic communities and put forth a greater sense of cosmopolitanism that significantly appeals to cinema audiences.

Art-house aesthetics and style

The second characteristic of the Malaysian postethnic cosmopolitan cinema is its art-house aesthetics. This characteristic signifies a break in style, as the MDI abandons the Indian melodramatic style, which profoundly influences Malaysian mainstream cinema. Instead, the MDI heavily borrows from Italian neo-realism to tell the 'truth' about working-class and urban living conditions. To project a slice-of-life scenario that focuses on social reality, the use of non-commercial actors enhances

---

9. The use of Bahasa Malaysia subtitles to compensate for the lack of understanding of another dialect or language is common in Tamil, Hindi, Korean, Latin American, and Japanese television programmes in Malaysia.

the films' naturalistic aesthetics; natural lighting, diegetic sounds, and location shooting provide a sense of immediacy; and the minimalist and low-budgeted settings display a sense of authenticity and realism while emphasising a sense of emptiness, meaninglessness, and purposelessness (Chaudhuri 2005, 7). Non-professional actors play characters that lack a clear causal motivation and deal with psychological problems such as alienation and a 'lack of communication'. Simultaneously, the verisimilitude of space in its mise-en-scène employs location shooting and non-Hollywood lighting schemes (Bordwell 1985, 206). While cosmopolitan cinema focuses on a thematic concern of the globe or internationalism by 'thinking and feeling beyond the nation' (Schwartz 2007, 160), the MDI borrows heavily from art cinema in differentiating itself from commercial Malaysian mainstream cinema.

Similar to art cinema, MDI films exist alongside commercial cinema. The MDI employs a greater thematic depth with an inclination towards experimentation in form and style, is produced for a niche audience, and is auteur-driven with a critical discourse that focuses on the filmmaker's role and vision as the artist (Chapman 2003, 42–43). The narratives in these films disregard the use of a linear causal chain, have haphazard events, and promote uncertainty in the form of an open-ended quest that leaves the film without an ending (Chaudhuri 2005, 7–8). These films have a looser and ambiguous narrative structure (Bordwell 1985, 206). By using ambiguity and uncertainty, the audience is placed within a moral/political position that enables the construction of an ideal positive or negative figure for emulation or criticism (Berry 1994, 101). Such forms of ambiguity create a reflective space that invites the audience to individually interpret and examine their critical understanding of the subjectivity of the film's development and meaning.

To take a specific example: art-house aesthetics and styles are used in James Lee's *The Beautiful Washing Machine*. Written and directed by Lee, the film uses psychological and social realism to explore the alienating effects caused by urbanisation through the main character, Teoh. Teoh, the morose-looking, bespectacled chain-smoker, lives without aim as he emerges from a broken relationship. He is confined to cramped spaces and narrow corridors, living alone, and occupying a single cubicle in an office painted in dull grey. His sense of loneliness, psychological anxiety, and moral confusion is shown through his non-verbal actions of walking with his head bent down and avoiding eye contact during conversations. His boss also chides him for his aimlessness and gloominess, which have affected his work and his co-workers' morale. Teoh eventually rediscovers a sense of purpose through his relationship with a new companion. This mysterious unnamed woman suddenly emerges in the middle of the night consuming a bowl of instant noodles while sitting beside the temperamental, broken-down, second-hand washing machine Teoh recently purchased. While she does not fulfil his need for love, lust, or recognition, Teoh's experience with alienation and loneliness is filled as he profits from her doing his daily chores and from making her a prostitute. Being character- rather than plot-led allows the film to carry on when Teoh mysteriously does not appear in the film

'Beyond Multiculturalism'   117

after being beaten up by an unsatisfied client. During the scuffle, the woman runs into Mr. Wong, who shelters her and coincidentally owns a faulty washing machine. Her presence, however, is naturally resented by his daughter, Yuen, as her boyfriend, Yap (also Teoh's colleague), and brother, Dee, have developed a fondness for her.[10]

The narrative in the film is presented in a non-melodramatic way through the use of non-professional actors. Using 'real' everyday people, Lee avoids contrived performances and melodramatic acting while allowing for a look of authenticity. In his search for performances that closely resemble the daily life of 'real' people, all the characters are similarly unmotivated by the achievement of ambitions, desires, or goals. In enhancing the slice-of-life situation that allows the actor to blend in with the working-class subject matter, these characters, through simple acts of eating instant noodles or sharing a cigarette, often appear subtle without displaying too much emotion and seem devoid of overt self-consciousness.

The film melancholically uses silence and minimal dialogue without any extra-diegetic sound, to capture sadness effectively, stifled passion, and fear. The female character often maintains a blank, expressionless gaze throughout the film, without displaying any signs of emotion and without ever uttering a word. Her silence is an unspoken remonstration against the display of mindless capitalist profiteering and consumption in a rapidly urbanising city. She willingly accepts any instructions put to her, and dutifully carries out her chores and dresses according to how others deem fit, without any resistance. Her silence also figuratively reflects how society often pretends not to see injustice, captured through a scene where Yap rapes her. Even though she hardly resists his confrontation, her facial expressions display her displeasure. The entire occurrence is witnessed by Mr. Teoh, who silently peeks through the door without protesting. Throughout the movie, silence is also used in appropriate scenes to highlight the social conditions of solitude and boredom. The characters often appear wary of each other's presence in situations that warrant chattiness and conversation. The use of silence is contrasted in two different scenes. In the first scene, Mr. Wong, Yap, and Yuen sit together at the dinner table. Mr. Wong eagerly waits for their approval concerning the quality of a new dish he cooked. Despite staring at them and waiting for their feedback, Mr. Wong receives no compliments. In contrast, the reclusive Teoh often breaks his silence by speaking to the washing machine. The washing machine becomes his companion during meals and is treated as a companion when he persuades it to function and wishes it a good night.

---

10. While James Lee often uses a recurrent cast of non-commercial actors, he casts the iconic Patrick Teoh as Mr. Wong in this film. As a former radio DJ and television newscaster known as the 'Voice of Malaysia', Patrick Teoh is also an award-winning actor. He has acted in commercial and independent films, is an active stage actor, author, blogger, restaurateur, and owner of the post-production studio Addaudio.

The use of lighting is kept to a minimum in order to achieve such effects. To accentuate a sense of realism and draw on the characters' and audiences' emotional response, natural/available light is predominantly used without any form of added lights to illuminate the scenes. This form of lighting is preferred over stylised lighting, three-point lighting, and constructed mise-en-scène often used by mainstream cinema in Malaysia. The use of natural/available lighting to create a sense of authenticity is fully exploited whenever possible by shooting on location, whether it is outdoors, in a supermarket, or a restaurant. To avoid interrupting a scene, Lee uses long takes, minimalist camera movements, and places the camera at a distance to capture an entire dialogue without cuts.

These long takes consciously generate tension in anticipating that an incident is about to occur, yet nothing happens in most cases. The camera also often functions as the third person in such situations by utilising hand-held shots to allow the audience to intrude and look voyeuristically into these scenes. The long shot is utilised so that the viewer, rather than the character, is invited to react to the situation. For example, the static camera is often placed at a distance. The entire scene is allowed to play without interruption as the mysterious female character is often seen at a distance doing household chores for Teoh or Mr. Wong. The camera is often placed outside the kitchen door frame, voyeuristically looking in as Teoh sits on a stool in the kitchen with a cigarette in hand while speaking to the mysterious woman. As she listens, she sits on the floor beside the washing machine, while the sunlight penetrates through the windows.

The film ends in ambiguity after Yuen purportedly accidentally stabs the mysterious woman in the kitchen. The climax and resolution are missing from this film, deconstructing, and fragmenting the narrative line, which often ends a film without an expected resolution. As Yuen fearfully runs away, she comes to her senses and returns to the kitchen only to find the mysterious woman has vanished without a trace. The disappearance of the mysterious woman affects Mr. Wong emotionally, as he often describes her as his lover. Mr. Wong attempts to cover his emotions by wearing a Japanese superhero's mask to hide his feelings. The same mask is also put on by Mr. Wong in two earlier incidences, once as he watches gay porn and the other as he looks in the mirror and starts to flex his muscles. The mask in these incidents reflects his attempts to be someone else or provide him with the means of transforming his personality in looking for a new identity. The ending of the film is ultimately left to the interpretation of the audience. As Mr. Wong prepares to pay for his purchases at the check-out counter of a supermarket, he looks up and notices that the cashier is an exact likeness of the mysterious woman. While he does not display any curiosity about whether the cashier is indeed the mysterious woman or is surprised at their resemblance, he attempts to confirm her identity by asking for her name. She curtly tells him to mind his own business as the film abruptly ends with a mid-shot of Mr Wong staring at the cashier.

Direct criticism of state policies and highlighting the voice of the marginalised

The third characteristic of the Malaysian postethnic cosmopolitan cinema is its direct criticism of state policies. MDI filmmakers represent a generation of highly intellectual, middle-class, well-educated, and articulate Malaysians unafraid of expressing their views on and displeasures at injustice. They are comprised mainly of the urban-based generation born after the 13 May 1969 race riots and have a deep sense of political and social consciousness after being primarily exposed to the socio-cultural and political conditions arising from Malay-centric nation-building policies. The majority were educated under the NEP and the NCP, favouring the rise of the middle-class *Bumiputeras*. Although receiving their elementary education in Malaysia, filmmakers such as Woo Ming Jin, Teck Tan, Amir Muhammad, and Ho Yuhang received an overseas tertiary education.[11]

Overseas studies have placed them in a situation where hard work is rewarded with success. This situation exposed them to social inequality in Malaysia caused by affirmative action policies favouring specific ethnic communities. Being internet savvy further allowed them to be exposed to the unrestricted inflow of information and materials. The internet propagated and encouraged emancipation through Western notions of secularism, democracy, meritocracy, and liberal speech and has revealed a greater understanding of egalitarianism, civil rights, and social equality.[12]

Being exposed to and aware of the discrimination and problems caused by ethnic segregation and inequality, MDI filmmakers highlight how ethnic segregation prevents unity. This subtle struggle for national unity carried out by both *Bumiputera* and non-*Bumiputera* filmmakers surpasses the need for ethnic identification. In line with the search for a national identity, their films incorporate local cultures blended with contemporary issues to contest and negotiate socio-politics and class conflict. These films contest notions of 'Malaysian-ness' by presenting a dichotomy of a 'new' multi-ethnic cinema versus the 'old' Malay-centric cinema through issues of belonging and marginalisation, race and ethnicity, religion, and sexuality depicted through the daily struggles of the filmic characters. MDI filmmakers understand that, so long as Malaysians fail to disregard the nation's attachment to ethnic allegiance, and so long as race- and ethnic-based politics continue to exist, Malaysia will continually search for its elusive national identity. The postethnic perspective is, therefore, essential in the negotiation of race and ethnic and cultural diversity.

---

11. Teck Tan completed his law and arts degrees at the University of Melbourne and then pursed filmmaking at the Australian Film TV and Radio School in Sydney. Ho Yuhang studied engineering at Iowa State University; Amir Muhammad read law at the University of East Anglia and studied film at New York University. Brenda Danker pursued her Master of Arts degree in screen drama direction at Goldsmiths College London.

12. For a detailed discussion regarding the online *Reformasi* movement and the impact of the emergence of a virtual civil society, see Tan 2010.

Examples of such audacity in highlighting sensitive and controversial issues which contest state social policies can be found in Amir Muhammad's films. His films *The Big Durian* (2003), *Lelaki Komunis Terakhir* (2006), *Apa Khabar Orang Kampung* (2007), and *Malaysian Gods* (2009) criticise the rise of autocratic power slowly replacing democracy.[13] His employment of themes regarding communism and *Reformasi* is considered 'touchy' and 'sensitive' issues for the state. While his films are neither revolutionary nor oppositional and do not directly discuss these issues, his film titles indirectly speak volumes. His opinion on politicians can be summed up through the title of his book, *Malaysian Politicians Say The Darndest Things*. The title *Malaysian Gods* is an ironic reference to Malaysians exalting their politicians as superior 'God-like beings' (Amir 2010b). These films and their titles demonstrate his political values that depart from state-sanctioned ideologies.

MDI directors also criticise the Malaysian education system and the NEP, which has led to non-Malay sentiments of being deprived of equal educational opportunities, having a negative impact on ethnic integration (Lee 2006).[14] Deepak Kumaran Menon explores this issue through the plights of the marginalised communities sidelined in the plantations.[15] *Chemman Chaalai* (2005) and *Chalanggai* (2007) highlight the plight of the Indian ethnic community who reside in plantations and urban Kuala Lumpur and who have been deprived of a proper education in two eras. Deepak's films separately tell Shantha and Uma's journeys and the difficulties they face as they aspire to obtain higher education. Both films inadvertently criticise the education system, which has sidelined the Indian ethnic community and which causes ethnic segregation. The importance of education is highlighted in his director notes, which state that the 'way forward would be [through] education', as the film 'emphasis [*sic*] on the importance of education for the growth of the community and nation'.[16]

Education is also given great emphasis in the ethnic Chinese community and is highlighted by criticising the Malaysian education system. In *Spinning Gasing*, Harry Lee was scolded by his father as a 'fool', 'failure', and 'disgrace' for failing his

---

13. Chapter 2 discusses Amir Muhammad's films and censorship.
14. Article 153 legalises Malay privileged access to educational scholarships, training, and enrolment. Simultaneously, the National Education Act (1971) introduced several ethnic preferential policies, including ethnic quotas, to increase Malay enrolment in higher education. For a detailed study on the Malaysian education policies and system, see Hazri and Nordin (2010) and Lee (2009). Non-Malay students have found difficulty securing places in local public universities. At the same time, Malay enrolment at the tertiary level is ensured through almost exclusively Malay-only programmes and institutions such as the Majlis Amanah Rakyat (Council of Trust for the Indigenous Peoples or MARA), MARA University of Technology (UiTM), MARA Junior Science Colleges, the Residential Secondary School system, the two-year matriculation programmes, and ethnic quota admission policies (Lee 2006; Santhiram and Sua 2010). As such, non-Malay students had to look for other avenues to pursue higher education, thereby creating ethnic enclaves in the education system (ibid.). For more information regarding the discussion of ethnic segregation in Malaysian schools, see Lee 2010a.
15. Chapter 1 discusses how the Indians arrived in the Malay Peninsula as plantation workers. They remained in the plantations because of the British policy of divide and rule.
16. Taken from (now defunct) http://www.deepakmenon.info/filmography.html.

'Beyond Multiculturalism' 121

Figure 3.1: Film poster of *Gadoh*.
Source: Brenda Danker.

exams. In *Gadoh* (2009), Heng is scolded by his father for not doing his best in school. There is a moment of silence in the conversation between Mak Inom and Kak Yam about Jason's failure to obtain a scholarship despite getting better results than Orked in *Sepet*.[17]

In *Gadoh*, directors Nam Ron and Brenda Danker have expressed their concerns about the need to overcome the dichotomisation of *Bumiputeras* against the Others, caused by the Malaysian education system. As Malaysians, both Danker and Nam Ron have personally experienced racism. They understand that an education system that promotes racial ideologies or maintains the political and social hegemony of particular ethnic groups must be abandoned, for education in Malaysia should not belong to any particular race. Such actions demonstrate an arrogance towards creating a selective history that benefits those who profit from such an ideology (Azly 2009). *Gadoh* is aimed at making Malaysian youths comprehend their Malaysian identity and exercising their right to freedom of speech and expression by being critical and unafraid to question (Kwan 2009).

Gadoh achieves this by highlighting how Malaysian students are segregated by clinging to their ethnic groups, to suggest a worrying institutionalisation of racism that constructs a sense of disunity among students from different ethnic groups to maintain the existing status quo. The film, therefore, propagates the need for unity through *Bangsa* Malaysia. The statement '*Aku Bangsa Malaysia*' (I am of the

---

17. The importance of education in Chinese society can be traced to the examination system that originated in the Han dynasty. The need to select government officials based on merit and a Chinese society that valued educated men led to aspiring candidates sitting for examinations based on their knowledge of Confucian classics. Success in the provincial civil service examinations would allow candidates to occupy positions as scholar-officials, bureaucrats, and top officials. The promise of prestige, honour, and social mobility that came with these positions led many candidates to continue pursuing success in such examinations. For more information regarding the Chinese examination system in Ancient China, see Tamura et al. 1997, 19–35.

Figure 3.2: The student cast of *Gadoh*. Source: Brenda Danker.

Malaysian race) on the film's poster aims at creating a united Malaysian nation suffused with a 'One people, one nation' mentality. This statement is also carried throughout the film, as Cikgu Azman continuously blames the system as the cause for ethnic segregation.[18] Azman directly calls for the education system to unite rather than divide and for education curricula and syllabi to be revised, planned, democratised, and closely monitored without coercion or domination in promoting greater inter-ethnic understanding and tolerance (Syed 2008, xxiii).

Cikgu Azman also demonstrates his support for *Bangsa* Malaysia. When his colleague Cikgu Ann asks about his quest in life, he replies, '*Aku nak buat sesuatu untuk bangsa aku*' (I'd like to do something for my race). She says, '*Melayu?*' (The Malays?). He answers, '*Malaysia. Bangsa Malaysia*'. Therefore, the film criticises the Malaysian education system that causes segregation and then directly criticises the taboo issue of discrimination and increased polarisation in society caused by the division into *Bumiputeras* and non-*Bumiputeras*. While *Sepet* and *S'kali* (2006) have subtly discussed the NEP and its effects, *Gadoh* openly criticises the NEP within education and workspace contexts. The film criticises how the NEP has shaped and defined Malaysian society according to race, ethnicity, culture, language, and religion (Farish 2009).[19] It also explores how conflicting issues of the national

---

18. 'Cikgu' can be translated as a teacher in Bahasa Malaysia. It is commonly added unofficially to a teacher's name in a show of respect and authority.
19. *Gadoh* is an addition to the KOMAS *Bangsa Malaysia Series*, a collection of videos used as resource tools for education and discussion on various racism topics in Malaysia. The videos can be viewed at http://www.engagemedia.org/Members/Komas/freedomfilmfest-fff-videos/videos. KOMAS or the Community Communications Centre (a Malaysian communications centre that focuses on assisting and organising the needs of groups involved in a whole range of local issues) organises the annual Freedom Film Festival. This festival highlights films and documentaries with themes encompassed by the Universal Declaration of Human Rights (UDHR) with hopes of spreading justice, peace, equality, and democracy. For more information regarding KOMAS and the Freedom Film Fest, see http://www.komas.org/.

'Beyond Multiculturalism'

identity, culture, and language remain unresolved because the nation is continually segregated into Malays, Chinese, Indians, and lain-lain (the 'other' indigenous communities).

Being unafraid to question puts MDI filmmakers in a situation to reclaim their positions as Malaysians. They continuously experience a longing for the nation as they have been pushed to the margins. They long for their nation as they remain 'nationless' in a 'nationless' state as Malaysians continue to pursue a concept that unites them (Zawawi 1998). In recent years, the racial and ethnic tensions caused by the fixation of the *Bumiputera* Self and the Others have worsened. This also means that the Malaysian society is shaped and defined according to race, ethnicity, culture, language, and religion rather than political ideologies (Farish 2009). MDI filmmakers highlight this sense of longing for the nation using cosmopolitan themes to envision a postethnic nation.

A cosmopolitan framework imagining a postethnic society allows the MDI to emphasise humanitarian issues beyond race and ethnic contestations. Such issues are portrayed through tales of individual struggles in society, dilemmas of the urban young in a modernising nation, and alienation and solitariness caused by an urbanised society's superficiality. These issues are portrayed through characters who long for and desire someone forcefully taken away from them. For example, Ping from *Love Conquers All*, Tung from *Rain Dogs* (2006), and Yun Ding from *The Elephant and the Sea* (2007) similarly suffer the harshness of experiencing separation or the loss of a loved one. These characters wander around aimlessly searching for love, answers, and recognition as they seek their sanctuary. This sense of longing and emptiness alienates them from the rest of society. Their displays of sadness and loneliness represent their sense of homelessness or 'nationless', of being driven by a forbidden desire of reclaiming their homeland, as individuals deterritorialised in search of their identity. These displays, in turn, reflect the individual experiences of MDI filmmakers who have personally experienced marginalisation.

The MDI shifts the focus of the subject matter onto stories of simple people living everyday lives. Tales of society's limitations, alienation of urban youth and marginalised working class, and mindless capitalist consumption are presented non-pretentiously in a non-melodramatic way. This method allows the audience to empathise with the characters, for it is, in general, a story about and for them. The MDI politicises the urban landscapes to provide a space for challenging current representations of ethnicity, race, and sexuality to promote creative expression and creative thinking. This cinema produced films with an underlying social commentary by highlighting the eventual moral breakdown in society caused by urbanisation, the breakdown of the traditional family and human relationships, increased violence in society, and the effects of being a consumer-driven society. Such themes portraying the alienation of youths in urban settings, as everyday people with everyday struggles, are a critique and social commentary about society's decadence.

For example, MDI films use the consumption of food to present its social commentary and critique. In mainstream cinema in Malaysia, a dining scene is often for courtship and is extravagantly portrayed regardless of its location, be it at home, posh restaurants, or hotels. For example, in an overtly exaggerated dining scene in *Pisau Cukur* (Gold Diggers, 2009), 'gold diggers' Bella and Intan share a meal with the affluent Datuk Zakaria. Dressed in exaggerated hats and brightly coloured dresses, they attempt to win the heart of Datuk Zakaria as they dine on a cruise ship. While the use of food is in line with Malaysia being a popular culinary destination and Malaysians for their gastronomic enthusiasm, the MDI uses food to represent social interaction. The use of food and its consumption signifies three social implications. Firstly, the act of eating can represent the breakdown of the traditional family and human relationships. For example, the characters in James Lee's and Ho Yuhang's films often consume a bowl of instant noodles alone at an empty table or on the couch. The use of instant noodles as food for the 'underprivileged' is also present in *Spinning Gasing*, when the characters are forced to eat instant noodles after having invested all their money in their musical band. The consumption of instant noodles alone, then, tells of the effects of being impoverished, lonely, and insolvent in a consumer-driven society. The characters' choice of eating alone represents a form of social dysfunction, being rejected by or withdrawn from society caused by the lack of friends or family members.

Second, eating can be simplified as the basic need to satiate hunger. Eating is an initiated desired act, as hunger encourages and compels an individual to eat to satisfy this hunger (Lee 2014; Newman 1997, 215). Scenes of eating to satisfy hunger are present in *Lips to Lips* (2000) and *Room to Let* (2002). In these films, the act of eating goes beyond the need to satisfy a sense of biological hunger. The characters are eating to satisfy the hunger for belonging and for recognition as Malaysians. This hunger represents the need for equality, as the NEP has seemingly marginalised them. Thus, this act of eating represents the characters fulfilling an inaccessible and unreachable desire to attain equal status as Malaysians, regardless of ethnic or racial backgrounds. While eating provides a sense of comfort, as food is easily accessible to all Malaysians regardless of background, the marginalised characters in MDI films accept their position at the periphery, incapable of receiving handouts from the state. This ideological preference is portrayed through characters eating instant noodles and not gastronomic meals, for instant noodles are often recognised for their simplicity, cheapness, and unhealthiness. This portrayal also symbolises MDI filmmakers' independence, making low-budget films instead of relying on state funds.

Third, the act of dining as a family represents a form of social acceptance of positive nation-building. As the nation's idea is represented by the family unit (Smith 1991), the family as the basis of a political community becomes a sanctuary that unites its members (Honohan 2008, 73). Meals at the dinner table present opportunities for family members to bond, communicate, and learn from one another; sitting around a table for a meal, returning home for a meal, or being welcomed

'Beyond Multiculturalism' 125

to join in a meal represents family unity. This family unity, therefore, represents national unity. In the *Elephant and the Sea*, Long Chai's mother chides him for not returning home for meals. While she grumbles that she might not have enough food to feed him and his friend Yun Ding, who turned up unannounced, they still find their place at the table and join in the meal. It is relatively uncommon for Chinese and Malays to dine together, because religion and food are important markers for ethnic identification due to the refusal of certain individuals from the Chinese and Malay communities to share utensils (Chee 2010, 98–99). *Flower in the Pocket* highlights how religious and ethnic boundaries need not bind individuals through a simple act of eating together. Ayu's (Malay) mother looks beyond the ethnicity of Ayu's (Chinese) friends, Li Ahh and Li Ohm. She instead sees them as two children longing for parental love and guidance as their father becomes a workaholic after their mother's passing. The acceptance of Li Ahh and Li Ohm goes beyond the simple act of feeding two hungry children. The feeding of children deprived of food and love from a different ethnic and religious background signifies the universality of love, humility, and humanity. This sharing of a meal goes beyond religious and ethnic boundaries. This possible postethnic coexistence beyond ethnic recognition leads towards the deconstruction of stereotypes.

The MDI provides a voice for the marginalised by challenging stereotypes. By deconstructing the need to categorise according to groups, marginalised individuals overcome the boundaries that distinguish them and the Others. This deconstruction allows marginalised individuals to acknowledge that differences present an opportunity to learn about one another and, in so doing, confront and recognise diversity to embrace multiple belongings through coexistence (Appiah 2006, xv). This sense of diversity deconstructs stereotypes as cosmopolitanism, creates the awareness of human diversity within communities, and recognises human plurality and the bonds of affinity between diverse groups (Lu 2000, 258). Stereotypes circulated through mainstream cinema in Malaysia have naturalised the unbalanced power relations, as audiences accept these stereotypes as mere entertainment (see this discussion in Chapter 1). The MDI attempts to overcome such stereotypes using cosmopolitan themes to discuss taboo issues, the marginalised, and the disadvantaged.

One issue boldly discussed by the MDI is sex and sexuality. In Malaysia, open discussions about sex remain taboo and sensitive. As this Muslim majority nation frowns upon public representations of sex, all locally produced or foreign films must be approved by the LPF before being shown in cinemas. Scenes or elements of nudity or sex or the involvement of lesbian, gay, bisexual, and transgender queer (LGBTQ) individuals, eroticism, skimpy outfits, and kissing are prohibited. Malaysia also takes a strict stand towards issues of LGBTQ people in society, as the act of sodomy is punishable by law.[20]

---

20. *Rozana Cinta '87* (Rozana's Love, 1987) became the first Malaysian film to portray LGBTQ characters. The film was a melodrama about romance and not about highlighting the plight of these marginalised characters. The film was never criticised for its thematic content or portrayal of homosexuality.

Film censorship regulations have also banned representations of LGBTQ individuals and themes. This regulation, coupled with the disapproval of religious authorities, has led to the negation of LGBTQ individuals within Malaysian society. Prior depictions of LGBTQ individuals in Malaysia were made famous by the limp-wristed Sam played by Imuda in Othman Hafsham's television sitcom *2+1*. Such characters were used as material for comic relief that caused negative perceptions of LGBTQ individuals. In 2011, *Dalam Botol* (In a Bottle), made by Khir Rahman, became the first Malaysian LGBTQ film. The film, said to be based on actual events, was deemed controversial due to its theme, original title (*Anu Dalam Bottle*/Penis in a Bottle; the LPF required the word 'Anu' be dropped), and thematic content. In *Spinning Gasing*, LGBTQ issues are represented with a certain degree of frankness that transcends ethnicity and religion. The film makes a bold approach to contesting homosexuality through Ariff's openness about his sexual preference. As Ariff attempts to reclaim his position in society, the film displays compassion for him rather than using his sexuality as comic relief. The film, through Ariff, also displays the marginalisation of LGBTQ individuals in society, when Ariff, who works as a male prostitute, is bullied by Tan Sri's bodyguard. Ariff, however, gains personal and societal empowerment, as he can negotiate his sexuality freely within the setting of his musical band.

Osman Ali took discussions about sex and LGBTQ individuals to a different level by highlighting the plight of sex workers in Kuala Lumpur. His film *Bukak Api* took a different turn by speaking out for marginalised transsexuals (in Bahasa Malaysia, the transsexual is *mak nyah*), drug users, and commercial sex workers.[21] Being rejected and marginalised by society has led them to a community of individuals of a similar fate, which provides them with support, comfort, and a sense of camaraderie.[22] Rather than taking a reproachful line of passing judgment and casting social shame on them, the film allows these characters to speak about how they have been marginalised and harassed in the notorious Chow Kit Road where they commonly work.

Real-life sex workers are interviewed at their homes and workplaces to highlight social and critical realism elements. It was by speaking to these individuals that allowed them to have a voice. *Bukak Api* gave them a platform to inform and explain their decision to become sex workers personally. They said that, despite knowing that their choice of occupation goes against society's morality, their sexual orientation left them with little choice but to earn a living as sex workers. The use of

---

21. According to Teh (2008), male-to-female transsexuals (regardless of whether they have undergone sex-change operations or not) are locally known as *mak nyah* (*mak* means 'mother', and *nyah* indicates feminine behaviour). In 1987, an unofficial society of transsexuals termed themselves as *mak nyah* to differentiate them from a *pondan* (effeminate man) or *bapok* (homosexuals). These terms are deemed derogatory.

22. Teh (2008) states that the majority of transsexuals or *mak nyahs* are involved in the sex industry, a third of them earning below the poverty line with MYR500 (US$125) per month. Seventy-four per cent have received secondary education, and 4 per cent have received tertiary education. The majority of *mak nyahs* choose the sex trade because of the obstacles and discrimination they face from society.

'Beyond Multiculturalism' 127

interviews allows them to speak about intimidation and harassment by the authorities and violent clients. At the same time, they allowed the camera to enter into their previously unknown lives intimately. In line with the film's theme of creating sexual and HIV/AIDS awareness, characters in simulated acts of sexual intercourse are recorded, to highlight graphically the importance of protected sex.[23]

The subject matter of transsexual sex workers is similarly highlighted in Poh Si Teng's *Pecah Lobang* (Busted, 2008).[24] This documentary, like *Bukak Api*, was shot in Chow Kit Road and similarly explores the plights and anxieties faced by sex workers through the lived experiences of Natasha. As one of the winning entries at the 2008 Freedom Film Fest, this documentary explores how being a sex worker means she is always faced with offensive threats from the authorities. Her profession is not one chosen out of free will but is the result of her failure to gain employment in society due to her sexuality. *Spinning Gasing*, *Bukak Api*, and *Pecah Lobang* similarly have become influential social commentaries that expose Malaysia's unseen side. The films shine a sympathetic light on marginalised LGBTQ individuals. These films are both postethnic and cosmopolitan by not portraying LGBTQ individuals as comic relief or sinful people but as individuals with feelings, emotions, and problems like everyone else. Although discussions of LGBTQ issues are taboo in society, these films negate the clichés and stereotypes. They differ from mainstream Malaysian films such as *Dalam Botol* (2011), as the characters are not forced to morally 'repent' their ways by denouncing their sexual preference. In 2021, the film *Miss Andy* (2020), which narrates the struggles of a transgender person, premiered in Taiwan. Without including Tsai Ming Liang's *I Don't Want To Sleep Alone* (2006), *Miss Andy* became the fifth Malaysian film produced within the post-2000 period that discusses the theme of an LGBTQ character, after *Bukak Api*, *Pecah Lobang*, *Waris Jari Hantu* (Heir of the Ghost Finger, 2007) and *2 Alam* (2 Universes, 2010).[25]

Survival Guide Untuk Kampong Radioaktif (Survival Guide for Radioactive Village, 2011) is an ideal example of how MDI filmmakers criticise the state and provide a voice for the marginalised. This project aims to create awareness about how the building of the proposed Australian Lynas rare earth mining plant will

---

23. *Bukak Api* was co-sponsored by Malaysian NGO movement Pink Triangle and the Malaysian AIDS Council.
24. Poh Si Teng is a journalism graduate from San Francisco State University and has worked at the *Miami Herald* and Associated Press news service. According to the film's official website, *Pecah Lobang* can be translated as 'busted'. The documentary was written, directed, and photographed by Poh Si Teng and co-produced by Big Pictures Production, KOMAS, and Konrad Adenauer Stiftung. The documentary has been screened at various international film festivals: the Social Justice Film Festival (Washington, 2009), the 33rd Frameline LGBTQ International Film Festival (San Francisco, 2009), the Nigah Festival (New Delhi, 2009), This Human World Film Festival (Vienna, 2009), the Mezipatra Festival (Prague, 2009), the Kanish-Mumbai International Queer Film Festival (2010), and Freedom Film Fest Singapore (2010).
25. The films *2 Alam* and *Waris Jari Hantu* (Heir of the Ghost Finger, 2007) use the horror genre to highlight sexual transgressions by transsexuals or the *mak nyah* as wrong, sinful, and immoral. In these mainstream horror films, the characters are rejected and stigmatised by society and family. In *2 Alam*, the narrative of the film depicts the notion that, because of their gender change, transsexuals would face problems not only in life but also during the hereafter, which is reflective of the film's title (2 Universes).

Figure 3.3: Lee Ah Seng appears on television. Source: Liew Seng Tat.

affect the environment and health of Malaysians, regardless of race and ethnicity. The online project, which consists of five short films, a trailer, a teaser, and a three-part investigative news segment, became a platform to create awareness. The films were produced mostly in Bahasa Malaysia and translated into English and Mandarin with subtitles. While there have been protest movements against the building of this government-approved plant, the apathy of Malaysians, supposed media blackout, and harassment faced by the villagers in the town of Gebeng has led these filmmakers to launch this online campaign.

As this campaign is carried on via the internet, it is a form of challenge of mainstream media's state control. The three-part investigative 'news segment', *TV Tiger's Lee Ah Seng Reports on the Malaysian Rare Earth Issue* (2011), criticises how the state controls information about the Lynas plant. It is a parody of the late environmental journalist Karam Singh Wahlia, who reported for local television station TV3. This parody uses an imaginary television station and journalist to criticise both TV3 and the state for their failure to highlight the risks associated with the building of this plant. This parody then criticises the way the mainstream media have portrayed this issue. Lee Ah Seng mimics Karam Singh, who was famous for his use of poetry, his beard and hand gestures, and used phrases such as 'the public should also use their brains', 'don't be easily misled' and 'believe only what's on TV'. Only by being online is this parody able to bypass political restrictions and travel across transnational networks.[26]

---

26. The videos can be seen on YouTube on the channel Kampong Radioaktif. The site can be accessed at http://www.youtube.com/kampongradioaktif. This online campaign has also been widely publicised through its Facebook page, and by online news portals, blogs, and forums.

'Beyond Multiculturalism'

Launched in November 2011, *Survival Guide Untuk Kampong Radioaktif* was pioneered by Tan Chui Mui. She brought together filmmakers Yeo Joon Han, Liew Seng Tat, Woo Ming Jin, and Azharr Rudin, political and environmental activists, and politicians to highlight a postethnic issue that goes beyond race and ethnic contestation. The fictional storylines in *Welcome to Kampong Radioactive* (2011), *Orang Minyak XX* (The Oily Man XX, 2011), and *Masakan Cinta* (Love Dish, 2011) are allegories about postapocalyptic conditions after a radiation plant has hazardously altered the environment. These short films employ black humour, exaggerations, and parodies to create awareness about the environmental dangers. In each film, the villagers are faced with problems of genetic mutation. In *Orang Minyak XX*, the radioactive poisoning is so intense that it even affects the mystical powers of the mythical *Orang Minyak*.[27] *Welcome to Kampong Radioaktif* speaks about a radioactively contaminated village. Two soldiers venture into the village in search of survivors. One of them is affected by the radiation and realises that his penis has mutated into a third hand.

In the same village, a family prepares to visit their grandfather during Eid-al-Fitr. As this middle-class family has been left behind, they demonstrate what needs to be done to survive for their journey. They create self-made radioactive suits and protect their car with aluminium foil. In another example, *Masakan Cinta* is a parody of a famous television chef preparing a dish. Among her ingredients are a two-headed chicken with three legs, a squid with a fish head, and a blue carrot. After 'cleaning' the ingredients of real and make-believe metals such as thorium, leukemium, mutanium, and monsterium, she serves the dish, consisting of little black specks, to her waiting guests: a Malaysian Chinese man, a Malaysian Indian man, and a Malaysian Indian lady. This act of serving radioactive food to her multi-ethnic guests demonstrates how a radioactive disaster affects all regardless of race and ethnicity.

Survival Guide Untuk Kampong Radioaktif also employs elements of love, hope, and humanism. *Lai Kwan's Love* (2011) documents a mother's daily struggles with her mentally challenged son. The documentary traces Lai Kwan, who worked in the Mitsubishi rare earth plant as a bricklayer in the 1980s. The plant, which had a radiation leak, affected a then-pregnant Lai Kwan. Her son, Cheah Lok Peng, was born disabled due to her exposure to radioactive waste. He continually craves her attention, and she spends twenty-two hours a day with him. The documentary serves as a warning of the dangers of radiation poisoning and the risk of it recurring. The use of a cosmopolitan framework in this documentary allows for emphasising humanitarian issues beyond race and ethnic contestations.

---

27. Based on the director's notes made available on YouTube, the *Orang Minyak* is an evil being who covers his entire body with oil to avoid capture. He is a burglar who rapes virgins to enhance his black magic prowess and is invisible to most people.

Figure 3.4: A scene from *Welcome to Kampong Radioaktif*. Source: Liew Seng Tat.

The films discussed in this section have become postethnic and cosmopolitan by criticising state policies and providing a voice for marginalised groups. MDI films that adopt themes of postethnicity, cosmopolitanism, and liberalism are produced in a society that does not espouse such thinking. These films, which go beyond discussions of race and ethnicity, are forms of cultural and political resistance which depict a more positive construction of an even-handed representation of society.

Targeting overseas film festivals

The fourth characteristic of the Malaysian postethnic cosmopolitan cinema is its targeting of overseas film festivals. Chapter 2 has analysed the importance of film festivals for MDI films to search for alternative sources of funding, distribution, and exhibition. A discussion of how the employment of postethnic and cosmopolitan themes enables the MDI to use film festivals as the focal site where filmmakers from world cinema, cosmopolitan cinema, accented cinema, and Third Cinema converge in the same purposes is the focus in this section.

MDI films with postethnic and cosmopolitan themes capably travel across national boundaries via dispersed networks and transborder formations. While film festivals are targeted as an alternative network with the hope of attracting international distributors by attaining international visibility, recognition, and reputation (Chaudhuri 2005), these festivals also provide a communal space. In this communal space, the most cosmopolitan audiences from most communities are allowed to view non-commercially viable films (Chan 2011, 253). These communal spaces are also preferred because of the resistance MDI filmmakers face from local regulators and censors. The humanistic themes that appeal to a diverse and global population

'Beyond Multiculturalism' 131

(Cubitt 2004) allow MDI films to share a desire for a worldwide community of human beings. The humanistic themes portraying social conditions of human suffering, struggles with emotions and sentiments, and the sense of inequality in MDI films are channelled through persistent flows of images within international film festivals as cosmopolitan spaces. Film festivals, therefore, become cosmopolitan spaces for audiences to participate in a concentrated cultural tour of the world and a space that regulates different social, economic, political, and cultural forces (Chan 2011, 253).

Deepak Kumaran Menon's second film, *Chalanggai*, became transnational through its distribution and exhibition on international film festival circuits.[28] Although modestly screened in Malaysia, the film, which is described as an 'equally rare instance of Tamil-language Malaysian filmmaking' (Stephens 2011), was widely exhibited across four continents. It was screened in Asia (Jakarta International Film Festival, 12th BIFF, 17th Fukuoka International Film Festival, 20th Tokyo International Film Festival, 9th Osian's Cinefan Festival of Asian & Arab Cinema, 5th Bangkok International Film Festival, 31st Hong Kong International Film Festival); in Europe (37th Festival International Du Film De La Rochelle, 36th Rotterdam International Film Festival); in Africa (Back Lot International Film Festival, 28th Durban International Film Festival); and in the Americas (Rio De Janeiro International Film Festival, Brazil, 30th Asian American International Film Festival, USA). *Chalanggai* also won the Special Mention Best Asian-Middle Eastern Award (20th Tokyo International Film Festival), NETPAC Best Film (9th Osian's Cinefan International Film Festival), and NETPAC Special Mention (36th International Film Festival Rotterdam).

Woo Ming Jin's *The Elephant and the Sea* became transnational through its distribution and exhibition at international film festivals.[29] It was previously titled *The Monkey Sea, The Ocean Circus*, and *The History of Pink Elephants*, but the filmmaker settled on *The Elephant and the Sea*. Written and directed by Woo, the film was produced by his production house, Greenlight Pictures, on a budget of MYR150,000 (US$50,000) that was partially state-funded and partially from the Hubert Bals Fund. The film was shot using DV technology over twenty days and made a return of MYR1,000 (US$250). *The Elephant and the Sea* premiered in 2007 at the Rotterdam International Film Festival. It was exhibited in more than thirty film festivals across Europe (Karlovy Vary International Film Festival, Warsaw Film Festival), Asia (Hong Kong International Film Festival, Taiwan International Film Festival), and the US (Los Angeles International Film Festival, Seattle International Film Festival). Along the way, *The Elephant and the Sea* was presented with five awards: the Special Jury Prize (Torino International Film Festival, 2007), Best Director Award and Critics Award (Cinema Digital Seoul Film Festival, 2007), Best

---

28. I was unable to see the film, as my efforts to obtain a copy from the director failed.
29. For the filmmaker's thoughts and production notes, see http://theelephantandthesea.blogspot.com/.

Film (Lisbon Village Film Festival, 2008), and Best Director (Diba Barcelona Film Festival, 2008). The film eventually premiered in Malaysian commercial cinemas in 2008, after the filmmaker removed two scenes that purportedly included sexual intercourse.[30]

Film festivals have become dependent on the input of world cinema films for exhibition. These festivals cannily benefit by investing in the works of an international auteur and ride on his or her global popularity, tapping into the established niche market of the auteur's globally dedicated audience to reach into secondary markets of the internet, television, and DVD releases (Elsaesser 2005, 499–500). Film festivals have also begun to foster the production of such films by offering 'development aid'. For example, production and distribution support specifically for first-time filmmakers from developing nations is provided by the Rotterdam Film Festival (Hubert Bals Fund) and the Berlin Film Festival (Berlin Film Festival World Cinema Fund) (503).[31] Deepak Kumaran Menon's *Chemman Chaalai* and *Chalanggai* were both funded by the Script Development Fund of the Hubert Bals Fund.

The Berlin Film Festival with the German Federal Cultural Foundation (Kulturstiftung des Bundes) established the World Cinema Fund to support filmmakers from developing nations. Having an annual budget of €500,000 (US$660,000) and a maximum grant amount of €100,000 (US$132,000), the fund aims to assist Latin American, African, Middle Eastern, and Asian filmmakers through funding, production, and distribution support. For a film to receive funding, a German partner is needed, but the film does not necessarily have to be co-produced. In 2011, Liew Seng Tat received the World Cinema funding award at the 14th Berlin Film Festival. The jury granted Liew the highest production award of €50,000 (US$66,000) for his next feature, *In What City Does It Live?*

The employment of cosmopolitan and postethnic themes has enabled films such as *Spinning Gasing*, *The Big Durian*, and *Karaoke* to travel along with the transnational networks of international film festivals.

The emergence of an auteur system of filmmaking

The fifth characteristic of the Malaysian postethnic cosmopolitan cinema is the emergence of an auteur system of filmmaking. The term 'auteur' originates from the *Cahiers* French film critics' theoretical writings and 'new avant-garde' filmmakers. The auteur is generally a filmmaker whose films have a strong personal style and

---

30. While Da Huang Pictures officially distributes the film's DVD, copies of the film were made available through online purchase by Malaysian businesses supporting Malaysian authors, filmmakers, and artists, Silverfish Books and the now defunct Rock Corner. The filmmaker has also innovatively utilised the internet to promote the film through trailers made available on its official website, YouTube, and Facebook, which ultimately mean direct to purchase of the film on the Da Huang website.

31. For more information regarding the World Cinema Fund, see http://www.berlinale.de/en/das_festival/world_cinema_fund/wcf_profil/index.html.

'Beyond Multiculturalism'

are truly cinematic and expressive with high technical and artistic achievements (Thomson-Jones 2008). The auteur places the filmmaker as the essential individual in the production of a film. It is a mark of respect for filmmakers whose films carry the filmmaker's recognisable and discernible style, recurrent stylistic signatures (art form, visual and aesthetic style), and thematic motifs (Goss 2009). Specifically, a filmmaker is characterised as an auteur based on three characteristics. Firstly, a filmmaker with technical competence and elementary flair in creating good films is propelled as an auteur. Secondly, the filmmaker's personality, signature, thoughts, stylistic characteristics, and feelings must be exhibited and recur over a group of films. Thirdly, the filmmaker's 'interior meaning' is caused by the unavoidable and ambiguous tension between a filmmaker's personality and a film's material (Sarris 2005).

The term 'auteur' is generally understudied in Malaysian cinema studies, possibly due to the lack of filmmakers befitting of such qualities and characteristics.[32] The inability to recognise Malaysian filmmakers as auteurs inevitably raises the question: what are the barriers preventing the emergence of Malaysian auteurs? Firstly, economic pressures require a filmmaker to reproduce another individual's work faithfully and self-effacingly. This situation leads to filmmakers being incapable of proficiently conveying personal expressions and styles. Over the years, however, Malaysian cinema has produced several 'metteurs-en-scène'. Talented filmmakers such as Aziz M. Osman and Shuhaimi Baba are at the mercy of their scripts. Rather than altering these materials, they adeptly adapt any given material without any true personal style (Buscombe 1973). Secondly, political restrictions possibly hamper the emergence of more Malaysian auteurs, as the LPF and FINAS have become the ultimate determinants of suitable content in scripts and films. These restrictions, which curb filmmakers' creativity and ideology, have prevented the emergence of more Malaysian auteurs.

MDI filmmakers, however, are not bound by economic and political restrictions. Their independence and transnational methods allow their films to employ their style, signature, characteristics, and feelings. This independence allows them to emphasise their thematic content and subject matter, work around cinematic and censorship regulations, and abandon the styles and systems of mainstream cinema in Malaysia which they view as stale and uncinematic. In other words, MDI filmmakers have produced works capable of winning against the system (Sarris 1968). This move is similar to the *André Bazin*-led *Cahiers* group sidestepping the 'sclerotic' and 'ossified' French cinema (Hayward 1996). François Truffaut, through *Cahiers*, dubbed French Cinema *'le papa de cinéma'* for its tedious repetitions of

---

32. U-Wei Saari's works have often taken an uncompromising approach in his recurrent addressing of the same subject matters and themes, studying issues of displacement, relationships, alienation, and identity of the Malay community. His works that fit within these qualities (*Perempuan, Isteri dan . . . ?*, 1993; *Kaki Bakar*, 1995; and *Jogho*, 1999) were made during the 1990s and did not fit within this study of post-2000 Malaysian cinema.

monotonously script-led films devoid of social realism and redolent with safe psychology (1996). The MDI is reflective of the French New Wave's 'auteur versus scenario-led films' (1996), as MDI filmmakers abandon making films commissioned by production companies that control the elements of themes and subject matter, production, exhibition, and distribution. In the following discussion, I deploy focussed case studies of James Lee and Yasmin Ahmad to analyse how their works distinguish them as auteurs in post-2000 Malaysian cinema.

Born in 1973, Lee is a trained graphic designer and a theatre actor and director. His theatre involvement eventually led to the film industry through *Lips to Lips*. Before this, Lee was single-handedly making digital short films through his production house, Doghouse73 Pictures. His film career began with the thriller *Snipers* (2001). His works are heavily inspired by John Cassavetes, David Lynch, Jim Jarmusch, Hou Hsiao-Hsien, Tsai Ming-Liang, and Wong Kar-Wai. As a prominent filmmaker and pioneer of the MDI, his filmography consists of several shorts and feature films such as *Ah Yu's Story* (1999), *Ah Beng Returns* (2001), *Beautiful Man* (2001), *Sometimes Love is Beautiful* (2005), *Bernafas Dalam Lumpur* (Breathing in Mud, 2008), and *I'll Call You Next Century* (2008). Lee remains the most versatile MDI filmmaker, as his production, distribution, and exhibition methods go beyond race and ethnicity, language, and gender. The fact that his award-winning films have been screened throughout different continents demonstrates that moving beyond multiculturalism is beneficial and advantageous for Malaysian films. In recognition of his contribution to Malaysian and Asian cinema, in 2007, Lee became the first Malaysian to be dubbed 'a talent to watch' and receive the special mention during the 9th Deauville Asian Film Festival in France.

Lee independently finances his films using overseas, personal, and private funding. For example, *Before We Fall in Love Again* was co-funded by The Hubert Bals Fund (Rotterdam) and The Global Film Fund (California). Lee often works with a minimal crew and budget and practises individual role-switching between productions. He has eminently featured in other filmmakers' works while collaborating with different production houses such as Da Huang Pictures, Paperheart Productions, and Red Films. As discussed in Chapter 2, this close rapport has seen him working as an actor in Amir Muhammad's *Lips to Lips* and Liew Seng Tat's *Flower in the Pocket*. He was the producer for Amir Muhammad's *The Big Durian* and *Tokyo Magic Hour* (2004), Ng Tian Hann's *First Take, Final Cut* (2004), Tan Chui Mui's *South of South* (2005) and *Company of Mushrooms* (2005), and Ho Yuhang's *Sanctuary* (2004); and executive producer for Tan Chui Mui's *Love Conquers All*. He then photographed Nam Ron's *Gedebe* (2002), Azharr Rudin's *Majidee* (2005), and Tan Chui Mui's *Love Conquers All*. His films have been widely circulated at international film festivals around different continents. *Before We Fall in Love Again* has also been screened at the Pusan International Film Festival and Tokyo International Film Festival. Lee heavily utilises the internet as a networking and promotional tool for distributing his work, to minimise costs. The Da Huang

'Beyond Multiculturalism' 135

Pictures website distributes his works and provides links to reviews, trailers, discussions, and feedback of his films on (the now defunct) doghouse73pictures.posterous.com, YouTube, and Facebook.

Lee is effectively the only Malaysian filmmaker who makes a vast number of cross-genre films. He also makes independent and mainstream commercial films. His independent films are from the genres of experimental (*Sunflowers*, 2000), gangster (*Man From Thailand*, 1999), romance (*Waiting for Love*, 2008), art-house drama (*Room to Let*, 2002), and horror (*Visits. Hungry Ghost Anthology*, 2004). His mainstream features *Histeria* (2008), *Tolong! Awek Aku Pontianak* (Help! My Girlfriend is a Pontianak, 2011), *Sini Ada Hantu* (Here Got Ghost, 2011), and *Claypot Curry Killers* (2011) are horror films. His mainstream martial art feature *Petaling Street Warriors* (2011) is co-directed with Hong Kong filmmaker Sampson Yuen Choi-Hin. The film features Malaysian and Singaporean talents Mark Lee and Yeo Yann Yann. This film exemplifies his ability to make cross-genre films and one with diverse languages and dialects. In *Petaling Street Warriors*, English, Mandarin, Bahasa Malaysia, Cantonese, Hailam, Hokkien, and Japanese are used. His second feature is another martial arts film titled *The Collector* (2012).[33]

This self-taught filmmaker made his name through his fourth DV feature, *The Beautiful Washing Machine*, when it won the Best Asian Picture and as the first Malaysian film to win the FIPRESCI Prize at the Bangkok International Film Festival (2005).[34] Shot over ten days by a four-person production team carrying different roles, this black humour film thrusts Malaysian audiences into the world of independent art-house cinema by exploring the effects of urbanisation. Lee's works also display a form of exquisite cinematographic style and a unique sense of film language that closely resembles that of Tsai Ming-Liang and Wong Kar-Wai. The *Jakarta Post* describes Lee's films as 'probably the least accessible of all contemporary Malaysian independent cinema', as his film work 'challenges cinematic conditions even further' with its 'strong heavy-handed experiments of strong visuals, deep semiotics, and non-traditional storytelling methods' (Agusta 2004). For example, Lee's love trilogy closely resembles Wong's love trilogy of *Days of Being Wild* (1990), *In the Mood for Love* (2000), and *2046* (2004). Lee's trilogy is *Before We Fall in Love Again* (2006), *Things We Do When We Fall in Love* (2007), and *Waiting for Love* (2008).

While the storylines of these three films do not interlink, the films are connected through recurring cast members. This is done through the repeated theme of an exposed love triangle by a couple whose relationship faces uncertainty and has become mundane, of couples falling in love or out of love through acts of betrayal and unfaithfulness, and the non-present third person within the secret love affair.

---

33. To date, James Lee has made another three feature films, *KL24: Zombies* (2017), *Kill-Fist* (2019), and *Two Sisters* (2019).

34. Lee's debut film, *Snipers*, premiered at Cinemanila.

The use of non-professional actors, natural lighting, diegetic sounds, and borrowed apartments or filming on the streets provide a sense of immediacy. Simultaneously, the settings display a sense of minimalism that carries along with them a sense of emptiness, meaninglessness, and purposelessness. This sense of minimalism is highlighted using visuals to express meanings. The minimal expressions (or lack of them), styles, and dialogues of the characters heavily reflect Tsai Ming-Liang's works. These feelings echo the themes in his films that highlight the sense of aimlessly struggling with commercialisation and urbanisation, reinforced with non-professional actors. The sense of simplicity in these films and the localisation of habits and characteristics allow the audience to identify with the characters in the film. For example, cigarettes and instant noodles are often consumed by the characters in *Beautiful Washing Machine* and *Room to Let*, who often loudly slurp as they eat the noodles.

The second MDI filmmaker who can persuasively be considered an auteur is Yasmin Ahmad, the director of *Sepet*, a case study that forms the final section of this chapter.[35] In the press, she is described by the *New Straits Times* as 'an independent filmmaker to be reckoned with in the country' (Sittamparam 2004).[36] *The National* labels her a 'director at the forefront of the independent film industry in Malaysia' (2009), and *Variety* describes her as a 'fast-rising helmer' who is a 'master at breezy, warm-hearted and sexually open repartee' (Weissberg 2007). Her style carries her signature through all six feature films: a blend of commercial and independent aesthetics and production methods that employ multi-ethnic and humanistic themes to challenge the Malaysian psyche.[37] Yasmin Ahmad started as an award-winning creative director for commercials for Malaysian and Singaporean television. Her commercials were often aired during festive seasons, particularly for Merdeka (Malaysian Independence Day).[38] Like her television commercials, her films have a very distinct style that deals with recurrent subject matter and themes. Yasmin also uses her works to challenge essentialist views on auteurship. She subverts and manipulates the cinema industry's expectations and was a female Muslim filmmaker working in a male-dominated industry. Her works resist the economic and political restrictions of the industry by employing transnational methods that allow her films to maintain her personal style, signature, characteristics, and feelings, work around regulations of censorship, as well as to abandon the stale and uncinematic

---

35. Certain parts of the section of this chapter were published as Lee Yuen Beng 2015. Yasmin Ahmad: Auteuring a New Malaysian Cinematic Landscape (*Wacana Seni Journal of Arts Discourse* 14: 87–109).

36. One of the biggest regrets I have in this book's writing is that I never met her in person. The arranged meeting we planned was postponed and never occurred, as she passed away soon after.

37. Yasmin's works bear similarities to those of Indonesia's Nia Dinata. Nia, who is similarly overseas trained and has a background in advertising, is often at odds with the Indonesian film censorship board. Her works contest social and Islamic values in Indonesia. While Nia's works do not contest inter-ethnicity, her works are social commentaries touching on cosmopolitan issues of homosexuality, migrant workers, and polygamy. Her filmography includes *Ca-bau-kan* (2002), *Arisan!* (2003), *Berbagi Suami* (2006), and *Arisan! 2* (2011).

38. Yasmin Ahmad was at the time holding a position with advertising agency Leo Burnett Malaysia. She held a degree in arts, majoring in politics and psychology, from Newcastle University in England.

Figure 3.5: Orked, Pak Inom, and Mak Atan during a birthday celebration. Source: Orked Ahmad.

styles and systems employed in commercial Malaysian mainstream cinema (Lee 2015). Inspired by the works of Charlie Chaplin, Satyajit Ray, Pedro Almódovar, Takeshi Kitano, and Yasujiro Ozu, Yasmin directed six feature films. Besides the made-for-television *Rabun* (2003), her other films, *Sepet*, *Gubra* (2006), *Mukhsin* (2007), *Muallaf* (2008), and *Talentime* (2009), were all commercial-oriented, aimed at a mass audience with independent features that resist the conventional cinematic methods employed by mainstream cinema in Malaysia.[39]

Yasmin was the oldest of three children, and her first four films are personal renditions of her life, *Rabun* based on her parents' characters. Yasmin's talent for the arts was directly influenced by her father being a musician and her mother a theatre director. The characters of Orked (named after Yasmin's biological sister), Pak Atan, and Mak Inom, all regulars in her films, were cinematic versions of her family members. It could be argued that her films' contestation with inter-ethnic and religious affairs was based on her personal life, for both her marriages were inter-ethnic. Her first husband was of Indian ethnic background, and her second husband was Chinese. The song 'Hujan' in *Mukhsin* was composed by her father. At the end of *Mukshin*, Pak Atan and Mak Inom make an appearance during the end credits playing the piano and singing 'Hujan'.

Yasmin's films are considered the bridge between commercial mainstream and independent films. They mix stylistic elements from independent cinema, commercial cinema, and television aesthetics. They have been both self-financed and financed by FINAS grants and were produced using a film crew with individual and specialised roles. However, her production methods contest the hegemony of a Malay-centric cinema, as she worked with multiracial casts and crews for all her

---

39. *Rabun* was initially planned for television. The plot for this telemovie was based on the personal lives of her parents. The telemovie attracted criticism for the open display of the husband-and-wife characters of Pak Atan and Mak Inom bathing together although there was no nudity involved. See https://www.yasminthestoryteller.com/.

films. While her films are not made with a minimal crew and budget, she practised role-switching to support other MDI filmmakers' productions. She is described as an easy-to-approach, supportive, and encouraging person. When Tan Chui Mui required funding for her short film *A Tree in Tanjung Malim* (2004), Yasmin became her sponsor without asking questions. In return, the money Tan won for the short film was used to finance Liew Seng Tat's *Flower in the Pocket*.[40] Yasmin also acted in Ho Yuhang's *Min* (2003), *Rain Dogs*, and *At the End of Daybreak* (2009), and in Amir Muhammad's *Susuk* (2008), and made cameo appearances in *Mukhsin* and *S'kali*. She was the executive producer for Azharr Rudin's short films *Raining Amber* (2005) and *The Amber Sexalogy* (2006).

Her films are distributed by commercial and independent companies such as Columbia Tristar Pictures and Lighthouse Pictures. Except *Rabun*, they premiered and were exhibited at international film festivals before making their Malaysian premiere.[41] All her films have received awards and were widely circulated at local and international film festivals. They were premiered overseas due to her choice of dealing with politically, culturally, and religiously sensitive topics. This defiance has made her a common enemy of the LPF. Her films that are critical of society's insincerity and hypocrisy have frequently become subjects of controversy and censorship targets. Due to their habit of criticising the Malaysian psyche, they were highly publicised in the media.

Yasmin was a filmmaker and a scriptwriter, and her works place her as the most prolific Malaysian filmmaker since P. Ramlee. Her works that generally criticise the failings of Malaysian society and, in particular, the Malay community and are recognised by scholars and the press (Hassan 2006b; Koay 2009) as similar to the works of Ramlee. Yasmin's films can be described as a form of social commentary, for she daringly exposes on the cinematic screen taboos and hypocrisies of society by criticising society's ignorance and its tendency to look away from practising racial prejudice and chauvinism while at the same time proclaiming itself to be a multiethnic and tolerant nation.

Yasmin's work on Malaysian society has been described as 'poetry in the lives of everyday and ordinary people', for it deeply examines the lives of ordinary Malaysians (Agusta 2004). She achieves this by intertwining romance with religious and ethnic conflicts to demonstrate that there remain obstacles and barriers from certain quarters that continue to frown upon interethnic relationships and marriages in Malaysian society. Yasmin ignores ethnic history by highlighting society's resistance to inter-ethnic relationships. Such differences are brought about by the

---

40. This fact was mentioned during my conversation with Wong Tuck Cheong on 26 July 2010, in Kuala Lumpur.
41. On 7 October 2009, I saw *Muallaf* at the Australian Malaysian Film Festival 2009 in Melbourne, before the film made its Malaysian premiere. After the screening, I held conversations with Affandi Jamaludin (who edited all Yasmin films), Sharifah Aleysha Syed Zainal Rashid (who acted in *Muallaf*), and Jacklyn Victor (who acted in *Talentime*). Each reminisced about how they missed Yasmin and how she had altered the landscape of Malaysia's filmmaking.

'Beyond Multiculturalism'

issue of conversion, a change in identity and lifestyles, and societal and familial objections, as a marriage between a Muslim and non-Muslim can become a site of contestation involving individuals, families, communities, and state; this leads to contestations between conservative and liberal Islamic forces (Jones, Chee, and Maznah 2009, 3). By drawing from her personal experience of being married inter-ethnically, she capably highlights that, in a nation made up of various ethnic communities and cultures, the rise of inter-ethnic relationships and marriages is inevitable.[42] By drawing from her personal experiences, she has allowed her films to be 'deeply personal and intensely humanistic' (Catsoulis 2008). As a result, she adds a personal touch to her films that emanates a raw authenticity that touches her audiences.

Yasmin's films drew audiences from multi-ethnic backgrounds by breaking social taboos and crossing ethnic boundaries. This style has led to her labelling as the 'taboo-breaker of Malaysian cinema' (The *National* 2009). She is also best known for her works that cross cultural and religious barriers, and her employment of humour, love, and humanism highlight society's hypocrisy and the importance of the family unit. According to Yasmin, her films are 'all about feelings'; she often reminded her audiences of the importance of love, respect, and tolerance (Bissme 2006).

Her films' thematic content upholds cosmopolitan values to blur the boundaries between ethnic communities, as these films envision the imaginary postethnic nation transcending cultural differences. Her films are controversial yet inspiring, as she focuses on a liberal outlook to imagine and construct a link that contests ideas about multiculturalism and ethnic relations. For example, her films *Rabun*, *Sepet*, *Gubra*, and *Mukhsin* focus on Orked's family as a unit for the nation. Her family members deconstruct the homogenous portrayal of middle-class families by consciously departing from those commonly portrayed in mainstream cinema. In her films, most middle-class Malay families resist being portrayed as rich and glossy, as projected by state imaginings. They instead demonstrate the struggles faced by everyday Malaysians and how identities are respected, and individuals need not be contained within boundaries. Yasmin achieves this by portraying Malay families as the Self (nation), welcoming and accommodating the Others.

Her films further challenge hegemony in Malaysian cinema using multi-ethnic themes. These themes are raised through representations of inter-ethnic relationships and work within the interstices of dominant languages by employing elements of melodrama, romance, and comedy. Her films lack the existence of the lone protagonist, as the characters from different ethnic backgrounds similarly struggle with the differences in identity politics caused by ethnocentrism. Her films are

---

42. In a marriage between a Muslim and a non-Muslim, non-Muslims are required by law to convert to Islam. In effect, marriage and divorce become issues intricately mixed with religious conversion (Jones, Chee, and Maznah 2009, 2–3).

Figure 3.6: Yasmin Ahmad in her office. Source: MHz Film.

shot using 35 mm film celluloid (except for *Rabun*, which was shot using digital technology). She employs non-professional actors and favours using long takes. She avoided shooting at posh and glamorous locations, preferring austere locations such as schools, houses, Malay *kampongs*, or even the streets of small towns such as Ipoh. Her film settings are kept to a bare minimum, and the characters in her films converse in Manglish, Chinese dialects, and Bahasa Malaysia. Such characteristics enable Malaysian audiences to identify with the characters and settings of the film. However, this simplicity denotes a sense of straightforwardness capable of transcending borders and is easily understood by overseas audiences.

Yasmin's filmmaking career lasted only six years. As an auteur 'granted insufficient time to reach her full potential' (Edwards 2009), she died at the age of fifty-one in 2009, while planning two feature films: a Japanese co-production called *Wasurenagusa* and a Singaporean film *Go Thaddeus!*. While Yasmin's death ended her inter-ethnic integration discourse through her films, her works have continually generated other filmmakers' impetus to contest and change the landscape of Malaysian cinema. Her influences in Malaysian and Asian cinema were so immense that a year after her passing in 2010, she posthumously became the first Malaysian to win the Best Director Award at the 54th Asia-Pacific Film Festival in Taipei. Her films continue to be discussed in the Malaysian media and academic circles, and she

'Beyond Multiculturalism'   141

remains the Malaysian filmmaker whose life and work are prominently discussed over all media forms. Her works continue to be discussed through forums, conferences, and on the internet. Her fans have also set up numerous memorial sites on Facebook to commemorate her works and contributions.[43]

Sepet: Envisioning a Postethnic Malaysian Cinema

Before examining how Yasmin Ahmad and *Sepet* have influenced the Malaysian cinematic landscape, it is essential to introduce the film.[44] *Sepet* is described as an 'eye-opening' film with its combination of an 'excellent theme, intelligent camera work, free-flowing dialogue and relaxed acting' (Sittamparam 2004). It was produced by MHZ Film and distributed by Columbia Tristar Film Distributors International and the independent Lighthouse Pictures Singapore. The film was shot over twenty-three days using 35 mm film celluloid instead of the DV format. Produced on an MYR900,000 (US$225,000) budget, the film, was only screened in nine cinemas in Malaysia and made a return of MYR522 000 (US$130,500).[45] *Sepet* has a relatively straightforward storyline.

The film is a classic 'boy meets girl' love story between two individuals professing unconditional love for each other. Jason and Orked are school leavers awaiting university entrance. The plot is best explained by the slogan on the film's poster that reads 'One Chinese boy. One Malay girl. One unforgettable love story'. Their paths cross in the most unlikely locations during an improbable business transaction. Jason, the Chinese boy, meets Orked, the Malay girl, when she searches for a copy of a bootlegged VCD commonly sold at open or night markets. This encounter at the open market is highly relevant to the development of the film's plot. Orked's search for a Takeshi Kaneshiro film leads her to meet Jason, who operates a stall at the open market selling these VCDs. This meeting place was important, for Jason and Orked had only been shown separately in the film's opening within the contexts of their respective religious and cultural settings. This setting and plot device becomes a reflexive commentary on the film's social role as instigator of newly imagined relationships and an apt metaphorical comment on how the director sees her filmic enterprise. The open market also provided the location and marketplace for Malaysians from diverse religious, cultures, and languages to assemble and meet while accommodating different isolated individuals in one location. After this brief encounter, their friendship rapidly blossoms into a romantic relationship. They

---

43. Amir Muhammad describes Yasmin's blogs as an excellent introduction to her voice. It's a voice that can still be heard—because it's still needed (2010b). Yasmin's blogs, however, are no longer accessible: http://yasminthestoryteller.blogspot.com.au/ and http://yasminthefilmmaker.blogspot.au/.
44. The term *Sepet* can be loosely translated as 'slit eye'. It is a derogatory term used to refer to Chinese ethnic individuals.
45. The film was partially funded by a FINAS grant of MYR400,000 (US$100,000). Chapter 2 discusses the difficulties that Yasmin faced in her search for funding for *Sepet*.

142   *Malaysian Cinema in the New Millennium*

experience moments of happiness, but their relationship becomes broken as they struggle with fidelity.

While both individuals have recently come from failed relationships, Jason's past comes back to haunt him. His past lover, Maggie, the sister of the gang leader who employs him, accuses Jason of impregnating her. Jason decides that it is his responsibility to take care of Maggie until the baby is born. Feeling betrayed, Orked ignores Jason and accepts a scholarship to pursue her studies overseas. As she departs for the airport, Jason also travels to the airport, hoping to ask Orked for forgiveness. During the journey, she finally relents by reading a letter Jason had left her. The letter reveals Jason's remorse and his pleas for redemption, for Maggie has decided to abort the baby. Upon realising her love for him, Orked decides to call Jason to inform him of her feelings.

The relationship between these two unlikely characters—a gang member who sells bootlegged VCDs but has a penchant for romantic films, and Orked, a middle-class Malay girl with a liberal mindset—allows the film to move postethnically, beyond ethnic divisions, class consciousness, and religious sensitivities. Jason, for example, displays his comfort in embracing a sense of 'Malay-ness' as he walks into the room and places a CD into a player. In full view of his Chinese companions, he dances, oblivious to the Malay song's rhythm, 'Dia Datang'.[46] The characters are not homogenously mono-ethnic and resist the stereotypical appearances, mindsets, and personalities of characters commonly portrayed in ethnocentric Malaysian cinema.

Polylingualism in *Sepet*

Sepet was criticised for its use of language, as incorrectly promoting the Malaysian culture through its use of Manglish. However, the use of Manglish and various other languages in the film challenges the idea that 'Malaysian-ness' in cinema means homogenously speaking in Bahasa Malaysia. Being polylingual allows *Sepet* to fit within the framework of a postethnic cosmopolitan cinema. The characters converse interchangeably in Manglish, Bahasa Malaysia, Mandarin, Cantonese, and Hokkien. Orked, for example, walks into a Chinese coffee shop dressed in a *baju kurung*.[47] As she catches a glance of roasted meat being sliced, she exclaims in Cantonese, '*Huiyoh, hou hou mei yah!*' (Wow, looks tasty!) and proceeds to walk into the coffee shop.

The juxtaposing of shots in the opening scene demonstrates the use of poly-lingualism. The film opens with the Qur'anic verse 'بسم الله الرحمن الرحيم' (In

---

46. The song 'Dia Datang' was paradoxically sung as a stage performance during the 50th Asian Film Festival. It was the same festival during which Yasmin Ahmad withdrew participation for *Sepet*. She also vowed never to submit her film for a Festival Filem Malaysia (Malaysian Film Festival) (Yasmin 2006).

47. The *baju kurung* is a two-piece, loosely fitting traditional Malay garment for women.

'Beyond Multiculturalism'

the Name of God, the Most Gracious and Most Merciful) (bismi-llāhi r-raḥmāni r-raḥīm).[48] The black and white verse is not recited verbally or translated through subtitles, for it is widely and promptly known and recognised.[49] The use of the words 'compassionate' and 'merciful' rightly addresses the recurrent theme of humanism to indicate that all beginning comes from God. The verse is commonly recited by Muslims requesting God's blessings and for a beginning of everything good. It simultaneously asserts the importance of religions in Malaysia, by demonstrating humility and submission to God and calling for God's blessings upon the nation.[50] As the scene continues, an intimate moment between a mother and her son is introduced. A male voice speaks in Mandarin. His hair coloured blonde, Jason reads a translation of the poem *The Judge* by Rabindranath Tagore as he sits on the floor beside his mother, who is wearing the Peranakan *baju kebaya*.[51] Jason's mother expresses her contentment in Bahasa Malaysia and demands to know the author. He playfully answers her inquiry with a question in Cantonese regarding the author's nationality. She guesses from mainland China, but Jason reveals it is India. She expresses her amazement that she can relate to a foreign poem by stating, 'Strange, a different culture. A different language. And yet we can feel what was in his heart'. Jason nods in agreement. Orked's voice reciting the *Yasin* overlaps this scene.[52] Dressed in a *telekung*, she ends her prayer by reciting, 'God has spoken the truth'.[53] She opens her wardrobe only to reveal posters of Takeshi Kaneshiro pasted inside the doors as a voice calls out *'Orked, Orked, turun makan'* (Orked, come down for dinner). She replies, 'Okay, coming'.

---

48. The verse 'In the Name of God, the Most Gracious and Most Merciful' is used in every film made by Yasmin Ahmad, *Rabun* being the exception. In *Muallaf*, the verse is translated into Mandarin and written '奉大仁大慈真主的尊名' (Feng Da Ren Da Ci Zhen Zhu De Zun Ming). In *Talentime*, the script is translated into Tamil and written 'பிஸ்மில்லாஹிர்ரஹ்மானிர்ரஹீம்'.

49. However, the beginning of films displaying a Quranic recital or citation is not unusual in Malaysian cinema. It usually is associated with films from the horror or supernatural genre and usually accompanied by a compulsory disclaimer—this disclaimer functions as a declaration that the film is merely a work of fiction.

50. The importance of religion in Malaysia is visible through three official discourses. Firstly, Article 3 (1) of Malaysia's Federal Constitution places Islam as the Federation's official religion. At the same time, Article 11 provides that every person has the right to profess and practise their religion. Secondly, the 'Negaraku' (My Country), the Malaysian national anthem, honours God's existence through the verse, *'Rahmat bahagia, Tuhan kurniakan'*, which can be translated as, 'May God bestow blessings of happiness'. Thirdly, the *'Rukunegara'* or National Pledge places the importance of God's existence in the sentence *'Kepercayaan kepada Tuhan'*, which can be translated as 'belief in God'.

51. The *Peranakan* community is a distinct ethnic community of ethnic Chinese embracing the Malay culture. This community emerged from marriages between the local Malay women and Chinese immigrants dating to the fifteenth century. The *Peranakan* community is distinguished by their cuisine, dress, and language. Conversing in Bahasa Malaysia, a female member of the *Peranakan* community is known as a *Nyonya* and the male a *Baba*. The term *Peranakan* is also discussed in *Sepet* between Keong and Jason in the hospital. For more information regarding the *Peranakan* community, see Lim 2003.

52. The 'Yasin' or 'Surah/Surat Yasin' is one of the most popularly read chapters of the Qur'an and is commonly read for *barakah* (blessings and protection), in the mornings, at times of mourning, for meditative purposes, for guidance, and healing purposes.

53. The *telekung* is a white garment usually worn by Malay women during prayers. It covers the devotee from head to toe, leaving only room for the face.

144   *Malaysian Cinema in the New Millennium*

This scene has been edited to surprise the audience through the way the various languages are used. The Arabic verses, followed by the recital of a Bengali poem in Mandarin, Jason's conversation with his mother in Bahasa Malaysia and Cantonese, and Orked's reply to the call for dinner in English demonstrate a linguistic universalism that blurs the boundaries of ethnoracial communities that identify the insider from the outsider (Chee 2010, 107). The reading of a poem about the universality of parental love for a child, written in the Bengali language by an Indian author (rather than reading a poem in Mandarin), and Orked's preference for Takeshi Kaneshiro strongly deconstruct the identification by phenotypical and cultural markers (Lim 2008). These characteristics deconstruct the basis for ethnic identification by straightforwardly characterising individuals into a race community based on physical differences (Cashmore 2004; Corlett 2003, 2007; Gracia 2007; Hollinsworth 2006; Fenton 1999).[54]

As a filmmaker from the Malay ethnic background, Yasmin incorporates elements of 'Chinese-ness' in *Sepet* to show her vision of a postethnic nation. One example that shows how the concepts of culture and ethnicity in Malaysia are not fixed or static but remain open for negotiation is through the characters of Mak Inom (Orked's mother) and Kak Yam (the family household help). They openly display their obsession with Cantonese television programmes throughout the film. This obsession is most evident in a scene when they capably sing as a duet the words to the Francis Yip song '上海灘' (Sheong Hoi Tan / Shanghai Bund, the theme song of Cantonese television drama series *The Bund*) as they stand and watch Jason speak to Orked in private outside their home. Yasmin again displays her move beyond multiculturalism by choosing Cantonese rather than Malay songs for the film's soundtrack, using popular Hong Kong entertainer Sam Hui's songs. The song 'Shi Shi Ru Qi' (世事如棋, Life is like a Chess Game) plays as the entrance theme of the film, 'Li Wo Qian Xiao' (梨渦淺笑, Dimpled Smile) is heard during a montage of the courtship between Loong and Orked, and 'Lang Zi Xing Shen' (浪子心聲, From the Heart of a Loafer) plays as the end credits roll.

The use of subtitles, while allowing for the language authenticity to be retained, also translates the various languages and Chinese dialects to make the film more appealing and accessible. It also gives a sense of familiarity about the existence of different cultures in Malaysia. Such familiarity can be reread using Mak Inom and Kak Yam's example of watching a Cantonese television programme. While television programmes in Malaysia are targeted at specific audiences according to ethnicity and language (Leong and Yap 2007), without subtitles, Cantonese serials from Hong Kong would also be limited to those who understand the Cantonese dialect. However, these serials can appeal universally to Malaysians across the ethnic divide through the everyday use of Bahasa Malaysia subtitles. This scenario is referenced

---

54. The inclusion of Rabindranath Tagore by Yasmin Ahmad is due to her liking his works. As her favourite poet, his works were quoted four times in her now defunct online blog: http://yasminthestoryteller.blogspot.com/.

'Beyond Multiculturalism' 145

again as Pak Atan repairs his car. He realises that it is time for evening prayer and asks Mak Inom where Orked is. Mak Inom, however, chides him for distracting her from her Cantonese programme. As she ignores him, he says, '*Bukannya faham cerita Cina*, you're reading the subtitles' (It's not like you understand Cantonese; you're merely reading the subtitles). He continues, '(I) can never understand how you can watch this so religiously (for you) don't even understand the language'. Pak Atan's statement of 'merely reading the subtitles' without understanding the language demonstrates how subtitles can make a film more appealing and accessible to other cultures. The heavy use of Cantonese in the film suggests that Malaysia's multiculturalism is an evolving rather than a closed system, as different cultures can be openly embraced.

The assortment of languages in *Sepet* demonstrates the blurring of ethnic and racial boundaries. The characters conversing in Bahasa Malaysia, Manglish, and Cantonese dialects suggest a fluidity in switching between languages to provide a slice-of-life depiction of Malaysia's multi-ethnicity. The hybridity of languages promotes an alternative vision of the nation by amalgamating cultural differences between the different ethnic communities. The film depicts the nation as one great family speaking the same language (Smith 1991, 79). The ability to transcend ethnic and language barriers through hybridity suggests that Malaysia's multiculturalism is evolving, rather than a closed system (Azly 2009, 442). The concepts of culture and ethnicity in Malaysia are not fixed or static and remain open for negotiation.

Art-house aesthetics and style in *Sepet*

Sepet should be discussed according to the controversies surrounding its approach towards the Malay culture. The film should also be studied by its positioning within the Malaysian filmmaking system's interstices that competently adapt both independent and commercial features. Firstly, Yasmin acknowledges that *Sepet* is aimed at a mass audience (Ong 2004) by employing the stereotypical 'boy meets girl' storyline. Secondly, other aspects, such as the film's cinematography, editing, mise-en-scène, soundtrack, narrative structure, and choice of non-professional actors, are a blend of art-house and commercial aesthetics. The cinematography in *Sepet* incorporates a mixture of independent and commercial filmmaking methods. The use of long takes, long shots, silence, and camera placements at a distance are typical methods of the MDI. Such methods are reflective of Tsai Ming-Liang's films. *Sepet* departs from Tsai's films, as Yasmin uses these methods to allow for human emotions and feelings to unfold through the employment of melodrama slowly. In short, rather than strictly positioning *Sepet* as a film with art-house aesthetics or commercial styles, we should see it as a landmark film that successfully bridged the gap between commercial and independent filmmaking. *Sepet* thus became the first Malaysian film to incorporate independent filmmaking features into a commercially oriented film.

Two instances powerfully demonstrate how Yasmin incorporates art-house aesthetics and styles with commercial features into *Sepet's* narratives. To melodramatically draw out the universal feelings of love, hope, and humanism, the camera stands at a distance without the use of close-ups or shot reverse shots. Only diegetic sounds and silence are used, without any non-diegetic background music or sound to complement the mood. The first instance occurs as a broken-hearted Jason finds solace in his mother.[55] The mise-en-scène is austere. Jason sits on a reclining chair, and she beside him on a wooden stool. The scene shows a bare home with obsolete items. This scene is like *Sepet's* opening sequence, which also displays an obsolete and minimal amount of furniture.

This minimalist arrangement of furniture differs from the customary lavish arrangements of furniture set in Malaysia's mainstream cinema. The entire scene is shot using two long takes. The first uses a long shot showing a broken-hearted Jason sitting alone. His mother then appears on-screen. In the same take, no words are exchanged, for his mother understands his facial expression. She does not question him. No diegetic music is used. Both Jason and his mother sit in silence. This use of silence tensely reflects the moment of sadness. The camera then cuts closer to Jason and his mother from the same angle. His mother, thinking that Jason is worried about his family objecting to his inter-ethnic relationship, comforts him by saying, 'I know why you're sad. You're in love with a Malay girl, aren't you? Don't worry son, I'm not angry with you'. In the same take, Jason buries his head in her lap. His mother silently strokes his hair and places a reassuring hand on his back.[56]

The second example occurs as Orked journeys to the airport. The setting in this scene that leads to the film's climax is also simple: the interior of an old car. This car contrasts with the luxury vehicles often driven by characters in commercial mainstream cinema [Shuhaimi Baba's *Ringgit Kasorrga*, 1995, and Yusof Haslam's *Pasrah* (Surrender), 2000]. As Orked finally reads Jason's letter, the camera is again placed unintrusively at a distance to capture only Orked and Mak Inom. The entire scene is shot using two long takes and mid-shots. Only Orked and her mother are visible in the frame, while Pak Atan appears offscreen. While this scene is melodramatic, Orked reading aloud Jason's letter and openly weeping with her mother, no music or sound effects are used to intensify Orked's emotions. Neither is this

---

55. I draw reference from this scene to the opening scene as Jason read the poem to his mother. The conversations in the earlier scene prefigure this event. As the reading of *The Judge* is juxtaposed with the Quranic verse, it serves as an admonition that any judgment should be left to God in criticising racial prejudice in society. The phrase reads, 'Say of him what you like, but I know my child's failings. I do not love him because he is good, but because he is my child. How can you know how sweet he is when all you do is measure the good and the bad? When I must punish him, he becomes, even more, a part of me. When I make him weep, I weep with him. I alone have the right to judge him, for only he who loves may chastise.'

56. This display of humanism was recorded through Yasmin Ahmad's statement, 'I cried when I was writing it. My crew cried when we were shooting the scene and when the film was played in cinemas, the audience cried too' (Faridul 2008).

'Beyond Multiculturalism'

scene intensified using close-ups or shot-reverse shots. The scene continues with Mak Inom continually kissing and embracing Orked. The emotional impacts in these scenes were created through long takes, moments of silence, the absence of non-diegetic music and sound effects, and placing the camera at a distance. Such styles conform to art-house aesthetics and style while drawing out melodramatic elements.

The film's ending is another example of *Sepet* blending art-house aesthetics and style with melodrama. In this scene, Orked decides to call Jason after reading his letter. The film dramatically builds anticipation towards its climax by cross-cutting shots of Orked and Mak Inom weeping in the car and of Jason weaving through traffic on a motorcycle. The conventional cause-and-effect narrative would show Jason answering his mobile phone or the two meeting at the airport in the following scene. The scene, however, cuts to a mobile phone ringing on the road as Jason lies motionless in a pool of blood. The viewer is left to assume that Jason has either been killed or left unconscious in a motor accident. The scene then cuts back to Orked, and we hear Jason's phone being answered. Jason's voice saying 'hello' is heard off-screen, and she pours her feelings out to him. While the film has a proper ending, this dreamlike sequence paradoxically is not logical. The film's ambiguous ending is open for the audiences' critical interpretation. This form of ending deconstructs and fragments the narrative line, as an expected resolution is not given.

Sepet cast popular actor Harith Iskander and actress Ida Nerina to play the roles of Orked's parents. The other cast members who were inexperienced and not imbued with commercial value were cast to play the roles of Orked's parents. *Sepet* also abandons the use of famous singers as seen in mainstream films like *Sembilu* (Heartache, 1994) and *Gemerlapan* (Glittering, 1997) and refuses to portray the successful, wealthy middle-class Malays seen in films such as Rahim Razali's *Abang* (1981) and Yusof Haslam's *Maria Mariana* (1996). The casting of actors with virtually no experience to play the lead characters of Jason and Orked helped project a slice-of-life scenario.[57] Casting virtual unknowns to portray 'everyday people' with 'everyday problems' allowed the film to construct a sense of social reality. The character of Jason was played by first-time actor Ng Choo Seong, who worked as an art director for Yasmin at Leo Burnett Advertising. Orked was played by Sharifah Amani Syed Zainal Rashid (daughter of Fatimah Abu Bakar, a Malaysian actress

---

57. Born of Scottish and Malay parentage, Harith Iskander Musa is a well-known Malaysian standup comedian, theatre, television and film actor, and celebrity host. He is best known for his roles as a television comedian in *Ah-ha* and *Phua Chu Kang*, for his acting roles in *Anna and the King* (1999) and *Cuci* (Wash, 2008), and his sole directorial feature, *Hanya Kawan* (Just Friends, 1997). Ida Nerina Hussain was already an award-winning actress when she played the role of Mak Inom in *Sepet*. She has starred in many Malaysian telemovies and television dramas but is best known for her roles in Shuhaimi Baba's films *Selubung*, *Layar Lara* (1997) and *Pontianak Harum Sundal Malam* (2004); for her participation in the 2008 series of *The Amazing Race Asia*; and as a talent coach in local reality television series *Akademi Fantasia*.

148   *Malaysian Cinema in the New Millennium*

and acting coach) who previously only held supporting roles in Shuhaimi Baba's
Selubung (1992) and *Mimpi Moon* (2000).[58]

The above discussions locate *Sepet* as a film with an experimental narrative
structure. Its thematic style that blends independent and commercial forms and
styles, the auteur-driven narrative, art-house aesthetics and style, and uncertainty at
the film's ending locates *Sepet* within Malaysian cinema's interstices.

Sepet: Targeting overseas film festivals

To bypass the restrictions set by the LPF and discuss 'sensitive' issues of inter-ethnic
relationships in her films, Yasmin chose to release *Sepet* overseas. It premiered in
2004 at the inaugural Malaysian Film Festival held in Singapore. Originally known
as *Ah Loong dan Intan*, *Sepet* was dubbed by Yasmin the 'little' and 'small' film. This
'little' and 'small' film, however, won the Best Feature Film in the ASEAN category
at the Ninth Malaysian Video Awards (2004), the Grand Prix du Jury Award at
the Creteil International Festival of Women's Films in France, Best Asian Film at
the 18th Tokyo International Film Festival (2005), Best Film at the Global Chinese
Golden Arts Malaysia (2005), and Best Film at the Anugerah Era Malaysia (2005).

Besides being screened at the Malaysian Film Festival in Singapore, *Sepet* was
screened at the Fourth Commonwealth Film Festival (2005), Barcelona Asian Film
Festival (2005), and 48th San Francisco International Film Festival (2005). Since
Sepet, Yasmin chose overseas film festivals as an alternative site to exhibit her film.
Sepet has been well-received at overseas film festivals. Yasmin's (now defunct) blog
'The Storyteller' noted some of the reviews *Sepet* received at international film
festivals. Firstly, she stated why the panel at the Creteil International Festival of
Women's Films awarded *Sepet* the Le Grand Prix du Jury. It was the film's sensibility,
originality, humour, great acting, and sensitive approach of sending the message
of love to overcome differences. In the same posting, Yasmin published the official
invitation from the San Francisco Film Festival, which described *Sepet* as 'quite a
charming and original work', which in their opinion would be 'very well received by
our audiences'. Secondly, in an excerpt written by Roger Garcia of the San Francisco
International Film Festival, *Sepet*, despite its 'provocative title', is a film with a heart-
felt plea for tolerance and has its subtle way of standing as a point of reference film
which altered the Malaysian cinema landscape.[59]

Every Yasmin Ahmad film premiered at overseas film festivals before finally
returning to Malaysia. Although there were times when she reluctantly adhered to

---

58. Jason's role has landed Ng Choo Seong the Most Promising Actor award at the 18th Malaysian Film Festival,
    but he has yet to participate in any feature film. After winning the Most Promising Newcomer award at the
    same festival, Sharifah Amani continued to play recurrent roles in Yasmin Ahmad's films, such as *Gubra*,
    Mukhsin, and *Muallaf*.

59. Sourced from (the now defunct): http://yasminthestoryteller.blogspot.com.au/2004/09/that-double-edged-
    sword-called.html; http://yasminthestoryteller.blogspot.com.au/2005_03_01_archive.html and http://yas-
    minthestoryteller.blogspot.com.au/2005/04/excerpt-from-write-up-on-sepet-at-48th_03.html

Figure 3.7: Yasmin Ahmad during the *Talentime* premiere in Kuala Lumpur, Malaysia. Source: Orked Ahmad.

the conditions set by the LPF, it was done so that Malaysian audiences could see her films. *Sepet* was only allowed to be screened in Malaysian cinemas in 2005, after Yasmin agreed to the LPF removing eight scenes from the film.

Direct criticism of state policies in *Sepet*

Sepet brings to attention a desire to envision a postethnic nation that transcends cultural differences. By imagining and constructing a common link binding its characters through cosmopolitanism, the film's contestation of the existing differences in nationality, ethnicity, and status is also a direct criticism of Malaysia's socio-cultural and political policies.

Yasmin forcefully maintained creative control throughout her films without using the stale and uncinematic styles and Malaysian mainstream cinema systems. This control has allowed *Sepet* to alter the socio-political and cultural landscape of Malaysia and its cinema. While *Sepet* emerged as the first Malaysian film to win against the system (Sarris 1968) successfully, cosmopolitan themes to depict a postethnic nation were seen as challenging the Malay psyche and the establishment of the Malay cinematic identity and culture. Sepet was produced in an era when ethnicity became the most relevant basis for people's recognition. It became only the second film in Malaysian cinematic history after L. Krishan's *Selamat Tinggal Kekasihku* (1955) to have received a considerable amount of positive and negative criticism.[60] While inter-ethnic romance was also discussed in Malaysian commercial

---

60. As discussed in Chapters 1 and 2, *Selamat Tinggal Kekasihku*'s narrative of a Malay male and a Chinese female love affair received a significant amount of protest.

mainstream cinema in *Paloh* (2003) and *Sembilu* 2005 (Heartache, 2005), these films did not resist the Malay cinematic identity or receive any resistance from society. In contrast, the use of cosmopolitan themes in envisioning a postethnic nation in *Sepet* was (mis)interpreted and sparked much debate among the Malaysian public and within the context of Malaysian cinema. These debates were briefly highlighted in Chapter 2 and will be discussed in detail using two examples.

First, *Sepet* became the first Malaysian film to cause a broad impact on the internet, across local and overseas media, and even in parliament. The film envisioned a postethnic nation using cosmopolitan themes while criticising the rising racial and cultural divides that boast of their multi-ethnic elements. The film's challenge to the hegemonic representation of the Malay(sian) culture on screen led to mixed responses. *Sepet* angered those who accused the film of tarnishing the Malay culture reputation, while others greatly admired it (Wong 2007). *Sepet* was labelled *pencemar budaya* (cultural smearing) because the postethnic and cosmopolitan nation envisioned in the film departs from the homogenous cinema of mono-ethnic, monolingual, and mono-cultural portrayal of ethnicity.

As mentioned in Chapter 2, this designation emerged from a forum entitled *Sepet dan Gubra Pencemar Budaya* (*Sepet* and *Gubra*, Corrupters of Malay Culture) televised on a national programme, *Fenomena Seni*. Certain forum members questioned the potentially negative consequences of depicting an inter-ethnic relationship in Yasmin Ahmad's films that might corrupt the Malay culture. Statements such as '*Malaysia Melayu punya*' (This country belongs to the Malays) and '*Orked sebagai perempuan Melayu digambarkan mempunyai didikan agama yang teguh tetapi dia hanya sesuai untuk seorang lelaki Cina penjual CD dan VCD haram yang boleh diketegorikan sebagai penjenayah*' (How could Orked, a Malay girl portrayed with a strong religious background, possibly be matched with a Chinese criminal that peddles bootlegged CDs and VCDs?) were made (Mohd Arif Nizam 2006). Individual forum members also criticised Orked, a girl with a firm Islamic religious upbringing, for being in a relationship with a Chinese *kafir* (infidel) with a problematic background. Discussions about *Sepet* continued in parliament when a lawmaker described the film as 'nothing great' because it did not reflect the Malaysian national identity. The central focus of the lawmaker's argument was Orked's deconstruction of the Malay woman. He claimed that Orked was not an ideal image for a Malay woman, for despite having a solid religious background, she could fall in love with a 'Chinese criminal' (Wong 2007). Yasmin Ahmad responded to her critics, who labelled her films *pencemar budaya* through a scene in *Mukhsin*. The villagers discover an almost lifeless chicken as Bujang, the family cat, lingers around it in the scene. A villager then states to the cat, '*Bujang bujang. Betullah kau ni. Pencemar budaya*' (Bujang, you really are smearing our culture).

Second, the controversy drew from *Sepet*'s triumph over Saw Teong Hin's multi-million-dollar production, *Puteri Gunung Ledang* (2004), during the Festival Filem Malaysia 18. *Sepet*'s victory was deemed controversial, as the win was seen

'Beyond Multiculturalism' 151

Figure 3.8: Yasmin Ahmad on set for *Mukhsin* 2006. Source: Hassan Muthalib.

as displacing it from the mainstream by offering an alternative narrative from the representations propagated by commercial Malaysian mainstream cinema. *Sepet*'s victory counteracted the hegemony of Malaysian cinema that focused on race, ethnic, and class issues.

This aesthetic articulation in the Malaysian cinematic space also deconstructed and challenged stereotyped representations in commercial Malaysian mainstream cinema. The cosmopolitan and postethnic themes in *Sepet* marked a conscious departure from the more ethnocentric Malaysian commercial mainstream cinema. According to NEP state imaginings, the film's victory also marked the deconstruction of the homogenous portrayal of a new generation of middle-class Malays (as discussed in Chapters 1 and 2). The portrayal of Orked's family as a simple middle-class family living in a house with minimal furniture, and her father who drives an old car, further deconstructs the official state envisioning of a modern and wealthy middle-class Malay represented as 'glossy and glamorous'. While maintaining strong attachments with their Islamic faith, the Malay family have more significant leanings towards liberal views and a preference for foreign lifestyles and cultures. This deconstruction of homogeneity represents a rhetorical shift in Malaysian cinema. The narrative, characters, themes, and subject matter in *Sepet* that contested ongoing conflicts and negotiations faced by individuals bound by familial, societal, and religious obligations are more cosmopolitan. The employment of cosmopolitanism

152   *Malaysian Cinema in the New Millennium*

allowed the film to envision a postethnic nation by bringing to the centre the struggles of everyday Malaysians within and between cultures and religions.

In Malaysia, state policies are often criticised and contested within the safety of the familial space because public criticism about state policies is not tolerated in Malaysia. These issues, however, become public when openly discussed in *Sepet*. This situation is exemplified when Mak Inom and Kak Yam sit watching a Cantonese television drama while discussing Orked's tertiary education.[61] They sit facing the audience as if speaking to them. In an overt criticism of the NEP and the standard of education in Malaysia, Mak Inom states that Orked has managed to get a scholarship despite getting only five As in her national exams. Without any show of expression, Kak Yam states her gratitude to God and leads the audience into speculation by saying, 'Jason scored 7As'. Mak Inom responds with a silent stare at Kak Yam. While the scene does not develop any further, the non-verbal gesture of the silent stare suggests that the audience understand the matter being discussed and are then made to think about the issue of inequality in the NEP that has become collectively familiar to Malaysians: Jason, although obtaining better results than Orked, is denied a scholarship because of his ethnic background (Ong 2008; Lee 2009; Iraiputtiran 2010; Hazri and Nordin 2010).

The characters in *Sepet* often meet at the dining table. The dining table exemplifies a platform that allows for a pragmatic, intimate and down-to-earth place for the characters to seek refuge and solace with their family. It also represents a place where the discussions of private and intimate matters are usually safely confined within private space. This discussion occurs as Orked, Jason, and Keong are seated at an eatery. All three sit awkwardly facing the camera to create a sense that they are communicating with the audience who are watching them. They openly criticise how Malaysians stereotype according to ethnicity. Keong states, 'Not every Chinaman is a cheat and not every Malay is lazy'. Orked, however, quips, 'That's where you are wrong. Every Malay is lazy'.[62] This dialogue seems to have been messily removed from the film. Such dialogue allows for (at times humorous) contestations of ethnic prejudice. In another example, Jason's family, despite their differences, still make time to gather as a family for a meal. During dinner, they converse using various languages, to represent the nation's many different languages and cultures metaphorically: Jason's mother converses in Bahasa Malaysia, his sister-in-law speaks Mandarin, and Jason's father speaks Cantonese.[63] The dinner table also represents

---

61. As discussed, Mak Inom and Kak Yam's obsession with Cantonese television programmes is also highlighted through their ability to fluently sing the words to Francis Yip's song '上海灘' (Sheong Hoi Tan). This fluency is shown as they watch Jason speak to Orked in private outside their home.

62. For a detailed discussion regarding the rise of the 'myth' of the lazy Malay, see Syed Hussein (1977) and Mahathir (1970).

63. According to their dialectic clans, Malaysia's Chinese community is segregated by preferences for food, dialectic language, and territory. The growing demand for tin in the twentieth century spurred the British government to search for a more significant workforce through immigrant labour, which saw the influx of Chinese immigrants in the Strait Settlements towns and Malay states (Verma 2004, 25). They are five significant

'Beyond Multiculturalism' 153

the sanctuary for Jason's family. It is also the only time everyone gathers, to high-light family values' importance in an increasingly consumer-driven society. Jason and Orked are also often seen dining together. Jason's companionship with Orked symbolises his hunger for a sense of belonging and recognition as a Malaysian.

Sepet resists the homogeneity in commercial Malaysian mainstream cinema by focusing on the problems and lifestyles of the other ethnic communities. This resist-ance is also towards state policies that favour one ethnic community over the others, such as the NCP and NEP (as discussed in Chapters 1 and 2). The film removes the perception that Malaysia consists of Malays or that only the Malay problems are highlighted. *Sepet* also represents the diverse community of other Malaysians formerly excluded from Malaysian cinema. By deconstructing ethnic identification that characterises ethnic and racial communities based on physical differences, the other ethnic communities previously sidelined are reintroduced to the centre.

The portrayal of intimacy in the Malay family challenges the conservative views predominant in certain Malay quarters. The LPF had suggested that the portrayal of Malay women wearing a sarong tied at the bosom or *berkemban* was too revealing and unsuitable for the viewers.[64] In deconstructing how a Malay family is conven-tionally built, functions, and behaves, *Sepet* brings to light certain forbidden and taboo matters that usually are not for open discussion. Such deconstruction forms are visible as the Pak Atan and Mak Inom dance in their sarongs at home. Their dance is suggestive, as Mak Inom plucks a grape and teases Pak Atan with it. Other 'controversial and inappropriate' scenes were Pak Atan and Mak Inom discussing Orked's love affectionately in bed; and an intimate scene with Orked, Mak Inom, and Kak Yam seated on a staircase dressed in sarongs while combing each other's hair. While these scenes were retained in the film, the scene when Pak Atan's sarong drops revealing him in nothing but his underwear was removed. These scenes sym-bolise the need to balance the new and the old, the modern and traditional, by char-acters placed in a postcolonial nation deeply embedded in religion and culture. This deconstruction of homogeneity in cinema represents a rhetorical shift in Malaysian cinema. Such characters previously unseen in Malaysian cinema reintroduce side-lined non-Malay and Malay communities.

The film also discusses the issue of conversion and inter-ethnic marriage. *Sepet* highlights religious freedom in Malaysia and the general supposition of religion's

---

communities from the south-eastern Chinese provinces of Fujian and Guangdong, the Hokkien (southern Fujian province), Cantonese (Guangdong), Teo Chew (Chaozhou Prefecture in the Guangdong Province), Hainanese/Hylam (Hainan Island), and Hakka (comprising the Hakka from Guangdong and the Khak of Fujian province) (Jenkins 2008, 41).

64. *Berkemban* is the dressing of women in a sarong tied at the midriff or the chest. The sarong is a traditional one-piece garment often worn by men (tied at the midriff) or women (tied at the chest) with plants or animal prints. The *berkemban* drew controversy in *Perempuan, Isteri dan ...?* when the character Zaleha was shown taking a bath in the sarong tied at the chest. The *berkemban* drew controversy again in *Rabun* when the characters of Pak Atan and Mak Inom were bathing each other dressed in sarongs. The *berkemban*, however, was never criticised when it was shown in P. Ramlee films such as *Panggilan Pulau* (Island Call, 1954).

importance to Malaysians (Jones, Chee, and Maznah 2009, 15–16).[65] Keong questions Jason about accepting a different religion and ethnic identity, as he would need to convert to Islam should he and Orked marry. In Malaysia, a non-Muslim and Muslim marriage requires the non-Muslim to convert to Islam before the marriage can be legalised. Keong then mentions the complication of converting to another religion, with statements concerning the need for a change in ethnic identity. He asks if Jason is ready to leave his religion and ethnicity, because Jason would not be able to consume pork (it is forbidden in Islam), would need to be circumcised, and change his surname.[66] Keong highlights this matter again as he states, 'How come hundreds of years ago it's so easy? Inter-ethnic marriages were not a problem. But today, when we're supposed to be civilised, it's hard'. Keong's statement reflects a time when issues of sex, marriage, and religion were viewed differently, and marriages were associated with monogamy, fidelity, and easy dissolution (Jones, Chee, and Maznah 2009, 4).

The scenes discussed above allow for the envisioning of a postethnic nation transcending cultural differences. Rather than focusing on existing differences in nationality, ethnicity, and status, the scenes suggest a liberal outlook to imagine and construct a link that binds, using cosmopolitanism that contests Malaysia's socio-cultural and political situations today.

In summary, the above discussion of *Sepet* frames the film as a clear example of postethnic cosmopolitan cinema. The film's envisioning of a postethnic nation that upholds cosmopolitan values blurs the boundaries between ethnic communities, to demonstrate the possibility of coexistence. The need to 'condition' the love between Orked and Jason does not pertain to *Sepet*. As they were free to affiliate with 'other' communities, the problems and conflicts they faced did not arise due to differences in religion, ethnicity, and class (Hollinger 1998). Throughout the film, Orked's family never pressure Jason into converting, as the narrative never presents any severe objections from their respective families or society. The pressure, however, came from the LPF, which questioned why Orked never attempted to convert Jason (Lau 2005).

Sepet presents a progressive cultural utopianism in a move beyond multiculturalism, as both Jason and Orked freely enter each other's cultural worlds. While the cosmopolitan themes resist the hegemonic Malay psyche and establishment of the Malay cinematic identity, the film regrettably failed to overcome the barrier of inter-ethnic love affairs. This failure is shown, for Jason was punished for his transgression. The film's ending suggests that Orked and Jason may have ultimately

---

65. As conversion to Islam is intertwined with the Malay identity, converts are recommended to change their surname to an Islamic name of 'bin' or 'binti' Abdullah (Lindenberg 2009, 228–229).

66. These questions are based on the belief that conversion signals a decisive break from the lives of the Chinese individuals, as conversion to Islam also means to *masuk Melayu* or to enter the Malay ethnic community, which requires one to instantaneously follow a Malay and Islamic lifestyle and customs (Lindenberg 2009, 228).

'Beyond Multiculturalism'

been prevented from being together despite Jason already planning to move abroad to study with her. Such forms of liberalism, however, were seen as offensive and improper in certain quarters, due to the rising tide of religious conservatism that has altered the face of this modern but moderate Muslim nation. These examples represent how *Sepet* used cosmopolitan themes to discuss the Malay psyche and Malay cinematic identity.

Auteur style of filmmaking in *Sepet*

Using *Sepet*, one can argue that Yasmin's works position her as an auteur for two reasons. Firstly, she maintains her style and control by authoring a Malaysian social landscape, which leads to a critical examination of Malaysia's reality today and the nation as envisioned by Yasmin. Secondly, her works are recognised through her cinematic style, which blends independent filmmaking features into a commercially oriented film.

Firstly, in positioning Yasmin as an auteur in the independent cinematic sense, *Sepet*, as in her first feature, *Rabun*, contests multiculturalism's reality while continuing to employ a sense of realism. Her films similarly envision a 'cinematic imagined community' bordering on a utopian Malaysia existing as a postethnic cosmopolitan society.[67] In 2006, in an interview (posted on her blog) with Lorna Tee of Focus Films, Yasmin clarified her embrace of cosmopolitanism in her films. This cosmopolitan and liberal outlook examines the lives of 'everyday people' in their daily struggles with emotional upheavals (as discussed in the previous section about the auteur filmmaking system). In justifying the universal values of love, hope, and humanism that have influenced her works, she modestly sees herself as an individual holding 'up a mirror to Mankind' and as a filmmaker observing 'the human condition' caused by the different cultures in multiracial Malaysia, if not the world. This constant focus throughout her body of work on cosmopolitan themes and subject matter allows *Sepet* to be universally understood, as these issues blur the boundaries of ethnoracial communities.

The use of ethnic terms in labelling Jason as 'Chinese' and Orked as 'Malay' (as evident on the film poster) has inadvertently placed ethnic referencing upon them. This reference unintentionally redirects the film's focal point from a love affair to contestation of ethnicity. The filmmaker, however, continually insists that *Sepet* is not about ethnicity or race but first love between two individuals from different backgrounds. She justifies this by stating that racism is merely an excuse to conceal

---

67. In defence of her works being accused of romantically imagining a utopian Malaysia, a seemingly puzzled Yasmin states (through her blog) that she fails to understand how her films are depicted as utopian. She states that although her films contain moments of light-heartedness and humour, they are actually 'quite dark' with instances of embezzlement (*Rabun*), death (*Sepet* and *Gubra*), and heartbreak (*Mukhsin*).

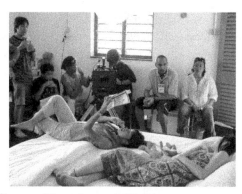

Figure 3.9: On the film set of *Sepet*. Source: MHz Film.

human weaknesses such as fear or greed (Yasmin 2004).[68] This statement is also present in the film, as Orked states her point of view about inter-ethnic love affairs after her friend Lin teases her about having a preference for Chinese men. In her defence, Orked tells Lin, 'You like who you like. Who cares if that someone likes the other someone because of their race? It's when you hate them, that's the problem'. Her film dealing with the struggles of two teenage lovers has been misinterpreted as a film about the contestation of ethnicity. As an auteur, Yasmin has the ability to focus on postethnicity and cosmopolitanism, which can be seen as her signature across all her films, including *Sepet*.

Second, Yasmin's style of continuously challenging the ideological restrictions, formal styles, and narrative themes conditioned by political pressures within Malaysian cinema, by the LPF and FINAS, is constant through her films (as discussed). She achieves this through her ongoing discussion of the 'sensitive' issue of inter-ethnic relations, to maintain the illusion that Malaysia's dreamed image remains as an objective mirror of the actual nation. Along these lines, *Sepet*, as a commercially oriented film with independent features, resists the conventional cinematic methods of Malaysian mainstream commercial cinema by continuing the MDI convention of contesting the official discourse of 'Malay-ness' in cinema. Instead of using the stereotypical storylines of mainstream cinema (as discussed in Chapter 2) and themes of monotonous entertainment with melodramatic elements of *suka* (love), *duka* (tragedy), and *jenaka* (humour), Yasmin employs cosmopolitan themes to maintain the blurring of ethnic and racial boundaries and to demonstrate the possibility of coexistence. The use of cosmopolitan themes negotiates the Malay psyche and the already established Malay cinematic identity. Cosmopolitanism allows the film's narrative, characters, themes, and subject matter to resist the Malay

---

68. In her blog, Yasmin wrote that her inspiration about first love was through Wislawa Szymborska's poem *First Love*.

psyche by demonstrating the struggles faced by everyday Malaysians within and between cultures and religions.[69] It becomes a platform to contest, criticise, and renegotiate state policies and societal taboos related to ethnicity, religion, politics, and sexuality. Cosmopolitanism thus allows Yasmin through *Sepet* to contest subject matters and themes that are more socially, culturally, and politically localised and subject matters closely related to Malaysians.

Yasmin's employment of cosmopolitanism in envisioning a postethnic nation has allowed the characters in *Sepet* to have a liberal outlook that overcame religious and ethnic barriers. This outlook is in line with her role as an auteur. Throughout her work, she continuously maintained her authoring of a postethnic Malaysian landscape by discussing issues related to ethnicity, race, and religion while upholding her cinematic style that incorporates both independent and commercial features.

Figure 3.10: Yasmin Ahmad taking a break during the production of *Sepet*. Source: MHz Film.

---

69. Yasmin Ahmad withdrew *Sepet*'s participation in the 50th Asia Pacific Film Festival due to the immense negative criticism from certain quarters. She also stated that threats were made against her should the film be run at the festival.

4
'The Malaysian Decade of Horror':
The Malaysian Horror Renaissance

The horror genre has become a site where the Malaysian Digital Indies (MDI) and mainstream Malaysian cinema converge. As discussed, the MDI heralded new filmmaking methods that diverged from those of the mainstream. The previous chapters have shown how independent and transnational filmmaking methods have allowed the MDI to emerge as an informal film culture with new funding, production, exhibition, distribution, and representation to contest the Malay-hegemonic mainstream cinema. The MDI and the mainstream, however, both participate in the production of new genres.

The horror genre has set itself distinctively apart from its high cinematic output, successful box-office returns, and broad thematic appeal. The horror genre, which was formerly banned for its anti-Islamic elements, has made its return as 'the decade of horror'. The horror genre uses *filem seram* (horror films) to bring to the fore contentious and haunting political and public-cultural issues that refuse to go away in a rapidly changing Malaysian nation.[1]

Issues that are causing high anxiety are related to the rise of inter-ethnic disparity and race supremacy: issues regarding nationhood, religious revivalism and extremism (nationally and internationally), political uncertainty, and the increased incidence of reported crime. Both current and urgent, these issues pose a threat to socio-economic and political stability if they continue to be left unresolved. How these anxieties are vividly portrayed in Malaysian horror films through representations of localised 'monsters' threatening to destabilise any form of normalcy will be examined. To understand the current (re)popularisation of Malaysian horror cinema, we must firstly unravel the cultural, political, social, and historical contexts that underlie the monster's metaphorical presence in the horror narrative. The term '(re)popularisation' rather than just 'popularization' is used, for horror films were popular before they were banned. Secondly, the horror genre has been easily re-popularised because the belief in horror, supernatural, myths, and occultism has

---

1. The term is translated into Bahasa Malaysia as *filem* (film) *seram* (horror) to localise and contextualise the horror film.

long existed in Malaysia. Before the coming of religion (Buddhism, Hinduism, Islam, and Christianity) through trade, animistic beliefs, tribal beliefs, and shamanism had long been practised in the country. The belief in the supernatural has led to the rise of mythical creatures, spirits, and ghosts, for example, *Hantu Laut, Hantu Raya, Hantu Penanggalan, Pontianak, Langsuir, Toyol,* and *Pocong.*

This chapter examines the Malaysian horror genre from cinematic, socio-cultural, political, and religious perspectives. It examines this genre within the context of ongoing national anxieties felt within this postcolonial nation by highlighting issues concerned with the philosophy of freedom within the framework of 'spectral nationality' (Cheah 2003) and postcolonial haunting (O'Riley 2007). This examination is done by looking at films from the 'Malaysian horror renaissance', producing over fifty films within eleven years. This periodisation of films is based on my research framework (2000–2011) and the sudden surge of interest from filmmakers, spurring them to make horror films brought on by new social anxieties and transnational production methods. The previous banning of films with mythical creatures such as the *pontianak*, ghosts, and ghouls is part of the Malay culture but considered 'anti-Islamic' (Ruzita 2008). It bespeaks lurking anxiety within culture and religion, and concerns over political stability and national security.

The Malaysian horror renaissance can be studied from a socio-cultural perspective, by examining public responses to the films. The popularity of horror films is reflected in the Festival Filem Malaysia 24 (24th Malaysian Film Festival) when a record twenty horror films were nominated for awards. This number is historic, as it was the first time such a high number of horror films were nominated; each category had at least one horror film. For example, *Senjakala* (Twilight, 2011) was nominated for the categories of Best Editing, Best Director, Best Actor, and Best Actress; *Khurafat: Perjanjian Setan* (Superstition: Satan's Pact, 2011) was nominated for the categories of Best Visual Effects, Best Original Musical Score, Best Editing, Best Sound Effects, Best Original Story, Best Script, Best Cinematography, and Best Supporting Actress; *Hantu Kak Limah* (Kak Limah's Ghost Returns Home, 2011) was nominated for Best Costume, Best Supporting Actor, and Best Original Story; and *Damping Malam* (Night Guardian, 2010) was nominated in the category for Best Child Actor.

These films highlight how the horror genre has (re)established itself through a proliferation of different sub-genres. The proliferation of different sub-genres is done in order to improve market response and become more commercially viable. Since the horror genre is already financially successful and in line with other cultural and social factors, sub-genres have emerged to make available more variations of proven themes (Tudor 1989, 23). These sub-genres are merely marketing ploys, whereby the horror genre is packaged in a different form to create a sense of innovation and freshness in the minds of the audience so that greater profits can be generated. These sub-genres are categorised as: horror from myths

Figure 4.1: Film poster of *Zombitopia*. Source: Woo Ming Jin.

Figure 4.2: Behind the scenes of *Zombitopia*. Source: Woo Ming Jin.

and legends: *Pontianak Harum Sundal Malam* and *Karak* (2011); supernatural and ghost films: *Jangan Pandang Belakang* and *Congkak* (2008); comedy horror: *Hantu Bonceng* (Pillion Rider Ghost, 2011) and *Zombie Kampung Pisang* (Zombie of Pisang Village, 2007); parody horror: *Jangan Pandang Belakang Congkak* (2009) and *Jangan Pandang Belakang Congkak 2* (2010); slasher films: *Seru* and *Penunggu Istana* (2011); religious horror: *2 Alam* (2 Universes, 2010) and *Rasuk* (Possess, 2011) and zombie apocalypse; *Zombi Kampung Pisang* (2007), *KL Zombi* (2013), *Belaban Hidup: Infeksi Zombie* (2020), and *Zombitopia* (2021).

The monster/supernatural entity in Malaysian horror films is often female. This employment of female monstrosity, however, does not only articulate male fears about female empowerment. Instead, one could suggest that the use of female monstrosity poses a broader challenge to a sense of normality and cultural and religious beliefs, particularly the anxieties over the construction of gender in the Malay culture. This situation implies that the horror genre's rise epitomises a series of intensifying anxieties over religion/culture, which symbolise political-economic anxieties. Since the horror film reflects the social, cultural, and political anxieties of its time, it is essential to understand it by analysing the monster's historical and cultural functions in these horror narratives. The study of the monster is essential in explaining the continued survival of the horror genre and explaining the social-cultural and political anxieties reflected at particular moments.

The discussion is divided into two sections. After a brief introduction about the revival of the horror genre in post-2000 Malaysian cinema, the global horror genre through a historical examination of its generic and industrial aspects and monster figures' social function (Cohen 1996) will be defined. The cultural, political, social, and historical contexts of Malaysian horror cinema are discussed in detail within three distinct phases: The Golden Age of Malaysian cinema, the Independent *Bumiputera* era, and post-2000 Malaysian cinema (a periodisation discussed in Chapter 1). The second section examines the contemporary Malaysian horror cinema's distinct characteristics in both mainstream and MDI variants. This section then examines whether the (re)popularisation of horror is affected by the Asian Horror Wave led by Japan and South Korea, or it is merely a commercial ploy of filling the void caused by the absence of horror films in a culture deeply rooted in the supernatural, horror, and superstition.

The (Re)popularisation of Horror Cinema in Malaysia

From roughly the mid-2000s until the turn of the decade, Malaysian horror cinema experienced a revival. On 20 May 2004, the first *pontianak* film in thirty years, Shuhaimi Baba's *Pontianak Harum Sundal Malam* (2004) 'return[ed] with a vengeance' (Faridul 2004b) to Malaysian cinema. Co-produced with FINAS at a budget of MYR2.5 million (US$625,000), it was proposed that the title of the film be changed to *Pontianak Harum Sedap Malam*, for the word '*Sundal*' literally means a tramp or a harlot in Bahasa Malaysia (Hafidah 2004).[2] However, the use of the term 'Harum Sundal Malam' is based on the name of a strongly scented white flower (*Polianthes tuberosa*) with supposed mysterious properties. The use of the word *sundal* was eventually approved only after the then-information minister's intervention (Hafidah 2003). The film (re)popularised the horror genre and achieved critical and commercial success by exploiting the infamous *pontianak* myth with deep mythical roots in Asia. In Malay folklore, the *pontianak* is a fearsome mythical female creature with vampire-like qualities. Popularised through films in the 1950s to the 1970s, she is recognised through her high-pitched shrieks, flowing hair, and fondness for children's blood (Ng 2009).

In one of the most contemporary discussions about the *pontianak* in folklore and popular culture, Ng attributes the *pontianak* as possessing similar qualities to the Western vampire, as a hybrid creature blending Eastern and Western vampiric characteristics. He says that the cinematic representations of the *pontianak* have blurred the boundaries between traditional belief and popular culture. This is a result of the *pontianak* having become a recalibration of Malay and Western folklore and popular culture. She was created with fangs, ghost-like traits, and subdued using a sharp object (nail at the back of the neck) (2009). Ng highlights the erroneous belief in the use of the term *pontianak* in current cinematic representation. Using Skeat's 1965 study on folklore in Malaysia, Ng says that the *pontianak* is the child of the *langsuyar/langsuir*, a creature that has similar characteristics. According to Skeat, the *langsuyar/langsuir* is an incredibly beautiful lady who died giving birth, of shock upon hearing her stillborn child has become a *pontianak*. She claps her hands and flies onto a tree. Glass beads are placed in her mouth, a chicken egg is placed under her armpits, and needles are pierced through her palms to prevent such a transformation. This act is done to prevent the dead woman from shrieking and flying, as her arm movements have been limited. The *langsuyar* is fond of fish and can be recognised through her green robe, long fingernails, and long jet-black hair. She may be subdued by cutting her nails and hair and stuffing them into a hole in her neck. In doing so, she becomes a woman and can be a wife and a mother (1965).

Pontianak Harum Sundal Malam became a local success (Santhi 2004) as it was screened at twenty-nine commercial cinemas. The film made a return of MYR3.2 million (US$800,000) and received accolades for Best Editing and Best Male Supporting Actor at the Festival Filem Malaysia 17 (17th Malaysian Film Festival). These included ten awards (Best Film Production, Best Cinematography, and Best Editing) at the 2004 Malaysian Film Workers Association (PPFM) Oscars. According to Shuhaimi, the film was more popular than were the Japanese and Korean horror films, as Malaysian audiences could easily relate to the Malay language and localised

---

2. In another instance, the title of U-Wei Saari's *Perempuan, Isteri dan Jalang* was renamed *Perempuan, Isteri dan ... ?* (1993) when the word *Jalang* was removed (Hafidah 2003).

pontianak (Looi 2011). The film is the first local horror film in the post-2000 era to be commercially screened overseas and at festivals in Spain, London, Bangkok, and Singapore. The film also won Best Director, Best Cinematography, and Best Music at the Estepona Horror and Fantasy Film Festival (Spain, 2004), and Best Actress at the Asia Pacific Film Festival (Japan, 2004). The local media, which extensively covered the film's accomplishments, helped the film gain extensive popularity while (re)popularising the horror genre. The 'wave' of popular horror films in Malaysia can therefore be attributed to this film. The above exemplifies the continued attraction and fascination of Malaysians with horror films. This phenomenon will form the basis of my examination of contemporary Malaysian horror and explain its sudden (re)popularisation in Malaysian cinema.

Defining the horror genre

Academic studies of horror films have often employed Freudian psychoanalysis (Creed 1996, 2005; Gearhart 2005; Schneider 2004; Tudor 2004; Wood 2004). In many ways, the horror film is comparable to a form of a cultural nightmare that develops materials that are simultaneously attractive yet repellent, displayed but obfuscated, desired and repressed (Pinedo 2004). Such repressions occur, it is argued, because patriarchal capitalism and society demand that sexual energy, bisexuality, and children's sexuality be repressed and considered as the 'Other' (Wood 1985). The horror film, like a nightmare, becomes the site for everything repressed or oppressed by society to emerge (Wood 1979). In this sense, the horror genre is considered as a form of 'dreamworld' (Tudor 1989). It is often suggested that it should be analysed using psychoanalytical methods to interpret how mental anxieties, fears, fantasies, and wishes were unconsciously repressed during childhood (Schneider 2004). While this book does not attempt to discredit psychoanalysis in the study of horror films, it does not employ a psychoanalytic framework. Even though psychoanalysis has been widely used to understand elements of horror films, Freudian psychology should not be seen as the only key to understanding a horror film (Allen 1999), especially in its focus on individual-psychic rather than collective-social processes for psychoanalysis. It has either fallen short of or failed to provide a comprehensive account of horror figures (Carroll 1990). Such frameworks remain inconclusive and do not bring about any detailed theoretical consequences (Tudor 1997).

This analysis of Malaysian horror abandons the psychoanalytical perspective.[3] Since the horror genre is filled with cultural and political awareness (Wood 2004), it is proposed that horror cinema can most effectively be examined through its mediation of cultural-political change. As the history of horror films reflects the historical

---

3. For a detailed discussion regarding the objections of psychoanalytic accounts of horror, see Levine (2004), Tudor (2004), and Turvey (2004).

anxieties of the twentieth century (Wells 2000, 3), it is thus necessary to examine how the various horror narratives reflect different cultural moments and the evolution of horror in adapting to anxieties of the given moment within the location of the film's production (Cherry 2009). The characteristics that constitute the horror genre are, therefore, not fixed.

Horror is a flexible genre open to varying interpretations. It varies according to the different audiences located within different contexts and moments. It is built on familiar conventions, using different cultural resources drawn upon by both filmmaker and audience (Tudor 1989). A genre is firstly in the most basic sense is seen as a collection of films related to one another through their joint possession of a nearly invariant narrative pattern in which we all know 'how it will end' (Jancovich 2002, 11). To perform its function of providing regulation and variety, genres are not systems but systematisation processes that carry out cinematic institutions' roles (Neale 1980). The grouping of films based on genre thus performs a variety of collective functions. Such forms of recognition allow critics to address industry activities, audience, and culture simultaneously. Secondly, it helps avoid financial losses by providing a set framework that capitalises on previous successful models. Thirdly, it provides a set of precepts according to audience expectations to help categorise their viewing choices and provides reviewers with a critical framework that organises the uniqueness and recognises the success of the product according to the needs of its target audience (Watson 1996). To meet the audiences' expectations with a sense of familiarity, the genre uses the formula of successfully repeating 'familiar stories with familiar characters in familiar situations' (Grant 2003, xv). In short, a genre performs a role that goes beyond merely generically cataloguing films based on characteristic similarities. According to the genre, this categorical placement of films has an integral role in helping to facilitate according to the needs of the industry, audience, critics, and reviewers. Therefore, the horror genre should be understood as a collection of related but often very different categories. As an overlapping and evolving set of conceptual categories, the horror genre is in a constant state of flux rather than being a distinct and unified set of films with shared conventions (Cherry 2009).

The simplest definition of a horror film is one that intends to horrify and thrill a captive audience (Creed 2005; Davis and Natale 2010). This statement is a paradox, as it is self-contradictory by containing two very conflicting emotions: the paradox of the horror film lies in its alluring appeal to horrifying audiences. While the term 'horror' itself denotes feelings of fear, shock, disgust, and abjection, when put to screen, horror films can cross cultural, religious, and class boundaries by drawing on and appealing to a range of audiences from different classes, localities, and beliefs. Horror films, as one of the most lucrative genres in the cinema industry, have the ability to continue drawing audiences to experience new frights and horrifying sights through morbid preoccupations with fear, death, and monsters, leading to the eternal question that has fascinated and bewildered critics and academics alike

(Carroll 1990, 2001; Mazur 2011; Ochoa 2011; Worland 2007): How do audiences continue to be attracted to something that causes fear and disgust?

This phenomenon of horror film's remarkable popularity and its continued acceptance by audiences has made horror films one of the more provocative and controversial genres in cinema (Hutchings 2008). To further define and understand the term 'horror', it is appropriate to distinguish between the nature of the threat implied through 'horror' and 'terror'. The atrocities and acts of graphic violence in a horror film have led to horror being deemed 'aesthetically cheap and ethically suspect'. In contrast, terror is deemed more 'artful and unsettling' (Worland 2007, 10). These two concepts are further distinguished by understanding their impact on audience preferences and reactions. The first difference between horror and terror is its impact on the imagination and senses of the audience. The concepts of horror and terror are of significant variance, as the former 'contracts, freezes and nearly annihilates them' while the latter 'expands the soul' (Radcliffe 1826, 145–152). To further analyse the emotions of audiences, horror and terror can then be differentiated as between an 'awful apprehension and sickening realisation: between the smell of death and stumbling against a corpse, for horror resorts to a cruder presentation of the macabre while terror creates an intangible atmosphere of spiritual physic dead' (Varma 1966, 130). Both concepts are associated with the interpretation of fear: terror causes feelings of extreme fear, while horror causes extreme fear characterised by an unknown threat to normalcy and the eventual feeling of disgust over its impending consequences (Tamborini and Weaver 1996). To create frightening thoughts in an audience's mind, terror, which requires the audience's intellectual and active participation, exists as an aesthetic approach that evolves meticulously towards the creation of a suspenseful moment, towards the probability of an unfortunate occurrence. At the same time, horror produces moments of anxiety and revulsion through the direct display of unrestrained frightening scenes (Worland 2007). As horror relates to the current feeling of a spectator, it creates a sense of immediacy and contemporaneity, rather than speculation, and can be metaphorically explained as the occurrence of a nightmarish experience through the realisation that an unfortunate incident has occurred and is still occurring (Wierzbicka 1999). In short, terror causes moments of fear due to the anticipation of waiting for a horrifying scene; horror is the disgust felt upon being shocked and scared to witness a frightful and grotesque scene.

The horror film has emerged from being seen as a form of low culture to being understood as a form that often reflects the social, cultural, and political anxieties of the time of its making. It explores fundamental questions about the nature of human existence and the new sense of the world by intensely conveying synchronic associations and ideological and social messages of a particular historical moment (Prince 2004). As the horror film is meant to draw negative emotions from the audience, it was once seen as a common form of culture (Prince 2004), as an 'outsider', 'forbidden fruit', 'distasteful', 'tainted', and 'cultural other', existing at the margins of the mainstream with a taboo status (Cherry 2009). Despite its marginal status, the horror genre has persisted since the inception of cinema. Audiences' perception of the horror genre has evolved since the days of early cinema. Horror has been a durable genre that has evolved from one generation to the next. The turnaround of horror from a genre existing on the fringes to a driving force in the mainstream locates it as possibly the most sustainable genre in cinematic history.

Before seeking the reasons why the repulsive and fearful horror film continues to draw attraction (Carroll 1990), it is necessary to trace its origins to a medium predating cinema: late eighteenth- and early nineteenth-century English Gothic literature. Today's horror films are often linked to the most enduring Gothic tales of terror published, Mary Shelly's *Frankenstein* (1818) and Dr John Polidori's *The Vampyre: A Tale* (1819) are examples (Kendrick 2010). Horror films and Gothic literature share the similarity of dealing with the effects, fears, and anxieties caused by change. Gothic literature emerged during an era of change, upheaval, and uncertainty. Even when religious dogma was questioned and rejected, Gothic narratives maintained the power to make sense of the uncanny, the inexplicable, and the irrational in many aspects of individual and social life (Worland 2007). Gothic narratives often depict the struggles between good and evil forces in the search for law and order and problematise the distinction between the sacred and the profane, between what is barbaric and civilised (Wells 2000). Gothic literature narratives are also intended to frighten the reader, using suggestions of supernatural threats (Worland 2007). Such imagery and themes are similarly produced in horror cinema (Hutchings 2008). This situation leads to narratives that dramatise the reclamation of normality through a battle between good and evil.

The battle between good and evil in horror films began with George Méliès's three-minute *Le Manoir du diable* (1896). The horror genre flourished through the 1920s and the 1930s as German Expressionist movements recalled the horrors of the First World War through Robert Wiene's *The Cabinet of Dr Caligari* (1920) and F. W. Murnau's *Nosferatu* (1922). In the Hollywood studio era of the 1930s to the 1950s, the horror film was made as the B-movie second feature/double bill to attract a larger audience (Manchel 1990, 651). The commercialisation of horror films by Hollywood resulted in low-cost productions that returned high profits through Tod Browing's *Dracula* (1931) and Karl Freund's *The Mummy* (1932). This form of low-brow mass entertainment fare lasted into the 1950s with exploitation films of teenage horror such as Gene Fowler Jr.'s *I Was A Teenage Werewolf* (1957) and Herbert Strock's *I Was A Teenage Frankenstein* (1957). Sci-fi horror films from the 1950s include Robert Wise's *The Day the Earth Stood Still* (1951) and Ishirô Honda's *Godzilla, King of the Monsters!* (1956). The turbulent and troubled 1960s to 1990s in the US, which grew with increasing civil rights movements, political assassinations, the Cold War, and the Vietnam War, led to horror films' resurgence. Alfred Hitchcock's *Psycho* (1960) led the way to slasher films such as Tobe Hooper's *The Texas Chainsaw Massacre* (1974) and Sean S. Cunningham's *Friday the 13th* series

(1980); to the religious horror films such as William Friedkin's *The Exorcist* (1973) and Richard Donner's *The Omen* (1976); to the sci-fi and horror hybrids such as Ridley Scott's *Alien* (1979) and John Carpenter's *The Thing* (1982); to the horror of Hannibal Lecter in Jonathan Demme's *Silence of the Lambs* (1991) and Brett Ratner's *Red Dragon* (2002).

Today, the horror cycle continues during a time of ever-increasing paranoia caused by looming threats about security and economic uncertainty through random acts of terrorism and financial crises through James Wong's *Final Destination* (2000) and Danny Boyle's *28 Days Later* (2002). The popularity of horror films during this decade is exemplified by the subsequent sequels of the *Final Destination* series directed by different individuals. The series continued to revolve around the ill-fated Flight 180: David R. Ellis directed *Final Destination 2* (2003), James Wong directed *Final Destination 3* (2006), David R. Ellis directed *The Final Destination* (2009), and Steven Quale directed *Final Destination 5* (2011). Filmmakers continu-ously exploit visual, aural, and narrative elements using newer and contemporary approaches that appeal to audiences. Today, horror films attempt to project a sense of immediacy in an effort at portraying realism, as if events were indeed unfolding in real life or from the recordings of a 'lost tape'. Examples of such films began with Daniel Myrick and Eduardo Sánchez's *The Blair Witch Project* and Jaume Balagueró and Paco Plaza's *[Rec]* (2007). The global horror film scene of today has also wit-nessed the rise of Asian horror (discussed in detail below) through the J-Horror (Japanese horror) phenomenon with Hideo Nakata's *Ringu* (1998) and Takashi Shimizu's *Ju-on: The Grudge* (2002). These films eventually led to the revitalisation of horror in Hollywood through the remaking of J-Horror films. The horror film also persists during these times because it examines emotions of fear and anxiety and helps to provide a sense of justification to the ongoing moments of disorder and chaos by giving a rationalisation for the paranoia (Winstead 2011): the existence of pure and inexplicable evil (Nelson 2010).

Horror films formerly existed in the form of B-movies and on the fringes of film culture as low-budget and independent productions, cult, and low-brow or trash cinema from the 1930s to the 1960s. Horror cinema eventually became a big-budget and a driving force within the mainstream due to its profitability and cul-tural longevity within popular culture (Cherry 2009).[4] The horror genre has since established itself across cultural distinctions and hierarchies by producing upmar-ket horrors, downmarket horrors, and middlebrow horror films across different markets (Hutchings 2008) and is no longer so frequently a target of moral panic or labelled as a marginal, subversive, or disreputable form of popular culture criticised for its aesthetics (Mazur 2011). To continually scare audiences, the boundaries of the genre have been wholly shifted over time to continually revitalise, evolve, trans-form, and hybridise into an incredibly diverse set of subgenres and new forms to

---

4. For a detailed history of horror films, see Jancovich (2002), Mundorf and Mundorf (2002), and Wells (2000).

offer thematic variations to its audience (Cherry 2009). The genre is further categorised into subgenres such as: Gothic films, based on adaptations of monsters of classic horror tales, e.g., Frankenstein, vampires, and mummies; supernatural, occult and ghost films, with spirits, witchcraft, the Devil and other uncanny entities, e.g., *The Haunting* (1999) and *The Others* (2001); psychological horror films exploring psychological states and psychoses, e.g., *Cat People* (1942) and *Psycho*; monster films about invading 'natural and secular' creatures causing death and destruction, e.g., *The Birds* (1963) and *Cloverfield* (2008); slasher films about a stalker menacing teenagers, e.g., *Scream* (1996) and *I Know What You Did Last Summer* (1997); body horror, splatter, and gore films, exploring the abject and disgust of the human body, e.g., *The Brood* (1979) and *The Fly* (1986); and exploitation cinema, video nasties or explicit violence films, focusing on violence, torture, and rape, e.g., *Saw* (2004) and *Hostel* (2005) (Cherry 2009, 5–6). Therefore, the durability of the horror genre can be explained through its ability to relate to the audience's perception of fear in line with shifting times.

To understand the ideological issues carried in a particular horror film, the horror film cycle's historical and social contexts need to be examined. The next section explores the horror movie's cultural functions by examining the social function of monster figures in the global horror genre to consider the monster's function in the new wave of Malaysian horror specifically.

The monster fear factor

This section analyses the social functions of the horror film by examining the monster in the horror narrative. The monster is not only used to arouse fear, frighten, disturb, shock, and provoke, but its omnipresence also indicates certain historical, social, and cultural functions. Since the monster plays the most significant role in the horror film narrative's progression, what, then, is the metaphorical significance of the monster?

The horror film narrative is centred on the existence of a monster. The monster causes a conflict due to its incongruity, being at odds with normality (Russell 1998). To restore normative order, humans try—ineffectually—to contain or defeat the violently rampaging monster (Pinedo 2004). The narrative of the horror film revolves around variations of the 'seek and destroy' pattern containing three familiar phases: the introduction of the monster's threat in a stable situation, the destruction caused by the monster and the attempts to restrain it, and the restoration of order as the monster is annihilated (Mazur 2011; Tudor 1989). The narrative structure of the horror film has been further explored beyond this formula. Carroll suggests a four-act complex discovery plot that consists of onset, discovery, confirmation, and confrontation (1990, 99–108). Ochoa discusses the many different variations of a horror film narrative and provides a generalised two-act structure: the attack and the final battle (2011, 38–46).

The monster in a horror film is a representation of specific cultural anxieties. In horror films based on Western mythologies and imagination, monsters can be classified into the supernatural (ghosts, evil spirits, witches, demons, Satan, vampires, werewolves, and mummies); supranatural (human-made monsters such as Frankenstein and Godzilla); and human (serial killers, psychotics, and chainsaw-wielding cannibals) (Mazur 2011, 233). Every horror film, regardless of ideology, centres on some monstrosity that represents opposition to the dominant ideological standpoint (Cherry 2009) as a form of social marginalising in creating 'the Other' (Wood 1985). While arousing dread and horror, the uncanny monster problematises the symbolic order through the evocation of fear, unease, disquiet, and gloom (Creed 2004).

In the narrative, the monster is often redefined based on the development of social and cultural history. It conventionally appears as a form of evil that tests the human condition's boundaries while shifting the boundaries between good and evil (Wells 2000). Horror films characteristically represent a culture. The dominant designation of the monster must necessarily be 'evil'. What has been repressed in the individual and culture will ultimately return as a threat perceived by the consciousness as ugly, terrible, and obscene (Wood 1985).

The monster's threat occurs as it crosses or threatens to cross the 'border' by doing something that is not permitted by society. In its crossing of the border, the monster is represented as abject, a being that threatens the symbolic order's stability (Creed 1996). The horror film disrupts and disorients any sense of presupposed reality, as the monster blurs boundaries by creating impurity and danger (Pinedo 2004). As the monster does not respect borders, it threatens the political and cultural status quo (Magistrale 2005). The monster in the narrative is thus presented as an abnormal being that threatens classificatory systems essential for the permanence of human society (Mazur 2011).

For the restoration of order to occur, the cause behind the threat needs to be destroyed. While audiences are perversely drawn to the abject for its threat towards understanding the self and society, the abject needs to be rejected before it becomes too threatening (Creed 2004). Some argue that horror films are watched to re-establish a feeling of essential normality, for the witnessing of a monster reminds the audience of a sense of normalcy (King 1981). As such, the monster needs to be destroyed for the re-establishment of social order. This re-establishment can be achieved by getting rid of the abject and redrawing the boundaries by repressing the monster's threat (as the irrational Other) when the monster is indeed dead and decayed (Pinedo 2004).

The monster's defiance and acts of destruction can also be presented differently as an object of sympathy and fascination (Wood 1985). The monster, therefore, also appeals to audiences as its acts demonstrate the possibility of having alternate visions, of showing how transformation can emerge through acts of destruction, as such acts also represent the hidden urges usually repressed in society (Magistrale

2005). The audience becomes entertained by allowing itself to be frightened yet fascinated simultaneously, as the members understand that such horrific occurrences in the narrative are a work of fiction that will remain remote from ever becoming a reality (Worland 2007). As the monsters are often located 'over there' in a remote and faraway location, the threat does not seem too intimidating (Prince 2004). Through the monster, the horror film becomes a site for the emergence of taboo feelings repressed by culture, such as terror and rage (Pinedo 2004).

For these reasons, the monster in the horror narrative carries greater significance than merely horrifying the audience. From a socio-cultural and political perspective, the horror film and its monster can be used to bolster a status quo under threat. The monster projected as the unfamiliar needs to be feared. It causes harm and destruction and can metaphorically represent an incompatible issue or contradictory or threatening to the current status quo. In creating 'landscapes of fear' through the monster, the horror film generates a social construction of fear in society (Tudor 1989, 5). To return to normalcy and departure from a fearful landscape, the solution is to destroy the monster, which is, in effect, a dismissal and rejection of the incompatible and contradictory issues. These points will be further examined below in my exploration of dominant themes in contemporary Malaysian horror cinema.

Horror in Malaysia: The history of the Malaysian *filem seram*

The Malaysian horror film uses localised monsters, entities, beliefs, mythologies, and superstition. The emergence of rationalised thinking, scientific advancement, and secularism has led to the gradual abandoning of superstitious elements of local religious cultures by the more middle-class and upper-class Malaysians from diverse ethnic communities (DeBernardi 2004). Such beliefs and practices persist in the Malaysian way of life, and to a certain extent represent the multiethnic identity.[5] These beliefs have allowed Malaysians to develop a deep sense of 'cultural verisimilitude' that invokes a deep sense of plausibility, motivation, justification, and belief (Neale 2003) due to familiarity with the monsters in these films. For example, the

---

5. Centuries-old religious customs and superstition continue to be adhered to and observed by the Malay, Chinese, and Indian communities and govern the regulations and conventions related to rites practised during events such as births, weddings, funerals, and religious festivals. For example, weddings are discouraged by the Chinese community during the seventh lunar month of the Chinese calendar, as 'ghost month' is considered an inauspicious period. The seventh lunar month (August in the Gregorian calendar) of the Chinese calendar is also known as the Chinese ghost month. According to Daoist and Buddhist beliefs, the gates of the Lower Realm of hell are opened for the deceased's spirits to visit relatives for twenty-nine days. During this period, religious and cultural rites such as the burning of incense, joss sticks, food offerings, and concerts are held to appease the spirits. It is often considered inauspicious for weddings, business ventures, or funerals during this month. Originating from China, the festival is widely practised by the Chinese communities in Malaysia, Singapore, and Taiwan. The month ends with the Hungry Ghost Festival. For a detailed history and taboos of the Hungry Ghost Festival, see Montillo (2009).

'The Malaysian Decade of Horror'

release of *Pontianak* (1957) caused individual members of the audience to lose consciousness, as the images were reported to be too shocking (Koay 2005a).[6]

The ideological imperatives of the horror film reflect the specific social, cultural, and political anxieties of its time. Given this, it will be useful to briefly examine the anxieties conveyed through the synchronic associations and ideological and social messages of a horror film within a particular time or historical moment through the monster (Prince 2004). The popularisation of the horror film can be divided into three cycles. This examination is essential, as the genre conveys particular social, religious, and cultural meanings. It has been challenging to identify the first Malaysian-made horror film. This difficulty is caused by the lack of substantial academic literature written on the horror genre pre-dating the Second World War and the difficulty in locating cinematic artefacts due to the lack of preservation or difficulty in accessing materials such as film posters, newspaper articles, and promotional items. In outlining the history of the horror genre in Malaysian cinema, the film *Mata Hantu* (Ghost Eye, 1938–1942) stands out as the probable first horror film made locally. *Mata Hantu* was produced by the Shaw Brothers between 1938 and 1941 and is the last film to be locally made before the Japanese Occupation in the Malay Peninsula (Kahn 2006; Barnard 2010). As discussed in Chapter 1, the Shaw Brothers ceased all cinematic productions during the Second World War. Their absence thus effectively marked the end of the horror film production during that time.

The first cycle: Horror in the 1950s–1970s

The first cycle falls within the Golden Age of Malaysian cinema (1955–1965) until 1970.[7] This phase coincides with the first phase of Malaysian cinema during the era of colonisation and de-colonisation that centred on the nation's independence (1957); the continuous threat of the communist insurgency and the declaration of the Emergency period from 1948 to 1960; the formation of Malaysia (1963); the eventual secession of Singapore from Malaysia in 1965; and the 13 May 1969 race riots.[8] Cathay-Keris rivalled the Shaw Brothers' MFP. The intense competition between these two studios led to the release of a substantial number of horror films. The studios employed transnational production methods and used mythical entities from Malay and Asian folklore. The most significant monster to appear during this period was the *pontianak*.

As the directors were originally from India (as discussed in Chapter 1), the horror films based on Malay folklore carried Indian influences. They produced

---

6. The historical significance of this event to the nineteenth-century incident that occurred during the first screening of *L'Arrivée d'un train en gare de La Ciotat* (1896) that reportedly caused the audience to duck and run from the theatre (Jess-Cooke 2009) is drawn.
7. For a detailed discussion on the Golden Age of Malaysian cinema, see Chapter 1.
8. These events have been discussed in Chapter 1.

horror films with melodramatic effects and song-and-dance sequences. The first horror films released were MFP's *Roh Membela* (Defending Soul, 1955) and *Hantu Jerangkong* (Skeleton Ghost, 1957). Cathay-Keris produced the first *pontianak* film, B. N. Rao's *Pontianak*. *Pontianak* was released as the film coincided with the celebrations of Eid-al-Fitr (*The Straits Times*, 1 May 1957). The film was released in the Malay language and dubbed in Cantonese for Hong Kong audiences and was popular even with the local Indian and Chinese communities. It was screened in major cinemas for nearly two months, which was unusual for a Malay film then (Barnard 2011, 46). The *pontianak* films proved to be a winning formula, a total of five films being released.

The *pontianak*, until today, remains the most recognisable monster. *Pontianak* starred Maria Menado, and the scriptwriter was her husband, Abdul Razak.[9] *Pontianak* narrates the tale of the female protagonist Chomel's transformation into a *pontianak*. Abandoned as a baby, she is adopted by an older man working as an author. However, she grows up ugly and hunchbacked and is ostracised by the villagers. At the older man's death bed, Chomel is instructed to burn all his belongings. She follows his instructions but stumbles upon a book that reveals the secret to obtaining good looks. She naturally keeps the book and formulates a mixture for beautifying herself. Based on the book's instructions, she drinks the mixture during a full moon and passes out. However, she overlooks a clause prohibiting her ever to taste blood. When she awakens as a beautiful woman, her life takes a turn for the better, and she eventually marries the son of a village head. Her transformation into a *pontianak* occurs when a snake bites Chomel's husband. In a bid to rescue him, she sucks the venom from his leg, but the taste of blood tempts her to drain his body of blood. She vanishes but emerges as a *pontianak* who returns during the night to visit her daughter, terrorise the village, and kill men after seducing them (Koay 2005a).[10] The film's success led to two sequels, *Dendam Pontianak* (Pontianak's Vengeance, 1957) and *Sumpah Pontianak* (Pontianak's Curse, 1958). As a commercial filmmaking enterprise, these sequels were produced as 'commercial feature films to continue telling familiar stories with familiar characters in familiar situations' (Grant 2003, xv).

Cathay-Keris employed B. N. Rao and Maria Menado for the sequels based on the genre formula of 'repetition and sameness' (Neale 2003, 171). Another two *pontianak* films, *Pontianak Kembali* (Pontianak Returns, 1963) and *Pontianak Gua Musang* (Pontianak of Gua Musang, 1964) were directed by B. N. Rao.[11] The genre's success eventually led to spin-offs and imitations by MFP. In 1958, MFP released

---

9. Maria Menado was born in 1932 in Sulawesi, Indonesia. She received her breakthrough as an actress at 17, when she won a beauty contest in Singapore. During her acting career that spanned from 1951 to 1962, Menado acted in twenty films. Besides her role as the *pontianak*, she has starred in and produced *Korban Fitnah* (Victim of Defamation, 1959), *Siti Zubaidah* (1961), and *Raja Bersiong* (Fanged King, 1963).

10. There no longer exists a copy of the film.

11. Gua Musang (literally, Civet Cave) is a town located on the Malaysian Peninsular eastern coast. Gua Musang is also the largest district in Kelantan.

Ramon Estella's *Anak Pontianak* (Pontianak's Child). The film displayed technical superiority to Cathay-Keris's films through better camera movements (virtuoso tracking shots), lighting techniques (neo-Expressionist use of shadows), and visual effects (pseudo-Gothic lettering for the opening credits). It was comparable to the horror films of James Whale (Guneratne 2003, 164). However, MFP only produced two *pontianak* films, the other being *Pusaka Pontianak* (The Accursed Heritage, 1964).[12]

Besides the *pontianak*, MFP and Cathay-Keris produced horror films using other mythical and supernatural creatures such as the *Orang Minyak* (Oily Man) and *Harimau Jadian* (Were-tiger). The cinematic trend at that moment was the initial release of a film by one studio, followed by the emulation of the subject matter by the other (sometimes even extending to a direct copy of the title). MFP (and Merdeka Studios after 1964) released *Pancha Delima* (Ruby Necklace, 1957), *Orang Minyak* (Oily Man, 1958), *Sumpah Orang Minyak* (Oily Man's Curse, 1958), *Azimat* (Amulet, 1958), *Gergasi* (Giant, 1958), *Hantu Kubor* (Ghost of the Grave, 1958), *Batu Belah Batu Bertangkup* (Haunted Cave, 1959), *Anak Setan* (Satan's Child, 1974), *Raja Bersiong* (1968), *Sitora Harimau Jadian* (Sitora the Were-tiger, 1964), *Puaka* (Demon, 1974). Cathay-Keris produced *Serangan Orang Minyak* (Attack of the Oily Man, 1958) *Orang Lichin* (Slippery Man, 1958), *Hantu Rimau* (Tiger Ghost, 1960), *Badang* (1962), *Mata Syaitan* (Satan Eyes, 1962), *Raja Bersiong* (1963), *Puaka* (Demon, 1970), and *Harimau Jadian* (Were-tiger, 1972). The intense rivalry between MFP and Cathay-Keris led to the increased output of horror films. This phenomenon needs to be analysed through the horror film's narratives, which reflect the social and political anxieties of their historical moments.

The first cycle of horror cinema occurred after the Second World War. In the build-up to independence in 1957, unresolved issues related to national identity, culture, citizenship, economic stability, and language remained a conflict source (Embong 2001, 60). What was needed was a uniting factor. The *pontianak*'s emergence in 1957 coincided with one of the most turbulent eras in the nation's history. The horror film managed to sustain its popularity as it delved into the central issue of fear and uncertainty. Arguably, horror movies become popular during such times, as audiences are distracted with an instinctive form of therapeutic escape (Skal 1993). They painfully recall acts and moments of unprecedented violence and trauma (Bishop 2010).

The *pontianak* became the most famous monster figure, as she represents a form of ambiguity. During this uncertain period, her ambiguity helped represent and culturally process the ongoing disorder and chaos (Winstead 2011). To collectively deal

---

12. For more discussions about the *Pontianak* in the Golden Era of Malaysian cinema, transnationalisation of the *Pontianak*, and gender roles of the *Pontianak*, see Lee Yuen Beng and Sarata Balaya. 2016. From international horror films to the local *filem seram*: Examining the cinematic identity and roles of the Malaysian Pontianak. *KEMANUSIAAN the Asian Journal of Humanities* 23 (Supp. 2): 161–174, https://doi.org/ 10.21315/ kajh2016.23.s2.9.

174   *Malaysian Cinema in the New Millennium*

with the effects and anxieties of change, the *pontianak* was projected as the common enemy. We might speculate that the *pontianak* indirectly represented the Second World War's horrors, the end of colonial rule, the communist ideology, the spectre of Singapore, and economic uncertainty. For the return and re-establishment of social order, these events (symbolised by the *pontianak*) needed to be culturally processed and symbolically overcome (destroyed). This interpretation allows us to see the *pontianak* as embodying specific meanings according to this period's historical and cultural changes. The act of dismissing the *pontianak* is, in effect, a wishful dismissal and rejection of incompatible and contradictory issues for the original status quo to be reinstated.

The second cycle: Horror in the 1970s to 1990

The second cycle coincides with cinema's nationalisation and the rise of the Independent *Bumiputera* filmmakers (as discussed in Chapter 1).[13] *Pontianak* (1975) became the eighth and final *pontianak* film released before the thirty-year hiatus in *pontianak* films. This parody was a transnational venture co-produced by Hamid Bond Organisation and Kobe Trading Company. Abdul Razak wrote the script, and the cast consisted of actors from Singapore (Sharif Medan), Malaysia (Jeniffer Kaur), Thailand (Piya Johnny), and Indonesia (Herdawati). Locally made horror films also lost their lustre with Malaysian audiences, and the horror genre became almost non-existent. It must be noted that, although no *pontianak* films were produced during this period, the horror genre did continue to be explored on a smaller scale although it failed to capture the imagination of audiences.

Even in its state of deficiency, this (near-) absence of horror films is a phenomenon reflecting the socio-political and cultural events of its time. As discussed in Chapters 1 and 2, the cinema industry's nationalisation meant the mobilisation of state-led policies such as the NEP and the NCP. This book focuses on the revival of Islam through the *dakwah* movement.[14] This Islamisation process meant that Islam became more than a spiritual guide; it became the central element to comprehend the state, politics, law, and society (Milne and Mauzy 1999, 82).[15]

---

13. The cinema industry experienced a decline due to the closure of the Chinese studios, and the introduction of television programmes and films from Hong Kong, India, and Indonesia. Local audiences also became more critical and intolerant of local films with shallow storylines using outdated techniques and recycled themes (as discussed in Chapter 1).

14. See Chapter 1 for a brief outline of the *dakwah* movement.

15. The process of Islamisation during the tenure of Mahathir Mohamad included the inclusion of Qur'anic quotations into political speeches; the establishment of religious administrations under the respective state governments, Islamic courts (*Syariah* courts), Islamic financial institutions (*Bank Islam*), Islamic institutions of higher education (International Islamic University), and Islamic think tanks (Institute for Islamic Thought and Civilisation/ISTAC and Malaysian Institute of Islamic Understanding/IKIM); the upgrading of the *Pusat Islam* (Islamic Centre); the building of colossal mosques; the broadcasting of the *azan* (Muslim call to prayer) on national television and radio stations; and the employment of *ulamas* (clerics) in the Department for Islamic Development in the Prime Minister's Office and Ministry of Education (Reid and Gilsenan 2007; Riddell 2005; Saat 2010).

Both *adat* and Islam remain essential features in the lives of Malays (Khoo 2006).[16] Because the Malays are attached to both Islam and *adat* (Verma 2004), the *dakwah* movement called for the revival of Islamic beliefs and challenged animistic notions and beliefs.[17] *Adat* has roots predating Islam, as Islam only arrived during the fifteenth-century Malaccan Sultanate Empire.[18] The close attachment Malays have to their sultans, and their cultural heritage based on *adat, nama* (name, reputation or title), and obedience meant the continued belief in magic, superstition, spirit worship, and taboos (Verma 2004).[19] Based on the *dakwah's* call for spiritual renewal, modernity, religious reform, and the 're-Islamisation of knowledge', such traditional symbols and systems of meaning were reinterpreted as 'un-Islamic' (Shamsul 1995). *Adat* and customs (magic, superstition, spirit worship, taboos), shamanic practices and beliefs (*pawang, dukun* or *bomoh*) which predate Islam have existed continuously in Malay culture but are viewed by Islamic fundamentalists as challenging Islam (Shamsul 2005).

Regarding gender relations and sexuality, although the *adat* is patriarchal, it practises greater tolerance towards displays of sexuality and sensuality while encouraging the empowerment and autonomy of women (Khoo 2006). In contrast, the *dakwah* movement employed strategies for 'recasting' Malay women's identity according to the Islamic mould based on two assumptions: first, women were relatively ignorant about the demands of Islam; and, second, their weakness and naivety meant they needed to be protected (Sharifah Zaleha 2002). Measures such as segregating men and women in public spaces are taken to restrain uncontainable feelings of *nafsu* (lust) by controlling a woman's physical appearance (Frisk 2009). The woman's *aurat* (parts of the body that should not be exposed) is covered to avoid shame and preserve modesty; concealing body parts such as the hair with a *tudung* (headscarf) sets Muslim women apart from the 'modern' (Western) women who neglect their morality and modesty (Sharifah Zaleha 2002).

---

16. In politics, with the *dakwah* movement gaining momentum, the two most influential Malay political parties, UMNO and PAS, both claiming to be the defender of Islam, attempted to outdo one another in their bids for the Malay vote by upholding differing opinions regarding the laws of Islam and the establishment of the Islamic state. UMNO declared itself the party of the Malays, defender of Islam and its values, and against theologically conservative Islamic policies of PAS (Verma 2004, 113).

17. The practice of *adat* or the Malay way of life is then divided into the matrilineal *Adat Perpatih* and patrilineal *Adat Temenggung*. While the followers of *Adat Perpatih* remain a minority to *Adat Temenggung*, the practice of *Adat Perpatih* that favours the female in heritage remains one of the most distinctive features of the Malay culture.

18. Before the arrival of Islam in South-east Asia, animistic beliefs in spirits (*semangat*), Buddhism, and Hinduism were widely practised (Frisk 2009). This pre-Islamic belief in spirits and magic has been continued through superstition, and ritualistic practices not derived from Islam remain among Malaysian Muslims today (McAmis 2002).

19. The term 'Malay-ness', politically constitutes the three elements of *bahasa* (language/Malay), *agama* (religion/Islam), and *raja* (royalty/sultan or chiefs) (Shamsul 1997).

The *dakwah* movement has also influenced Malaysian cinema. Because Islam is indistinguishable from the Malay identity (Verma 2004), this conflict and tension between Islam and *adat* led to the horror genre's eventual banning.[20] During this period, Malaysian filmmakers faced more significant challenges and restrictions than did many of their Asian counterparts, due to the banning of the supernatural, ghosts, and witchcraft elements. The banning of these elements reflects the authority and influence of the *dakwah* movement. Despite the ban, certain films with horror elements did manage to escape censorship (Khoo 2006, 112). In the 1980s, a series of such films were produced. These include *Perjanjian Syaitan* (Satan's Pact, 1981), *Toyol* (1981), *Anita Dunia Ajaib* (Anita in Wonderland, 1981), *Setinggan* (Squatters, 1982), *Perawan Malam* (Night Virgin, 1982), *Ilmu Saka* (Perennial Knowledge, 1984), *Mangsa* (Victim, 1985), and *Rahsia* (Secret, 1987). These commercially unsuccessful films managed to be released in cinemas despite having film titles and thematic content depicting supernatural and spiritual beings such as *toyol*, *hantu* (ghost), and *syaitan* (Satan).

In the 1990s, the only (possible) horror films are *Main-Main Hantu* (Playing with Ghosts, 1990) and *Fantasi* (Fantasy, 1993). *Fantasi*, however, was initially banned for depicting supernatural creatures, which contradicts Islam. In 1993, *Fantasi* was finally released after the intervention of Mahathir Mohamad. The film title changed from *Fantasia* to *Fantasi* and the unIslamic scenes removed (Nora and Dara exchanging vows; Dara's spirit entering Nora's body; Kana's explanation about Silbi's origins; and Nora and Rahmat meeting Dara's spirit).[21]

The MDI in Contemporary Malaysian Horror Cinema

Contemporary Malaysian horror cinema has partially blurred the lines between the mainstream and the MDI. However, while commercial and MDI filmmakers converge in their production of mainstream horror films, their works continue to diverge through the employment of different thematic representations and subject matter. The MDI filmmakers have released just one independent horror film titled *Visits: Hungry Ghost Anthology*, but their venture into the commercial horror genre has been more successful. Amir Muhammad, James Lee, and Woo Ming Jin have directed horror films produced and financed by the two major commercial film

---

20. The Malaysian New Wave directors have critiqued this clash between modern and traditional, and religion (Islam) and customs and traditions (*adat*) in films such as *Selubung* (1992) and *Perempuan, Isteri dan . . . ?* (1993) (as discussed in Chapter 1). These films challenged such constructions by 'reclaiming *adat*' by portraying mystical elements and the empowerment of women through the portrayal of women in sarongs (*berkemban*), mainly through the films of Shuhaimi Baba (Khoo 2006). Such challenges also bring back such scenes commonly found in the films during the Golden Age of Malaysian cinema, such as P. Ramlee's *Musang Berjanggut* (Bearded Fox, 1959) and *Panggilan Pulau* (1954).

21. While the film's original title *Fantasia* is similar to a 1940 Walt Disney animation film, it is inferred that the logic behind the name change is for the LPF to remind audiences that the film's events are nothing but (a) *Fantasi* (Fantasy).

companies, Primeworks Studios and Tayangan Unggul. These films were made after procuring the necessary FINAS permits. Except for *Seru*, all the films have been rated 'U' (suitable for general viewers of all ages) by the LPF. This condition allows the horror films by MDI filmmakers to be released in local commercial circuits. These films have also been circulating at international film festivals. *Histeria* was screened at the 2011 San Francisco International Asian American Film Festival, 21st Singapore International Film Festival, and 2009 Hong Kong International Film Festival. *Seru* was screened at the 2011 Udine Far East Film Festival and the 2011 Puchon International Fantastic Film Festival. *Claypot Curry Killers* (2011) premiered at the 2011 Indonesia International Fantastic Film Festival.[22]

While Amir Muhammad was the first MDI filmmaker to co-direct a mainstream commercial film, the venture into commercial filmmaking through the horror genre was successfully led by James Lee. Lee became the first Malaysian filmmaker who continuously migrates between working in independent and in mainstream commercial filmmaking. What makes his career unique is his ability to change modes, from being a filmmaker who always produces works that appeal only to a niche market of independent cinema followers to making films that commercially appeal. Already dominating the independent cinematic scene with his unique cinematographic style and transnational filmmaking methods, Lee entered through the horror genre into the Malay-dominated mainstream cinema. His career in commercial horror cinema started with *Histeria*, *Sini Ada Hantu*, and *Tolong! Awek Aku Pontianak*. Lee's commercial horror cinema efforts received further recognition when *Sini Ada Hantu* was nominated for Best Original Theme Song during the Festival Filem Malaysia 24 (24th Malaysian Film Festival). His horror films employ commercial aesthetics and cinematography and are commercially financed, produced, distributed, and exhibited. His films diverge from the mainstream through their resistance to Islamisation and local cinematic guidelines for the horror genre, employment of non-Malay casts, storylines, and language, and feature at international film festivals. The horror films of James Lee are more inclined to employ a postethnic cosmopolitan cinema (as discussed in Chapter 3). This section outlines how MDI filmmakers' commercial horror films, including Lee's, diverge from mainstream horror filmmakers based on two characteristics: their different representations of Islam and their inclination towards pan-Asian themes. This latter represents the MDI filmmakers' persistence in employing transnational cultural flows from the Asian region to contest national issues.

---

22. The LPF has twice denied Lee's latest horror feature, *Claypot Curry Killers,* a commercial release. The film, however, internationally premiered at the Indonesian International Fantastic Film Festival in 2011.

The MDI and representations of religion

MDI filmmakers and mainstream filmmakers diverge in their treatment of religion. James Lee's *Sini Ada Hantu* revolves around two employees of a freight company, Ah Meng and Bakri. One night, they are assigned a last-minute dispatch of delivering a corpse and its coffin to a wake being held in a village located far from the city. During the journey, they exchange ghost stories to keep themselves awake. The stories they tell are popular Malaysian ghost stories, supernatural entities, and ghosts commonly known to Malaysians regardless of race and ethnicity, language, or religion.

The first tale is about the *hantu pokok pisang* (The 'banana tree spirit'). The spirit of a beautiful woman is believed to reside inside the banana tree. She can be summoned on a Friday, at midnight, during a full moon, by tying one end of a red cloth around the banana tree and the other onto the ends of the bed. The second tale is about the *hantu nombor ekor* (The 'lottery spirit'). It is believed that spirits in a cemetery can be summoned to predict winning lottery numbers. In exchange for these numbers, the spirit must first be appeased using offerings such as the blood from a dog or a chicken. The third tale is about the *hantu asrama* (The 'boarding school spirit'). Malaysia is nation that experienced Second World War atrocities, so tales of buildings being haunted by former soldiers or victims of war crimes are not uncommon (see the discussion of *Rasuk* above). One of the more famous ghost stories is buildings (in this case, boarding schools) haunted by Japanese soldiers' spirits.

Sini Ada Hantu diverges from mainstream filmmakers' horror films in that it does not contain religious elements. First, the film does not employ religion as the core theme and subject matter, nor does it become a platform to inform of the dangers of transgressing religion. There is no religious verse at the beginning of the film. A disclaimer, however, is placed at the film's beginning stating, '*Cerita yang bakal anda saksikan tiada kena mengena dengan sesiapa sama ada yang masih hidup ataupun yang telah meninggal dunia. Ia semata-mata sebuah karya rekaan penulis yang kononnya pernah terjumpa hantu*'. (The story you are about to see has nothing to do with any living or dead person. It is merely a work of fiction by the writer who claims to have previously seen a ghost.) While denouncing events and characters in the film as fictional, this disclaimer also mocks the requirement of placing it in the film. It also makes fun of Ah Meng and Bakri, who claim to have either seen a ghost or heard about it from someone else.

While the events in the three ghost stories told by Ah Meng and Bakri do transgress the boundaries of religion, for they involve the invocation of spirits for worldly pleasures, the moral message put forth by this film is, in fact, about the exploration of the human conscience. They transgress because the stories of the *hantu pokok pisang* and *hantu nombor ekor* involve acts of betraying friends for selfish purposes. Neither is *Sini Ada Hantu* an attempt at highlighting religion, as no religious

'The Malaysian Decade of Horror'   179

authorities are portrayed in this film. While the horror film guidelines require the film to conclude with the triumph of good over evil, in these stories, religion has not been used as *the* required element to defeat or overwhelm a destructive evil force. The spirits in all three stories are never conquered or destroyed.

Second, the women in the film are not portrayed as hapless victims, nor are they powerless. In this film, a reversal of gender roles has occurred, as the *hantu pokok pisang* and the *hantu nombor ekor* are female spirits, while their victims are males. Both stories conclude with the male victims being killed for their transgressions, but the female spirits are never destroyed. As such, the repression of women does not occur in these two stories. The stereotypical representations of the woman requiring a male figure to rescue her do not happen. *Sini Ada Hantu*, therefore, diverges from the mainstream when it does not present religion as the 'social safety valve' that rescues the victims. Third and finally, the film also diverges from the mainstream, as the portrayal of ghost stories told by one Chinese and one Malay character is different from the portrayal in horror films of mainstream filmmakers, for this film is not mono-ethnic and revolves around different ethnic communities. This situation, in effect, is reflective of the postethnic and cosmopolitan approach of the MDI filmmakers, as discussed in Chapter 3.

In another example, Woo Ming Jin teams up with mainstream horror filmmaker Pierre Andre to co-direct *Seru*. *Seru* narrates the story of a film crew trapped in a jungle. After two crew members, Sari and Julie, becomes possessed and become hysterical, the group seeks shelter at base camp. Tony and Sham venture into the jungle to search for Julie, who has run off. At base camp, the others begin arguing about whether the location has been *dipagar* (cleansed and protected from evil spirits) and how they are behind schedule. A crew member mentions that she read about a girl murdered there. As they continue to quarrel, they locate two Orang Asal (Indigenous community) villagers, Pakcik Ungkai and his wife, Makcik Aneng. They help exorcise the possessed Sari, and she is sent to the hospital. As the others are about to leave, they recall that Tony and Sham have not returned. Someone spots Sari outside a window. She has returned, still possessed, and begins to kill them. Jeff, the sole survivor, manages to escape, but he is captured by a possessed Azman who is the production manager. The latter drags him to a site where Pakcik Ungkai and Mak Cik Aneng carry out a ritual. Pak Cik Ungkai mentions that Azman has helped 'fulfil all the conditions' required to resurrect his dead daughter Mislila, using Julie's body.

Seru employs filmmaking techniques similar to those of *The Blair Witch Project* (1999), *Cloverfield* (2008), and *Quarantine* (2008). Closer to home, the film is similar to Singapore's *Haunted Changi* (2010). *Seru*, like *Haunted Changi*, employs the storyline of events being recorded on a tape that 'reveals' the murder of every character as an exposé about the 'true' events that have taken place. By witnessing the events as they unfold, unedited realism is projected with a sense of immediacy. *Seru* begins with a close-up of Jeff. Looking defeated and drenched in sweat, he states, 'To whomever discovers this tape, please hand it over to the police. This tape contains evidence of what happened to us. My name is Jeff.' As members of a film crew amid the production of a horror film, the entire event is conveniently recorded, as a camera is already within reach. Since the events are being recorded in an uncontrolled environment, the camerawork seems 'amateurish' and 'clumsy'. However, this form of camerawork forms the aesthetics of a shaky frame caused by an unsteady camera movement as if the jib arm and steadicam are not used. The Dutch angle is also commonly used to signify a psychological mood of disorientation or unease. It is used during shocking moments, times of madness, or to denote an invisible demonic force (Cherry 2009, 65).

In *Seru*, religious elements are simply not present. Being isolated in the jungle, the crew members must save themselves, as there are no religious figures being summoned. They are being murdered because they just happen to be at the wrong place at the wrong time, as Pakcik Ungkai, and Makcik Aneng have been searching for sacrificial victims. However, Seru goes against religion and the cinematic regulations in contemporary Malaysian horror cinema through the scene of a deceased person being resurrected.[23] The excessive amount of blood in the film also escapes censorship. As the film does not seem to carry any form of moral message, the compulsory disclaimer that denounces the following acts and characters in the film as works of fiction is not used. Neither is religion sought as the final solution, and good does not triumph over evil, as all the film characters are killed. Pakcik Ungkai and Makcik Aneng successfully resurrect their dead daughter through the body of Julie.

In summary, while the horror genre partially blurs the boundaries between the works of the MDI directors and mainstream filmmakers, their works diverge in the extent of their representation of religious themes and subject matter. MDI filmmakers' horror films do not use religion as the final solution. Given this, MDI filmmakers' horror films seem more closely related to pan-Asian horror's cultural flows, since the works of other Asian horror filmmakers similarly avoid religion as the core theme or subject matter of their films.

The MDI pan-Asian horror film connection

The employment of famous ghost stories in Malaysian horror cinema is aligned with the superstitious beliefs in the wider Asian region. While both MDI and mainstream horror filmmakers have heavily employed this subject matter, the non-employment of religion by MDI filmmakers points towards their association with the current wave of pan-Asian horror.

---

23. In 1964, M. Amin's *Rumah Itu Duniaku* (Home Sweet Home) was initially banned by the LPF because of a scene depicting a deceased man's children wailing beside his body. The ban was based on Islamic law that prohibits any forms of wailing for the dead (Hamzah 2004).

Horror cinema has always been popular in Asia. Asian audiences have historically been entertained with Malaysian *pontianak* films such as *Sumpah Pontianak* and *Anak Pontianak* in the 1950s to the 1970s; and Indonesian horror films *Mystics in Bali* (1981) and *Pengabdi Setan* (1982) that explored the mystical and supernatural in the 1980s. From Hong Kong are the Chinese (hopping) vampire films in the 1990s, such as *Encounters of the Spooky Kind* (1980) and *Mr Vampire* films. In Malaysia, James Lee's *Claypot Curry Killers* bears certain similarities to the cannibalistic acts in Fruit Chan's short film *Dumplings* in the *Three . . . Extremes* (2004) compilation: here, human flesh is used to enhance a particular dish's flavour and saleability. It makes sense to examine how MDI filmmakers' horror films are influenced by the current wave of pan-Asian cinematic horror. Not to be confused with the Hollywood remakes of popular Asian titles such as *Ringu* and *Dark Water* (2002), produced using big budgets, stars, and special effects, Asian horror began as low-budget and independently produced, without the presence of renowned stars or special effects (Rawle 2010).[24] This current wave of cinematic horror is greatly aided by the rise of digital filmmaking technology and the internet. The release of *Ringu* and its subsequent sequels and prequel created shockwaves across the region and worldwide.[25]

Beginning regionally in Asia, the *Ringu* phenomenon sparked immense discussions on the internet, in the media, academia, and the cinematic world. *Ringu*, a low-budget independent production (Lim 2009; Rawle 2010), has similarly influenced Malaysian horror (as discussed throughout this chapter). The image of a slim-figured Sadako dressed in a long white garment, with long straight hair, parted to reveal only her left eye, crawling out of a television, and the curse of certain death after the viewing of a videocassette and the receiving of a phone call has dramatically influenced the horror genre. This image of Sadako has influenced the portrayal of Meriam the *pontianak* in *Pontianak Harum Sundal Malam* and the *hantu nombor ekor* in *Sini Ada Hantu*. The possibility of such a horrendous being emerging from simple everyday appliances shocked and horrified millions of viewers regionally and worldwide, as this image and storyline tore down the boundaries between what was possible and factual while questioning the fragility of life. The success of *Ringu* and the theatrical releases of its sequels *Ringu 2* (1999) and *Ring 0: Birthday* (2000) led to the emergence of the J-Horror movement and the eventual rise of the horror wave across Asia.[26] Worldwide, *Ringu* and J-Horror's success led to DreamWorks's

---

24. The film has a similar name to that of Koji Suzuki's horror anthology and is based on Suzuki's short story *Floating Water*. In 2005, Hollywood released a remade version of the film, also known as *Dark Water* (Walter Salles).
25. Nakata's *Ringu* was inspired by Koji Suzuki's 1991 novel of the same name. The film's title was changed to *The Ring* for marketing purposes during its release in the US. To avoid confusion, as the film was remade as *The Ring* in an English version, the title *Ringu* will be used throughout this chapter.
26. The popularity of *Ringu* also led to the release of *Ringu* as a radio drama and two television series in Japan.

182   *Malaysian Cinema in the New Millennium*

remake as *The Ring* (2002).[27] This wave occurred, as horror is a cinematic genre capable of transcending borders; fear as a universal emotion has allowed the horror genre to move cross-culturally (Rafferty 2008) quickly.

The pan-Asian horror film represents the incorporation of contemporary regionalism and globalisation that exists at the intra-, inter-, and extra-textual levels; is successfully exhibited and distributed across the Asian region and globally through Hollywood adaptations; and taps into themes with vital regional and international significance (Knee 2009, 69).[28] In pan-Asian horror cinema, most filmmakers and producers prefer regional and global production approaches because of their cosmopolitan backgrounds and overseas educations. In contrast, the rise and popularity of the internet and digital media have allowed audiences access to local and national cinemas across Asia (Choi and Wada-Marciano 2009). Human and technological capital's transnationality also causes the cultural exchanges illustrated by the current horror boom across Asia. Cinematic representations in pan-Asian horror, however, differ from Hollywood-established patterns. Many ghosts in Asian horror films are created with likenesses and traits similar to Sadako's. Known as the *onryo*, they are females dressed in the long flowing white gown of the burial kimono, have long straight hair, lifeless eyes on an expressionless face, and move by crawling in a spider-like motion. They embody female murder victims returning from the dead as spirits seeking revenge, as seen in Takashi Shimizu's *Ju-on: The Grudge 2* (2003).[29] While the cultural exchanges illustrated by the current horror boom across Asia are caused by the transnationality of human and technological capital, the MDI works are locally funded and produced in Malaysia. Their themes, style, and exhibition patterns, however, carry vital regional and international significance. The thematic content of the MDI filmmakers' horror films differs from the established thematic content of horror films by mainstream Malaysian filmmakers. This difference is through shared themes and collective experience of the MDI filmmakers horror films within the Asian region, their embrace of spiritual themes, and their liberal use of blood and gore.

Many Asian nations possess shared cultural, historical, and social characteristics, as cultural flows have quickly occurred across borders. The influences from such diverse belief systems can be physically seen through the urban architecture

---

27. As *Ringu* became one of the highest-earning Japanese films with a gross estimate of US$6.6 million in Japan, *The Ring* earned US$8.3 million during its opening two weeks in Japan (Xu 2007, 152). *The Ring* remade at US$40 million was directed by Gore Verbinski. The rights to *Ringu* were purchased for US$1.2 million. The film made a gross return of US$130 million domestically and US$230 million internationally.

28. The success of J-Horror, low-budgeted digital filmmaking, and the ability of horror films to cross cultures and borders across Asia led to the emergence of prominent titles from several Asian nations; from South Korea: Kim Ji-Woon's *The Quiet Family* (1998); Thailand: Nonzi Nimibutr's *Nang Nak*; Indonesia: Rizal Mantovani's *Jelangkung* (2001); Singapore: Djinn's *Return to Pontianak* (2001); the Philippines: Chito S. Roño's *Feng Shui* (2004); and Malaysia: Shuhaimi Baba's *Pontianak Harum Sundal Malam*. This list is by no means exhaustive, but these films represent some of the pioneering works from different Asian countries, emerging after the success of *Ringu*.

29. In 2004, Hollywood released a remake of the *Ju-on* series titled *The Grudge*, directed by Takashi Shimizu.

of various shrines, monuments, and sacred buildings; socially through the mainte-
nance of patriarchal and Confucian societies formed by the definition of roles played
by males and females; and politically through systems and policies maintained by
various Asian states. Equally strong in Asia are beliefs in the supernatural, urban
legends, and mythologies of religious diversity and animistic beliefs. Particularly
salient are feng shui (风水) beliefs, luck, numerals, and colours among the Chinese
in Asia. The number 8 and the colour red are believed to bring fortune. In contrast,
the number 4 and the colour black (and/or white) means death.

A significant number of horror films in the current wave of Asian horror, while
extensively influenced by the Noh and Kabuki-influenced *shunen* (revenge) and
kaidan (ghost mystery stories) of *Ringu*, also employ localised elements of religious
beliefs, customs, traditions, and values. Common themes often explored in Asian
horror are curses, urban legends, and mythical tales, such as the masked woman
with a mutilated face in *Carved* (2007), vengeance for a transgression in *Shutter*
(2004), and tales of haunted buildings or houses that represent a displacement of
being 'unreconciled to the past and unconsoled by the present' (Parry 2004, 193),
through spectral nationalities and postcolonial hauntings as captured in *The Maid*
(2005).[30] The horror films of MDI filmmakers are more influenced by folk belief
systems derived regionally.[31] Their works are derived from beliefs in spirits (*semangat*), magic, Buddhism, and Hinduism, practices and religions commonly found in
Asia.[32] This use of regional themes places their works within an 'Asian Cinematic
Imagined Community' of different locations, classes, and nationalities.[33]

As a single entity with an internal diversity homogenised in false unity, 'Asia'
is a literary and psychological construct imposed by the West (Weightman 2002).
Emerging as postcolonial nations after the Second World War, many Asian nations
have experienced the need to deconstruct ideological Eurocentric supremacy and
domination (Said 1978, 43).[34] The collective rise as new nations also meant the col-

---

30. In 2008, Hollywood released *Shutter*, a remake of the 2004 Thai horror film.
31. The belief in horror and the supernatural has always been popular within the Malaysian popular culture.
    Besides horror films, horror has been well established in Malaysian television through popular programmes
    such as *Misteri Nusantara* and *Seekers*, respectively investigating mysterious occurrences in the Asian region
    and paranormal activities. In literature, magazines such as *Mastika* and books such as *44 Cemetery Road*, and
    Hantus and Spells with Survival Guidelines reinforce such beliefs. To demonstrate the popularity of horror and
    the supernatural in Asia, a random search on the internet using the word *hantu* (ghost) generated more than
    27 million hits, websites claiming tales of close encounters with ghosts. Some were equipped with video and
    photographic evidence from Malaysian, Brunei, Indonesia, and Singapore.
32. Asia is the birthplace of Christianity, Islam, Buddhism, Hinduism, Shinto, and various other religions. Pre- or
    non-modern religious and ethical belief systems maintain a stronghold in many Asian nations.
33. Benedict Anderson's concept of the Imagined Community (1991) is borrowed.
34. The need for providing and receiving collective support through protectionism, cooperation, and defence
    through groups such as The Association of Southeast Asian Nations (ASEAN) or EAEC (East Asia Economic
    Caucus) is for trade agreements such as the ASEAN Free Trade Agreement (AFTA). For more details regard-
    ing ASEAN, see http://www.aseansec.org/. For more details regarding EAEC, see Lincoln (2004).

184   *Malaysian Cinema in the New Millennium*

lective need to redefine themselves politically, socially, and economically.[35] This led to rapid urbanisation and mass migration from the rural to urban areas and the problems that came along with it, such as the rise of crime, alienation, and poor living conditions (as discussed in Chapter 3). This anxiety is captured in pan-Asian horror through spirits and ghosts emerging in urban spaces. For example, Mun in *The Eye* (2002), who, after having her eyesight restored through corneal transplants, begins to have visions of ghostly figures that ubiquitously appear around her in very public spaces as in an elevator, in a restaurant, and even during traffic jams.[36] The emergence of spirits and ghosts in modern and contemporary urban spaces is a form of displacement of archaic figures affected by rapid modernisation. These archaic figures are left with no place to go but haunt the cities and buildings that rapidly emerged due to modernisation. In short, these phenomena represent a sense of postcolonial fear in South-east Asian nations such as Malaysia, Singapore, and the Philippines.

Therefore, the horror genre has always been popular among Asian audiences due to its deep rooting in religious and superstitious beliefs and fears arising from postcolonial haunting. Many Asian nations similarly experienced the need to deconstruct ideological Eurocentric supremacy and domination after emerging as postcolonial nations after the Second World War (Said 1978, 43). One of the most shared historical experiences in much of Asia was Japanese atrocities during the Second World War. In Asian horror, this historical trauma is represented through shared tales of haunting and wandering spirits belonging to the victims and perpetrators of such events. These spirits are commonly reported to be sighted in buildings built on cemeteries or old colonial buildings used as the centre of operations during the war, where beheadings, murders, and executions are believed to have taken place. Spirits of Japanese soldiers feature in a hologram-like form in *Sini Ada Hantu* (see discussion above). They are not visible in Singapore's *Haunted Changi*. Their ambiguous presence in haunted buildings represents a haunting memory shared regionally. The horror film deals with social anxieties and repressed memories of conflicts and war. These spirits that continue to emerge in pre-colonial buildings represent the lurking anxiety of the need to eradicate memories of the colonial era. Besides highlighting the memories of conflict and war, the categorisation of horror stories according to race and ethnicity in *Sini Ada Hantu* is a spectre of colonial racism representing lurking anxiety still unresolved (Cheah 2003).

This clash between modernisation and traditionalism is highlighted in *Sini Ada Hantu's hantu nombor ekor*. The group of friends seeking quick financial gains

---

35. Rapid industrialisation after decolonisation has seen Singapore, Hong Kong, Taiwan, and South Korea surge ahead as Newly Industrialised Economies (NIE). The 1990s, in particular, is a time of immense economic growth that led to the rise of the 'Asian Tigers' (as discussed in Chapter 1). As the economy prospered in Asia, other Third World nations in Asia, such as Malaysia, similarly sought NIE status.

36. After *The Eye*'s success, the Pang Brothers made two sequels to the film, *The Eye 2* (2004) and *The Eye 10* (2005). The film was remade with a similar storyline into an Indian version, *Naina* (2005), and in Hollywood as *The Eye* (2008).

summon a female spirit who can supposedly predict winning lottery numbers. In *Seru*, the production crew's trespassing in a jungle is not welcomed. They symbolise modernity's intrusion into the space of traditionalism. The 'migration' of supernatural entities from the rural to the urban is highlighted in *Tolong! Awek Aku Pontianak*. The romantic relationship between Bob and Maya, a *pontianak*, highlights anxieties about traditionalism and modernisation and how the past and present, the old and new, attempt to coexist. This storyline of humans and supernatural entities falling in love is similar to Thailand's *Zombie Love* (1984), and Hong Kong's *A Chinese Ghost Story* (1987) trilogy, *Esprit d'amour* (1983), and *Spiritual Love* (1987).[37] This clash between past and present is represented by Maya and her *pontianak* sister, Liyana, who live in a city apartment. Although Maya and Liyana, who originate from the *kampung*, manage to conceal their real appearances (by inserting a needle into the base of their necks), they are constantly reminded that they are spiritually and territorially 'out of place'. They then promise to return to where they have come from should Aaron Slam Bach, the 'celebrity *bomoh*', help them defeat their evil sister, Nadia, who kidnapped Bob's colleague, Kamal.

The effects of urbanisation and the clash between modernisation and traditionalism are highlighted in the film through Bob. He was recently dumped for not making enough money as he struggles to make ends meet in the urbanised city of Kuala Lumpur. During Bob's first date with Maya, he comments on her 'old-fashioned' handbag as they take a stroll along the streets. This handbag represents how traditionalism—while being 'out of place'—continues to exist in a modernised world. As she attempts to conceal her real age by lying that the handbag belonged to her mother, a motorcyclist snatches it from her. This theft firstly highlights how crime is a common occurrence in public spaces. It also highlights the negative effects caused by modernisation and urbanisation. To survive, certain individuals are driven to committing a crime. Bob is beaten up by the motorcyclist's accomplices and passes out in his attempt to retrieve the handbag. Maya then transforms into a *pontianak* who floats and hovers in the air. She scares them away through her high-pitched shrieks. This act represents the incompatibility between modernisation and traditionalism. This incompatibility is highlighted as Liyana constantly reminds Maya that *pontianaks* and humans do not fall in love. This act of falling in love represents how the laid-back Bob struggles to keep up with modernity through his relationship with Maya. At the end of the film, Maya and Liyana's success at finding true love ultimately lifts the curse. This success allows them to become human again. Bob and Maya's unity represents how *Tolong! Awek Aku Pontianak* goes against the LPF's horror film guideline, which requires the *pontianak*'s demise. The belief in the *pontianak* transforming into a human echoes the superstitious beliefs in themes

---

37. Looking beyond Asia, examples of romance between vampires and humans in a film can be found in *The Vampire Lovers* (1970), *The Hunger* (1983), *Bram Stoker's Dracula* (1992), *Let the Right One In* (2008), and *Twilight* (2008).

of folktales and superstition in pan-Asian horror. This capability of transforming also challenges the understanding and stereotyping of how women in cinema need to be objectified. The *pontianak*'s transformation from a beautiful to a horrifying being illustrates a sense of empowerment as she is in charge of her sexuality and is not subjected to a passive role nor is a source of visual pleasure (Lee 2016). This also goes against the portrayal of women negatively, which stereotypes women as evil beings that are able to destabilise society's normalcy (Lee and Balaya 2016). The portrayal of the *pontianak* as a figure of authority and intelligence, which departs from the stereotyped portrayals of woman as passive and in need of being rescued, also symbolically becomes a castration threat towards the patriarchal structure. The portrayal of the *pontianak* in more positive manners is a trait that is similarly shared by many horror films of other Asian cinemas.

In other similarities between MDI horror and pan-Asian horror, the MDI filmmakers' embracing of non-religious figures resonates with pan-Asian horror film's frequent thematisations of local folk beliefs and superstitions. Non-religious authorities feature in MDI horror films: *bomohs* such as Pakcik Ungkai and the Dukun Dewannga featur in *Seru* and *Susuk*, as the services of a *bomoh* rather a religious figure is sought after in these films. In *Tolong! Awek Aku Pontianak*, Aaron Slam Bach is employed, and in *Sini Ada Hantu*, a former *dukun* is called to rescue Zam from the *hantu pokok pisang*.

These similarities point to the MDI inclination towards pan-Asian horror films, which centralise urban legends, superstitions, and myths. Pan-Asian horror films often involve spirits, folk religion, possession, exorcism, shamanism, and ghosts. In Mr. Vampire films, the Daoist priest performs rites of subduing the *Geong Si* using a combination of religious chants, a handbell, martial arts, joss sticks, and sticking a yellow talisman with Chinese characters on the *Geong Si*'s forehead. Local folk beliefs, exorcism rituals, and religious authorities' representation are found in the Thai horror-comedy *Buppah Rahtree* (2003). In the film, the vengeful spirit of Rahtree refuses to leave an apartment Rahtree is haunting. Mrs. See, the landlord, is becoming increasingly apprehensive as Rahtree's spirit haunts the apartment block's tenants. To avoid losing more tenants, Mrs. See attempts to exorcise Rahtree's spirit. Rahtree's spirit, however, refuses to leave. Rahtree chases away the local police; religious rituals and exorcisms by a false 'Monkey God'-like shaman named Maew, his teacher, Master Tong, two Roman Catholic priests, and a Cambodian shaman remain ineffective.

The use of an excessive amount of blood and the failure of good to defeat evil are common characteristics of pan-Asian horror films such as *To Sir with Love* (2006) and Park Chan-wook's short film *Cut* (2004). The horror films of MDI filmmakers share this characteristic. The majority of horror films by mainstream filmmakers such as Ahmad Idham and Syamsul Yusof closely adhere to LPF guidelines. Their films contain a 'moral message', conclude with good triumphing over evil, and contain hardly any blood. However, while working within the mainstream's

'The Malaysian Decade of Horror'

confines, the MDI filmmakers have chosen to disregard such guidelines. MDI film-makers' horror films contain an incredible amount of blood and do not contain a moral message. In them, good does not necessarily triumph over evil. In *Sini Ada Hantu*, the *hantu pokok pisang*, *hantu nombor ekor*, and *hantu asrama* are not defeated or killed off; the *bomoh* in *Tolong! Awek Aku Pontianak*, *Seru*, and *Susuk* remain undefeated. As discussed, it is difficult to ascertain the moral message in *Seru*, in which the film crew just happen to be at the wrong place at the wrong time. In *Seru* and *Histeria*, the audience is teased into imagining that something widespread and routine could unexpectedly turn into a spine-chilling experience. Schoolgirls serving detention are killed one after another, or film production in the jungle turns into a nightmare. Such events are similar to events in *The Eye*.

As *Seru* belongs to the slasher subgenre, an excessive amount of blood and gore is used. This use of excessive amounts of blood and gore is similar to the films of pan-Asian horror such as *The Wig* (2005), *Red Shoes* (2005), *Cello* (2005), and *Dream Home* (2010). In *Seru*, blood is splattered over the floors and walls at their base camp. The clothing of the characters is soaked with blood, and their faces are often stained with blood.

This shock is reflected in a statement uttered by Jeff, '*Banyaknya darah*' (So much blood), as a point-of-view shot shows him staring at a pool of blood. The violence in *Seru* is directly portrayed and is shocking and appalling. The possessed Sari kills her victims using weapons such as a sword, a knife, or a sickle; she mutilates her hand to escape when she is tied to a kitchen sink using a metal chain and is hit with a plank of wood by Jeff as she rampages uncontrollably. The slashers in *Oldboy* (2003), *The Chaser* (2008), and *I Saw The Devil* (2010) kill in acts of vengeance or are psychologically disturbed. Being from the slasher subgenre, Seru also borrows the plot of Hollywood's *Fallen* (1998) and Singapore's *Haunted Changi*, of an evil spirit possessing a particular individual to kill others. The excessive amount of blood and gore in *Seru* is similar to that of the pan-Asian horror films noted above that depict similar features. The violence portrayed in pan-Asian horror is done directly, with nothing left to the imagination. The scenes are often violent, shocking, and appalling compared to Hollywood's horror films, with acts of decapitation, mutilation, and torture, often filled with blood and gore.

In a second example, although the scenes depicting blood and gore in *Histeria* do not match those in *Seru*, the film does relate in other ways to the films of pan-Asian horror. *Histeria* revolves around tales of haunting in an all-girls' boarding school. The schoolgirls are being punished for pulling a prank, by remaining in detention during the school holidays. They are haunted and killed by a monster known as the *Hantu Raya Jembalang Kuning* during this time. This monster has been unexpectedly evoked by the schoolgirls' chanting of a mantra (spell) summoning it. This act has caused the monster to 'shift its allegiance' to its new owner, Murni, the timid schoolgirl who chanted the mantra. This unexpected turn of events catches its previous owner, the school gardener, by surprise, and his efforts to subdue the monster are in vain. The monster thus begins to kill Murni's friends, as they have often bullied her. This storyline is similar to that of other Asian 'schoolgirl horrors' such as South Korea's *Memento Mori* (1999), Taiwan's *My Whispering Plan* (2005), and Japan's *Wizard of Darkness* (1995).

Murni remains the sole survivor in the monster's killing rampage, as the final scene shows the monster being her *sahabat* (friend). Her transformation from a naive schoolgirl often bullied by her peers into a ruthless killer is similar to Asami in *Audition* (1999), who transforms from an innocent-looking individual into a monstrous figure. Murni, who murders all her friends, is like Asami, who giggles while amputating her lover's (Aoyoma) foot with a wire and tortures him with needles. Both characters are left without any sense of conscience. The end of *Histeria* also leaves the audience in a state of ambiguity: was it Murni who killed all her friends, or the monster? This sense of ambiguity occurs because the film's beginning does not correlate with the end. At the beginning of the film, a doctor has diagnosed Murni with depression, while the policeman investigating the murders strongly believes that Murni is in a healthy state of mind and capable of the murders. At the film's ending, the hospitalised Murni comfortably speaks to the monster at her bedside. The audience needs to speculate if the monster is a figment of her imagination, created due to her psychosis, or if it exists. This method of blending rationality, psychology, and horror in *Histeria* is similar to the method in *Suicide Club* (2001), *A Tale of Two Sisters* (2003), *APT* (2006), and *Blood Ties* (2009).[38] At the end of the films, the audience ponders whether the girls or a supernatural force carried out the murders.

The violence, blood and gore portrayed in these films echo how pan-Asian horror treats these elements: nothing is left to the imagination. The scenes are often directly portrayed using a 'no-holds-barred' method. They are violent, shocking, and appalling as acts of decapitation, mutilation, and torture are unflinchingly portrayed and often saturated with blood and gore. Other examples of scenes in *Histeria* with blood and gore occur when blood profusely sprays from Kerek's neck when Tini slashes her during a heated argument. The possessed Junita bites Cikgu Helmi's head off when he attempts to bed her. Marina is attacked and killed by the *Hantu Raya Jembalang Kuning* in a toilet cubicle, and when Riz's decapitated head rolls onto the floor and it stops at the feet of Murni and Lis. These scenes are captured using gritty and gloomy cinematography and mise-en-scène to tease the audiences psychologically. Tension is built by placing the uncanny within the mise-en-scène without the need to draw attention to it. Characters stuck in a schoolyard, or a jungle, are similar to those in *Dark Water*, where the haunting scenes in an apartment create a sense of claustrophobia.

The use of the haunted school is also similar to pan-Asian horror films such as Thailand's *Dorm* (2006), Hong Kong's *The Haunted School* (2007), and South Korea's

---

38. In 2009, Hollywood released a remake of *A Tale of Two Sisters* as *The Uninvited*.

Whispering Corridors (1998) and *Voice* (2005). These storylines are often based on schoolchildren living in dormitories, sharing urban legends of haunting in schools passed down by individual 'seniors', fears of using toilets alone at night, and students being killed due to certain transgressions. The use of the Malaysian schoolgirl in *Histeria* is also similar to the way schoolgirls are depicted in J-Horror. While the schoolgirls in *Histeria* are not sexualised, except for a short kiss between Lis and Zeta, J-Horror reverses the sexualised fetish of 'cute' or *kawaii* often associated with the Japanese schoolgirl and transforms her into a ruthless and cold-blooded killer. *Histeria* similarly achieves this. The schoolgirl dressed in a school uniform of a *baju kurung*, or skirt and blouse, similarly becomes a feared killer like her Japanese counterpart dressed in a short plaid skirt, socks, flat shoes, and white blouse. Examples of schoolgirls becoming vicious killers in J-Horror films are Ami, who uses her prosthetic machine-gun arm in seeking revenge against the Yakuza-Ninja clan for the death of her brother in *The Machine Girl* (2008); schoolgirls becoming flesh-seeking zombies or a 'Stacy' in *Stacy: Attack of the Schoolgirl Zombies* (2001); cold-blooded killers who turn against friends in order to survive a 'death-game' on a deserted island in *Battle Royale* (2000); or a teenage vampire and Frankenstein in *Vampire Girl vs Frankenstein Girl* (2009). In drawing similarities between *Seru* and *Histeria* with pan-Asian horror cinema, the two films can be similarly categorised as 'gore films'. These films are similar to their pan-Asian counterparts due to the too-graphic and realistic depiction of violence, torture, and murder that reveals bloodshed, bone, flesh, and school and schoolgirl themes.

In short, the horror films of MDI filmmakers depart from their mainstream counterparts by contesting national issues by embedding transnational themes and styles from the pan-Asian wave of cinematic horror. All the horror films produced by MDI filmmakers have endings like those in pan-Asian films. They end with the monster emerging victorious, contain excessive amounts of blood and gore, tease the audience psychologically, and are heavily influenced by folktales and superstition. Pan-Asian themes are easily incorporated within the MDI works because of the existing familiarity and popularity of specific themes and styles in a regional horror film; these make the Malaysian examples easily cross national borders and find a regional audience.

Conclusion: Towards the Fourth Phase of Malaysian Cinema

As the existing scholarship on Malaysian cinema has been inadequate to date, this study of post-2000 Malaysian cinema has added comprehensive and detailed examination to complement existing scholarship. First, the continuous progression of Malaysian cinema as a transnational cinema through three different phases has been explored. The purpose of outlining these three phases was to examine cinema's political economy alongside the nation's corresponding socio-cultural milieu at each given moment. This historical examination outlined Malaysian cinema's progression through a directory of filmmakers and films produced, while critically assessing the national policies that influenced Malaysian cinema at each historical moment. This historical outline showed how Malaysian cinema has consistently been influenced by transnational forces and has progressed from a cinema built for capitalist purposes in the 1940s to the 1960s to the attempted nationalising and Islamisation of cinema in the 1970s to the 1990s, and finally to a cinema heavily influenced by globalisation in the post-2000 period. In short, Malaysian cinema has remained transnational. It progressively shifted from Chinese ownership and control to a Malay-centric industry and eventually to the emergence of a postethnic cosmopolitan cinema of the MDI.

Second, the way the MDI has significantly revived a lacklustre Malaysian cinema has been explored. Even though the ratio of mainstream to MDI films stood recently at approximately 3:1 (see Appendices I and II) and are located at the margins, MDI films managed to surpass mainstream films in aesthetics, subject matter, and themes and gained greater overseas prominence and standing. This transition from the national to the transnational was achieved through the MDI's employment of globally resonant aesthetics, cosmopolitan themes, and transnational funding, production, exhibition, and distribution. While these transnational networks provided opportunities for co-productions, funding, exhibition, and distribution, MDI filmmakers could access these networks because they employed postethnic and cosmopolitan themes. These transnational networks have also provided a space that allowed the MDI to critique national issues. The MDI, therefore, emerged as a platform that contested national issues such as hegemonic state-led policies on

Conclusion

race and ethnicity, culture, and national identity. As a result, MDI films were globally exhibited across Asia, Europe, the Americas, and Africa. In turn, mainstream filmmakers themselves began to emulate this practice of procuring overseas coproductions and exhibition and distribution sites. This progressive transition from the local to the global led by the MDI has allowed Malaysian films to be exhibited and circulated more extensively than ever before.

Third, MDI's emergence alongside a series of state policies and national developments has been investigated. The five national policies are: the New Economic Policy (NEP) (1971), National Culture Policy (NCP) (1971), Vision 2020 (1991), National Development Policy (NDP) (1991), and the Multimedia Super Corridor (MSC) (1996). The three developments in society are: the awakening of civil society, censorship and rampant piracy, and the Malaysian 'New Wave' filmmakers, who have indirectly shaped the MDI.

These policies and developments have introduced *Bangsa* Malaysia, inexpensive DV equipment, and the internet. MDI filmmakers have also contested these policies, which institutionalised class and ethnic segregation, modernisation which led to rapid urbanisation, and the institutionalisation of race and ethnicity in Malaysian cinema. While inexpensive DV equipment allowed for easier filmmaking access, and the internet helped democratise social space, the adoption of *Bangsa* Malaysia and an increased cultural and political awareness has led MDI filmmakers to contest race and ethnicity, national identity. They have also provided a voice for the marginalised. MDI filmmakers employed the *Bangsa* Malaysia and its call to create an egalitarian society and cosmopolitan themes to move 'beyond multiculturalism'.

These cosmopolitan themes have enabled the MDI to intervene in debates about interracial relationships, cultural and ethnic diversity, humanistic philosophies and universalism, and ideals of global justice. Without needing to focus on race and ethnicity, the MDI envisioned creating a nation that is both postethnic and cosmopolitan. It was this postethnic cosmopolitan orientation that distinguished the MDI from the ethnocentricity of mainstream cinema.

Fourth, this book has examined the MDI's incorporation into the mainstream. The subsequent popularity of the MDI also meant its reincorporation into the mainstream. As discussed in Chapter 4, the horror genre has allowed mainstream and independent filmmakers to converge. This shift is comparable to that of the Sixth Generation Chinese filmmakers who continuously shift between the independent and the mainstream or do well within the conventional film establishment. James Lee, Amir Muhammad, and Woo Ming Jin are MDI filmmakers constantly shifting between underground and mainstream filmmaking. Nam Ron, Woo Ming Jin, and James Lee have ventured into the occasional mainstream production through the horror genre. Besides *Seru*, Woo Ming Jin has directed horror features such as *KL Zombi* (2013) and *Zombitopia* (2021). Amir Muhammad is the managing director of Kuman Pictures which produced *Roh*, Tamil-language horror film *Irul: Ghost*

Hotel (2021), and James Lee's *Two Sisters* (2019). As the fourth phase witnesses these independent filmmakers venturing into commercial Malaysian mainstream cinema as filmmakers, producers, or actors, this shift represents their flexibility in shuttling freely between the periphery and the centre and back again. Although their commercial films have been screened in commercial mainstream cinemas across Malaysia, online, and are made available in bootlegged DVD copies, they have continued making independent films. Their incorporation into the mainstream could be paradoxically understood as their acceptance of mainstream filmmaking methods and themes, particularly the acceptance of dominant discourses of race and ethnicity in Malaysian cinema.

Instead of writing off these filmmakers as sell-outs by producing mainstream horror films, we should note that their films diverge from those of the long-time mainstream filmmakers by not entirely conforming to conventional methods and themes. As this book focuses on their horror films, a different opinion is uncovered. MDI filmmakers' horror films are more inclined towards pan-Asian aesthetics and themes, as their films refuse to comply with the guidelines set by the LPF. These films tend towards the employment of characteristics synonymous with pan-Asian horrors such as blood and gore, superstition and myths, and high-level violence. By refusing to conform, MDI filmmakers continue their approach of defying and confronting accepted conventions and norms even when working inside mainstream genres and filmmaking structures.

The developments of the three phases of Malaysian cinema have been explored in this book. In particular, it scrutinises the MDI located within the third phase of Malaysian cinema. Although MDI film production has generally slowed down and ended in 2011, the planned relocation of Da Huang Pictures to Beijing and the incorporation of MDI filmmakers into the mainstream represent the latest development in Malaysian cinema. Speculatively, these developments are shifting Malaysian cinema from the third phase into an unfolding fourth phase. Bearing in mind that Da Huang has been supportive and responsible for the growth and development of Malaysian cinema, their far-sightedness in a planned relocation to Beijing will likely offer new and emerging filmmakers more access to transnational filmmaking opportunities. It is also crucial to explore how this fourth phase is likely to witness the continued democratisation of Malaysia's social and political spaces. Malaysians have become bolder and more intrepid in speaking out against injustice and discrimination. This mindset is likely to be increasingly applied to Malaysian cinema. The resistance to state policies and the democratisation of cinematic rules and regulations could lead to the democratisation of cinematic space and the acceptance of more MDI filmmakers into the mainstream.

Given that MDI filmmakers have now successfully demonstrated that it is possible to resist conforming to the restrictiveness of cinematic rules and guidelines through the horror genre, they need to look for other prospective genres which would enable them to contest from within the confines of mainstream issues related

Conclusion 193

(for example) to politics, race and ethnicity, and marginalised communities. These filmmakers' audacity in calling for an egalitarian society without restriction by race and ethnicity or oppressive cinematic regulations could lead towards the material realisation of the postethnic and cosmopolitan society envisioned in the MDI films and possible changes in the fourth phase of Malaysian cinema. Examples of such films are as *Ola Bola, Jagat, The Journey, Guang, Miss Andy,* and *Lelaki Harapan Dunia.*

The fourth phase of Malaysian cinema therefore holds possibilities for further prospective research. In such a fourth phase, research could focus on how Da Huang Pictures' efforts to penetrate the China market could lead to more opportunities for funding, co-productions, and distribution and exhibition circuits. One such example is Tan Chui Mui's third feature film, *Barbarian Invasion* (2021), which was produced after a decade. Produced by Da Huang Pictures on a budget of RMB1 million (MYR640,000), the film was funded by China's Heaven Pictures and Hong Kong International Film Festival Society under a new initiative known as 'Back to Basic (B2B: A Love Supreme)'. The film was co-produced by Woo Ming Jin and Bianca Baibuena from the Philippines. The film, which also starred Tan Chui Mui as the lead actor, Moon Lee, who is given the opportunity to jumpstart her career as an actress through a martial arts film, went on to win the Jury Grand Prix at the 2021 Shanghai International Film Festival. This win was widely covered by the Malaysian mainstream press.

The fourth phase also witnesses more opportunities for the emergence of new filmmakers as digital filmmaking and the Internet provide easier access to cheaper equipment, better ideas, and a wider platform for transnational funding, co-productions, exhibition, and distribution opportunities. As cinema halls in Malaysia that were shuttered during the various lockdown phases slowly reopen, in 2021, Malaysia's first online cinema service Film Wallet Premium Video-on-Demand (PVOD), an over-the-top (OTT) service offering hundreds of on-demand content from various continents was launched. The availability of online streaming channels such as Astro First, Netflix, and Disney+ Hotstar provide Malaysian films with greater avenues of premiering their films and as exhibition sites with more than 100 Malaysian films such as *Jagat, One Two Jaga* (2018), *Mukhsin, Talentime,* and *Bunohan* made available. *Roh,* which premiered at the 2019 Singapore International Film Festival, was also screened at the 2019 Jogja-Netpac Asian Film Festival, 2020 Udine Far East Film Festival in Italy (July 2020), New York Asian Film Festival 2020, and at the Italy TOHorror Fantastic Film Fest 2020. It has been acquired by New York–based North American distributor of independent and foreign films company Film Movement to distribute theatre and virtual cinema release as well as home entertainment and digital roll-out in North America in the fourth quarter of 2021. In 2021, Chiu Keng Guan released the film *On Your Mark,* a co-production with the Chinese Jiangsu Hao Di Cultural Development, Sports Culture Development Center of the State General Administration of Sports (China Sports Museum),

Figure 5.1: Film poster of *Barbarian Invasion*. Source: Woo Ming Jin.

Figure 5.2: Behind the scenes of *Barbarian Invasion*. Source: Woo Ming Jin.

Conclusion

and Astro Shaw. The film, which stars Chinese actors Wang Yanhui, Marco Zhang, and Gong Beibi, topped the Chinese box office on its opening day with a return of MYR8.7 million (US$2.18 million), going on to collect MYR24 million (US$3 million) over the next two days.

The progress made by Malaysian films in securing transnational opportunities beyond Malaysian shores has led towards more awareness of, and interest and involvement in, the world of filmmaking among Malaysians. For example, the number of film festivals and competitions has increased throughout the years with the emergence of the Kuala Lumpur Eco Film Festival (KLEFF), SeaShorts Film Festival, BMW Shorties, Borneo Eco Film Festival (BEFF), Pesta Filem Kita, Freedom Film Festival, and Petron Vision. In addition, film-related events and screenings are consistently held at independent locations to screen past and present films in Kuala Lumpur, Penang, and Ipoh. In addition to Kelab Seni Filem, The Working Title Film Drinks and Film Lovers of Malaysia are examples of online filmmaking communities on Facebook that actively gather a network and community of filmmakers and film lovers to share information about events, launches, and premieres.

A study about Malaysian cinema should not be confined to the filmmaking activities and filmmakers from Peninsular Malaysia. The fourth phase also presents opportunities for the emergence of 'many first of its kinds' within the realms of Malaysian cinema. The reason is that filmmakers from the East Malaysian states of

Figure 5.3: Film screening of the Freedom Film Festival Georgetown Penang 2018. Source: Brenda Danker.

Sabah and Sarawak have been making their presence felt in the filmmaking industries of Malaysia and worldwide. From Sabah, prominent names such as Nadira Ilana, Soon King Yaw, and Katak Chua have been producing films that best capture the narratives of everyday people and their struggles in that state and abroad. Nadira Ilana's documentary, *Silent Riot* (2013), which documents the Sabah riots of 1986, became the first film from East Malaysia to be awarded the Justin Louis Grant from the Freedom Film Festival. Sabah also plays host to the Kota Kinabalu Film Festival (KKIFF). Its 11th edition in 2020 was disrupted due to the COVID-19 pandemic.

In Sarawak, besides the Sarawak-born Tsai Ming-Liang who is based in Taiwan, and Hollywood filmmaker James Wan, the more prominent filmmakers from Sarawak are Ray Lee and Bjarne Wong. Ray Lee's Dayak film, the first of its kind which featured Malay-Iban dialogue, *Belaban Hidup: Infeksi Zombie* (Fighting for Life: Zombie Infection, 2021), features a Dayak warrior who battles against zombies. This horror-romance film recently won the Best Feature Film award at the 2021 World Film Carnival in Singapore, was nominated for Best Feature Film and Best Horror awards at the International Symbolic Art Film Festival (ISAFF) St. Petersburg, Russia, and received a nomination at the Los Angeles Marina Del Rey Film Festival (LAMDRFF). In Sarawak, Wan Zulfadli Ad-Dinnie Wan Azmi, fondly known as Cikgu Dinnie, won the Best Film by Popular Jury at the Brazilian Film Festival for student work for the short animation *B.B. Batuh Bijanji* (The Promised Stones, 2020). Although Cikgu Dinnie was not born in Sarawak, this full-time teacher and self-taught filmmaker uses his time after school hours to make films using rotoscope animation to inspire his students. Cikgu Dinnie also had his film *Hana* premiere at the 2018 Busan International Kids and Youth Film Festival, South Korea *Cikgu Hana* (2019) and won the National Digital Storytelling Animation award, and *Alice* (2019) was shortlisted as a BMW Shorties' top 10 finalist.

The fourth phase of Malaysian cinema should theoretically intersect with Vision 2020 through the realisation of a postethnic and cosmopolitan nation that looks beyond race and ethnicity in society and films. In 2020, however, the Malaysian society and its cinema remain fragmented. Vision 2020, which failed to materialise, was 'postponed' by Mahathir Mohamad in 2019 to the year 2030, through a new policy dubbed the Shared Prosperity Vision (SPV) 2030. According to SPV 2030, from 2021 to 2030, a government blueprint outlines the steps to be taken in order to increase the incomes of all ethnic groups (especially the *Bumiputera* lower-income group), the hardcore poor, the economically poor, the indigenous communities of *Orang Asal* and *Bumiputeras* of Sabah and Sarawak, the differently abled, youths, women, children, senior citizens, and individuals in economic transition. During this time, Malaysian politics and society continue to search for a postethnic political party that is capable of looking beyond race and ethnicity and does not need to be identified by identity politics. In a speech about SPV 2030 by then prime minister Muhyiddin Yassin in September 2020, he stated how the country continues to be plagued by racial tension and segregation.

Conclusion

In the fourth phase of Malaysian cinema, there has been a rise in the cinematic outputs of Malaysian films in the Malaysian Chinese cinema and within the Malaysian Tamil cinema. From 2012 to 2021, over sixty films from the Malaysian Tamil cinema were released, and more than seventy films are in the Chinese language. This number of releases in both Malaysian Chinese and Tamil cinemas does indeed signify firstly, further progress being made in Malaysian cinema in cinematic output; and secondly, the emergence of Malaysian films that have capably broken away from the Malay-centric films using mostly dialogue in Bahasa Malaysia and featuring stereotypical storylines revolving around the tiresome, 'tried and tested', monotonous films containing melodramatic elements of *suka* (love), *duka* (tragedy), and *jenaka* (humour). While the films released by the Malaysian Chinese and Tamil cinemas do explore the genres of horror, action, comedy, and romance, they contain mostly Chinese or Tamil film titles and dialogues, and feature a mostly mono-ethnic cast. Such efforts signify a departure from the Malay-centric cinema that mostly featured Malay actors, speaking in the Malay language, and highlighting issues faced by the Malay community. An increase in the Malaysian Chinese and Tamil films puts forth the understanding that Malaysia does indeed consist of other ethnic communities and that their issues are also important to discuss within the medium of film. The Chinese and Indian characters in such films also do not speak or behave in stereotypical comical accents or behaviours.

The emergence of the Malaysian Chinese and Tamil cinemas, however, puts forth a question of whether these films are moving in the direction of unintentionally developing into an ethno-centric cinema that departs from the notion of moving 'beyond multiculturalism' and elements of race and ethnicity in the effort to develop a postethnic cosmopolitan cinema. Would the emergence of these films that feature a fully Malaysian Chinese or Indian cast speaking in a single language or dialogue be capable of moving away from the labels of ethnic identity and segregation in a postethnic nation? Or, is the emergence of a Malaysian Chinese and Tamil cinema eventually capable of collectively forming what could be known as the elusive Malaysian cinema? Or, would the fourth phase of Malaysian cinema witness the production of a film that can truly be identified as a Malaysian film capably capturing what Malaysia truly is that is inclusive of and representing the societies of Peninsular and East Malaysia?

As the nation continues to struggle with the COVID-19 pandemic, cinema halls have been shutting down or merging, and film productions are being put on hold. How, then, will Malaysian cinema recover in the post COVID-19 era? These questions are indeed essential to examine and should be further studied. Malaysian cinema has been and is projected to continue being a vibrant cinema industry that is located within a society that is still in search of its unifying national identity, as efforts of moving 'beyond multiculturalism' in the formation of a postethnic cosmopolitan society that looks beyond elements of elements of race and ethnicity continue to be negotiated.

Filmography: Malaysian Films

10 Tahun Sebelum Merdeka (10 Years Before Merdeka). Directed by Fahmi Reza, 2007.

1413 (In *Visits. Hungry Ghost Anthology*). Directed by Low Ngai Yuen. Red Films, 2004.

18? Directed by Danny Lim, 2004.

1957. Hati Malaya (1957. Malayan Heart). Directed by Shuhaimi Baba. Pesona Pictures, 2007.

2 Alam (2 Universes). Directed by Harie Othman and Ed Zarith. Dr. Movie Production, 2010.

A Day in a Beggar's Life. Directed by Ahmad Yazid, 2003.

A Note of Love. Directed by Linus Chung. Nokia, 2007.

A Tree in Tanjung Malim. Directed by Tan Chui Mui. Da Huang Pictures, 2004.

Abang (The Elder Brother). Directed by Rahim Razali. Fleet Communications, 1981.

Abang 92 (The Elder Brother 92). Directed by Rahim Razali. ASA XX, 1993.

Absent Without Leave (不即不离). Directed by Lau Kek-Huat and Chen Jin-Lian. Hummingbird Production, 2016.

Ah Beng Returns. Directed by James Lee. Doghouse73 Pictures, 2001.

Ah Kew the Digger. Directed by Khoo Eng Yow. Da Huang Pictures, 2004.

Ah Lok Café. Directed by Anwardi Jamil. N. Finity Production, 2004.

Ah Yu's Story. Directed by James Lee. Doghouse73 Pictures, 1998.

Aku Bukan Tomboy (I'm Not a Tomboy). Directed by Syamsul Yusof. Skop Productions, 2011.

Aku Kaya The Movie (I'm Rich: The Movie). Directed by Murali Abdullah. Boommax and A&A Pictures, 2003.

Aku Masih Dara (I'm Still a Virgin). Directed by Ahmad Idham. Metrowealth Movies, 2010.

Aku No. 1 (I'm Number 1). Directed by Aznil Nawawi. Boommax and A&A Pictures, 2004.

Aku Tak Bodoh (I'm Not Stupid). Directed by Boris Boo. Primeworks Studios, 2010.

Alamak Toyol. Directed by Ismail Bob Hashim. Metrowealth Movies, 2011.

Al-Hijab. Directed by Pierre Andre. Empat Samudra Plantation, 2011.

Ali Baba Bujang Lapok (Ali Baba and the Broke Bachelors). Directed by P. Ramlee. Malay Film Productions, 1961.

Ali Setan. Directed by Jins Shamsuddin. Amir Communications, 1985.

Amok. Directed by Adman Salleh. Nizarman Productions, 1995.

Anak Bapak (Daddy's Boy). Directed by P. Ramlee. Merdeka Film Productions, 1968.

Anak Halal (Legal Child). Directed by Osman Ali. Tayangan Unggul, 2007.

Anak Pontianak (Pontianak's Child). Directed by Ramon Estella. Malay Film Productions, 1958.

Anak Sarawak (Sarawak Child). Directed by Rahim Razali. ASA XX, 1989.

Anak Setan (Satan's Child). Directed by Omar Rojik. Merderka Film Productions, 1974.

Anak Tunggal (Only Child). Directed by M. Osman. Rozhadi Film Productions, 1980.

Anakku Sazali (Sazali My Son). Directed by Phani Majumdar. Malay Film Productions, 1958.

Anaknya Sazali (Sazali His Son). Directed Jack Ad'Din. Eurofine, 2000.

Anita Dunia Ajaib (Anita in Wonderland). Directed by Omar Mohd Said, 1981.

Antara Dua Darjat (Between Two Classes). Directed by P. Ramlee. Malay Film Productions, 1960.

Antoo Fighter. Directed by Azizi Chunk. Primeworks Studios, 2007.

Anybody Home? (In *Visits: Hungry Ghost Anthology*). Directed by Ho Yuhang. Red Films, 2004.

Apa Kata Hati? (What Does the Heart Say?). Directed by Saw Teong Hin. Tayangan Unggul, 2008.

Apa Khabar Orang Kampung (Village People Radio Show). Directed by Amir Muhammad. Da Huang Pictures, 2007.

Appalam. Directed by Afdlin Shauki. Tayangan Unggul, 2011.

At the End of Daybreak. Directed by Ho Yuhang. M&FC, October Pictures, and Paperheart, 2009.

Awang Spanar. Directed by Z. Lokman. S.V. Productions, 1989.

Awas (Caution). Directed by Abdul Aziz Razak. Medanmas, 1995.

Azimat (Amulet). Directed by Rolf Bayar. Malay Film Productions, 1958.

B.B. Batuh Bijanji (The Promised Stones). Directed by Cikgu Dinnie. SK Temong, Serian, 2020.

Badang. Directed by S. Roomai Noor. Cathay-Keris Films, 1962.

Baik Punya Cilok (Good Action). Directed by Afdlin Shauki. Tayangan Unggul, 2005.

Bakun (The Dam). Directed by Bernice Chauly, 1995.

Bas Konduktor (The Bus Conductor). Directed by Z. Lokman. Zahari Film Productions, 1986.

Barber Kubur (The Graveyard Barber). Directed by Lee Yuen Beng. Adrian Lee's Reel Heritage Series, 2017.

Batu Belah Batu Bertangkup (Haunted Cave). Directed by Jamil Sulong. Malay Film Productions, 1959.

Beautiful Man. Directed by James Lee. Doghouse73 Pictures, 2001.

Before We Fall in Love Again. Directed by James Lee. Da Huang Pictures, 2006.

Belaban Hidup: Infeksi Zombie (Fighting for Life: Zombie Infection). Directed by Ray Lee. Hornbill Films Sdn. Bhd. and Harry Aziz Entertainment Sdn. Bhd., 2021.

Bernafas Dalam Lumpur (Breathing in Mud). Directed by James Lee. Red Films, 2008.

Bini-Biniku Gangster (My Wives are Gangsters). Directed by Ismail Bob Hashim. Metrowealth Movies, 2011.

BoBoiBoy Movie. Directed by Nizam Razak. Animonsta Studios, 2016.

BoBoiBoy Movie 2. Directed by Nizam Razak. Animonsta Studios, 2019.

Bohsia: Jangan Pilih Jalan Hitam (Bohsia: Don't Choose the Wrong Path). Directed by Syamsul Yusof. Skop Production and Primeworks Studio, 2009.

Brainscan: Aku dan Topi Ajaib (Brainscan: Me and the Magical Hat). Directed by Ahmad Idham. Metrowealth Movies, 2008.

Buai Laju-Laju (Swing Quickly). Directed by U-Wei Saari. Lebrocquy Fraser, 2003.

Budak Lapok (Broke Kid). Directed by Anwardi Jamil. Matahari Animation and Production, 2007.

Bujang Lapok (Broke Bachelors). Directed by P. Ramlee. Malay Film Productions, 1957.

Bujang Lapok Kembali Daa (The Return of the Broke Bachelors). Directed by Aziz Sattar. A. Sattar Film Production, 1986.

Bukak Api (Open Fire). Directed by Osman Ali. Pink Triangle Malaysia, 2000.

Bukit Kepong (Kepong Hill). Directed by Jins Shamsuddin. Jins Shamsuddin Production, 1982.

Buli (Bully). Directed by Afdlin Shauki. Primeworks Studios, 2004.

Buli Balik (Bully Returns). Directed by Afdlin Shauki. Primeworks Studios, 2006.

Buloh Perindu (The Magical Bamboo). Directed by B.S. Rajhans. Cathay-Keris Films, 1953.

Bunohan (Bunohan: Return to Murder). Dain Iskandar Said. Apparat Sdn. Bhd., 2012.

Call If You Need Me. Directed by James Lee. Da Huang Pictures, 2011.

Castello. Directed by Bade Azmi. Suhan Movies and Trading, 2006.

Ceritaku Ceritamu (Your Story, My Story). Directed by Saadiah. Anang Enterprise Production, 1979.

Chalanggai (Dancing Bells). Directed by Deepak Kumaran Menon. One Hundred Eye, 2007.

Checkpoint (In *6horts*). Directed and produced by Amir Muhammad, 2002.

Chemman Chaalai (The Gravel Road). Directed by Deepak Kumaran Menon. One Hundred Eye, 2005.

Chermin (Mirror). Directed by Zarina Abdullah. Starry Eye Production, 2007.

Chocolate (In *15Malaysia*). Directed by Yasmin Ahmad. P1, 2009.

Choice. Directed by Patrick Lim, 2003.

Cicakman (Lizardman). Directed by Yusry Abd Halim. KRU Studios, 2006.

Cicakman 2: Planet Hitam (Lizardman 2: Black Planet). Directed by Yusry Abd Halim. KRU Studios, 2006.

Cikgu Hana. Directed by Cikgu Dinnie. SK Temong, Serian, 2018.

Cikgu Romantik (Romantic Teacher). Directed by Z. Lokman. Berjaya Film Trading, 1993.

Cinta (Love). Directed by Kabir Bhatia. Primeworks Studios, 2006.

Cinta 200 Ela (200 Yards Love). Directed by Shadan Hashim. JAS Production, 2002.

Cinta Kita (Our Love). Directed by A. Razak Mohaideen. Berjaya Film Production, 1995.

Cinta Kolestrol (Cholesterol Love). Directed by A. Razak Mohaideen. Metrowealth Productions, 2003.

Ciplak (Pirated). Directed by Khairil M. Bahar. FYI Films, 2006.

Company of Mushrooms. Directed by Tan Chui Mui. Da Huang Pictures, 2006.

Congkak. Directed by Ahmad Idham. Metrowealth Movies, 2008.

Cuci (Wash). Directed by Hans Isaac. Tune Entertainment Group and Tall Order Productions, 2008.

Cun. Directed by Osman Ali. Nuansa and Tayangan Unggul, 2011.

Dalam Botol (In a Bottle). Directed by Khir Rahman. Pengedaran JAS, 2011.

Damping Malam (Night Companion). Directed by Ahmad Idham. Metrowealth Movies, 2010.

202   Filmography

Darah Muda (Young Blood). Directed by Jamil Sulong. S.V. Productions, 1963.

Darah Satria (Knight's Blood). Directed by Aziz Sattar. Indra Film Productions, 1983.

Dari Jemapoh Ke Manchestee (From Jemapoh to Manchester). Directed by Hishamuddin Rais. Picairn Films, Paya Dara Productions, and Halim Sabir Production, 1998.

Dendam Pontianak (Pontianak's Vengeance). Directed by B.N. Rao. Cathay-Keris Films, 1957.

Di Ambang Misteri (At the Threshold of Mystery). Directed by Silver Chung. Cosmos Discovery, 2004.

Do Re Mi. Directed by P. Ramlee. Merdeka Film Productions, 1966.

Don't Play Play. Directed by Liew Seng Tat, 2002.

Dream #1 She Sees A Dead Friend (In *All My Failed Attempts*). Directed by Tan Chui Mui. Da Huang Pictures, 2009.

Dream #2 He Slept Too Long (In *All My Failed Attempts*). Directed by Tan Chui Mui. Da Huang Pictures, 2009.

Dream #3 We Need You to Save the World (In *All My Failed Attempts*). Directed by Tan Chui Mui. Da Huang Pictures, 2009.

Duit Kecil (Loose Change). (In *15Malaysia*). Directed by Johan John. P1, 2009.

Dukun (Shaman). Directed by Dain Iskandar Said. Astro Shaw, 2018.

Dunia Baru The Movie (New World: The Movie). Directed by Yeop Hitler. Primeworks Studios, 2008.

Duyung (Mermaid). Directed by A. Razak Mohaideen. KRU Studios, Primeworks Studios, and Lineclear Motion Pictures, 2008.

Ejen Ali: The Movie (Agent Ali: The Movie). Directed by Usamah Zaid Yasin. WAU Animation, 2019.

Embun. Directed by Erma Fatima. Filem Negara Malaysia and FINAS, 2002.

Enam Jahanam (Six Devils). Directed by P. Ramlee. Merdeka Film Productions, 1969.

Esok Masih Ada (There Is Still Tomorrow). Directed by Jins Shamsuddin. Jins Shamsuddin Productions, 1979.

Esperando Por Felicidad. Directed by Tan Chui Mui. 2003.

Estet (Estate). Directed by Mamat Khalid. Naga VXS, 2010.

Ethirkaalam. Directed by C. Kumar. Super Arts Production, 2006.

Everyday Everyday. Directed by Tan Chui Mui. Da Huang Pictures, 2009.

Evolusi KL Drift (KL Drift Evolution). Directed by Syamsul Yusof. Skop Production and Primeworks Studio, 2008.

Evolusi KL Drift 2 (KL Drift Evolution 2). Directed by Syamsul Yusof. Skop Production, 2010.

Fang. Produced by Red Films and Ground Glass Images. 2005.

Fantasi (Fantasy). Directed by Aziz M. Osman. Teletrade, 1993.

Femina. Directed by Aziz M. Osman. S.V. Productions, 1993.

Fenomena. Directed by Aziz M. Osman. Teletrade, 1990.

First Take, Final Cut. Directed by Ng Tian Hann. Doghouse73 Pictures, 2004.

Flat 3A. Directed by Azhari Mohd Zain. Metrowealth Movies, 2010.

Flower in the Pocket. Directed by Liew Seng Tat. Da Huang Pictures, 2007.

Friday (In *6horts*). Directed and produced by Amir Muhammad, 2002.

Gadoh (Fight). Directed by Brenda Danker and Nam Ron. KOMAS, 2009.

Gangster. Directed by Bade Azmi. Tayangan Unggul, 2005.

Gedebe (Gangster). Directed by Nam Ron. Cipta Films, 2003.

Gemerlapan (Glittering). Directed by A. Razak Mohaideen. Primeworks Studio, 1997.

Geng: Pengembaraan Bermula (Gang: The Adventure Begins). Directed by Nizam Razak. Les' Copaque Production, 2009.

Gerak Khas The Movie (Special Forces: The Movie). Directed by Yusof Haslam. Skop Productions, 2001.

Gerak Khas The Movie 2 (Special Forces: The Movie 2). Directed by Yusof Haslam. Skop Productions, 2002.

Gergasi (Giant). Directed by Dhiresh Gosh. Malay Film Productions, 1958.

Gerhana (Eclipse) (In *15Malaysia*). Directed by James Lee. P1, 2009.

Gerimis (Drizzle). Directed by P. Ramlee. Malay Film Productions, 1968.

Getaran (Vibrations). Directed by V. Nagaraj. S.V. Productions, 2001.

Gila Bola (Football Madness). Directed by Zulkiflee Md. Said. Nizarman Productions, 2003.

GK3 The Movie. Directed by Yusof Haslam. Skop Productions and Five Star AV, 2005.

Gol dan Gincu (Goal and Lipstick). Directed by Bernard Chauly. Red Films, 2005.

Gong. Directed by Sandosh Keshavan. Primeworks Studios, 2006.

Goodbye Boys. Directed by Bernard Chauly. Red Films, 2007.

Great Day. Directed by Chiu Keng Guan. Astro Shaw, 2011.

Guang. Directed by Quek Shio Chuan. Reservoir Production, 2018.

Gubra (Anxiety). Directed by Yasmin Ahmad. Nusanbakti Corporation, 2006.

Halal (Kosher). (In *15Malaysia*). Directed by Liew Seng Tat. P1, 2009.

Hana. Directed by Cikgu Dinnie. SK Temong, Serian, 2017.

Hang Jebat. Directed by Hussain Haniff. Cathay-Keris Films, 1961.

Hang Tuah (The Legend of Hang Tuah) Directed by Phani Majumdar. Malay Film Productions, 1956.

Hantu Bonceng (Pillion Rider Ghost). Directed by Ahmad Idham. Excellent Pictures, 2011.

Hantu Jerangkong (Skeleton Ghost). Directed by K. M. Basker. Malay Film Productions, 1957.

Hantu Kak Limah Balik Rumah (Kak Limah's Ghost Returns Home). Directed by Mamat Khalid. Tayangan Unggul, 2011.

Hantu Kak Limah (Kak Limah's Ghost). Directed by Mamat Khalid. Astro Shaw, Infinitus Production, 2018.

Hantu Kubor (Ghost of the Grave). Directed by Chow Cheng Kok. Malay Film Productions, 1958.

Hantu Rimau (Tiger Ghost). Directed by L. Krishnan, B. N. Rao, and S. Roomai Noor. Cathay-Keris Films, 1960.

Hantu Siang (Day Ghost). Directed by A.R. Badul. Fuego Productions, 1986.

Hanya Kawan (Just Friends). Directed by Harith Iskander. Nizarman Productions, 1997.

Harimau Jadian (Were-tiger). Directed by M. Amin. Cathay-Keris Films, 1972.

Healthy Paranoia (In *15Malaysia*). Directed by Khairil M. Bahar. P1, 2009.

Hikayat Merong Mahawangsa (The Malay Chronicles: Bloodlines). Directed by Yusry Abd Halim. KRU Studios, 2011.

Histeria (Hysteria). Directed by James Lee. Tayangan Unggul, 2008.

House (In *15Malaysia*). Directed by Linus Chung. P1, 2009.

Husin, Mon dan Cit Pakai Toncit. Directed by Mamat Khalid. Tayangan Unggul, 2013.

I Know What You Did Last Raya. Directed by A. Razak Mohaideen. Primeworks Studios and MIG Beats, 2004.

Ibu Mertuaku (Mother In-law). Directed by P. Ramlee. Malay Film Productions, 1962.

Ice Kacang Puppy Love. Directed by Ah Niu. Asia Tropical Films, 2010.

Ilmu Saka (Perennial Knowledge). Directed by M. Osman. Asmah Film Productions, 1984.

I'll Call You Next Century. Directed by James Lee. Doghouse73 Pictures, 2008.

I'm Not Single. Directed by Pierre Andre. Metrowealth Movies, 2008.

Impak Maksima (Maximum Impact). Directed by Ahmad Idham. Excellent Pictures, 2007.

Jagat. Directed by Shanjey Kumar Perumal. Skyzen Studios, 2015.

Jangan Pandang Belakang (Don't Look Behind). Directed by Ahmad Idham. Metrowealth Movies, 2007.

Jangan Pandang Belakang Congkak. Directed by Ahmad Idham. MIG Production, 2009.

Jangan Pandang Belakang Congkak 2. Directed by Ahmad Idham. MIG Production, 2010.

Jangan Tegur (Don't Speak). Directed by Pierre Andre. Metrowealth Movies, 2009.

Jangan Tinggal Daku (Don't Leave Me). Directed by P. Ramlee. Merdeka Film Productions, 1971.

Jasmin. Directed by Jamil Sulong. Kay Film Productions, 1984.

Jimi Asmara (Jimi Love). Directed by Erma Fatima. BNE Studio, 1995.

Jin Notti (Naugthy Genie). Directed by Azhari Mohd Zain. KRU Studios, 2009.

Jogho (Champion). Directed by U-Wei Saari. Gambar Tanah Licin, 1999.

Kaki Bakar (The Arsonist). Directed by U-Wei Saari. Satu Gitu and Gambar Tanah Licin, 1995.

Kala Malam Bulan Mengambang. Directed by Mamat Khalid. Tayangan Unggul, 2008.

Kami (Us). Directed by Patrick Yeoh. Indra Filem, 1982.

Kami: The Movie. Directed by Effendee and Fariza Azlina. Primeworks Studios, 2008.

Kamunting (In 6horts). Directed and produced by Amir Muhammad, 2002.

Karak. Directed by Yusry Abd Halim. KRU Studios, 2011.

Karaoke. Directed by Chris Chong. Tanjung Aru Pictures, 2009.

Kayuh (Cycle). Directed by Soh Sook Hwa, 2009.

Keluarga 69 (Family 69). Directed by P. Ramlee. Merdeka Film Productions, 1967.

Keluarga Si Comat (Comat's Family). Directed by Aziz Sattar. Sabah Filem, 1975.

Kerana Korana (Because of Corona). Directed by Kabir Bhatia. Astro Shaw and Wildsnapper, 2021.

Khurafat: Perjanjian Setan (Superstition: Satan's Pact). Directed by Syamsul Yusof. Skop Production and Primeworks Studio, 2011.

Kinta 1881. Directed by C. L. Hor. Blackbox Pictures, 2008.

KL Gangster. Directed by Syamsul Yusof. Skop Production, 2011.

KL Menjerit (KL Screams). Directed by Bade Azmi. Tayangan Unggul, 2002.

KL Menjerit 2 (KL Screams 2). Directed by Bade Azmi. Tayangan Unggul, 2005.

Kongsi (Syndicate). Directed by Farid Kamil. Metrowealth Movies, 2011.

Konstabel Mamat (Constable Mamat). Directed by Z. Lokman. Perkasa Filem, 1992.

Kopi O Khau Sikit Kurang Manis (Unsweetened Coffee). Directed by Andrew Sia. 2006.

Korban Fitnah (Victim of Defamation). Directed by P.L. Kapur. Maria Menado Production and Cathay-Keris Films, 1959.

Kurus (Days of the Turquoise Sky). Directed by Woo Ming Jin. Greenlight Pictures, 2008.

Malaysian Films 205

Labu dan Labi (Labu and Labi). Directed by P. Ramlee. Malay Film Productions, 1962.
Lady Boss. Directed by A. Razak Mohaideen. Metrowealth Movies and Gitu-gitu Productions, 2005.
Lagi-Lagi Senario (Scenario Again). Directed by Aziz M. Osman. Primeworks Studios and Paradigm Film, 2001.
Lai Kwan's Love (In *Survival Guide Untuk Kampung Radioaktif*). Directed by Tan Chui Mui, 2011.
Laila Majnun. Directed by B.S. Rajhans. Motilal Chemical, 1933.
Laksamana Do Re Mi (Admirals Do, Re and Mi). Directed by P. Ramlee. Merdeka Film Productions, 1972.
Layar Lara (The Sad Screen). Directed by Shuhaimi Baba. Pesona Pictures, 1997.
Lee Chong Wei: Rise of the Legend. Directed by Teng Bee. CB Pictures and Mahu Pictures, 2018.
Leftenan Adnan (Liutenant Adnan). Directed by Aziz M. Osman. Primeworks Studios and Paradigm Film, 2000.
Lelaki Harapan Dunia (Men Who Save the World). Directed by Liew Seng Tat. Everything Films, Volya Films, Flying Moon Filmproducktion and Mandra Films, 2014.
Lelaki Komunis Terakhir (The Last Communist). Directed by Amir Muhammad. Red Films, 2006.
Lips to Lips. Directed by Amir Muhammad. 2000.
Lollipop (In *15Malaysia*). Directed by Nam Ron. P1, 2009.
Los dan Faun (Los and Faun). Directed by Afdlin Shauki. Vision Works, 2008.
Lost (In *6horts*). Directed and produced by Amir Muhammad, 2002.
Love Conquers All. Directed by Tan Chui Mui. Da Huang Pictures, 2006.
Lumpur (Mud) (In *15Malaysia*). Directed by Kamal Sabran. P1, 2009.
M for Malaysia. Directed by Dian Lee and Ineza Rousille. Project M Media, 2020.
Madu Tiga (Three Wives). Directed by P. Ramlee. Malay Film Productions, 1964.
Magika (Magically). Directed by Edry Abdul Halim. KRU Studios, 2010.
Mahsuri. Directed by B.N. Rao. Cathay-Keris Films, 1958.
Main-Main Hantu (Playing with Ghosts). Directed by Junaidi Dahalan and Tommy Chung. Solid Gold Publishers, 1990.
Majidee. Azharr Rudin. 2005.
Makar (Assault). Directed Silver Chung. Cosmos Discovery, 2004.
Malaikat Di Jendela (An Angel at the Window). Directed by Osman Ali. Nuansa, 2001.
Malaysian Gods. Directed by Amir Muhammad. Da Huang Pictures, 2009.
Man From Thailand. Directed by James Lee. Doghouse73 Pictures, 1999.
Mangsa (Victim). Directed by Zalina Mohd Som. Darul Makmur Film Productions, 1981.
Man Laksa. Directed by Mamat Khalid. Tayangan Unggul, 2006.
Mantra. Directed by Azhari Mohd Zain. MIG Productin, 2010.
Maria Mariana. Directed by Yusof Haslam. Skop Production and Primeworks Studio, 1996.
Maria Mariana 2. Directed by Yusof Haslam. Skop Production and Primeworks Studio, 1998.
Masam-masam Manis (Bittersweet). Directed by P. Ramlee. Merdeka Film Productions, 1965.
Masakan Cinta (Love Dish) (In *Survival Guide Untuk Kampung Radioaktif*). Directed by Woo Ming Jin, 2011.

206 Filmography

Mata Hantu (Ghost Eye). Directed by (Miss) Yen and Wan Hai Ling. Produced by Shaw Brothers, 1938–1942.

Mata Syaitan (Satan Eyes). Directed by Hussain Haniff. Cathay-Keris Films, 1962.

Matinya Seorang Patriot (Death of a Patriot). Directed by Rahim Razali. Zsa Holdings, 1984.

Maut (Death). Directed by Bade Azmi. Tayangan Unggul, 2009.

May 13. Directed by Ahmad Mahmud. Ahmad Mahmud Production, 1984.

Me, My Mother and Mosquito. Directed by K. Shanmugan. 2001.

Mekanik (Mechanic). Directed by Othman Hafsham. Syed Kechik Production, 1983.

Menanti Hari Esok (Waiting for Tomorrow). Directed by Jins Shamsuddin. Jins Shamsuddin Productions, 1977.

Meter (In *15Malaysia*). Directed by Benji, Bahar. P1, 2009.

Mimpi Moon (Moon's Dream). Directed by Shuhaimi Baba. Pesona Pictures and Primeworks Studio, 2000.

Min. Directed by Ho Yuhang. 2003.

Miskin (Poverty). Directed by K.M. Basker. Malay Film Productions, 1952.

Misteri Jalan Lama (Mystery of the Old Road). Directed by Afdlin Shauki, 2011.

Mistik. Directed by A. Razak Mohaideen. Metrowealth Movies, 2003.

Momok Jangan Panggil Aku (Phantom Don't Call Me). Directed by M. Jamil. Galaksi Seni, 2011.

Momok The Movie (Phantom: The Movie). Directed by M. Jamil. Galaksi Seni, 2009.

Mona (In *6horts*). Directed and produced by Amir Muhammad, 2002.

Monday Morning Glory. Directed by Woo Ming Jin. Greenlight Pictures, 2005.

Moris Rasik. Directed by Haanim Bamadhai. 2003.

Mr. Cinderella. Directed by Ahmad Idham. Kuasatek Pictures and Skop Production, 2002.

Mr. Os. Directed by A.R. Badul. S.V. Productions, 1987.

Muallaf (The Convert). Directed by Yasmin Ahmad. MHZ Film, 2008.

Mukhsin. Directed by Yasmin Ahmad. Primeworks Studio, 2006.

Munafik. Directed by Syamsul Yusof. Skop Productions, 2016.

Munafik 2. Directed by Syamsul Yusof. Skop Productions and President Productions, 2018.

Musang Berjanggut (Bearded Fox). Directed by P. Ramlee. Malay Film Productions, 1959.

My Father and His Celluloid. Directed by Devan R., 2001.

My Spy. Directed by Afdlin Shauki. KRU Studios, 2009.

Nasi Lemak 2.0. Directed by Namewee. Prodigee Media, 2011.

Nasib Do Re Mi (Do Re and Mi's Fate). Directed by P. Ramlee. Merdeka Film Productions, 1966.

Nasib Si Labu dan Labi (Labu and Labi's Fate). Directed by P. Ramlee. Malay Film Productions, 1963.

Nenek Unta (Grandma Ostrich). Directed by Bernard Chauly. Red Films, 2005.

Ngangkung. Directed by Ismail Bob Hashim. Metrowealth Movies, 2011.

Nien Resurrection. Produced by Young-Jump Animation, 2000.

Niyang Rapik. Directed by Ahmad Idham. Excellent Pictures, 2010.

Nobody's Girlfriend. Directed by Tan Chui Mui. Da Huang Pictures, 2007.

Nodding Scoop (In *Visits. Hungry Ghost Anthology*). Directed by Ng Tian Hann. Red Films, 2004.

Malaysian Films 207

Nujum Pak Belalang (Pak Belalang the Astrologer). Directed by P. Ramlee. Malay Film Productions, 1959.

Ola Bola. Directed by Chiu Keng Guan. Astro Shaw, Golden Screen Cinemas, Multimedia Entertainment Sdn. Bhd., 2016.

One Day. Directed by Anthony Tham. MotionLine Pictures, 2020.

One Future (In *15Malaysia*). Directed by Tan Chui Mui. P1, 2009.

Orang Lichin (Slippery Man). Directed by L. Krishnan. Cathay-Keris Films, 1958.

Orang Minyak (The Oily Man). Directed by P. Ramlee. Malay Film Productions, 1958.

Orang Minyak (The Oily Man). Directed by Jamal Maarif and C.K. Karan. Infohibur, 2007.

Orang Minyak XX (The Oily Man XX). (In *Survival Guide Untuk Kampung Radioaktif*). Directed by Yeo Joon Han, 2011.

Pagar-Pagar Cinta (Love Fences). Directed by A.R. Badul. Sabah Film Production, 1986.

Paloh. Directed by Adman Salleh. Filem Negara Malaysia and FINAS, 2003.

Panas (Heat). Directed by Nurhalim Ismail. Take One Production and Nur TV Production, 1998.

Pancha Delima (Ruby Necklace). Directed by P. Ramlee. Malay Film Productions, 1957.

Pang Yau (Friend). (In *6horts*). Directed and produced by Amir Muhammad, 2002.

Panggilan Pulau (Island Call). Directed by S. Ramanathan. Malay Film Productions, 1954.

Papadom. Directed by Afdlin Shauki. Tayangan Unggul, 2009.

PASKAL: The Movie. Directed by Adrian Teh. Asia Tropical Films, 2018.

Pasrah (Surrender). Directed by Yusof Haslam. Primeworks Studio and Skop Production, 2000.

Pecah Lobang (Busted). Directed by James Lee. Big Pictures Productions, 2008.

Penarik Becha (Trishaw Puller). Directed by P. Ramlee. Malay Film Productions, 1955.

Pendekar Bujang Lapok (Broke Bachelor Warriors). Directed by P. Ramlee. Malay Film Productions, 1959.

Pening-Pening Lalat (Dizziness). Directed by A.R. Badul. Berjaya Film Production, 1990.

Pensil (Pencil). Directed by M. Subash Abdullah. Genius Parade, 2008.

Penunggu Istana (Castle Guardian). Directed by Wan Hasliza. Primeworks Studios, 2011.

Penyair Malam (Night Poet). Directed by Kamal Ishak. Primeworks Studios, 1998.

Perawan Malam (Night Virgin). Directed by Aziz Sattar. Panshah Film Production, 1988.

Perempuan Melayu Terakhir (The Last Malay Woman). Directed by Erma Fatima, 1999.

Perempuan Isteri dan . . . ? (Woman, Wife, and Whore). Directed by U-Wei Saari. Berjaya Film Production, 1993.

Perjanjian Syaitan (Satan's Pact). Directed by S. Sudarmaji. Darul Makmur Film Productions, 1981.

Persona Non Grata. Directed by Azidi Al Bukhary. Nizarman Productions, 2006.

Petaling Street Warriors. Directed by James Lee and Sampson Yuen Choi-Hin. Juita Entertainment, 2011.

Piala Untuk Mama (Trophy for Mama). Directed by Bernard Chauly. Ten on Ten Pictures, 2003.

Pisau Cukur (Gold Diggers). Directed by Bernard Chauly. Red Films and Primeworks Studio, 2009.

Pontianak. Directed by B.N. Rao. Cathay-Keris Films, 1957.

208 Filmography

Pontianak. Directed by Roger Sutton. Hamid Bond Organisation and Kobe Trading Company, 1975.

Pontianak Gua Musang (Pontianak of Gua Musang). Directed by B. N. Rao. Cathay-Keris Films, 1964.

Pontianak Harum Sundal Malam (Pontianak. Scent of the Tuber Rose). Directed by Shuhaimi Baba. Pesona Pictures, 2004.

Pontianak Harum Sundal Malam 2 (Pontianak. Scent of the Tuber Rose 2). Directed by Shuhaimi Baba. Pesona Pictures, 2005.

Pontianak Kembali (Pontianak Returns). Directed by B.N. Rao. Cathay-Keris Films, 1963.

Pontianak Menjerit (Screaming Pontianak). Directed by Yusof Kelana. ME Communication and Skop Production, 2005.

Possessed. Directed by Bjrane Wong. Hock Star Entertainment Industry, 2006.

Potong Saga (In *15Malaysia*). Directed by Ho Yuhang. P1, 2009.

Potret Mistik (The Mystic Potrait). Directed by A. Razak Mohaideen. Metrowealth Movies and Primeworks Studios, 2004.

Prebet Sapu (Hail, Driver!). Directed by Muzzamer Rahman. Le Mediator Studio, Kristal Azmir Sdn Bhd dan Konda Kondi Studio, 2020.

Puaka (Demon). Directed by M. Amin. Cathay-Keris Films, 1970.

Puaka (Demon). Directed by Omar Rojik. Merdeka Film Production, 1974.

Puaka Tebing Biru (Demon of Tebing Biru). Directed by Osman Ali. Tayangan Unggul, 2007.

Punggok Rindukan Bulan (This Longing). Directed by Azharr Rudin. Da Huang Pictures, 2008.

Pusaka Pontianak (The Accursed Heritage). Directed by Ramon Estella. Malay Film Productions, 1964.

Putera (Prince). Directed by Zulkeflie M. Osman. J.D. Productions, 1995.

Puteri (Princess). Directed by Rahim Razali. ASA XX Film Productions, 1987.

Puteri Gunung Ledang (Princess of Mount Ledang). Directed by Saw Teong Hin. Enfiniti Productions, 2004.

Putih. Directed by Rashid Sibir. Fine Animation, 2001.

Qaisy dan Laila (Qaisy and Laila). Directed by Raja Ahmad Alauddin. Nizarman Productions and Serangkai Filem, 2005.

Rabun (My Failing Eyesight). Directed by Yasmin Ahmad. Primeworks Studios, 2003.

R.A.H.M.A.N. Directed by Zan Azlee. Fat Bidin Media, 2004.

Rahsia (Secret). Othman Hafsham. Cinematic Pictures, 1987.

Rain Dogs. Directed by Ho Yuhang. Focus Films, 2006.

Raining Amber. Directed by Azharr Rudin. 2005.

Raja Bersiong (Fanged King). Directed by Jamil Sulong. Malay Film Productions, 1968.

Raja Bersiong (Fanged King). Directed by Ramon Estella. Cathay-Keris Film, 1963.

Ranjau Sepanjang Jalan (The Thorny Road). Directed by Jamil Sulong. Kay-Sarimah Filem, 1983.

Rasuk (Possess). Directed by S. Baldev Singh. Sri Saheb Production and Merpati White Entertainment, 2011.

Rasukan Ablasa (Ablasa Possession). Directed by A. Razak Mohaideen. Primeworks Studios and Line Clear Motion Pictures, 2009.

Redha (Beautiful Pain). Directed by Tunku Mona Riza. Current Pictures Sdn. Bhd., 2016.

Malaysian Films 209

Red Haired Tumbler di Malaya (Red Haired Tumbler in Malaya). Directed by Eddie Pak. 2020 Productions, 1994.

Remp-It. Directed by Ahmad Idham. Metrowealth Movies, 2006.

Ringgit Kasorrga (High Society). Directed by Shuhaimi Baba. Pesona Pictures, 1995.

Roh (Soul). Directed by Emir Ezwan. Kuman Pictures, 2000.

Roh Membela (Defending Soul). Directed by B.N. Rao. Malay Film Productions, 1955.

Rojak (In *15Malaysia*). Directed by Suleiman Brothers. P1, 2009.

Room to Let. Directed by James Lee. Doghouse73 Pictures, 2002.

Rozana Cinta '87 (Rozana's Love '87). Directed by Nasir Jani. Amircom, 1987.

Sabarudin Tukang Kasut (Sabarudin the Cobbler). Directed by P. Ramlee. Merdeka Film Productions, 1966.

Salon (Saloon). Directed by Woo Ming Jin. Primeworks Studios, 2005.

Sanctuary. Directed by Ho Yuhang. Doghouse73 Pictures, 2004.

Santau (Curse). Directed by Azhari Mohd Zain. Metrowealth Movies, 2009.

Sayang Salmah (Loving Salmah). Directed by Mahadi J. Murat. Primeworks Studios and Perkasa Filem, 1995.

Sayang You Can Dance. Directed by Bjarne Wong. Hock Star Entertainment Industry, 2009.

Seed of Darkness. Directed by Michael Chuah. Evo Pictures, 2006.

Selamat Tinggal Kekasihku (Farewell My Lover). Directed by L. Krishnan. Cathay-Keris Films, 1955.

Sell Out! Directed by Yeo Joon Han. Astro Shaw, 2009.

Selubung (Veil of Life). Directed by Shuhaimi Baba. Identity Entertainers, 1992.

Seman. Directed by Mansor Puteh. Unity Filem, 1986.

Sembilu (Heartache). Directed by Yusof Haslam. Skop Productions, 1994.

Sembilu 2005 (Heartache 2005). Directed by Yusof Haslam. Skop Production, 2005.

Semerah Padi (Semerah Padi Village). Directed by P. Ramlee. Malay Film Productions, 1956.

Senario Asam Garam (Senario. Taste of Life). Directed by Hatta Azad Khan. MIG Production, 2010.

Senario Lagi (Senario. Again). Directed by Aziz M. Osman. Primeworks Studios and Paradigm Film, 2000.

Senario Pemburu Emas Yamashita (Senario. Hunter of Yamashita's Gold). Directed by Aziz M. Osman. Primeworks Studios, 2006.

Senario: The Movie Ops Pocot. Directed by Ismail Bob Hashim. Metrowealth Movies, 2011.

Senario: the Movie. Directed by Aziz M. Osman. Paradigm Film and Grand Brilliance, 1999.

Senario: The Movie: Episode 1. Directed by Ahmad Idham. MIG Production, 2008.

Senario: The Movie: Episode 2. Directed by Ahmad Idham. MIG Production, 2009.

Senario XX. Directed by Aziz M. Osman. Primeworks Studios, 2005.

Seniman Bujang Lapok (Broke Bachelors Artists). Directed by P. Ramlee. Malay Film Productions, 1961.

Senjakala (Twilight). Directed by Ahmad Idham. Excellent Pictures and MIG Production, 2011.

Sepet (Chinese Eyes). Directed by Yasmin Ahmad. MHZ Film, 2005.

Sepi (Lonely). Directed by Kabir Bhatia. Primeworks Studios, 2008.

Serangan Orang Minyak (Attack of the Oily Man). Directed by L. Krishnan. Cathay-Keris Films, 1958.

210   Filmography

Sergeant Hassan. Directed by Alberto Avellana. Malay Film Productions, 1958.

Seru (The Calling). Directed by Pierre Andre and Woo Ming Jin. Tayangan Unggul, 2011.

Seruan Merdeka (Call of Freedom). Directed by B. S. Rajhans. Malayan Arts Production, 1946.

Sesudah Subuh (After Dawn). Directed by P. Ramlee. Merdeka Film Production, 1967.

Setem (Stamp). Directed by Kabir Bhatia. Tayangan Unggul, 2009.

Setinggan (Squatters). Directed by Aziz Sattar. Indra Filem, 1981.

Si Badul. Directed by Aziz Sattar. Sabah Film Productions, 1979.

Si Jantung Hati (Heartthrob). Directed by A.R. Badul. Sabah Film Production, 1986.

Sifu dan Tongga (Sifu and Tongga). Directed by A. Razak Mohaideen. Primeworks Studios and Lineclear Motion Pictures, 2008.

Silat Lagenda (Legendary Silat). Directed by Hassan Abdul Muthalib. Peninsula Pictures, 1998.

Silent Riot. Directed by Nadila Ilana. Big Pictures Production and Pusat Komas, 2013.

Sini Ada Hantu (Here Got Ghost). Directed by James Lee. Astro Shaw, 2011.

Siti Subaidah. Directed by B. N. Rao. Maria Menado Production and Cathay-Keris Films, 1961.

Sitora Harimau Jadian (Sitora the Were-tiger). Directed by P. Ramlee. Merdeka Film Productions, 1964.

S'kali (Altogether). Directed by Arivind Abraham. Perantauan Enterprise and Asa'ad Entertainment Network, 2006.

Skrip 7707 (Script 7707). Directed by A. Razak Mohaideen. Primeworks Studios and Lineclear Motion Pictures, 2009.

Slovak Sling (In *15Malaysia*). Directed by Woo Ming Jin. P1, 2009.

Snipers. Directed by James Lee. Doghouse73 Pictures, 2001.

Soal Hati (Question of the Heart). Directed by Othman Hafsham. Serangkai Holding, 2000.

Soalnya Siapa? (Question is Who?). Directed by Othman Hafsham. Serangkai Filem, 2002.

Sometimes Love is Beautiful. Directed by James Lee. Doghouse73 Pictures, 2005.

South of South. Directed by Tan Chui Mui. Da Huang Pictures, 2005.

Spinning Gasing. Directed by Teck Tan. Niche Film and Spinning Gasing Films, 2000.

Suatu Ketika (Once Upon A Time). Directed by Prakash Murugiah. Kash Pictures Sdn. Bhd. and GSC Movies, 2019.

Subak. Directed by Justin Ong. NHK, KBS, and Caldecott Productions, 2008.

Suci Dalam Debu (Pure in Dust). Directed by Zukleflie M. Osman. Aarti Filem, 1992.

Sumo-lah (Sumo). Directed by Afdlin Shauki. Vision Works, 2007.

Sumpah Orang Minyak (Oily Man's Curse). Directed by P. Ramlee. Malay Film Productions, 1958.

Sumpah Pontianak (Pontianak's Curse). Directed by B. N. Rao. Cathay-Keris Films, 1958.

Sunflowers. Directed by James Lee. Doghouse73 Pictures, 2000.

Survivor. Directed by James Lee. Doghouse73 Pictures, 1999.

Susuk (Charm Needles). Directed by Amir Muhammad and Naeim Ghalili. Primeworks Studio, 2008.

Syaitan (Satan). Directed by Bade Azmi. Tayangan Unggul, 2007.

Syukur 21 (Praise 21). Directed by Eddie Pak. Metrowealth Movies, 2000.

Talentime. Directed by Yasmin Ahmad. Primeworks Studio, 2009.

Taman di dalam Sinkiku. Directed by Azharr Rudin, 2005.

Tentang Bulan (About the Moon). Directed by Ahmad Idham. Metrowealth Movies, 2006.

Tetangga (Neighbour). Directed by Desmond Ng. Ten on Ten Pictures, 2003.

The Amber Sexalogy. Directed by Azharr Rudin. 2006.

The Beautiful Washing Machine. Directed by James Lee. Doghouse73 Pictures, 2004.

The Big Durian. Directed by Amir Muhammad. Doghouse73 Pictures, 2003.

The Bird House. Directed by Khoo Eng Yow. Red Films, 2006.

The Elephant and the Sea. Directed by Woo Ming Jin. Greenlight Pictures, 2007.

The Journey. Directed by Chiu Keng Guan. Woohoo Pictures Production, 2014.

The Little Dhoby of Penang. Directed by Lee Yuen Beng. Adrian Lee's Reel Heritage Series, 2018.

The Need for Rites (In *All My Failed Attempts*). Directed by Tan Chui Mui. Da Huang Pictures, 2009.

The Pirate and the Emperor's Ship. Directed by Khoo Eng Yow. Da Huang Pictures, 2008.

The Red Kebaya. Directed by Oliver Knott. L'Agenda Production, 2006.

The Son (In *15Malaysia*). Directed by Desmond Ng. P1, 2009.

The Son. Directed by Bryant Low. Ten on Ten Pictures, 2003.

The Tiger Factory. Directed by Woo Ming Jin. Greenlight Pictures, 2010.

The Tree (In *15Malaysia*). Directed by Amir Muhammad. P1, 2009.

The Year of Living Vicariously. Directed by Amir Muhammad. Miles Films, 2005.

Things We Do When We Fall in Love. Directed by James Lee. Da Huang Pictures, 2007.

Think Positive! Directed by James Lee. Doghouse73 Pictures, 1999.

Tiada Esok Bagimu (No Tomorrow). Directed by Jins Shamsuddin. Jins Shamsuddin Productions, 1979.

Tiga Abdul (Three Abduls). Directed by P. Ramlee. Malay Film Productions, 1964.

Tiger Woohoo! Directed by Chiu Keng Guan. Astro Shaw, 2010.

To Say Goodbye. Directed by Tan Chui Mui. Da Huang Pictures, 2009.

Tokyo Magic Hour. Directed by Amir Muhammad. Doghouse73 Pictures, 2005.

Tolong! Awek Aku Pontianak (Help! My Girlfriend is a Pontianak). Directed by James Lee. Tayangan Unggul, 2011.

Toyol. Directed by Malik Selamat. Sabah Film Production, 1981.

Toyol Nakal (Mischievous Toyol). Directed by Z. Lokman. Artistik Pictures, 2011.

Trauma. Directed by Aziz M. Osman. Primeworks Studios and Paradigm Film, 2004.

Tsu Feh Sofia. Directed by Rahim Razali. ASA XX, 1986.

TV Tiger's Lee Ah Seng Reports on the Malaysian Rare Earth Issue Report 1. (In *Survival Guide Untuk Kampung Radioaktif*). Directed by Tan Chui Mui, Liew Seng Tat, Woo Ming Jin, and Yeo Joon Han, 2011.

TV Tiger's Lee Ah Seng Reports on the Malaysian Rare Earth Issue Report 2. (In *Survival Guide Untuk Kampung Radioaktif*). Directed by Tan Chui Mui, Liew Seng Tat, Woo Ming Jin, and Yeo Joon Han, 2011.

TV Tiger's Lee Ah Seng Reports on the Malaysian Rare Earth Issue Report 3 - FINAL (In *Survival Guide Untuk Kampung Radioaktif*). Directed by Tan Chui Mui, Liew Seng Tat, Woo Ming Jin, and Yeo Joon Han, 2011.

Tujuh Perhentian (Seven Stops). Directed by A. Razak Mohaideen. MIG Beats, Metrowealth Movies and Primeworks Studios, 2004.

Upin dan Ipin (Upin and Ipin). Produced by Les' Copaque Production, 2007.

Upin & Ipin: Keris Siamang Tunggal (Upin & Ipin: The Lone Gibbon Keris). Directed by Adam Amiruddin, Syed Nurfaiz Khalid Syed Ibrahim, Ahmad Razuri Roseli. Les' Copaque Production, 2019.

V3 Samseng Jalanan (V3 Street Thugs). Directed by Farid Kamil. MIG Production, 2010.

Waiting for Love. Directed by James Lee. Da Huang Pictures, 2007.

Waiting for Them (In *Visits. Hungry Ghost Anthology*). Directed by James Lee. Red Films, 2004.

Waris Jari Hantu (Heir of the Ghost Finger). Directed by Shuhaimi Baba. Pesona Pictures and Primeworks Studio, 2007.

Welcome to Kampung Radioaktif (Welcome to Radioactive Village). (In *Survival Guide Untuk Kampung Radioaktif*). Directed by Liew Seng Tat, 2011.

When Buddha Touched Tamaole. Directed by Anna Har. Red Films, 2003.

Wind Chimes. Directed by Deepak Kumaran Menon, 2004.

Woman on Fire looks for Water. Directed by Woo Ming Jin. Greenlight Pictures, 2009.

XX Ray. Directed by Aziz M. Osman. Nizarman Productions, 1992.

XX Ray 2. Directed by Aziz M. Osman. Nizarman Productions, 1995.

Yassin. Directed by Kamarul Ariffin. Kay Filem, 1988.

Your World, My World. Directed by Low Ngai Yuen. Red Films, 2003.

Zombie Kampung Pisang (Zombie of Pisang Village). Directed by Mamat Khalid. Tayangan Unggul, 2007.

Filmography: Non-Malaysian Films

[Rec]. Directed by Jaume Balagueró and Paco Plaza. Castelao Producciones, Filmax, and Television Española, 2007.

2046. Directed by Wong Kar-Wai. Jet Tone Films, Shanghai Film Group Corporation, and Orly Films, 2004.

28 Days Later. Directed by Danny Boyle. DNA Films and British Film Council, 2002.

30 Days of Night. Directed by David Slade. Columbia Pictures, Ghost House Pictures, and Dark Horse Entertainment, 2007.

A Chinese Ghost Story. Directed by Ching Siu-Tung. Cinema City Film Productions and Film Workshop, 1987.

A Tale of Two Sisters. Directed by Kim Jee-woon. B. O. M. Film Productions Co., and Masulpiri Films, 2003.

Alien. Directed by Ridley Scott. Brandywine Productions and Twentieth Century-Fox Productions, 1979.

Ang Pagdadalaga ni Maximo Oliveros. Directed by Auraeus Solito. Cinemalaya Foundation and UFO Pictures, 2005.

Anna and the King. Directed by Andy Tennant. Fox 2000 Pictures, and Lawrence Bender Productions, 1999.

Another Girl Another Planet. Directed by Michael Almereyda. Miramax, 1992.

APT. Directed by Ahn Byeong-ki. Toilet Pictures, 2006.

Arisan! Directed by Nia Di Nata. Kalyana Shira Film, 2003.

Arisan! 2. Directed by Nia Di Nata. Add Word Productions, Ezy Productions, and Kalyana Shira Film, 2011.

Audition. Directed by Takashi Miike. AFDF, Creators Company Connection, and Omega Project, 1999.

Back to the Future. Directed by Robert Zemeckis. Universal Pictures and Amblin Entertainment, 1985.

Battle Royale. Directed by Kinji Fukasaku. AM Associates, Battle Royale Production Committee, Fukasaku-gumi, 2000.

Be with Me. Directed by Eric Khoo. Zhao Wei Films (I) and Infinite Frameworks Pte. Ltd., 2005.

Ben Hur. Directed by William Wyler. Metro-Goldwyn-Myer, 1959.

Berbagi Suami. Directed by Nia Di Nata. Kalyana Shira Film, 2006.

Bicycle Thieves. Directed by Vittorio De Sica. Produzioni De Sica, 1948.

214   Filmography

Blood ties. Directed by Chai Yee Wei. Oak 3 Films, 2009.

Boxing Day. Directed by Kriv Stender. Horrorshow, Rising Sun Pictures, and Smoking Gun Productions, 2007.

Bram Stoker's Dracula. Directed by Francis Ford Coppola. American Zoetrope, Columbia Pictures Corporation, and Osiris Films, 1992.

Buppah Rahtree. Directed by Yuthlert Sippapak. Mahagan Films Co. Ltd., Mangpong Public Co. Ltd., and Nakomthai Picture Co. Ltd., 2003.

Ca-bau-kan. Directed by Nia Di Nata. Kalyana Shira Film, 2002.

Carved. Directed by Kôji Shiraishi. Tornado Film, For-side.com, and Twin Co. Ltd., 2007.

Cat People. Directed by Jacques Tourneur. RKO Radio Pictures, 1942.

Cello. Directed by Lee Woo-cheol, 2005.

Click in the Stories About Love. Directed by Cheah Chee Kong, 2000.

Cloverfield. Directed by Matt Reeves. Paramount Pictures and Bad Robot, 2008.

Crazy Safari. Directed by Billy Chan. Win's Movie Production Ltd. and Samico Films Production Company Ltd., 1991.

Dark Water. Directed by Hideo Nakata. Honogurai mizu no Soko kara Seisaku Iinkai, Kadokawa Shoten Publishing Co., and Nippon Television Network Corporation (NTV), 2002.

Days of Being Wild. Directed by Wong Kar-Wai. In-Gear Film, 1990.

Dorm. Directed by Songyos Sugmakanan. Hub Ho Hin Films, 2006.

Dracula. Directed by Tod Browning. Universal Pictures, 1931.

Dream Home. Directed by Pang Ho-Cheung. 852 Films and Making Film, 2010.

Durian Durian. Directed by Fruit Chan. Canal+, Golden Network, and Nice Top Entertainment, 2000.

Eliana, Eliana. Directed by Riri Riza. I Sinema, Miles Films, and Prima Entertainment, 2002.

Encounters of the Spooky Kind. Directed by Sammo Hung Kam-Bo. Bo Ho Film Company Ltd., and Golden Harvest Company, 1980.

Esprit d'amour. Directed by Ringo Lam. Cinema City Film Productions, 1983.

Feng Shui. Directed by Chito S. Roño. ABS-CBN Film Productions and Star Cinema Productions, 2004.

Final Destination. Directed by James Wong. New Line Cinema, Zide-Perry Productions, and Hard Eight Pictures, 2000.

Final Destination 2. Directed by David R. Ellis. New Line Cinema and Zide-Perry Productions, 2003.

Final Destination 5. Directed by Steven Quale. New Line Cinema, Practical Pictures, and Parallel Zide, 2011.

Friday the 13th. Directed by Sean S. Cunningham. Paramount Pictures, Georgetown Productions Inc., and Sean S. Cunningham Films, 1980.

Flash Point. Directed by Wilson Yip. Well Go USA Entertainment, 2007.

Godzilla, King of the Monsters! Directed by Ishirô Honda and Terry O. Morse. Toho Company and Jewell Enterprise Inc., 1956.

Going Home (In *Three*). Directed by Peter Chan. Applause Pictures, B.O.M. Film Productions Co., and Cinemasia, 2002.

Haunted Changi. Directed by Andrew Lau. Mythopolis Pictures, 2010.

Haura. Directed by Abdul Nizam, 2000.

Non-Malaysian Films

Hostel. Directed by Eli Roth. Hostel LLC, International Production Company, and Next Entertainment, 2005.

I Don't Want to Sleep Alone. Directed by Tsai Ming-Liang. Centre National de la Cinématographie (CNC), Dama Orchestra Malaysia, and EMI Music Taiwan, 2006.

I Know What You Did Last Summer. Directed by Jim Gillespie. Columbia Pictures Corporation, Mandalay Entertainment, and Summer Knowledge LLC, 1997.

I Saw The Devil. Directed by Kim Jee-woon. Softbank Ventures, Showbox/Mediaplex, and Peppermint & Company, 2010.

I Was A Teenage Frankenstein. Directed by Herbert L. Strock. Santa Rosa Productions, 1957.

I Was A Teenage Werewolf. Directed by Gene Fowler Jr. Sunset Productions (III), 1957.

Ichi the Killer. Directed by Takashi Miike. Omega Project, Omega Incott Inc., and Emperor Multimedia Group, 2001.

Infection. Directed by Masayuki Ochiai. Aozora Investments, Entertainment Farm, and Geneon Entertainment, 2004.

Infernal Affairs. Directed by Andrew Lau and Alan Mak. Media Asia Films and Basic Pictures, 2002.

In Public. Directed by Jia Zhang Ke. Sidus Pictures, 2001.

In the Mood for Love. Directed by Wong Kar-Wai. Block 2 Pictures, Jet Tone Production, and Paradis Films, 2000.

Jelankung. Directed by Rizal Mantovani and Jose Purnomo. Rexcinema Production, 2001.

Ju-on: The Grudge. Directed by Takashi Shimizu. Pioneer LDC, Nikkatsu, and Oz Company, 2002.

Ju-on: The Grudge 2. Directed by Takashi Shimizu. Pioneer LDC, Nikkatsu, and Oz Company, 2003.

Jurassic Park. Directed by Steven Spielberg. Amblin Entertainment, 1993.

L'Arrivée d'un train en gare de La Ciotat. Directed by Auguste Lumière and Louis Lumière. Lumière See, 1896.

Le Manoir du diable. Directed by Georges Méliès. Georges Méliès and Star-Film, 1896.

Let the Right One In. Directed by Tomas Alfredson. EFTI, Sandrew Metronome Distribution Sverige AB, and Filmpool Nord, 2008.

Life of Pi. Directed by Ang Lee. Fox 2000 Pictures, Dune Entertainment, Ingenious Media and Haishang Films, 2012.

Manila Skies. Directed by Raymond Red. Filmex Productions, Ignite Media, and Pacific Film Partners, 2009.

Mee Pok Man. Directed by Eric Khoo. 27 Productions, 1996.

Memento Mori. Directed by Kim Tae-Yong and Min Kyu-Dong, 1999.

Memories (In *Three*). Directed by Kim Ji-woon. Applause Pictures, B.O.M. Film Productions Co., and Cinemasia, 2002.

Mr. Vampire. Directed by Ricky Lau. Bo Ho Film Company Ltd., and Golden Harvest Company, 1985.

My Whispering Plan. Directed by Arthur Chu Yu-Ning. Oxygen Films, 2005.

Mystics in Bali. Directed by H. Tjut Djalil. Pusat Perusahaan Film and Video Tape Corp., 1981.

Naina. Directed by Shripal Morakhia. iDream Productions, 2005.

Nang Nak. Directed by Nonzee Nimibutr. Tai Entertainment, 1999.

216 Filmography

No Day Off. Directed by Eric Khoo. Screener, 2006.

Nosferatu. Directed by F. W. Murnau. Jofa-Atelier Berlin-Johannisthal and Prana-Film GmbH, 1922.

Number 9. Directed by Erin Davis and Nathan Edmondson, 2010.

Oldboy. Directed by Park Chan-wook. Egg Films and Show East, 2003.

One Missed Call. Directed by Takashi Miike. Kadokawa–Daiei Eiga K.K., 2003.

Pather Panchali. Directed by Satyajit Ray. Government of West Bengal, 1955.

Pengabdi Setan. Directed by Sisworo Gautama Putra. Rapi Films, 1982.

Platform. Directed by Jia Zhang Ke. Artcam International, Bandai Entertainment Inc., and Hu Tong Communications, 2000.

Postman. Directed by He Jianjun. United Frontline, 1995.

Premonition. Directed by Norio Tsuruta. Entertainment Farm, Fella Pictures, and Geneon Entertainment, 2004.

Psycho. Directed by Alfred Hitchcock. Shamley Productions, 1960.

Public Toilet. Directed by Fruit Chan. Digital Nega and Nicetop Independent Ltd., 2002.

Pulse. Directed by Kiyoshi Kurosawa. Daiei Eiga, Hakuhodo, Imagica, 2001.

Quarantine. Directed by John Erick Dowdle. Andale Pictures, Screen Gems, and Vertigo Entertainment, 2008.

Raise the Red Lantern. Directed by Zhang Yimou. ERA International, China Film Co., Century Communications and Salon Films, 1991.

Red Dragon. Directed by Brett Ratner. Universal Pictures, Dino De Laurentiis Company, and Metro-Goldwyn-Mayer (MGM), 2002.

Red Shoes. Directed by Kim Yong-gyun. Thousand Year Films, 2005.

René Besson's Boxes. Directed by Daniel Myrick and Edwardo Sanchez, 2000.

Return to Pontianak. Directed by Djinn. Shaw Organisation and Vacant Films, 2001.

Ring O: Birthday. Directed by Norio Tsuruta. Ring O: Birthday Seisaku Iinkai, 2000.

Ringu. Directed by Hideo Nakata. Omega Project, Imagica, and Asmik Ace Entertainment, 1998.

Ringu 2. Directed by Hideo Nakata. Kadokawa Shoten Publishing Co., Ring 2 Production Group, and Asmik Ace, 1999.

Rinne. Directed by Takashi Shimizu. Entertainment Farm, Geneon Entertainment, and Mainichi Broadcasting System (MBS), 2005.

Saw. Directed by James Wan. Evolution Entertainment, Saw Productions Inc., and Twisted Pictures, 2004.

Scream. Directed by Wes Craven. Dimension Films and Woods Entertainment, 1996.

Shutter. Directed by Matt Mickelson. Dobler's Pen Productions, 2004.

Silence of the Lambs. Directed by Jonathan Demme. Orion Pictures Corporation and Strong Heart/Demme Production, 1991.

Spiritual Love. Directed by David Lai and Taylor Wong. Golden Harvest Company and Johnny Mak Productions, 1987.

Stacy. Attack of the Schoolgirl Zombies. Directed by Naoyuki Tomomatsu. Synapse Films. 2001.

Still Life. Directed by Jia Zhang Ke. Xstream Pictures and Shanghai Film Studios, 2006.

Sueños lejanos. Directed by Alejandro Legaspi. Grupo Chaski, 2007.

Suicide Club. Directed by Shion Sono. Omega Project, Biggubito, and For Peace Co. Ltd., 2001.

Non-Malaysian Films

Teorema. Directed by Pier Paolo Pasolini. Aetos Produzioni Cinematografiche and Euro International Film (EIA), 1968.

The Adventures of Iron Pussy. Directed by Michael Shaowanasai and Apichatpong Weerasethakul. Kick the Machine, 2003.

The Birds. Directed by Alfred Hitchcock. Universal Pictures and Alfred J. Hitchcock Productions, 1963.

The Blair Witch Project. Directed by Daniel Myrick and Edwardo Sanchez. Haxan Films, 1999.

The Brood. Directed by David Cronenberg. Canadian Film Development Corporation (CFDC), Elgin International Films Ltd., and Mutual Productions Ltd., 1979.

The Cabinet of Dr. Caligari. Directed by Robert Wiene. Decia-Bioscop AG, 1920.

The Celebration. Directed by Thomas Vinterberg. Nimbus Film Productions, Danmarks Radio (DR), and Nordisk Film & TV Fond, 1998.

The Chaser. Directed by Na Hong-jin. Daishin Venture Capital, Fine Cut, and Hanhwa Venture Capital, 2008.

The Day the Earth Stood Still. Directed by Robert Wise. Twentieth Century Fox Film Corporation, 1951.

The Days. Directed by Wang Xiaoshuai. Creative Workshop and Image Studio, 1994.

The Exorcist. Directed by William Friedkin. Warner Bros. Pictures, Warner Bros., and Hoya Productions, 1973.

The Eye. Directed by David Moreau and Xavier Palud. Lionsgate, Paramount Vantage, and Cruise/Wagner Productions, 2008.

The Eye. Directed by Oxide Pang Chun and Danny Pang. Applause Pictures and Mediacorp Raintree Pictures, 2002.

The Eye 2. Directed by Oxide Pang Chun and Danny Pang. Applause Pictures and Mediacorp Raintree Pictures, 2004.

The Eye 10. Directed by Oxide Pang Chun and Danny Pang. Applause Pictures and Ruddy Morgan Productions, 2005.

The Final Destination. Directed by David R. Ellis. New Line Cinema, Practical Pictures, and Parallel Zide, 2009.

The Fly. Directed by David Cronenberg. Brooksfilms, 1986.

The Godfather. Directed by Francis Ford Coppola. Paramount Pictures and Alfran Productions, 1972.

The Haunted School. Directed by Man Kei Chin. Basic Pictures, STAR TV Filmed Entertainment, 2007.

The Haunting. Directed by Jan de Bont. DreamWorks SKG and Roth-Arnold Productions, 1999.

The Hunger. Directed by Tony Scott. Metro-Goldwyn-Mayer (MGM) and Peerford Ltd., 1983.

The Idiots. Directed by Lars Von Trier. Zentropa Entertainments, Danmarks Radio (DR), and Liberator Productions, 1999.

The King is Alive. Directed by Kristian Levring. Newmarket Capital Group, Good Machine, and Zentropa Entertainments, 2000.

The Machine Girl. Directed by Noboru Iguchi. Fever Dreams and Nikkatsu, 2008.

The Maid. Directed by Kelvin Tong. Dream Movie Entertainment Ltd., Media Development Authority (MDA), and Mediacorp Raintree Pictures, 2005.

The Mummy. Directed by Karl Freund. Universal Pictures, 1932.

The Music Teacher. Directed by James Toh, 2000.

The Omen. Directed by Richard Donner. Twentieth Century Fox Film Corporation and Twentieth Century-Fox Productions, 1976.

The Others. Directed by Alejandro Amenabar. Cruise/Wagner Productions, Sociedad General de Cine (SOGECINE) S. A., and Las Producciones del Escorpión S. L., 2001.

The Quiet Family. Directed by Kim Ji-woon. Myung Film Company Ltd., 1998.

The Ring. Directed by Gore Verbinski. DreamWorks SKG, MacDonald/Parkes Productions, and BenderSpink, 2002.

The Sound of Music. Directed by Robert Wise. Argyle Enterprises, Inc., 1965.

The Terminator. Directed by James Cameron. Hemdale Film Corporation, Pacific Western Productions, Euro Film Funding Cinema '84, 1994.

The Texas Chainsaw Massacre. Directed by Tobe Hooper. Vortex, 1974.

The Thing. Directed by John Carpenter. Universal Pictures and Turman-Foster Company, 1982.

The Twelve. Directed by Khavn de la Cruz, 2000.

The Wheel (In *Three*). Directed by Nonzeee Nimibutr. Applause Pictures, B.O.M. Film Productions Co., and Cinemasia, 2002.

Three Extremes . . . Box. Directed by Takashi Miike. Applause Pictures Limited, Applause Pictures, and Fortissimo Film Sales, 2004.

Three Extremes . . . Cut. Directed by Park Chan-wook. Applause Pictures Limited, Applause Pictures, and Fortissimo Film Sales, 2004.

Three Extremes . . . Dumplings. Directed by Fruit Chan. Applause Pictures Limited, Applause Pictures, and Fortissimo Film Sales, 2004.

To Sir with Love. Directed by Lim Dae-wung. Fineworks and U Zone Films, 2006.

Todo Todo Teros. Directed by John Torres. Peliculas Los Otros, 2006.

Twilight. Directed by Catherina Hardwicke. Summit Entertainment, Temple Hill Entertainment, and Maverick Films, 2008.

Uncle Boonmee Who Can Recall His Past Lives. Directed by Apichatpong Weerasethakul. Kick the Machine, Illuminations Films, and Anna Sanders Films, 2010.

Unknown Pleasures. Directed by Jia Zhang Ke. E-Pictures, Hu Tong Communications, and Lumen Films, 2002.

Uzumaki. Directed by Higuchinsky. Omenga Micott Inc., Shogakukan, and Space Shower TV, 2000.

Vampire Girl vs Frankenstein Girl. Directed by Yoshihiro Nishimura and Naoyuki. Tomomatsu. Concept Film, Excellent Film and Pony Canyon, 2009.

Voice. Directed by Choe Ik-hwan. Cinema Service, Cine-2000 Film Production, Chungmuro Fund, 2005.

Voodoo Girls. Directed by Thunska Pansittivorakul, 2003.

Whispering Corridors. Directed by Park Ki-hyeong, 1998.

Wizard of Darkness. Directed by Shimako Sato. GAGA and Tsuburaya Eizo, 1995.

Wonderful Town. Directed by Aditya Assarat. Pop Pictures, 2007.

Zombie Love (Det-Pee-Dip). Directed by Kaai Tip, 1984.

Appendix I: Database for the Malaysian Digital Indies, 2000–2011

Filmmaker	Film title	Year	Production Company	Language	Genre	Format	Length (mins)
Amir Muhammad	*Lips to Lips*	2000	Artsee.net, Kino-I	English	Drama	Digital	102
Chris Chong	*Minus*	2000	N/A	English	Short film	Digital	3
Ho Yuhang	*Semangat Insan – Masters of Tradition*	2000	Planet E!	English	Documentary	Digital	N/A
Osman Ali	*Bukak Api*	2000	Pink Triangle Malaysia	Bahasa Malaysia	Documentary	35 mm	80
Teck Tan	*Spinning Gasing*	2000	Niche Film, Spinning Gasing Films	English	Drama	35 mm	90
Ho Yuhang	*Good Friday at the Zoo*	2001	N/A	English	Short film	Digital	12
James Lee	*Sunflowers*	2001	Doghouse73 Pictures	Cantonese	Short film	Digital	8
James Lee	*Snipers*	2001	Artsee.net, Doghouse73 Pictures	English	Thriller	Digital	90
James Lee	*Beautiful Man*	2001	Doghouse73 Pictures	N/A	Experimental	Digital	14
James Lee	*Ah Beng Returns*	2001	Doghouse73 Pictures	Mandarin	Gangster	Digital	75
Osman Ali	*Malaikat Di Jendela*	2001	Nuansa	Bahasa Malaysia	Short film	Digital	N/A
K. Shanmugam	*Me, My Mother and Mosquito*	2001	N/A	N/A	Short film	Digital	8
Devan R	*My Father and His Celluloid*	2001	N/A	N/A	Short film	Digital	10
Amir Muhammad	*Lost* (In *6horts*)	2002	N/A	English	Short film	Digital	9
Amir Muhammad	*Friday* (In *6horts*)	2002	N/A	Bahasa Malaysia, Cantonese	Short film	Digital	8

Filmmaker	Film title	Year	Production Company	Language	Genre	Format	Length (mins)
Amir Muhammad	Mona (In 6horts)	2002	N/A	Bahasa Malaysia	Short film	Digital	6
Amir Muhammad	Checkpoint (In 6horts)	2002	N/A	English	Short film	Digital	7
Amir Muhammad	Kamunting (In 6horts)	2002	N/A	Bahasa Malaysia	Short film	Digital	15
Amir Muhammad	Pang Yau (In 6horts)	2002	N/A	Bahasa Malaysia, Cantonese	Short film	Digital	12
Amir Muhammad	Digital Compassion 02	2002	N/A	N/A	Short film	Digital	N/A
Ho Yuhang	Not Far From Here	2002	N/A	English	Short Film	Digital	38
James Lee	Think Positive!	2002	Doghouse73 Pictures	N/A	Short film	Digital	12
James Lee	Ah Yu's Story	2002	Doghouse73 Pictures	N/A	Short film	Digital	35
James Lee	Room to Let	2002	Doghouse73 Pictures	Cantonese	Drama	Digital	108
Linus Chung	Demolition Frog	2002	N/A	N/A	Short film	Digital	N/A
Liew Seng Tat	Don't Play Play	2002	N/A	N/A	Short film	Digital	6
Ahmad Yazid	A Day in Beggar's Life	2003	N/A	N/A	Short film	Digital	14
Anna Har	When Buddha Touched Tamaole	2003	Red Films	N/A	Documentary	Digital	18
Amir Muhammad	The Big Durian	2003	Doghouse 73 Pictures	Bahasa Malaysia, English, Mandarin, Hokkien, Cantonese	Documentary	Digital	75
Bryant Low	The Son	2003	Ten on Ten	N/A	Drama	Digital	45
Desmond Ng	Tetangga	2003	Ten on Ten	N/A	Drama	Digital	N/A
Haanim Bamadhai	Moris Rasik	2003	N/A	N/A	Short film	Digital	16
Ho Yuhang	Min	2003	N/A	Bahasa Malaysia	Drama	Digital	78
James Lee	Emu Kwan's Tragic Breakfast	2003	Doghouse73 Pictures	English	Short film	Digital	25
James Lee	Teatime with John	2003	Doghouse73 Pictures	English	Short film	Digital	9
Linus Chung	3-Minute Life	2003	N/A	English	Short film	Digital	3
Low Ngai Yuen	Your World My World	2003	Red Films	N/A	Short film	Digital	10

Appendix I 221

Filmmaker	Film title	Year	Production Company	Language	Genre	Format	Length (mins)
Nam Ron	*Gedebe*	2003	Pustaka Cipta	Bahasa Malaysia	Experimental	Digital	65
Ng Tian Hann	*First Take, Final Cut*	2003	Doghouse73 Pictures	Mandarin, Cantonese	Comedy	Digital	85
Patrick Lim	*Choice*	2003	N/A	N/A	Short film	Digital	23
Tan Chui Mui	*Esperando Por Felicidad*	2003	N/A	N/A	Short film	Digital	8
Tan Chui Mui	*Hometown*	2003	N/A	Mandarin	Short film	Digital	6
Woo Ming Jin	*Love for Dogs*	2003	Greenlight Pictures	Bahasa Malaysia, Chinese	Short	Digital	24
Yasmin Ahmad	*Rabun*	2003	Primeworks Studios	Bahasa Malaysia	Drama	Digital	90
Zan Azlee	*I May Be Malaysian, But I Carry a Big Stick*	2003	Fat Bidin Media	English	Short Documentary	Digital	2
Zan Azlee	*Popiahs, Murtabaks, and a Patriotic Donkey*	2003	Fat Bidin Media	English	Short Documentary	Digital	3
Zan Azlee	*The Black, White, and Grey*	2003	Fat Bidin Media	English	Short Documentary	Digital	13
Amir Muhammad	*Wait*	2004	N/A	English	Short film	Digital	3
Azharr Rudin	*Dancing Kites*	2004	Placebo Pictures, Strange Pictures	English, Bahasa Indonesia	Documentary short	Digital	11
Danny Lim	*18?*	2004	N/A	N/A	Short film	Digital	18
Deepak Kumaran Menon	*Wind Chimes*	2004	N/A	English	Short film	Digital	13
Ho Yuhang	*Anybody Home?* (In *Visits. Hungry Ghost Anthology*)	2004	Red Films	Mandarin	Horror	Digital	110
Ho Yuhang	*Sanctuary*	2004	Doghouse73 Pictures	Mandarin, Cantonese	Drama	Digital	80
James Lee	*Goodbye*	2004	Doghouse73 Pictures	Mandarin	Short film	Digital	33
James Lee	*The Beautiful Washing Machine*	2004	Doghouse73 Pictures	Mandarin	Drama	Digital	113

Filmmaker	Film title	Year	Production Company	Language	Genre	Format	Length (mins)
James Lee	*Goodbye to Love*	2004	Doghouse73 Pictures	N/A	Short film	Digital	16
James Lee	*Waiting for Them* (In *Visits. Hungry Ghost Anthology*)	2004	Red Films	Mandarin	Horror	Digital	110
Khairil M. Bahar	*Nicotine*	2004	N/A	English	Short film	Digital	10
Khoo Eng Yow	*Ah Kew the Digger*	2004	Da Huang Pictures	Mandarin, Hokkien, English	Documentary	Digital	68
Low Ngai Yuen	*1413* (In Visits. Hungry Ghost Anthology)	2004	Red Films	Mandarin	Horror	Digital	110
Ng Tian Hann	*Nodding Scoop* (In *Visits. Hungry Ghost Anthology*)	2004	Red Films	Mandarin	Horror	Digital	110
Tan Chui Mui	*A Tree in Tanjung Malim*	2004	Da Huang Pictures	Mandarin	Short film	Digital	24
Yasmin Ahmad	*Sepet*	2004	MHZ Film	Bahasa Malaysia, English, Cantonese, Hokkien, Mandarin	Drama	35 mm	105
Zan Azlee	*R.A.H.M.A.N.*	2004	Fat Bidin Media	Bahasa Malaysia, English	Documentary	Digital	30
Amir Muhammad	*Tokyo Magic Hour*	2005	Doghouse73 Pictures	Bahasa Malaysia	Experimental	Digital	60
Amir Muhammad	*The Year of Living Vicariously*	2005	Miles Films	Bahasa Indonesia	Documentary	Digital	63
Azharr Rudin	*Raining Amber*	2005	N/A	N/A	Short film	Digital	9
Azharr Rudin	*Majidee*	2005	N/A	Bahasa Malaysia	Short film	Digital	15
Azharr Rudin	*Taman di dalam Sinkiku*	2005	N/A	Bahasa Malaysia, English	Short film	Digital	14
Bernard Chauly	*Nenek Unta*	2005	Red Films	N/A	Drama	Digital	N/A

Appendix I

Filmmaker	Film title	Year	Production Company	Language	Genre	Format	Length (mins)
Deepak Kumaran Menon	*Chemman Chaalai*	2005	One Hundred Eye	Tamil, English, Bahasa Malaysia, Mandarin	Drama	Digital	92
James Lee	*A Moment of Love*	2005	Doghouse73 Pictures	Mandarin	Short film	Digital	10
James Lee	*Bernafas Dalam Lumpur*	2005	Doghouse73 Pictures	Bahasa Malaysia	Short film	Digital	18
Khairil M. Bahar	*Some Like it White*	2005	N/A	English	Short film	Digital	10
Red Films and Ground Glass Images	*Fang*	2005	Red Films and Ground Glass Images	N/A	N/A	N/A	N/A
Tan Chui Mui	*South of South*	2005	Da Huang Pictures	Hokkien	Short film	Digital	10
Woo Ming Jin	*Monday Morning Glory*	2005	Greenlight Pictures	Bahasa Malaysia	Drama	Digital	87
Woo Ming Jin	*It's Possible Your Heart Cannot be Broken*	2005	Greenlight Pictures	Bahasa Malaysia, Chinese	Short	Digital	16
Woo Ming Jin	*Catching the Sea*	2005	Greenlight Pictures	Bahasa Malaysia, Chinese	Short	Digital	13
Amir Muhammad	*Lelaki Komunis Terakhir*	2006	Red Films	Bahasa Malaysia, English, Tamil, Hokkien, Cantonese	Documentary	Digital	90
Andrew Sia	*Kopi O Khau Sikit Kurang Manis*	2006	N/A	English	Documentary	Digital	30
Arivind Abraham	*S'Kali*	2006	Perantauan Enterprise, Asa'ad Ent. Network	English, Bahasa Malaysia	Drama	35 mm	85
Azharr Rudin	*The Amber Sexalogy*	2006	N/A	Bahasa Malaysia, English	Short film	Digital	9
Chris Chong	*Tuesday be my Friend*	2006	N/A	Mandarin	Short film	Digital	10
Ho Yuhang	*Rain Dogs*	2006	Focus Films	Mandarin, Cantonese	Drama	Digital	105
James Lee	*Before We Fall in Love Again*	2006	Da Huang Pictures	Mandarin	Drama	Digital	99

Filmmaker	Film title	Year	Production Company	Language	Genre	Format	Length (mins)
Khairil M. Bahar	*Ciplak*	2006	FYI Films	English	Comedy	Digital	83
Khoo Eng Yow	*The Bird House*	2006	Red Films	Hokkien, Mandarin	Drama	Digital	97
Kit Ong	*The Flowers Beneath My Skin*	2006	N/A	N/A	Horror	Digital	70
Tan Chui Mui	*Company of Mushrooms*	2006	Da Huang Pictures	Bahasa Malaysia, Mandarin	Short film	Digital	30
Tan Chui Mui	*Love Conquers All*	2006	Da Huang Pictures	Bahasa Malaysia, Cantonese, Mandarin	Drama	Digital	90
Yasmin Ahmad	*Gubra*	2006	Nusanbakti Corporation	Bahasa Malaysia, English, Cantonese, Mandarin	Drama	35 mm	110
Yasmin Ahmad	*Mukhsin*	2006	Primeworks Studios	Bahasa Malaysia, English, Mandarin	Drama	35 mm	94
Zan Azlee	*Searching For Sheila*	2006	Fat Bidin Media	Bahasa Indonesia	Short documentary	Digital	17
Zan Azlee	*Tudung*	2006	Fat Bidin Media	Bahasa Malaysia	Short	Digital	3
Amir Muhammad	*Apa Khabar Orang Kampung*	2007	Da Huang Pictures	Bahasa Malaysia, Thai	Documentary	Digital	72
Bernard Chauly	*Goodbye Boys*	2007	Red Films	Bahasa Malaysia, Cantonese, English	Drama	Digital	88
Chris Chong	*Kolam*	2007	N/A	Bahasa Indonesia, English	Short film	Digital	14
Deepak Kumaran Menon	*Chalanggai*	2007	One Hundred Eye	Tamil, English, Bahasa Malaysia, Mandarin	Drama	Digital	99
Fahmi Reza	*10 Tahun Sebelum Merdeka*	2007	N/A	Bahasa Malaysia	Documentary	Digital	36
Ho Yuhang	*As I Lay Dying*	2007	Paperheart	Mandarin	Short film	Digital	10

Appendix I

Filmmaker	Film title	Year	Production Company	Language	Genre	Format	Length (mins)
James Lee	*Things We Do When We Fall in Love*	2007	Da Huang Pictures	Mandarin	Drama	Digital	89
James Lee	*Waiting for Love*	2007	Da Huang Pictures	Mandarin	Drama	Digital	70
Linus Chung	*A Note of Love*	2007	Nokia	Bahasa Malaysia, Hokkien, English	Drama	Digital	82
Tan Chui Mui	*Nobody's Girlfriend*	2007	Da Huang Pictures	French, English	Short film	Digital	20
Woo Ming Jin	*The Elephant and The Sea*	2007	Greenlight Pictures	Mandarin	Drama	Digital	100
Woo Ming Jin	*Blue Roof*	2007	Greenlight Pictures	Bahasa Malaysia, Chinese	Short	Digital	13
Azharr Rudin	*Eaten by Time*	2008	N/A	Bahasa Malaysia	Short film	Digital	3
Azharr Rudin	*Punggok Rindukan Bulan*	2008	Da Huang Pictures	Bahasa Malaysia	Drama	Digital	122
Brenda Danker	*Senandainya Aku Siti*	2008	Red Films	Bahasa Malaysia	Drama	Digital	N/A
Chris Chong	*Block B*	2008	Tanjung Aru Pictures	Tamil	Short film	Digital	20
James Lee	*Bernafas Dalam Lumpur*	2008	Red Films	Bahasa Malaysia	Drama	Digital	78
Justin Ong	*Subak*	2008	NHK, KBS and Caldecott Productions	English, Bahasa Indonesia	Documentary	Digital	N/A
Khoo Eng Yow	*The Pirate and the Emperor's Ship*	2008	Da Huang Pictures	Hokkien, English	Documentary	Digital	65
Liew Seng Tat	*Flower in the Pocket*	2008	Da Huang Pictures	Bahasa Malaysia, English, Cantonese, Mandarin	Drama	Digital	90
Poh Si Teng	*Pecah Lobang*	2008	Big Pictures Productions	Bahasa Malaysia	Short Film	Digital	30
Woo Ming Jin	*Kurus*	2008	Greenlight Pictures	Bahasa Malaysia	Drama	Digital	76
Yasmin Ahmad	*Muallaf*	2008	MHZ Film	Bahasa Malaysia, English, Cantonese	Drama	35 mm	80

Filmmaker	Film title	Year	Production Company	Language	Genre	Format	Length (mins)
Amir Muhammad	*Malaysian Gods*	2009	Da Huang Pictures	Tamil	Documentary	Digital	70
Amir Muhammad	*The Tree* (In *15Malaysia*)	2009	P1	Bahasa Malaysia	Short documentary	Digital	4
Benji, Bahir	*Meter* (In *15Malaysia*)	2009	P1	Bahasa Malaysia	Short film	Digital	8
Chris Chong	*Karaoke*	2009	Tanjung Aru Pictures	Bahasa Malaysia	Drama	35 mm	75
Desmond Ng	*The Son* (In *15Malaysia*)	2009	P1	Cantonese	Short film	Digital	5
Ho Yuhang	*At the End of Daybreak*	2009	M&FC, October Pictures, Paperheart	Mandarin	Drama	Digital	94
Ho Yuhang	*Potong Saga* (In *15Malaysia*)	2009	P1	English, Bahasa Malaysia, Mandarin	Short	Digital	6
James Lee	*Gerhana* (In *15Malaysia*)	2009	P1	Bahasa Malaysia	Short film	Digital	5
Johan John	*Duit Kecil* (In *15Malaysia*)	2009	P1	Bahasa Malaysia	Short film	Digital	7
Kamal Sabran	*Lumpur* (In *15Malaysia*)	2009	P1	Bahasa Malaysia	Short film	Digital	4
Khairil M. Bahar	*Healthy Paranoia* (In *15Malaysia*)	2009	P1	Bahasa Malaysia, English	Short film	Digital	6
Liew Seng Tat	*Halal* (In *15 Malaysia*)	2009	P1	Bahasa Malaysia	Short film	Digital	5
Linus Chung	*House* (In *15Malaysia*)	2009	P1	Tamil, English, Bahasa Malaysia	Short film	Digital	5
Nam Ron	*Lollipop* (In *15Malaysia*)	2009	P1	Bahasa Malaysia	Short film	Digital	5
Nam Ron	*Gadoh*	2009	KOMAS	Bahasa Malaysia, Chinese	Drama	Digital	70
Soh Sook Hwa	*Kayuh*	2009	N/A	Bahasa Malaysia	Documentary	Digital	30
Suleiman Brothers	*Rojak* (In *15Malaysia*)	2009	P1	Tamil	Short film	Digital	5
Tan Chui Mui	*To Say Goodbye*	2009	Da Huang Pictures	Mandarin	Short film	Digital	14

Appendix I

Filmmaker	Film title	Year	Production Company	Language	Genre	Format	Length (mins)
Tan Chui Mui	*One Future* (In *15Malaysia*)	2009	P1	English	Short film	Digital	5
Tan Chui Mui	*Everyday Everyday*	2009	Da Huang Pictures	Mandarin	Short film	Digital	18
Tan Chui Mui	*Dream #2 He Slept Too Long* (In *All My Failed Attempts*)	2009	Da Huang Pictures	Bahasa Malaysia	Short film	Digital	5
Tan Chui Mui	*The Need for Rites* (In *All My Failed Attempts*)	2009	Da Huang Pictures	Mandarin	Short film	Digital	13
Tan Chui Mui	*Dream#3 We Need You to Save the World* (In *All My Failed Attempts*)	2009	Da Huang Pictures	N/A	Short film	Digital	9
Tan Chui Mui	*Dream#1 She Sees A Dead Friend* (In *All My Failed Attempts*)	2009	Da Huang Pictures	English	Short film	Digital	8
Woo Ming Jin	*Woman on Fire Looks for Water*	2009	Greenlight Pictures	Mandarin, Cantonese, Korean	Drama	Digital	98
Woo Ming Jin	*Slovak Sling* (In *15Malaysia*)	2009	P1	Cantonese, English, Bahasa Malaysia	Short documentary	Digital	5
Yasmin Ahmad	*Talentime*	2009	Primeworks Studios	Bahasa Malaysia, English, Tamil	Drama	35 mm	110
Yasmin Ahmad	*Chocolate* (In *15Malaysia*)	2009	P1	Mandarin, Bahasa Malaysia	Short film	35 mm	4
Yeo Joon Han	*Sell Out!*	2009	Astro Shaw	English	Musical	35 mm	107
Tan Chui Mui	*Year Without a Summer*	2010	Da Huang Pictures	Bahasa Malaysia	Drama	Digital	87
Woo Ming Jin	*The Tiger Factory*	2010	Greenlight Pictures	Bahasa Malaysia, Cantonese, Mandarin	Drama	Digital	84

Filmmaker	Film title	Year	Production Company	Language	Genre	Format	Length (mins)
Ho Yuhang	*No One is Illegal*	2011	Cinema Reloaded, Paperheart	N/A	Short	Digital	N/A
Ho Yuhang	*Open Verdict*	2011	N/A	N/A	Short	Digital	N/A
James Lee	*Call If You Need Me*	2011	Da Huang Pictures	Mandarin	Gangster	Digital	104
Tan Chui Mui	*Yulu*	2011	Da Huang Pictures	Mandarin	Documentary	Digital	88
Woo Ming Jin	*60 Seconds of Solitude in Year Zero*	2011	Greenlight Pictures	English	Drama	Digital	60
Woo Ming Jin	*Masakan Cinta* (In *Survival Guide Untuk Kampung Radioaktif*)	2011	N/A	Bahasa Malaysia	Short film	Digital	5
Yeo Joon Han	*Orang Minyak XX* (In *Survival Guide Untuk Kampung Radioaktif*)	2011	N/A	Bahasa Malaysia	Short film	Digital	10
Liew Seng Tat	*Welcome to Kampung Radioaktif* (In *Survival Guide Untuk Kampung Radioaktif*)	2011	N/A	Bahasa Malaysia, Cantonese	Short film	Digital	14
Tan Chui Mui	*Lai Kwan's Love* (In *Survival Guide Untuk Kampung Radioaktif*)	2011	N/A	Hakka, Cantonese, English, Mandarin	Short film	Digital	10
Tan Chui Mui	*Cinta Lai Kwan* (In *Survival Guide Untuk Kampung Radioaktif*)	2011	N/A	Hakka, Cantonese, English, Mandarin	Short film	Digital	10
Tan Chui Mui, Liew Seng Tat, Woo Ming Jin, and Yeo Joon Han	*TV Tiger's Lee Ah Seng Reports on the Malaysian Rare Earth Issue Part 1, 2, and 3* (In *Survival Guide Untuk Kampung Radioaktif*)	2011	N/A	Bahasa Malaysia	Short film	Digital	4

Appendix II: Database for Commercial Mainstream Films in Post-2000 Malaysian Cinema, 2000–2011

Filmmaker	Film title	Year	Production Company	Language	Genre	Format	Length (mins)
Aziz M. Osman	*Senario Lagi*	2000	Primeworks Studios, Paradigm Film	Bahasa Malaysia	Comedy	35 mm	118
Aziz M. Osman	*Leftenan Adnan*	2000	Primeworks Studios, Paradigm Film	Bahasa Malaysia	War	35 mm	120
Eddie Pak	*Syukur 21*	2000	Metrowealth Movies	Bahasa Malaysia	Drama	35 mm	N/A
Jack Ad'Din	*Anaknya Sazali*	2000	Eurofine	Bahasa Malaysia	Comedy	35 mm	96
Othman Hafsham	*Soal Hati*	2000	Serangkai Holding	Bahasa Malaysia	Comedy	35 mm	117
Shuhaimi Baba	*Mimpi Moon*	2000	Pesona Pictures, Primeworks Studios	Bahasa Malaysia	Drama	35 mm	120
Young-Jump Animation	*Nien Resurrection*	2000	Young-Jump Animation	N/A	Animation	Digital	N/A
Yusof Haslam	*Pasrah*	2000	Primeworks Studios, Skop Production	Bahasa Malaysia	Romance	35 mm	N/A
Aziz M. Osman	*Lagi-Lagi Senario*	2001	Primeworks Studios, Paradigm Film	Bahasa Malaysia	Comedy	35 mm	110
Aziz M. Osman	*Seri Dewi Malam*	2001	Primeworks Studios, Paradigm Film	Bahasa Malaysia	Romance	35 mm	115
Azman Mohd Yusof	*Cinta Tiada Restu*	2001	Dreamwalk	Bahasa Malaysia	Romance	35 mm	105

Filmmaker	Film title	Year	Production Company	Language	Genre	Format	Length (mins)
Erwin Argh	*Cheritera*	2001	Matahari Animation & Production, Red Rocket Animation	Bahasa Malaysia	Animation	35 mm	82
Rashid Sibir	*Putih*	2001	Fine Animation	Bahasa Malaysia	Animation	35 mm	90
S. Mohan	*The Deadly Disiple*	2001	Dynacoral Productions	English	Action	35 mm	90
V. Nagaraj	*Getaran*	2001	SV Productions	Bahasa Malaysia	Musical drama	35 mm	115
Yusof Haslam	*Gerak Khas The Movie*	2001	Skop Production	Bahasa Malaysia	Crime	35 mm	N/A
Z Lokman	*No Problem*	2001	Metrowealth Movies	Bahasa Malaysia	Romantic comedy	35 mm	100
Mahadi J. Murat	*Putera Merdeka*	2001	Karya Impian	Bahasa Malaysia	Drama	35 mm	N/A
A. Razak Mohaideen	*Anak Mami The Movie*	2002	Primeworks Studios	Bahasa Malaysia	Comedy	35 mm	N/A
A. Razak Mohaideen	*Mami Jarum*	2002	MIG Production	Bahasa Malaysia	Comedy	35 mm	95
Ahmad Idham	*Mr. Cinderella*	2002	Kuasatek Pictures, Skop Production	Bahasa Malaysia	Comedy	35 mm	N/A
Aziz M. Osman	*Idola*	2002	Tayangan Unggul	Bahasa Malaysia	Comedy	35 mm	105
Bade Azmi	*KL Menjerit*	2002	Tayangan Unggul	Bahasa Malaysia	Action	35 mm	107
Erma Fatima	*Embun*	2002	FINAS, Filem Negara Malaysia	Bahasa Malaysia	War	35 mm	135
Othman Hafsham	*Soalnya Siapa?*	2002	Serangkai Filem	Bahasa Malaysia	Comedy	35 mm	132
Shadan Hashim	*Cinta 200 Ela*	2002	JAS Production	Bahasa Malaysia	Romance	35 mm	N/A
Yusof Haslam	*Gerak Khas The Movie 2*	2002	Skop Production	Bahasa Malaysia	Crime	35 mm	125
Z Lokman	*Mendam Berahi*	2002	Metrowealth Movies	Bahasa Malaysia	Drama	35 mm	100
A. Razak Mohaideen	*Mami Jarum Junior*	2003	Metrowealth Movies	Bahasa Malaysia	Comedy	35 mm	100
A. Razak Mohaideen	*Mistik*	2003	Metrowealth Movies	Bahasa Malaysia	Horror	35 mm	100
A. Razak Mohaideen	*Jutawan Fakir*	2003	Metrowealth Movies	Bahasa Malaysia	Comedy	35 mm	83

Appendix II

Filmmaker	Film title	Year	Production Company	Language	Genre	Format	Length (mins)
A. Razak Mohaideen	*Cinta Kolestrol*	2003	Cinta Kolestrol	Bahasa Malaysia	Comedy	35 mm	108
Adman Salleh	*Paloh*	2003	FINAS, Filem Negara Malaysia	Bahasa Malaysia	War	35 mm	120
Ambri Kailani	*Black Maria*	2003	Simfoni Makmur	Bahasa Malaysia	Action	35 mm	105
Aziz M. Osman	*Gila-gila Pengantin*	2003	Skop Production, Ace Motion Pictures	Bahasa Malaysia	Comedy	35 mm	120
Din CJ	*Mr. Cinderella 2*	2003	Kuasatek Pictures, Skop Production	Bahasa Malaysia	Comedy	35 mm	111
Mamat Khalid	*Lang Buana*	2003	Primeworks Studios	Bahasa Malaysia	Drama	35 mm	N/A
Murali Abdullah	*Aku Kaya The Movie*	2003	Boommax; A&A Pictures	Bahasa Malaysia	Comedy	35 mm	95
Rashid Sibir	*Laila Isabella*	2003	Tayangan Unggul	Bahasa Malaysia	Romantic comedy	35 mm	124
V. Nagaraj	*Iskandar*	2003	SV Productions	Bahasa Malaysia	Thriller	35 mm	110
Yusof Haslam	*Sembilu 2005*	2003	Skop Production, Lotus Five Star AV	Bahasa Malaysia	Drama	35 mm	110
Yusof Haslam	*Janji Diana*	2003	Skop Production	Bahasa Malaysia	Drama	35 mm	N/A
Yusof Kelana	*MX3*	2003	ME Comm., Skop Production	Bahasa Malaysia	Comedy	35 mm	N/A
Zulkeflie M. Osman	*Diari Romeo*	2003	Tayangan Unggul	Bahasa Malaysia	Comedy	35 mm	102
Zulkiflee Md. Said	*Gila Bola*	2003	Nizarman	Bahasa Malaysia	Comedy	35 mm	92
A. Razak Mohaideen	*Kuliah Cinta*	2004	Metrowealth Movies	Bahasa Malaysia	Romantic comedy	35 mm	106
A. Razak Mohaideen	*Hingga Hujung Nyawa*	2004	Metrowealth Movies	Bahasa Malaysia	Romance	35 mm	105
A. Razak Mohaideen	*I Know What U Did Last Raya*	2004	Primeworks Studios, MIG Beats	Bahasa Malaysia	Horror-comedy	35 mm	95

232   Appendix II

Filmmaker	Film title	Year	Production Company	Language	Genre	Format	Length (mins)
A. Razak Mohaideen	*Potret Mistik*	2004	Metrowealth Movies, Primeworks Studios	Bahasa Malaysia	Horror	35 mm	N/A
A. Razak Mohaideen	*Tujuh Perhentian*	2004	MIG Beats, Metrowealth Movies, Primeworks Studios	Bahasa Malaysia	Horror-romance	35 mm	95
A. Razak Mohaideen	*Tangkai Jering*	2004	Metrowealth Movies, Primeworks Studios	Bahasa Malaysia	Comedy	35 mm	70
Afdlin Shauki	*Buli*	2004	Primeworks Studios	Bahasa Malaysia	Romantic comedy	35 mm	114
Anwardi Jamil	*Ah Loke Café*	2004	N.Finity Production	English	Comedy	35 mm	90
Aziz M. Osman	*Biar Betul*	2004	Nizarman, Ace Motion Pictures, Gitu-gitu Productions	Bahasa Malaysia	Comedy	35 mm	N/A
Aziz M. Osman	*Bintang Hati*	2004	Tayangan Unggul	Bahasa Malaysia	Romantic comedy	35 mm	93
Aziz M. Osman	*Trauma*	2004	Tayangan Unggul	Bahasa Malaysia	Thriller	35 mm	N/A
Aznil Nawawi	*Aku No. 1*	2004	Boommax; A&A Pictures	Bahasa Malaysia	Comedy	35 mm	105
Bade Azmi	*Berlari ke Langit*	2004	Tayangan Unggul	Bahasa Malaysia	Drama	35 mm	100
Rashid Sibir	*Cinta Luar Biasa*	2004	Tayangan Unggul	Bahasa Malaysia	Romantic comedy	35 mm	119
Rosnani Jamil	*Bicara Hati*	2004	RJ Production	Bahasa Malaysia	Romance	35 mm	N/A
S. Baldev Singh, Aziz Sattar	*Father*	2004	Sri Saheb Production	English	Drama	35 mm	150
Saw Teong Hin	*Puteri Gunung Ledang*	2004	Enfiniti Productions	Bahasa Malaysia	Drama	35 mm	145
Shuhaimi Baba	*Pontianak Harum Sundal Malam*	2004	Pesona Pictures, Jugra Publication	Bahasa Malaysia	Horror	35 mm	115
Silver Chung	*Di Ambang Misteri*	2004	Cosmos Discovery	Bahasa Malaysia	Horror	35 mm	95

Appendix II

Filmmaker	Film title	Year	Production Company	Language	Genre	Format	Length (mins)
Silver Chung	*Makar*	2004	Cosmos Discovery	Bahasa Malaysia	Horror	35 mm	105
U-Wei Saari	*Buai Laju-laju*	2004	Lebrocquy Fraser	Bahasa Malaysia	Drama	35 mm	93
Zek Zukry	*SH3 The Movie*	2004	AD Niaga	Bahasa Malaysia	Comedy	35 mm	N/A
Zulkeflie M. Osman, Din Glamour	*Bisikan Remaja*	2004	Berjaya Film Production	Bahasa Malaysia	Romantic comedy	35 mm	N/A
A. R. Badul	*Tak Ori Tapi Ok*	2005	Nusanbakti Corporation	Bahasa Malaysia	Comedy	35 mm	N/A
A. Razak Mohaideen	*Anak Mami Kembali*	2005	Metrowealth Movies, MIG Beats, Gitu-gitu Productions	Bahasa Malaysia	Comedy	35 mm	104
A. Razak Mohaideen	*Cinta Fotokopi*	2005	Metrowealth Movies	Bahasa Malaysia	Comedy	35 mm	100
A. Razak Mohaideen	*Lady Boss*	2005	Metrowealth Movies, Gitu-gitu Productions	Bahasa Malaysia	Romantic comedy	35 mm	110
Afdlin Shauki	*Baik Punya Cilok*	2005	Tayangan Unggul	Bahasa Malaysia	Comedy	35 mm	115
Aziz M. Osman	*Senario XX*	2005	Primeworks Studios	Bahasa Malaysia	Comedy	35 mm	105
Aziz M. Osman	*Gila-Gila Pengantin Popular*	2005	Skop Production, Ace Motion Pictures	Bahasa Malaysia	Comedy	35 mm	115
Bade Azmi	*KL Menjerit 1*	2005	Tayangan Unggul	Bahasa Malaysia	Drama	35 mm	100
Bade Azmi	*Gangster*	2005	Tayangan Unggul	Bahasa Malaysia	Gangster	35 mm	90
Bernard Chauly	*Gol & Gincu*	2005	Red Films	Bahasa Malaysia	Romantic comedy	35 mm	102
Bjarne Wong	*The Legend of the Red Curse*	2005	Hock Star Ent. Industry	English, Mandarin, Bahasa Malaysia, Iban	Horror	35 mm	78
Mamat Khalid	*Rock*	2005	Primeworks Studios	Bahasa Malaysia	Comedy	35 mm	107
Meor Hashim Manap	*Kemarau Cinta*	2005	Nusanbakti Corporation	Bahasa Malaysia	Drama	35 mm	96

Filmmaker	Film title	Year	Production Company	Language	Genre	Format	Length (mins)
Premnath Pillai	*Uyir*	2005	Ambi Agency	Tamil	Horror	Digital	90
Raja Ahmad Alauddin	*Qaisy Dan Laila*	2005	Nizarman, Serangkai Filem	Bahasa Malaysia	Drama	35 mm	N/A
S. Baldev Singh, Aziz Sattar, Arjinder Singh	*Maaria*	2005	Sri Saheb Production	English	Horror	35 mm	150
Sandosh Kesavan	*Aandal*	2005	N/A	Tamil	Drama	Digital	100
Shuhaimi Baba	*Pontianak Harum Sundal Malam 2*	2005	Pesona Pictures	Bahasa Malaysia	Horror	35 mm	117
Woo Ming Jin	*Salon*	2005	Primeworks Studios	Bahasa Malaysia	Romantic comedy	35 mm	90
Yusof Haslam	*GK3 The Movie*	2005	Skop Production, Lotus Five Star AV	Bahasa Malaysia	Crime	35 mm	N/A
Yusof Kelana	*Pontianak Menjerit*	2005	ME Comm., Skop Production	Bahasa Malaysia	Horror-comedy	35 mm	105
A. R. Badul	*Salah Bapak*	2006	Nusanbakti Corporation	Bahasa Malaysia	Comedy	35 mm	100
A. Razak Mohaideen	*Bujang Senang*	2006	KSG Pictures	Bahasa Malaysia	Comedy	35 mm	97
A. Razak Mohaideen	*Main-Main Cinta*	2006	Metrowealth Movies	Bahasa Malaysia	Musical	35 mm	93
A. Razak Mohaideen	*Nana Tanjung*	2006	NAJ Productions, Lineclear Motion Pictures, Primeworks Studios	Bahasa Malaysia	Comedy	35 mm	96
Afdlin Shauki	*Buli Balik*	2006	Primeworks Studios	Bahasa Malaysia	Romantic comedy	35 mm	120
Ahmad Idham	*Tipah Tertipu The Movie*	2006	Excellent Pictures	Bahasa Malaysia	Musical	35 mm	93
Ahmad Idham	*Tentang Bulan*	2006	Metrowealth Movies	Bahasa Malaysia	Drama	35 mm	83
Ahmad Idham	*Remp-It*	2006	Metrowealth Movies	Bahasa Malaysia	Action	35 mm	92
Azidi Al Bukhary	*Persona Non Grata*	2006	Nizarman	Bahasa Malaysia	Drama	35 mm	92

Appendix II

Filmmaker	Film title	Year	Production Company	Language	Genre	Format	Length (mins)
Aziz M. Osman	*Senario Pemburu Emas Yamashita*	2006	Primeworks Studios	Bahasa Malaysia	Comedy	35 mm	100
Bade Azmi	*Bilut*	2006	Mega Wajasinar	Bahasa Malaysia	Drama	35 mm	120
Bade Azmi	*Castello*	2006	Suhan Movies & Trading	Bahasa Malaysia	Action	35 mm	110
Bjarne Wong	*Possessed*	2006	Hock Star Ent. Industry	Cantonese	Horror	35 mm	84
C. Kumar	*Ethirkaalam*	2006	Super Arts Production	Tamil	Action	35 mm	165
CL Hor	*The 3rd Generation*	2006	Blackbox Pictures	Cantonese	Drama	35 mm	115
Erma Fatima	*Diva Popular*	2006	Amazon Ent. Production	Bahasa Malaysia	Comedy	35 mm	107
FINAS & NOVISTA	*The Perak Man*	2006	FINAS & NOVISTA	English	Documentary	Digital	60
Jasmi Shahir	*Jejak Rasul - Muhammad s.a.w. Episod - Israk Mikraj*	2006	TV3	Bahasa Malaysia	Documentary	Digital	22
Kabir Bhatia	*Cinta*	2006	Primeworks Studios	Bahasa Malaysia	Romance	35 mm	112
Mamat Khalid	*Man Laksa*	2006	Tayangan Unggul	Bahasa Malaysia	Musical-comedy	35 mm	110
Michael Chuah	*Seed Of Darkness*	2006	Evo Pictures	Cantonese	Horror	Digital	90
Oliver Knott	*The Red Kebaya*	2006	L' Agenda Production	English	Drama	35 mm	100
Sandosh Kesavan	*Gong*	2006	Primeworks Studios	Bahasa Malaysia	Horror	35 mm	99
Young Juwahir	*Misi 1511*	2006	AV Vision	Bahasa Malaysia	Comedy	35 mm	117
Yusry Abd Halim	*Cicakman*	2006	KRU Studios	Bahasa Malaysia	Action	35 mm	107
A. Razak Mohaideen	*Otai*	2007	Primeworks Studios, Lineclear Motion Pictures	Bahasa Malaysia	Comedy	35 mm	N/A
A. Razak Mohaideen	*Nana Tanjung 2*	2007	Primeworks Studios, Lineclear Motion Pictures	Bahasa Malaysia	Comedy	35 mm	N/A

Filmmaker	Film title	Year	Production Company	Language	Genre	Format	Length (mins)
Afdlin Shauki	*Sumo-Lah*	2007	Vision Works	Bahasa Malaysia	Comedy	35 mm	140
Ahmad Idham	*Impak Maksima*	2007	Excellent Pictures	Bahasa Malaysia	Action	35 mm	N/A
Ahmad Idham	*Jangan Pandang Belakang*	2007	Metrowealth Movies	Bahasa Malaysia	Horror	35 mm	99
Ahmad Yazid Puad	*Making The Cut*	2007	Reel Networks	English	Documentary	Digital	24
Anwardi Jamil	*Budak Lapok*	2007	Matahari Animation & Production	Bahasa Malaysia	Animation	35 mm	90
Bade Azmi	*Syaitan*	2007	Tayangan Unggul	Bahasa Malaysia	Horror	35 mm	90
Felix Tan	*Hidden Summer In My Heart*	2007	Dreamteam Studio	Mandarin	Drama	Digital	110
Idzwan Junaidi	*Demi Kemanusiaan*	2007	Global Interway	Bahasa Malaysia	Documentary		30
Jamal Maarif, C.K. Karan	*Orang Minyak*	2007	Infohibur Production	Bahasa Malaysia	Horror	35 mm	98
Jamilah Taib	*The Woodsmiths*	2007	Reel Networks	English	Documentary	Digital	24
K.Annan	*Yantra*	2007	N/A	Tamil	Drama	N/A	135
Leong Hon Yuen	*Restoring Mederka*	2007	Discovery Channel	English	Documentary	Digital	23
Les' Copaque Production	*Upin & Ipin*	2007	Les' Copaque Production	Bahasa Malaysia	Animation	Digital	25
Mamat Khalid	*Zombie Kampung Pisang*	2007	Tayangan Unggul	Bahasa Malaysia	Horror-comedy	35 mm	118
Mazlan	*Rumah Degil*	2007	Akademi Seni Budaya Dan Warisan Kebangsaan	Bahasa Malaysia	Documentary	Digital	10
N.S krishna	*Manjari*	2007	N/A	Tamil	Drama	N/A	100
Osman Ali	*Anak Halal*	2007	Tayangan Unggul	Bahasa Malaysia	Drama	35 mm	115
Osman Ali	*Puaka Tebing Biru*	2007	Tayangan Unggul	Bahasa Malaysia	Horror	35 mm	130
Osman Ali	*Anak Halal*	2007	Tayangan Unggul	Bahasa Malaysia	Action	35 mm	115
Pierre Andre	*9 September*	2007	Metrowealth Movies	Bahasa Malaysia	Romance	35 mm	90
Raja Ahmad Alauddin	*Kayangan*	2007	Raden Pictures	Bahasa Malaysia	Drama	35 mm	106

Appendix II

Filmmaker	Film title	Year	Production Company	Language	Genre	Format	Length (mins)
Rosli Nordin	*Zara Gadis Semai*	2007	RTM, UNICEF	Bahasa Malaysia	Documentary	Digital	25
S. Baldev Singh	*Vittaghan... The Hacker...*	2007	Sri Saheb Production	Tamil	Thriller	Digital	86
Shadan Hashim	*Haru Biru*	2007	JAS Production	Bahasa Malaysia	Drama	35 mm	87
Sharad Sharan	*Diva*	2007	Astro Shaw	Bahasa Malaysia	Musical drama	35 mm	127
Shuhaimi Baba	*Waris Jari Hantu*	2007	Pesona Pictures, Primeworks Studios	Bahasa Malaysia	Horror	35 mm	110
Shuhaimi Baba	*1957: Hati Malaya*	2007	Pesona Pictures	Bahasa Malaysia	Drama	35 mm	117
VN Raj	*Aathma*	2007	Demaz Ent.	Tamil	Horror	Digital	105
Zaili Sulan	*Qabil Khushry Qabil Igam*	2007	Sonata Film	Bahasa Malaysia	Drama	35 mm	105
Zarina Abdullah	*Chermin*	2007	Starry Eye Production	Bahasa Malaysia	Horror	35 mm	98
Zulkeflie M. Osman	*Cinta Yang Satu*	2007	Wan's Production	Bahasa Malaysia	Romance	35 mm	94
A. Razak Mohaideen	*Cinta U-Turn*	2008	Lineclear Motion Pictures, Pyramid Saimira Theatre Chain	Bahasa Malaysia	Romantic comedy	35 mm	108
A. Razak Mohaideen	*Duyung*	2008	KRU Studios, Primeworks Studios, Lineclear Motion Pictures	Bahasa Malaysia	Romantic comedy	35 mm	94
A. Razak Mohaideen	*Sifu & Tongga*	2008	Primeworks Studios, Lineclear Motion Pictures	Bahasa Malaysia	Comedy	35 mm	104
Afdlin Shauki	*Los dan Faun*	2008	Vision Works	Bahasa Malaysia	Comedy	35 mm	105
Ahmad Idham	*Brainscan: Aku dan Topi Ajaib*	2008	Metrowealth Movies	Bahasa Malaysia	Drama	35 mm	90
Ahmad Idham	*Congkak*	2008	Metrowealth Movies	Bahasa Malaysia	Horror	35 mm	86

Filmmaker	Film title	Year	Production Company	Language	Genre	Format	Length (mins)
Ahmad Idham	*Senario The Movie: Episode 1*	2008	MIG Production	Bahasa Malaysia	Comedy	35 mm	87
Ahmad Idham	*Brainscan: Aku Dan Topi Ajaib*	2008	Metrowealth Movies	Bahasa Malaysia	Science fiction	35 mm	90
Amir Muhammad, Naeim Ghalili	*Susuk*	2008	Primeworks Studios	Bahasa Malaysia	Horror	35 mm	110
Azizi Chunk	*Antoo Fighter*	2008	Primeworks Studios	Bahasa Malaysia	Horror-comedy	35 mm	114
Barney Lee	*Anak*	2008	Box Lite Film	Bahasa Malaysia	Horror	35 mm	90
CL Hor	*Kinta 1881*	2008	Blackbox Pictures	Cantonese	Martial arts	35 mm	86
Effendee, Fariza Azlina	*Kami The Movie*	2008	Primeworks Studios	Bahasa Malaysia	Drama	35 mm	100
Hans Isaac	*CUCI*	2008	Tune Ent. Group, Tall Order Productions	Bahasa Malaysia	Comedy	35 mm	90
Hatta Azad Khan	*Wayang*	2008	UiTM - Universiti Teknologi Mara	Bahasa Malaysia	Drama	35 mm	110
Ike Ong	*Wirasiswi*	2008	London Filmmakers Studio	Bahasa Malaysia	Action	Digital	120
James Lee	*Histeria*	2008	Tayangan Unggul	Bahasa Malaysia	Horror	35 mm	91
Kabir Bhatia	*Sepi*	2008	Primeworks Studios	Bahasa Malaysia	Romance	35 mm	115
M. Subash Abdullah	*Pensil*	2008	Genius Parade	Bahasa Malaysia	Drama	35 mm	110
Mamat Khalid	*Kala Malam Bulan Mengambang*	2008	Tayangan Unggul	Bahasa Malaysia	Horror-comedy	35 mm	110
Mark Tan	*Jarum Halus*	2008	Sparky Pictures	English	Thriller	Digital	136
Martias Ali	*Malaysia's Sweetheart*	2008	N/A	Bahasa Malaysia	Drama	Digital	87
Naga	*Uruvam*	2008	N/A	Tamil	Drama	N/A	100
P. Rameesh	*Vikrant*	2008	Super Arts Production	Tamil	Action	Digital	165
Pierre Andre	*I'm Not Single*	2008	Metrowealth Movies	Bahasa Malaysia	Romance	35 mm	87

Appendix II 239

Filmmaker	Film title	Year	Production Company	Language	Genre	Format	Length (mins)
S.Gana	*Ganavin Ivanthaanda Hero*	2008	GV Media Broadcast	Tamil	Comedy	Digital	130
Saw Teong Hin	*Apa Kata Hati*	2008	Tayangan Unggul	Bahasa Malaysia	Romantic comedy	35 mm	94
Sharad Sharan	*Tipu Kanan Tipu Kiri*	2008	Astro Shaw, Metrowealth Movies	Bahasa Malaysia	Comedy	35 mm	N/A
Syamsul Yusof	*Evolusi KL Drift*	2008	Skop Production, Primeworks Studios	Bahasa Malaysia	Action	35 mm	101
Syed Mohamed	*Akhirat*	2008	Sri Saheb Production	Bahasa Malaysia	Drama	35 mm	112
Wan Azli	*Budak Kelantan*	2008	Primeworks Studios	Bahasa Malaysia	Drama	35 mm	100
Yana Samsudin	*Selamat Pagi Cinta*	2008	Metrowealth Movies	Bahasa Malaysia	Romance	35 mm	85
Yeop Hitler	*Dunia Baru The Movie*	2008	Primeworks Studios	Bahasa Malaysia	Drama	HD	90
Yusry Abd Halim	*Cicakman 2: Planet Hitam*	2008	KRU Studios, Primeworks Studios	Bahasa Malaysia	Action	35 mm	107
A. Razak Mohaideen	*Rasukan Ablasa*	2009	Primeworks Studios, Lineclear Motion Pictures	Bahasa Malaysia	Horror	35 mm	80
A. Razak Mohaideen	*Skrip 7707*	2009	Primeworks Studios, Lineclear Motion Pictures	Bahasa Malaysia	Horror	35 mm	92
Afdlin Shauki	*Papadom*	2009	Tayangan Unggul	Bahasa Malaysia	Comedy	35 mm	115
Afdlin Shauki	*My Spy*	2009	KRU Studios	Bahasa Malaysia	Comedy	35 mm	94
Ahmad Idham	*Syurga Cinta*	2009	MIG Production	Bahasa Malaysia	Comedy	35 mm	89
Ahmad Idham	*Jangan Pandang Belakang Congkak*	2009	MIG Production	Bahasa Malaysia	Horror-comedy	35 mm	90
Ahmad Idham	*Senario The Movie Episode 2: Beach Boys*	2009	MIG Production	Bahasa Malaysia	Comedy	35 mm	N/A
Along Kamaludin	*Cinta Terakhir*	2009	KSG Pictures	Bahasa Malaysia	Romance	35 mm	95

Filmmaker	Film title	Year	Production Company	Language	Genre	Format	Length (mins)
Azhari Mohd Zain	*Jin Notti*	2009	KRU Studios	Bahasa Malaysia	Comedy	35 mm	94
Azhari Mohd Zain	*Santau*	2009	Metrowealth Movies	Bahasa Malaysia	Horror	35 mm	83
Azmi Mohd Hata	*Duhai Si Pari-pari*	2009	Tayangan Unggul	Bahasa Malaysia	Comedy	35 mm	110
Bade Azmi	*Maut*	2009	Tayangan Unggul	Bahasa Malaysia	Horror	35 mm	90
Bernard Chauly	*Pisau Cukur*	2009	Red Films, Primeworks Studios	Bahasa Malaysia	Comedy	35 mm	100
Bjarne Wong	*Sayang You Can Dance*	2009	Hock Star Ent. Industry	Bahasa Malaysia	Drama	35 mm	94
Jak Othman and Ed Chard	*Inside Silat*	2009	N/A	English	Documentary	Digital	60
Jeffery Wong	*Jin Hutan*	2009	Image Filmhosting Ent., WFE Logistics, Primeworks Studios	Bahasa Malaysia	Thriller	35 mm	100
Kabir Bhatia	*Setem*	2009	Tayangan Unggul	Bahasa Malaysia	Comedy	35 mm	108
M. Subash Abdullah	*Jomlah C.I.U.M*	2009	Genius Parade	Bahasa Malaysia	Drama	35 mm	84
M.Jamil	*Momok The Movie*	2009	Galaksi Seni	Bahasa Malaysia	Horror-comedy	35 mm	102
Majed Salleh	*Lembing Awang Pulang Ke Dayang*	2009	Dayang Digital	Bahasa Malaysia	Action	35 mm	N/A
Muhammad Usamah Zaid Yasin	*Upin & Ipin: Kembara Ke Pulau Harta Karun*	2009	Les' Copaque Production	Bahasa Malaysia	Animation	Digital	19
Nazir Jamaluddin	*Jalang*	2009	De Baron	Bahasa Malaysia	Drama	35 mm	102
Nizam Razak	*Geng: Pengembaraan Bermula*	2009	Les' Copaque Production	Bahasa Malaysia	Animation	35 mm	95
P.Ramesh	*Uttrachai Kali*	2009	N/A	Tamil	Drama	N/A	62
Pierre Andre	*Jangan Tegur*	2009	Metrowealth Movies	Bahasa Malaysia	Horror	35 mm	83
Shahnun Hanif Shuhaimi	*Gaza*	2009	TV3	Bahasa Malaysia	Documentary	Digital	60

Appendix II   241

Filmmaker	Film title	Year	Production Company	Language	Genre	Format	Length (mins)
Suhaimi Kaswan	*Bumi Pribumi*	2009	Finas & Q-Plez Comm.	Bahasa Malaysia	Documentary	35 mm	N/A
Syamsul Yusof	*Bohsia: Jangan Pilih Jalan Hitam*	2009	Skop Production, Primeworks Studios	Bahasa Malaysia	Action	35 mm	88
Syirfan Indra Mitra Surya Hussin	*Rosli Dhoby - Pembunuh atau Pejuang*	2009	N/A	Bahasa Malaysia	Documentary	Digital	60
Uttam Kumar Thangiah	*Pulau Asmara*	2009	Alakazam Productions	Bahasa Malaysia	Drama	35 mm	104
A. Razak Mohaideen	*2 Hati 1 Jiwa*	2010	Primeworks Studios, Lineclear Motion Pictures	Bahasa Malaysia	Comedy	35 mm	109
A. Razak Mohaideen	*4 Madu*	2010	Primeworks Studios, Lineclear Motion Pictures	Bahasa Malaysia	Romantic comedy	35 mm	107
Aamigoz Sugu	*Panjamuni*	2010	N/A	Tamil	Drama	N/A	80
Ah Niu	*Ice Kacang Puppy Love*	2010	Asia Tropical Films	Bahasa Malaysia	Romantic comedy	35 mm	105
Ahmad Idham	*Adnan Semp-It*	2010	MIG Production	Bahasa Malaysia	Comedy	35 mm	90
Ahmad Idham	*Niyang Rapik*	2010	Excellent Pictures	Bahasa Malaysia	Horror	35 mm	90
Ahmad Idham	*Semerah Cinta Stilleto*	2010	Metrowealth Movies	Bahasa Malaysia	Drama	35 mm	87
Ahmad Idham	*Jangan Pandang Belakang Congkak 2*	2010	MIG Production	Bahasa Malaysia	Horror-comedy	35 mm	90
Ahmad Idham	*Cuti-Cuti Cinta*	2010	MIG Production	Bahasa Malaysia	Romance	35 mm	86
Ahmad Idham	*Aku Masih Dara*	2010	Metrowealth Movies	Bahasa Malaysia	Romance	35 mm	90
Ahmad Idham	*Damping Malam*	2010	Metrowealth Movies	Bahasa Malaysia	Horror	35 mm	90
Allen Tinggi	*Saloi The Movie*	2010	Allen Tinggie Trading	Iban	Comedy	Digital	147

Filmmaker	Film title	Year	Production Company	Language	Genre	Format	Length (mins)
Aminah Rhapor	*Lu Pikirlah Sendiri de Movie*	2010	SDAF Pictures	Bahasa Malaysia	Comedy	35 mm	90
Azhari Mohd Zain	*Zoo*	2010	MIG Production	Bahasa Malaysia	Comedy	35 mm	N/A
Azhari Mohd Zain	*Mantra*	2010	MIG Production	Bahasa Malaysia	Horror	35 mm	86
Azizi Chunk	*Kapoww!!*	2010	Tayangan Unggul	Bahasa Malaysia	Comedy	HD	110
Boris Boo	*Aku Tak Bodoh*	2010	Primeworks Studios	Bahasa Malaysia	Comedy	35 mm	95
Chiu Keng Guan	*Tiger Woohoo!*	2010	Astro Shaw	Mandarin	Drama	35 mm	95
Dean A. Burhanuddin	*Crayon*	2010	Zioss	English	Drama	35 mm	83
Dhojee	*Hooperz*	2010	Primeworks Studios, MHZ Films	Bahasa Malaysia	Drama	35 mm	103
Din CJ	*Andartu Terlampau 21 Hari Mencari Suami*	2010	Big Productions	Bahasa Malaysia	Romantic comedy	35 mm	90
Edry Abdul Halim	*Magika*	2010	KRU Studios	Bahasa Malaysia	Musical	35 mm	94
Farid Kamil	*V3 Samseng Jalanan*	2010	MIG Production	Bahasa Malaysia	Action	35 mm	N/A
Hatta Azad Khan	*Senario Asam Garam*	2010	MIG Production	Bahasa Malaysia	Comedy	35 mm	83
Ismail Bob Hashim	*Ngangkung*	2010	Metrowealth Movies	Bahasa Malaysia	Horror-comedy	35 mm	92
Jason Chong	*Belukar*	2010	Preston Zaidan Productions	Bahasa Malaysia	Action	35 mm	96
Julian Cheah	*Killer Clown*	2010	Julian Cheah Pictures	English	Horror	35 mm	79
M. Subash Abdullah	*Mannaan - Mencari Cahaya*	2010	Genius Parade	Tamil	Drama	Digital	60
Mamat Khalid	*Estet*	2010	Naga VXS	Bahasa Malaysia	Comedy	35 mm	101
Mamat Khalid	*Hantu Kak Limah Balik Rumah*	2010	Tayangan Unggul	Bahasa Malaysia	Horror-comedy	35 mm	100

Appendix II

Filmmaker	Film title	Year	Production Company	Language	Genre	Format	Length (mins)
S. Baldev Singh, Ikhzal Ideris	*Kecoh Betul*	2010	Sri Saheb Production, White Merpati Ent.	Bahasa Malaysia	Action	35 mm	155
Sharad Sharan	*Lagenda Budak Setan*	2010	Astro Shaw	Bahasa Malaysia	Romance	35 mm	106
Syamsul Yusof	*Evolusi KL Drift 2*	2010	Skop Production	Bahasa Malaysia	Action	35 mm	100
Hairie Othman, Ed Zarith	*2 Alam*	2010	Dr. Movie Production	Bahasa Malaysia	Horror	35 mm	86
Yeop Hitler	*Janin*	2010	Primeworks Studios	Bahasa Malaysia	Horror	35 mm	110
A. Razak Mohaideen	*Raya Tak Jadi*	2011	Primeworks Studios, Lineclear Motion Pictures	Bahasa Malaysia	Comedy	35 mm	93
Afdlin Shauki	*Appalam*	2011	Tayangan Unggul	Bahasa Malaysia	Comedy	35 mm	115
Afdlin Shauki	*Misteri Jalan Lama*	2011	Tayangan Unggul	Bahasa Malaysia	Thriller	35 mm	N/A
Ahmad Idham	*Senjakala*	2011	Excellent Pictures, MIG Production	Bahasa Malaysia	Horror	35 mm	90
Ahmad Idham	*Hantu Bonceng*	2011	Excellent Pictures	Bahasa Malaysia	Horror	35 mm	90
Azhari Mohd Zain	*Flat 3A*	2011	Metrowealth Movies	Bahasa Malaysia	Horror	35 mm	95
Chiu Keng Guan	*Great Day*	2011	Astro Shaw	Cantonese	Drama	35 mm	91
CL Hor, Jumaatun Azmi	*Haq*	2011	Kasehdia	Bahasa Malaysia	Science fiction	35 mm	90
Effendee, Fariza Azlina	*Songlap*	2011	Primeworks Studios	Bahasa Malaysia	Action	35 mm	N/A
Farid Kamil	*Kongsi*	2011	Metrowealth Movies	Bahasa Malaysia	Gangster	35 mm	90
Hatta Azad Khan	*Kembar Siang*	2011	Metrowealth Movies	Bahasa Malaysia	Comedy	35 mm	87
Ismail Bob Hashim	*Senario The Movie Ops Pocot*	2011	Metrowealth Movies	Bahasa Malaysia	Comedy	35 mm	83
Ismail Bob Hashim	*Alamak Toyol*	2011	Metrowealth Movies	Bahasa Malaysia	Horror-comedy	35 mm	85

Filmmaker	Film title	Year	Production Company	Language	Genre	Format	Length (mins)
Ismail Bob Hashim	*Bini-Biniku Gangster*	2011	Metrowealth Movies	Bahasa Malaysia	Comedy	35 mm	92
James Lee	*Sini Ada Hantu*	2011	Astro Shaw	Bahasa Malaysia, Mandarin, Cantonese	Horror	35 mm	98
James Lee	*Tolong Awek Aku Pontianak*	2011	Tayangan Unggul	Bahasa Malaysia	Horror-comedy	35 mm	102
James Lee	*Claypot Curry Killers*	2011	N/A	N/A	N/A	N/A	N/A
Kabir Bhatia	*Nur Kasih The Movie*	2011	Primeworks Studios	Bahasa Malaysia	Drama	35 mm	90
M.Jamil	*Momok Jangan Panggil Aku*	2011	Galaksi Seni	Bahasa Malaysia	Horror-comedy	35 mm	98
Namewee	*Nasi Lemak 2.0*	2011	Prodigee Media	Bahasa Malaysia, English, Mandarin, Tamil	Comedy	35 mm	90
Osman Ali	*Cun*	2011	Nuansa, Tayangan Unggul	Bahasa Malaysia	Romantic comedy	35 mm	105
Osman Ali	*Ombak Rindu*	2011	Astro Shaw	Bahasa Malaysia	Drama	35 mm	N/A
Othman Hafsham	*Karipap Karipap Cinta*	2011	Cinematic Pictures	Bahasa Malaysia	Comedy	35 mm	110
Pierre Andre	*Al-Hijab*	2011	Empat Semudra Plantation	Bahasa Malaysia	Horror	35 mm	90
Pierre Andre, Woo Ming Jin	*Seru*	2011	Tayangan Unggul	Bahasa Malaysia	Horror	35 mm	84
S. Baldev Singh	*Rasuk*	2011	Sri Saheb Production, White Merpati Ent.	Bahasa Malaysia	Horror	35 mm	90
Syamsul Yusof	*Khurafat*	2011	Skop Production, Primeworks Studios	Bahasa Malaysia	Horror	35 mm	80
Syamsul Yusof	*KL Gangster*	2011	Skop Production	Bahasa Malaysia	Gangster	35 mm	81
Syamsul Yusof	*Aku Bukan Tomboy*	2011	Skop Production	Bahasa Malaysia	Comedy	35 mm	97
Z Lokman	*Toyol Nakal*	2011	Artistik Pictures	Bahasa Malaysia	Comedy	35 mm	93

Appendix II

Filmmaker	Film title	Year	Production Company	Language	Genre	Format	Length (mins)
Naga	*Underground Rascals*	2010	N/A	Tamil	Crime	N/A	120
Khir Rahman	*Dalam Botol*	2011	Pengedaran JAS	Bahasa Malaysia	Drama	35 mm	90
Yusry Abd Halim	*Hikayat Merong Mahawangsa*	2011	KRU Studios	Bahasa Malaysia, English	Drama	35 mm	109
James Lee and Sampson Yuen Choi-Hin	*Petaling Street Warriors*	2011	Juita Ent.	English, Mandarin, Bahasa Malaysia, Cantonese, Hailam, Hokkien, and Japanese	Action	35 mm	106
Wan Hasliza	*Penunggu Istana*	2011	Primeworks Studios	Bahasa Malaysia	Horror	35 mm	90

Appendix III: Database for Horror Films in Post-2000 Malaysian Cinema, 2000–2011

Filmmaker	Film title	Year	Production Company	Language	Genre	Format	Length (mins)
A. Razak Mohaideen	*Mistik*	2003	Metrowealth Movies	Bahasa Malaysia	Horror	35 mm	100
A. Razak Mohaideen	*Potret Mistik*	2004	Metrowealth Movies, Primeworks Studios	Bahasa Malaysia	Horror	35 mm	N/A
A. Razak Mohaideen	*I Know What U Did Last Raya*	2004	Primeworks Studios, MIG Beats	Bahasa Malaysia	Horror-comedy	35 mm	95
A. Razak Mohaideen	*Tujuh Perhentian*	2004	MIG Beats, Metrowealth Movies, Primeworks Studios	Bahasa Malaysia	Horror-romance	35 mm	95
Ho Yuhang	*Anybody Home?* (In *Visits. Hungry Ghost Anthology*)	2004	Red Films	Mandarin	Horror	Digital	110
James Lee	*Waiting for Them* (In *Visits. Hungry Ghost Anthology*)	2004	Red Films	Mandarin	Horror	Digital	110
Low Ngai Yuen	*1413* (In *Visits. Hungry Ghost Anthology*)	2004	Red Films	Mandarin	Horror	Digital	110
Ng Tian Hann	*Nodding Scoop* (In *Visits. Hungry Ghost Anthology*)	2004	Red Films	Mandarin	Horror	Digital	110
Shuhaimi Baba	*Pontianak Harum Sundal Malam*	2004	Pesona Pictures, Jugra Publication	Bahasa Malaysia	Horror	35 mm	115

Appendix III

Filmmaker	Film title	Year	Production Company	Language	Genre	Format	Length (mins)
Silver Chung	*Di Ambang Misteri*	2004	Cosmos Discovery	Bahasa Malaysia	Horror	35 mm	95
Silver Chung	*Makar*	2004	Cosmos Discovery	Bahasa Malaysia	Horror	35 mm	105
Bjarne Wong	*The Legend of the Red Curse*	2005	Hock Star Ent. Industry	English, Mandarin, Bahasa Malaysia, Iban	Horror	35 mm	78
Premnath Pillai	*Uyir*	2005	Ambi Agency	Tamil	Horror	Digital	90
S. Baldev Singh, Aziz Sattar, Arjinder Singh	*Maaria*	2005	Sri Saheb Production	English	Horror	35 mm	150
Shuhaimi Baba	*Pontianak Harum Sundal Malam 2*	2005	Pesona Pictures	Bahasa Malaysia	Horror	35 mm	117
Yusof Kelana	*Pontianak Menjerit*	2005	ME Comm., Skop Production	Bahasa Malaysia	Horror-comedy	35 mm	105
Bjarne Wong	*Possessed*	2006	Hock Star Ent. Industry	Cantonese	Horror	35 mm	84
Kit Ong	*The Flowers Beneath My Skin*	2006	N/A	N/A	Horror	Digital	70
Michael Chuah	*Seed Of Darkness*	2006	Evo Pictures	Cantonese	Horror	Digital	90
Sandosh Kesavan	*Gong*	2006	Primeworks Studios	Bahasa Malaysia	Horror	35 mm	99
Ahmad Idham	*Jangan Pandang Belakang*	2007	Metrowealth Movies	Bahasa Malaysia	Horror	35 mm	99
Bade Azmi	*Syaitan*	2007	Tayangan Unggul	Bahasa Malaysia	Horror	35 mm	90
Jamal Maarif, C.K. Karan	*Orang Minyak*	2007	Infohibur Production	Bahasa Malaysia	Horror	35 mm	98
Osman Ali	*Puaka Tebing Biru*	2007	Tayangan Unggul	Bahasa Malaysia	Horror	35 mm	130
Shuhaimi Baba	*Waris Jari Hantu*	2007	Pesona Pictures, Primeworks Studios	Bahasa Malaysia	Horror	35 mm	110
VN Raj	*Aathma*	2007	Demaz Ent.	Tamil	Horror	Digital	105
Zarina Abdullah	*Chermin*	2007	Starry Eye Production	Bahasa Malaysia	Horror	35 mm	98

Filmmaker	Film title	Year	Production Company	Language	Genre	Format	Length (mins)
Mamat Khalid	*Zombie Kampung Pisang*	2007	Tayangan Unggul	Bahasa Malaysia	Horror-comedy	35 mm	118
Ahmad Idham	*Congkak*	2008	Metrowealth Movies	Bahasa Malaysia	Horror	35 mm	86
Amir Muhammad, Naeim Ghalili	*Susuk*	2008	Primeworks Studios	Bahasa Malaysia	Horror	35 mm	110
Barney Lee	*Anak*	2008	Box Lite Film	Bahasa Malaysia	Horror	35 mm	90
James Lee	*Histeria*	2008	Tayangan Unggul	Bahasa Malaysia	Horror	35 mm	91
Mamat Khalid	*Kala Malam Bulan Mengambang*	2008	Tayangan Unggul	Bahasa Malaysia	Horror-comedy	35 mm	110
Azizi Chunk	*Antoo Fighter*	2008	Primeworks Studios	Bahasa Malaysia	Horror-comedy	35 mm	114
A. Razak Mohaideen	*Skrip 7707*	2009	Primeworks Studios, Lineclear Motion Pictures	Bahasa Malaysia	Horror	35 mm	92
Azhari Mohd Zain	*Santau*	2009	Metrowealth Movies	Bahasa Malaysia	Horror	35 mm	83
Bade Azmi	*Maut*	2009	Tayangan Unggul	Bahasa Malaysia	Horror	35 mm	90
Pierre Andre	*Jangan Tegur*	2009	Metrowealth Movies	Bahasa Malaysia	Horror	35 mm	83
Ahmad Idham	*Jangan Pandang Belakang Congkak*	2009	MIG Production	Bahasa Malaysia	Horror-comedy	35 mm	90
M.Jamil	*Momok The Movie*	2009	Galaksi Seni	Bahasa Malaysia	Horror-comedy	35 mm	102
Ahmad Idham	*Niyang Rapik*	2010	Excellent Pictures	Bahasa Malaysia	Horror	35 mm	90
Ahmad Idham	*Damping Malam*	2010	Metrowealth Movies	Bahasa Malaysia	Horror	35 mm	90
Azhari Mohd Zain	*Mantra*	2010	MIG Production	Bahasa Malaysia	Horror	35 mm	86
Hairie Othman, Ed Zarith	*2 Alam*	2010	Dr. Movie Production	Bahasa Malaysia	Horror	35 mm	86
Julian Cheah	*Killer Clown*	2010	Julian Cheah Pictures	English	Horror	35 mm	79

Appendix III

Filmmaker	Film title	Year	Production Company	Language	Genre	Format	Length (mins)
Yeop Hitler	*Janin*	2010	Primeworks Studios	Bahasa Malaysia	Horror	35 mm	110
Ahmad Idham	*Jangan Pandang Belakang Congkak 2*	2010	MIG Production	Bahasa Malaysia	Horror-comedy	35 mm	90
Ismail Bob Hashim	*Ngangkung*	2010	Metrowealth Movies	Bahasa Malaysia	Horror-comedy	35 mm	92
Mamat Khalid	*Hantu Kak Limah Balik Rumah*	2010	Tayangan Unggul	Bahasa Malaysia	Horror-comedy	35 mm	100
Ahmad Idham	*Senjakala*	2011	Excellent Pictures, MIG Production	Bahasa Malaysia	Horror	35 mm	90
Ahmad Idham	*Hantu Bonceng*	2011	Excellent Pictures	Bahasa Malaysia	Horror	35 mm	90
Azhari Mohd Zain	*Flat 3A*	2011	Metrowealth Movies	Bahasa Malaysia	Horror	35 mm	95
James Lee	*Sini Ada Hantu*	2011	Astro Shaw	Bahasa Malaysia, Mandarin, Cantonese	Horror	35 mm	98
Pierre Andre	*Al-Hijab*	2011	Empat Semudra Plantation	Bahasa Malaysia	Horror	35 mm	90
Pierre Andre, Woo Ming Jin	*Seru*	2011	Tayangan Unggul	Bahasa Malaysia	Horror	35 mm	84
S. Baldev Singh	*Rasuk*	2011	Sri Saheb Production, White Merpati Ent.	Bahasa Malaysia	Horror	35 mm	90
Syamsul Yusof	*Khurafat*	2011	Skop Production, Primeworks Studios	Bahasa Malaysia	Horror	35 mm	80
Ismail Bob Hashim	*Alamak Toyol*	2011	Metrowealth Movies	Bahasa Malaysia	Horror-comedy	35 mm	85
James Lee	*Tolong! Awek Aku Pontianak*	2011	Tayangan Unggul	Bahasa Malaysia	Horror-comedy	35 mm	102
M.Jamil	*Momok Jangan Panggil Aku*	2011	Galaksi Seni	Bahasa Malaysia	Horror-comedy	35 mm	98
Yusry Abd Halim	*Karak*	2011	KRU Studios	Bahasa Malaysia	Horror	35 mm	90
Wan Hasliza	*Penunggu Istana*	2011	Primeworks Studios	Bahasa Malaysia	Horror	35 mm	90

References

Affendi, Jamaludin. 2009. Personal Conversation with Yuen Beng Lee. Melbourne, Australia, 7 October.

Agusta, Paul F. 2004. 'Malaysia's New Generation of Filmmakers Find Their Own Voices'. *The Jakarta Post*, 1 March.

Allen, Richard. 1999. 'Psychoanalytic Film Theory'. In *A Companion to Film Theory*, edited by T. Miller and R. Stam, 123–145. Oxford: Blackwell.

Althusser, Louis. 1972. 'Ideology and Ideological State Apparatuses: Notes Towards an Investigation'. In *Lenin and Philosophy and Other Essays*, 85–126. New York: Monthly Review Press.

Amir, Muhammad. 2006. *Coming to Korean TV*. Accessed 1 April 2010. http://lastcommunist.blogspot.com/2006_05_01_archive.html.

Amir, Muhammad. 2007. '"Non-Malaysian" Films Get Recognition'. *New Straits Times*, 18 January, 18.

Amir, Muhammad. 2010a. *Malaysiakini on "Malaysian Gods"*. Accessed 14 August 2010. http://amirmu.blogspot.com/2008/09/malaysiakini-on-malaysian-gods.html.

Amir, Muhammad. 2010b. Personal Conversation with Yuen Beng Lee. Kuala Lumpur, Malaysia, 25 July.

Amir, Muhammad. 2012. *Telling Stories to Her Nation: Six Commercials by the Late Malaysian Filmmaker Yasmin Ahmad*. Accessed 9 February 2012. http://www.movingimagesource.us/articles/telling-stories-to-her-nation-20100129.

Andaya, Barbara Watson, and Leonard Y. Andaya. 2001. *A History of Malaysia*. 2nd ed. Hampshire: Palgrave.

Anderson, Benedict. 1991. *Imagined Communities: Reflections of the Origin and Spread of Nationalism*. London: Verso.

Ang, Ien. 2010. 'Between Nationalism and Transnationalism: Multiculturalism in a Globalising World'. Paper read at Biennial Malaysian Studies Conference, at Penang, Malaysia.

Appadurai, Arjun. 1996. *Modernity at Large: Cultural Dimensions of Globalization*. Minneapolis: University of Minnesota Press.

Appiah, Anthony Kwame. 2006. *Cosmopolitanism: Ethics in a World of Strangers*. New York: W.W. Norton.

Armes, Roy. 1987. *Third World Film Making and the West*. Berkeley: University of California Press.

References

Asiaweek. 1995. 'One Nation, One People: Mahathir Lays the Groundwork for Stronger Unity'. Accessed 20 October 2008. http://edition.cnn.com/ASIANOW/asiaweek/95/1006/nat4.html.

Asthana, N. C., and A. Nirmal. 2009. *Urban Terrorism: Myths and Realities*. Jaipur, India: Pointer Publishers.

Awang, Azman Awang Pawi, and Khor Chooi Lian, eds. 2005. *P. Ramlee di cakera nusantara*. Kota Samarahan: Universiti Malaysia Sarawak.

Azly, Rahman. 2009. 'The "New Bumiputeraism" as Pedagogy of Hope and Liberation: Teaching the Alternative Malaysian Ethnic Studies'. In *Multiethnic Malaysia: Past, Present and Future*, edited by T. G. Lim, A. Gomes, and R. Azly, 429–446. Kuala Lumpur: SIRD.

Baharudin, Latif. 1983. *Krisis filem Melayu*. Kuala Lumpur: Insular Publishing House.

Baharudin, Latif, and Groves, Don. 1994. 'Film Censorship Board Termed Fickle, at Best'. *Variety*, 22–28 August, 38.

Baharudin, Latif, and Groves, Don. 1995. 'Censorship is Alive and Well'. *Variety*, 21–27 August, 54.

Balmain, Colette. 2008. *Introduction to Japanese Horror Film*. Edinburgh: Edinburgh University Press.

Banchoff, Thomas. 2007. 'Introduction'. In *Democracy and the New Religious Pluralism*, edited by T. Banchoff, 3–16. New York: Oxford University Press.

Barker, Thomas, and Lee Yuen Beng. 2017. 'Making Creative Industries Policy: The Malaysian Case'. *Kajian Malaysia* 35 (2): 21–37.

Barker, Thomas, and Lee Yuen Beng. 2018. 'Creating within Constraints: Creative Industries Policy in Malaysia'. In *Routledge Handbook of Cultural and Creative Industries in Asia*, edited by L. Lorraine and Hye-Kyung Lee, 13–26. London: Routledge.

Barnard, Timothy P. 2010. 'Filem Melayu: Nationalism, Modernity and Film in a Pre-World War Two Malay Magazine'. *Journal of Southeast Asian Studies* 41 (1): 47–70.

Basch, Linda, Nina Glick Schiller, and Cristina Szanton Blanc. 1994. *Nations Unbound: Transnational Projects, Postcolonial Predicaments, and Deterritorialized Nation-States*. London: Gordon and Breach.

Bernama. 2011. *Call for Tax Rebate for Malaysian Movies in Local Dialects*. Accessed 6 February 2011. http://web6.bernama.com/bernama/v3/bm/news_lite.php?id=562247.

Berry, Chris. 1994. 'Neither One Thing nor Another: Toward a Study of the Viewing Subject and Chinese Cinema in the 1980s'. In *New Chinese Cinemas: Forms, Identities, Politics*, edited by N. Browne, P. G. Pickowicz, V. Sobchack and E. Yau, 88–116. New York: Cambridge University Press.

Bhabha, Homi K. 1990. 'DissemiNation: Time, Narrative, and the Margins of the Modern Nation'. In *Nation and Narration*, edited by Homi K. Bhabha, 291–322. London: Routledge.

Bhabha, Homi K. 2004. *The Location of Culture*. London: Routledge.

Bishop, Kyle William. 2010. *American Zombie Gothic: The Rise and Fall (and Rise) of the Walking Dead in Popular Culture*. Jefferson, NC: McFarland.

Bissme, S. 2006. 'All about Feelings'. *The Sun*, 1 June.

Boase, Roger. 2005. 'Introduction'. In *Islam and Global Dialogue: Religious Pluralism and the Pursuit of Peace*, edited by R. Boase, 1–10. Aldershot, UK: Ashgate.

Bordwell, David. 1985. *Narration in the Fiction Film*. Madison: University of Wisconsin Press.

Brockopp, Jonathan E. 2000. 'Islam'. In *Death and the Afterlife*, edited by J. Neusner, 60–78. Cleveland, OH: The Pilgrim Press.

Brown, David. 1996. *The State and Ethnic Politics in Southeast Asia*. London: Routledge.

Brown, Michael E. 1997. 'The Impact of Government Policies on Ethnic Relations'. In *Government Policies and Ethnic Relations in Asia and the Pacific*, edited by M. E. Brown and Š. Ganguly, 511–576. Cambridge, MA: MIT Press.

Buscombe, Edward. 1973. 'Ideas of Authorship'. *Screen* 14 (3):75–85.

Carroll, Noël. 1990. *The Philosophy of Horror, or, Paradoxes of the Heart*. New York: Routledge.

Carroll, Noël. 2001. 'Why Horror?' In *Arguing about Art: Contemporary Philosophical Debates*, edited by A. Neill and A. Ridley, 297–316. London: Routledge.

Cashmore, Ellis. 2004. *Encyclopaedia of Race and Ethnic Studies*. London: Routledge.

Catsoulis, Jeannette. 2008. 'Mukhsin (2006)'. *The New York Times*.

Chaiworaporn, Anchalee, and Adam Knee. 2006. 'Thailand: Revival in an Age of Globalization'. In *Contemporary Asian Cinema: Popular Culture in a Global Frame*, edited by A. T. Ciecko, 58–70. Oxford: Berg.

Chan, Christine. 2010. '"Gadoh" Film Not Approved for Public Screening'. Accessed 12 August 2011. https://www.malaysiakini.com/news/141665.

Chan, Felicia. 2011. 'The International Film Festival and the Making of a National Cinema'. *Screen* 52 no. 2 (Summer): 253–260.

Chapman, James. 2003. *Cinemas of the World: Film and Society from 1895 to the Present*. London: Reaktion.

Chaudhuri, Shohini. 2005. *Contemporary World Cinema: Europe, the Middle East, East Asia and South Asia*. Edinburgh: Edinburgh University Press.

Cheah, Boon Kheng. 2002. *Malaysia: The Making of a Nation*. Singapore: Institute of Southeast Asian Studies.

Cheah, Boon Kheng. 2003. *Red Star over Malaya: Resistance and Social Conflict During and After the Japanese Occupation of Malaya, 1941–1946*. 3rd ed. Singapore: Singapore University Press.

Cheah, Boon Kheng. 2005. 'Ethnicity in the Making of Malaysia'. In *Nation Building: Five Southeast Asian Histories*, edited by G. Wang, 91–116. Singapore: ISEAS Publications.

Cheah, Boon Kheng. 2007. 'Malaysia: Envisioning the Nation at the Time of Independence'. In *Rethinking Ethnicity and Nation Building: Malaysia, Sri Lanka and Fiji in Comparative Perspective*, edited by A. R. Embong, 40–56. Selangor: Persatuan Sains Sosial Malaysia.

Cheah, Pheng. 2003. *Spectral Nationality: Passages of Freedom from Kant to Postcolonial Literatures of Liberation*. New York: Columbia University Press.

Chee, Kiong Tong. 2010. *Identity Ethnic Relations in Southeast Asia: Racializing Chineseness*. Dordrecht: Springer.

Cherry, Brigid. 2009. *Horror*. London: Routledge.

Cheung, Esther M. K., Gina Marchetti, and See-Kam Tan, eds. 2011. *Hong Kong Screenscapes: From the New Wave to the Digital Frontier*. Hong Kong: Hong Kong University Press.

Choi, Jinhee, and Mitsuyo Wada-Marciano. 2009. 'Introduction'. In *Horror to the Extreme: Changing Boundaries in Asian Cinema*, edited by Jinhee Choi and Mitsuyo Wada-Marciano, 1–12. Hong Kong: Hong Kong University Press.

Chok, Suat Ling, Ibrahim Anis, Eileen Ng, and Ahmad Arman. 2005. 'MPs Debate Merits of "Sepet"'. *New Straits Times*, 31 March, 22.

References 253

Chong, Debra. 2009. 'What Price Malaysia's Honour?' *The Malaysian Insider*, 2 December. http://www.themalaysianinsider.com/index.php/malaysia/45282-what-price-malaysias-honour-.

Chong, Terence. 2006. 'The Emerging Politics of Islam Hadhari'. In *Malaysia: Recent Trends and Challenges*, edited by Saw S. H. and K. Kesavapany, 26–46. Singapore: Institute of Southeast Asian Studies.

Codell, Julie F. 2007. 'World Cinema: Joining Local and Global'. In *Genre, Gender, Race, and World Cinema: An Anthology*, edited by J. F. Codell, 359–368. Malden, MA: Blackwell.

Cohen, Jeffrey Jerome. 1996. 'Monster Culture (Seven Theses)'. In *Monster Theory: Reading Culture*, edited by J. J. Cohen, 3–25. Minneapolis: University of Minnesota Press.

Corlett, J. Angelo. 2003. *Race, Racism and Reparations*. Ithaca, NY: Cornell University Press.

Corlett, J. Angelo. 2007. 'Race, Ethnicity and the Public Policy'. In *Race or Ethnicity? On Black and Latino Identity*, edited by J. J. E. Gracia, 225–247. Ithaca, NY: Cornell University Press.

Corliss, Richard. 2001. 'Bright Lights'. *Time*, 19 March. http://content.time.com/time/subscriber/article/0,33009,103002,00.html.

Cornelius, Sheila, and Ian Haydn Smith. 2002. *New Chinese Cinema: Challenging Representations*. London: Wallflower Press.

Cox, Oliver Cromwell. 2000. *Race: A Study in Social Dynamics*. New York: Monthly Review Press.

Creed, Barbara. 1996. 'Horror and the Monstrous-Feminine: An Imaginary Abjection'. In *The Dread of Difference: Gender and the Horror Film*, edited by B. K. Grant, 37–67. Austin: University of Texas Press.

Creed, Barbara. 2004. *Pandora's Box: Essays in Film Theory*. Melbourne: Australian Centre for the Moving Image with the Cinema Studies Program, University of Melbourne.

Creed, Barbara. 2005. *Phallic Panic: Film, Horror and the Primal Uncanny*. Carlton, Victoria: Melbourne University Press.

Cubitt, Sean. 2004. *The Cinema Effect*. Cambridge, MA: MIT Press.

D'Oliviero, Michael 2004. 'Exploring Film Censorship in Malaysia'. *Metro Magazine: Media & Education Magazine*: 106–107.

Daniels, Timothy P. 2005. *Building Cultural Nationalism in Malaysia*. New York: Routledge.

Darr, Brian. 2005. *Video as a Subversive Art: The 48th San Francisco International Film Festival, April 21–May 5, 2005*. Accessed 1 March 2010. http://archive.sensesofcinema.com/contents/festivals/05/36/sfiff2005.html.

Davis, Blair, and Kial Natale. 2010. '"The Pound of Flesh Which I Demand": American Horror Cinema, Gore, and the Box Office, 1998–2007'. In *American Horror Film: The Genre at the Turn of the Millennium*, edited by S. J. Hantke, 35–57. Jackson: University Press of Mississippi.

DeBernardi, Jean. 2004. *Rites of Belonging: Memory, Modernity, and Identity in a Malaysian Chinese Community*. Redwood City, CA: Stanford University Press.

de Valck, Marijke 2007. *Film Festivals: From European Geopolitics to Global Cinephilia*. Amsterdam: Amsterdam University Press.

de Valck, Marijke, and Skadi Loist. 2009. 'Film Festival Studies: An Overview of a Burgeoning Field'. In *Film Festival Yearbook 1: The Festival Circuit*, edited by D. Iordanova and R. Rhyne, 179–215. St Andrews: University of St Andrews.

Dennison, Stephanie, and Hwee Lim Song. 2006. 'Introduction. Situating World Cinema as a Theoretical Problem'. In *Remapping World Cinema: Identity, Culture and Politics in Film*, edited by S. Dennison and H. L. Song, 1–15. London: Wallflower Press.

Department of Statistics Malaysia. 2020. 'Current Population Estimates, Malaysia, 2020'. Accessed 1 May 2021. https://www.dosm.gov.my/v1/index.php?r=column/cthemeByCat&cat=155&bul_id=OVByWjg5YkQ3MWFZRTN5bDJiaEVhZz09&menu_id=L0pheU43NWJwRWVSZklWdzQ4TlhUUT09.

Dharmender Singh. 2010. 'New Film Censorship Rules on March 15'. *The Star*, 8 March.

Diani, Hera. 2008a. *Asia's Digital Cinema Only Serves as Training Ground*. Accessed 27 February 2010. http://m.thejakartapost.com/news/2002/12/22/asia039s-digital-cinema-only-serves-training-ground.html.

Diani, Hera. 2008b. *Malaysian Filmmaker Ready to Challenge Viewers*. Accessed 1 March 2010. http://m.thejakartapost.com/news/2003/01/05/malaysian-filmmaker-ready-challenge-viewers.html.

Donnelly, K. J. 2005. *The Spectre of Sound: Music in Film and Television*. London: BFI.

Drotner, Kirsten. 1999. 'Dangerous Media? Panic Discourses and Dilemmas of Modernity'. *Paedagogica Historica* 35 (3): 593–610.

Dunne, Tim. 2008. 'Liberalism'. In *The Globalization of World Politics: An Introduction to International Relations*, edited by J. Baylis, S. Smith, and P. Owens, 113–125. New York: New York University Press.

Edwards, Russell. 2009. 'Talentime'. *Variety*, 2 November. https://variety.com/2009/film/reviews/talentime-1200477636/.

Elsaesser, Thomas. 2005. *European Cinema: Face to Face with Hollywood*. Amsterdam: Amsterdam University Press.

Embong, Abdul Rahman. 2001. 'The Culture and Practice of Pluralism in Postcolonial Malaysia'. In *The Politics of Multiculturalism: Pluralism and Citizenship in Malaysia, Singapore and Indonesia*, edited by R. W. Hefner, 59–85. Honolulu: University of Hawai'i Press.

Embong, Abdul Rahman. 2007. *Rethinking Ethnicity and Nation-Building: Malaysia, Sri Lanka & Fiji in Comparative Perspective*. Selangor: Persatuan Sains Sosial Malaysia.

Eriksen, Thomas Hylland. 2002. *Ethnicity and Nationalism*. 2nd ed. London: Pluto Press.

Esposito, John L., and John O. Voll. 2001. *Makers of Contemporary Islam*. New York: Oxford University Press.

Ezra, Elizabeth, and Terry Rowden. 2006. 'General Introduction: What Is Transnational Cinema?' In *Transnational Cinema: The Film Reader*, edited by E. Ezra and T. Rowden, 1–12. London: Routledge.

Faridul, Anwar Farinordin. 2004a. 'Censorship Rules a Dampener'. *New Straits Times*, 27 January, 3.

Faridul, Anwar Farinordin. 2004b. '"Pontianak" Returns with a Vengeance'. *New Straits Times*, 1 May, 3.

Faridul, Anwar Farinordin. 2008. 'Getting into the Heart of Yasmin'. *New Straits Times*, 31 August.

Farish, A. Noor. 2009. *What Your Teacher Didn't Tell You: The Annexe Lectures (Volume 1)*. Petaling Jaya, Malaysia: Matahari Books.

Fenton, Steve. 1999. *Ethnicity: Racism, Class and Culture*. London: Macmillan.

References255

Fenton, Steve, and Stephen May. 2002. 'Ethnicity, Nation and "Race": Connections and Disjunctures'. In *Ethnonational Identities*, edited by S. Fenton and S. May, 1–20. New York: Palgrave Macmillan.

Freeland, Cynthia A. 1996. 'Feminist Frameworks of Horror Films'. In *Post-theory: Reconstructing Film Studies*, edited by D. Bordwell and N. Carroll, 195–218. Madison: University of Wisconsin Press.

Frisk, Sylva. 2009. *Submitting to God: Women and Islam in Urban Malaysia*. Seattle: University of Washington Press.

Fuller, Thomas. 2001. 'Criticism of 30-Year-Old Affirmative-Action Policy Grows in Malaysia'. *The New York Times*, 5 January.

Furnivall, J. S. 1948. *Colonial Policy and Practice: A Comparative Study of Burma and Netherlands India*. Cambridge: Cambridge University Press.

Gabriel, Teshome Habte. 1982. *Third Cinema in the Third World: The Aesthetics of Liberation*. Ann Arbor, MI: UMI Research Press.

Gandhi, Leela. 1998. *Postcolonial Theory: A Critical Introduction*. New Delhi: Oxford University Press.

Garnham, Nicholas. 1992. *Capitalism and Communication: Global Culture and the Economics of Information*. London: SAGE Publications.

Gatsiounis, Ioannis. 2005. 'The Search for a Malaysian Race'. *Asia Times*, 15 January.

Gazetas, Aristides. 2008. *An Introduction to World Cinema*. Jefferson, NC: McFarland.

Gearhart, Suzanne. 2005. 'Inclusions. Psychoanalysis, Transnationalism, and Minority Cultures'. In *Minor Transnationalism*, edited by F. Lionnet and S.-m. Shih, 27–40. Durham, NC: Duke University Press.

Gerstner, David A. 2003. 'The Practices of Authorship'. In *Authorship and Film*, edited by D. A. Gerstner and J. Staiger, 3–25. New York: Routledge.

Goh, Beng Lan. 2001. 'Rethinking Urbanism in Malaysia. Power, Space and Identity'. In *Risking Malaysia: Culture, Politics and Identity*, edited by M. Maznah and S. K. Wong, 159–178. Bangi: Universiti Kebangsaan Malaysia Press.

Goh, Daniel P. S. 2008. 'From Colonial Pluralism to Postcolonial Multiculturalism: Race, State Formation and the Question of Cultural Diversity in Malaysia and Singapore'. *Sociology Compass* 2 (1): 232–252.

Gomez, Edmund Terence. 2005. 'The Perils of pro-Malay Policies'. *Far Eastern Economic Review* 168 (8): 36–39.

Gomez, Edmund Terence. 2008. *Jockeying for Power in the New Malaysia*. Accessed 4 December 2008. www.e-invest.com.my/index.php?option=com_content&task=view&id=75&Itemid=32.

Gomez, Edmund Terence, and K. S. Jomo. 2001. *Malaysia's Political Economy. Politics, Patronage and Profits*. Cambridge: Cambridge University Press.

Goss, Brian Michael. 2009. *Global Auteurs: Politics in the Films of Almodóvar, von Trier, and Winterbottom*. New York: Peter Lang.

Gracia, Jorge J. E. 2007. 'Race or Ethnicity? An introduction'. In *Race or Ethnicity? On Black and Latino Identity*, edited by J. J. E. Gracia, 1–16. Ithaca, NY: Cornell University Press.

Grant, Barry Keith. 2003. 'Introduction'. In *Film Genre Reader III*, edited by B. K. Grant, xv–xx. Austin: University of Texas Press.

Grassilli, Mariagiulia. 2008. 'Migrant Cinema: Transnational and Guerrilla Practices of Film Production and Representation'. *Journal of Ethnic and Migration Studies* 34 (8): 1237–1255.

Gray, Gordon. 2010. *Cinema: A Visual Anthropology*. New York: Berg.

Grewal, Inderpal. 2005. *Transnational America: Feminisms, Diasporas, Neoliberalisms*. Durham, NC: Duke University Press.

Guarnizo, Luis E., and Michael Peter Smith. 1998. 'The Locations of Transnationalism'. In *Transnationalism from Below*, edited by M. P. Smith and L. E. Guarnizo, 3–34. New Brunswick, NJ: Transaction Publishers.

Guneratne, Anthony R. 2003. 'The Urban and the Urbane: Modernization, Modernism and the Rebirth of Singapore Cinema'. In *Theorizing the Southeast Asian City as Text: Urban Landscapes, Cultural Documents, and Interpretative Experiences*, edited by R. B. H. Goh and B. S. A. Yeoh, 159–190. Singapore: World Scientific Publishing.

Gupta, Akhil, and James Ferguson. 1992. 'Beyond "Culture": Space, Identity, and the Politics of Difference'. *Cultural Anthropology* 7: 6–23.

Hafidah, Samat. 2003. 'Censor's Bite at "Pontianak"'. *New Straits Times*, 23 June, 3.

Hafidah, Samat. 2004. 'Shuhaimi's Singing the Blues'. *New Straits Times*, 1 March, 3.

Hafidah, Samat, and Anwar Farinordin Faridul. 2004. 'Doing it for Themselves'. *New Straits Times*, 30 December, 11.

Hafidz, Mahpar. 2009. 'Rebel about the Cost'. *The Star*, 10 January, 37.

Hageman, Andrew. 2009. 'Floating Consciousness: The Cinematic Confluence of Ecological Aesthetics in Suzhou River'. In *Chinese Ecocinema: In the Age of Environmental Challenge*, edited by S. Lu and J. Mi, 73–92. Hong Kong: Hong Kong University Press.

Hall, Stuart. 1982. 'The Rediscovery of "Ideology": Return of the Repressed in Media Studies'. In *Culture, Society and the Media*, edited by T. Bennett, J. Curran, M. Gurevitch, and J. Wollacott, 56–90. London: Methuen.

Hall, Stuart 2002. 'Political Belongings in a World of Multiple Identities'. In *Conceiving Cosmopolitanism: Theory, Context and Practice*, edited by S. Vertovec and R. Cohen, 25–32. New York: Oxford University Press.

Hamzah, Hussin. 2004. *Memoir Hamzah Hussin: Dari Keris Filem ke Studio Merdeka (Memoirs of Hamzah Hussin: From Keris Films to Merdeka Studio)*. Bangi: Penerbit Universiti Kebangsaan Malaysia.

Hannerz, Ulf. 1996. *Transnational Connections: Culture, People, Places*. London: Routledge.

Harding, James, and Sarji Ahmad. 2002. *P. Ramlee: The Bright Star*. Subang Jaya: Pelanduk Publications.

Harper, Timothy Norman. 1996. 'New Malays, New Malaysians. Nationalism, Society, and History'. In *Southeast Asian Affairs*, edited by D. Singh and T. K. Liak, 238–255. Singapore: Institute of Southeast Asian Studies.

Harper, Timothy Norman. 1997. '"Asian Values" and Southeast Asian Histories'. *The Historical Journal* 40 (2): 507–517.

Harrison, Rachel. 2005. 'Amazing Thai Film: The Rise and Rise of Contemporary Thai Cinema on the International Screen'. *Asian Affairs* 36 (3): 321–338.

Hassan, Muthalib. 2006a. 'Lost Malaysian Films'. In *Lost Films of Asia*, edited by N. Deocampo, 43–50. Pasic City, Philippines: Anvil Publishing.

Hassan, Muthalib. 2006b. *Rabun: The Vision Is Blurred, but the Heart Is Clear*. Accessed 16 February 2010. http://www.criticine.com/review_article.php?id=12.

References 257

Hassan, Muthalib. 2007. 'The Little Cinema of Malaysia'. *A Journal for Film and Audiovisual Media (KINEMA)* (Spring): 1–8.

Hassan, Muthalib. 2005a. *Ho Yuhang's "Sanctuary": The Other Side of Malaysia*. Accessed 19 March 2010. http://www.criticine.com/review_article.php?id=7.

Hassan, Muthalib. 2005b. *Voices of Malaysian Cinema*. Accessed 19 March 2010. http://www.criticine.com/feature_article.php?id=17.

Hassan, Muthalib. 2009. *Sweet and Bitter Dreams: The Legacy of the AFM (Malaysian Film Academy)*. Accessed 1 March 2010. http://bengkelsenilayar.webs.com/about.htm.

Hassan, Muthalib. 2010. Personal conversation with Yuen Beng Lee. Kuala Lumpur, Malaysia, 28 July.

Hassan, Muthalib. 2011. Email to Yuen Beng Lee, 7 September.

Hassan, Muthalib. 2012. Email to Yuen Beng Lee, 8 February.

Hassan, Muthalib. 2017. 'From Shadow Play to the Silver Screen: Early Malay(sian) Cinema'. In *Early Cinema in Asia*, edited by Nick Deocampo, 240–254. Indiana: Indiana University Press.

Hassan, Muthalib, and Tuck Cheong Wong. 2002. 'Malaysia: Gentle Winds of Change'. In *Being and Becoming: The Cinemas of Asia*, edited by A. Vasudev, L. Padgaonkar, and R. Doraisamy, 81–100. New Delhi: Macmillan.

Hatta, Azad Khan. 1997. *The Malay Cinema*. Bangi: Penerbit Universiti Kebangsaan Malaysia.

Hayward, Susan. 1993. *French National Cinema*. London: Routledge.

Hayward, Susan. 1996. *Key Concepts in Cinema Studies*. London: Routledge.

Hazlin, Hassan. 2011. 'KL Horror Films Spook Islamists'. *The Straits Times*, 2 October.

Hazri, Jamil, and Abd. Razak Nordin. 2010. 'Ethnicity and Education Policy in Malaysia: Managing and Mediating the Ethnic Diversity'. *Journal of US-China Public Administration* 7 (1): 77–87.

Hefner, Robert W. 2001. 'Introduction: Multiculturalism and Citizenship in Malaysia, Singapore and Indonesia'. In *The Politics of Multiculturalism: Pluralism and Citizenship in Malaysia, Singapore and Indonesia*, edited by R. W. Hefner, 1–58. Honolulu: University of Hawai'i Press.

Held, David. 2002. 'Culture and Political Community: National, Global and Cosmopolitanism'. In *Conceiving Cosmopolitanism: Theory, Context and Practice*, edited by S. Vertovec and R. Cohen. New York: Oxford University Press.

Held, David. 2005. 'Principles of Cosmopolitan Order'. In *The Political Philosophy of Cosmopolitanism*, edited by G. Brock and H. Brighouse, 48–58. Cambridge: Cambridge University Press.

Heng, Pek Koon. 1998. 'Chinese Responses to Malay Hegemony in Peninsular Malaysia (1957–1996)'. In *Cultural Contestations: Mediating Identities in a Changing Malaysian Society*, edited by I. Zawawi, 51–82. London: ASEAN Academic Press.

Higson, Andrew. 1989. 'The Concept of National Cinema'. *Screen* 30 (4): 36–46.

Higson, Andrew. 1995. *Waving the Flag: Constructing a National Cinema in Britain*. Oxford: Clarendon Press.

Higson, Andrew. 2000. 'The Limiting Imagination of National Cinema'. In *Cinema and Nation*, edited by M. Hjort and S. Mackenzie, 57–68. London and New York: Routledge.

Hill, John. 1986. *Sex, Class and Realism: British Cinema 1956–1963*. London: BFI Publishing.

Hilley, John. 2001. *Malaysia: Mahathirism, Hegemony and the New Opposition*. London: Zed.

Hillier, Jim. 2001. 'Introduction'. In *American Independent Cinema: A Sight and Sound Reader*, edited by J. Hillier, ix–xvii. London: British Film Institute.

Hillier, Jim. 2006. 'American Independent Cinemas Since the 1980s'. In *Contemporary American Cinema*, edited by L. R. Williams and M. Hammond, 247–264. Maidenhead, UK: Open University Press.

Hjort, Mette. 2009. 'On the Plurality of Cinematic Transnationalism'. In *World Cinemas, Transnational Perspectives*, edited by N. Ďurovičová and K. Newman, 12–33. New York: Routledge.

Hjort, Mette, and Scott MacKenzie, eds. 2000. *Cinema and Nation*. London: Routledge.

Ho, Khai Leong. 2006. 'Competition, (Ir)Relevance and Market Determinations: Government Economic Policies and Ethnic Chinese Responses in Malaysia'. In *Southeast Asia's Chinese Businesses in an Era of Globalization: Coping with the Rise of China*, edited by L. Suryadinata, 191–204. Singapore: Institute of Southeast Asian Studies.

Ho, Yuhang. 2009a. Facebook message to Yuen Beng Lee, 9 December.

Ho, Yuhang. 2009b. Facebook message to Yuen Beng Lee, 11 December.

Ho, Yuhang. 2009c. Facebook message to Yuen Beng Lee, 21 December.

Hollinger, David. 1995. *Postethnic America: Beyond Multiculturalism*. New York: Basic Books.

Hollinger, David. 1998. 'Postethnic America'. In *Beyond Pluralism: The Conception of Groups and Group Identities in America*, edited by W. F. Katkin, N. Landsman, and A. Tyree, 47–62. Urbana: University of Illinois Press.

Hollinger, David. 2008. 'Obama, Blackness, and Postethnic America'. *The Chronicle Review* (54): B7.

Hollinger, Karen. 1996. 'The Monster as Woman: Two Generations of Cat People'. In *The Dread of Difference: Gender and the Horror Film*, edited by B. K. Grant, 346–358. Austin: University of Texas Press.

Hollinsworth, David. 2006. *Race and Racism in Australia*. South Melbourne: Thomson/ Social Science Press.

Holmlund, Chris. 2005. 'Introduction: From the Margins to the Mainstream'. In *Contemporary American Independent Film: From the Margins to the Mainstream*, edited by C. Holmlund and J. Wyatt, 1–19. London: Routledge.

Honohan, Iseult. 2008. 'Metaphors of Solidarity'. In *Political Language and Metaphor: Interpreting and Changing the World*, edited by T. Carver and J. Pikalo, 69–82. New York: Routledge.

Hopper, Paul. 2007. *Understanding Cultural Globalization*. Cambridge: Polity.

Hunt, Leon. 2005. 'Ong-Bak: New Thai Cinema, Hong Kong and the Cult of the "Real"'. *New Cinemas: Journal of Contemporary Film* 3 (2): 69–84.

Hunt, Leon, and Wing-Fai Leung. 2008. 'Introduction'. In *East Asian Cinemas: Exploring Transnational Connections on Film*, edited by L. Hunt and W.-F. Leung, 1–13. London: I. B. Tauris.

Hussin, Mutalib. 2008. *Islam in Southeast Asia*. Singapore: ISEAS Publications.

Hutchings, Peter. 2008. *The A to Z of Horror Cinema*. Lanham, MD: Scarecrow Press.

Ibrahim, Ariff, and Chen Chuan Goh. 1998. *Multimedia Super Corridor*. Kuala Lumpur: Leeds.

Iordanova, Dina. 2009. 'The Film Festival Circuit'. In *Film Festival Yearbook 1: The Festival Circuit*, edited by D. Iordanova and R. Rhyne, 109–126. St Andrews, UK: St Andrews Film Studies.

References

Iraiputtiran. 2010. *The Height of Racism in Malaysia — Educational Discrimination*. Accessed 24 May 2010. http://www.hrp-my.org/2010/05/24/the-height-of-racism-in-malaysia-educational-discrimination/.

Iwabuchi, Koichi. 2002. *Recentering Globalization: Popular Culture and Japanese Transnationalism*. Durham, NC: Duke University Press.

Jacklyn, Victor. 2009. Personal conversation with Yuen Beng Lee. Melbourne, Australia, 7 October.

Jamil, Sulong. 1990. *Kaca Permata: Memoir Seorang Pengarah*. Kuala Lumpur: DBP.

Jancovich, Mark. 1992. *Horror*. London: Batsford.

Jancovich, Mark. 2002. 'General Introduction'. In *Horror, the Film Reader*, edited by M. Jancovich, 1–20. London: Routledge.

Jenkins, Gwynn. 2008. *Contested Space: Cultural Heritage and Identity Reconstructions; Conservation Strategies within a Developing Asian City*. Berlin: LIT.

Jenkins, Richard P. 2008. *Rethinking Ethnicity*. 2nd ed. Los Angeles: SAGE.

Jess-Cooke, Carolyn. 2009. *Film Sequels: Theory and Practice from Hollywood to Bollywood*. Edinburgh: Edinburgh University Press.

Johan, Jaaffar. 2002. 'Spinning in the Right Spirit'. *New Straits Times*, 5 February, 9.

Johan, Saravanamuttu. 2001. 'Malaysian Civil Society–Awakenings?' In *Risking Malaysia: Culture, Politics and Identity*, edited by M. Maznah and S. K. Wong, 93–111. Bangi: Universiti Kebangsaan Malaysia Press.

Jomo, K. S. 2004. 'The New Economic Policy and Interethnic Relations in Malaysia'. Paper read at UNRISD Programme on Identities, Conflict and Cohesion, at Geneva.

Jones, Gavin W., Heng Leng Chee, and Mohamad Maznah. 2009. 'Muslim-non-Muslim marriage, Rights and the State in Southeast Asia'. In *Muslim-non-Muslim Marriage: Political and Cultural Contestations in Southeast Asia*, edited by G. W. Jones, H. L. Chee, and M. Maznah, 1–32. Singapore: Institute of Southeast Asian Studies.

Joseph, Cynthia. 2006. '"It Is So Unfair Here . . . It Is So Biased": Negotiating the Politics of Ethnic Identification in Ways of Being Malaysian Schoolgirls'. *Asian Ethnicity* 7 (1): 53–73.

Joseph, Cynthia 2014. *Growing up Female in Multi-Ethnic Malaysia*. New York: Routledge.

Kahn, Joel S. 1995. *Culture, Multiculture, Postculture*. London: Sage.

Kahn, Joel S., ed. 1998. *Southeast Asian Identities: Culture and the Politics of Representation in Indonesia, Malaysia, Singapore and Thailand*. Singapore: Institute of Southeast Asian Studies.

Kahn, Joel S. 2001. *Modernity and Exclusion*. London: Sage.

Kahn, Joel S. 2006. *Other Malays: Nationalism and Cosmopolitanism in the Modern Malay World*. Singapore: Singapore University Press.

Kahn, Joel S., and Kok Wah Francis Loh, eds. 1992. *Fragmented Vision: Culture and Politics in Contemporary Malaysia*. Sydney: Asian Studies Association of Australia in Association with Allen & Unwin.

Kearney, Michael. 1995. 'The Local and the Global: The Anthropology of Globalization and Transnationalism'. *Annual Review of Anthropology* 24: 547–565.

Kementerian Dalam Negeri. 2010. *4 Major Aspects of Film's Contents*. Accessed 18 April 2010. http://www.moha.gov.my/eng/template04.asp?SectionID=9&SectionContentID=113.

Kementerian Dalam Negeri. 2010. *Garis Panduan Penapisan Filem*. Putrajaya: Bahagian Kawalan Filem and Penguatkuasaan.

Kendrick, James. 2010. 'A Return to the Graveyard: Notes on the Spiritual Horror Film'. In *American Horror Film: The Genre at the Turn of the Millennium*, edited by S. Hantke, 142–158. Jackson: University Press of Mississippi.

Kerr, Philip. 2002. 'How to Become an Armchair Polyglot'. *New Statesman*, 46.

Khoo, Boo Teik. 1995. *Paradoxes of Mahathirism: An Intellectual Biography of Mahathir Mohamad*. Kuala Lumpur: Oxford University Press.

Khoo, Boo Teik. 2002. 'Nationalism, Capitalism and Asian Values'. In *Democracy in Malaysia: Discourses and Practices*, edited by F. Loh Kok Wah and Khoo Boo Teik, 51–74. Richmond, Surrey: Curzon.

Khoo, Boo Teik. 2003. *Beyond Mahathir: Malaysian Politics and Its Discontents*. London: Zed.

Khoo, Gaik Cheng. 2003. 'Shuhaimi Baba and the Malaysian New Wave: Negotiating the Recuperation of Malay Custom (Adat)'. In *Women Filmmakers: Refocusing*, edited by Jacqueline Levitin, Judith Plessis and Valerie Raoul, 229–238. New York: Routledge.

Khoo, Gaik Cheng. 2004a. 'Malaysian Independent Filmmaking: Rust- Do -FOR# -Yourself'. *Aliran Monthly*, 19–22.

Khoo, Gaik Cheng. 2004b. 'The Malaysian Indies, or "Oh, really"?' *Aliran Monthly*, 22.

Khoo, Gaik Cheng. 2006. *Reclaiming Adat: Contemporary Malaysian Film and Literature*. Singapore: Singapore University Press.

Khoo, Gaik Cheng. 2007. 'Just-Do-It-(Yourself): Independent Filmmaking in Malaysia'. *Inter-Asia Cultural Studies* 8 (2): 227–247.

Khoo, Gaik Cheng. 2008. 'Urban Geography as Pretext: Sociocultural Landscapes of Kuala Lumpur in Independent Malaysian Films'. *Singapore Journal of Tropical Geography* 29: 34–54.

King, Claire Sisco. 2004. 'Imaging the Abject: The Ideological Use of the Dissolve'. In *Horror Film: Creating and Marketing Fear*, edited by S. Hantke, 21–34. Jackson: University Press of Mississippi.

King, Stephen. 1981. *Stephen King's Danse Macabre*. New York: Everest House.

Knappert, Jan. 1980. *Malay Myths and Legends*. Kuala Lumpur: Heinemann Educational Books.

Knee, Adam. 2009. 'The Pan-Asian Outlook of *The Eye*'. In *Horror to the Extreme: Changing Boundaries in Asian Cinema*, edited by Jinhee Choi and Mitsuyo Wada-Marciano, 69–84. Hong Kong: Hong Kong University Press.

Kntayya, Mariappan. 2002. 'Ethnicity, Malay Nationalism, and the Question of Bangsa Malaysia'. In *Ethnonational Identities*, edited by S. Fenton and S. May, 198–226. New York: Palgrave Macmillan.

Koay, Allan. 2001. 'French Honour for Malaysian Director'. *The Star*, 16 November 2001, 6.

Koay, Allan. 2005a. 'Famed Foe, the Pontianak'. *The Star*, 5 August, 4.

Koay, Allan. 2005b. 'Sepet Continues its Winning Run'. *The Star*, 2 November, 24.

Koay, Allan. 2005c. 'Tale of the Bloodsucker'. *The Star*, 5 August.

Koay, Allan. 2009a. 'Kelab Seni Filem Malaysia Opens Its Doors'. *The Star*, 19 January.

Koay, Allan. 2009b. 'Yasmin's Footprints'. *The Star*, 1 March, 2.

Koay, Allan. 2010. 'Creative Control'. *The Star*, 12 March, 6.

References 261

Koshy, Susan. 2005. 'The Postmodern Subaltern: Globalization Theory and the Subject of Ethnic, Area and Postcolonial Studies'. In *Minor Transnationalism*, edited by F. Lionnet and S.-m. Shih, 109–131. Durham, NC: Duke University Press.

Koven, Mikel J. 2008. *Film, Folklore, and Urban Legends*. Plymouth, UK: Scarecrow Press.

Krich, John. 2003. *Free Spirits of Asian Cinema: Malaysia Underground*. Accessed 14 March 2010. http://thebigdurian.tripod.com/media/feer.html.

Krich, John. 2009. 'Camcorder Capers in Malaysia'. *Time*, 16 November.

Kwan, Brian. 2009. *Close up . . . Brenda Danker & Namron*. Accessed 1 March 2010. http://www.timeoutkl.com/film/articles/Close-up-Brenda-Danker-Namron.

Latif, Baharudin A. 2001. 'A Brief History of Malaysian Film'. In *Films in South East Asia: Views from the Region*, edited by D. Hanan, 120–145. Hanoi: SEAPAVAAA.

Lau, Jenny Kwok Wah. 2003. 'Globalization and Youthful Subculture: The Chinese Sixth-Generation Films at the Dawn of the New Century'. In *Multiple Modernities: Cinemas and Popular Media in Transcultural East Asia*. edited by J. K. W. Lau, 13–27. Philadelphia, PA: Temple University Press.

Lau, Leslie. 2005. 'KL Film Industry: It's a Black and White Script'. *The Straits Times*, 11 January.

Lee, Hock Guan. 2005. 'Affirmative Action in Malaysia'. In *Southeast Asian Affairs*, edited by D. Singh and T. K. Liak, 211–228. Singapore: Institute of Southeast Asian Studies.

Lee, Hock Guan. 2006. 'Globalisation and Ethnic Integration in Malaysian Education'. In *Malaysia: Recent Trends and Challenges*, edited by S. H. Saw and K. Kesavapany, 230–259. Singapore: Institute of Southeast Asian Studies.

Lee, Hock Guan. 2009. 'Language, Education and Ethnic Relations'. In *Multiethnic Malaysia: Past, Present and Future*, edited by T. G. Lim, A. Gomes, and R. Azly, 207–229. Kuala Lumpur: Strategic Information and Research Development Centre.

Lee, James. 2011. Personal conversation with Yuen Beng Lee. Kuala Lumpur, Malaysia, 22 June.

Lee, Julian C. H. 2010. *Islamization and Activism in Malaysia*. Singapore: ISEAS Publications.

Lee, Yuen Beng. 2010a. '*Gadoh*: Negotiating the Politics of Ethnic Identification in Malaysian Schools'. In *5th Singapore Graduate Forum on Southeast Asian Studies*. National University of Singapore, Singapore.

Lee, Yuen Beng. 2010b. 'Transnational Malaysian Cinema: Problematizing the National'. Paper read at 5th International Conference on Interdisciplinary Social Sciences, 2–5 August, University of Cambridge, Cambridge.

Lee, Yuen Beng. 2010c. '*Gadoh*: Platform for Ethnic Negotiations'. Paper read at the IAFOR Inaugural Asian Conference on Media and Mass Communication 2010 (MediAsia 2010): Brave New World, 28–30 October, Osaka, Japan.

Lee, Yuen Beng. 2014. 'The Art of Eating in Malaysian Cinema: The Malaysian Sinophone Hunger for National Identity'. In *Transnational Chinese Cinema: Corporeality, Desire and the Ethics of Failure*, edited by B. Bergen-Aurand, M. Mazzilli and W. S. Hee, 181–200. Piscataway, NJ: Transaction Publishers.

Lee, Yuen Beng. 2015. 'Yasmin Ahmad: Autering a New Malaysian Cinematic Landscape'. *Wacana Seni Journal of Arts Discourse* 14: 87–109.

Lee, Yuen Beng. 2016. 'The Villainous Pontianak? Examining Gender, Culture and Power in Malaysian Horror Films'. *Pertanika Journal of Social Sciences & Humanities* 24 (4): 1431–1444.

Lee, Yuen Beng, and Sarata Balaya. 2016. 'From International Horror Films to the Local Filem Seram: Examining the Cinematic Identity and Roles of the Malaysian Pontianak.' *KEMANUSIAAN the Asian Journal of Humanities* 23 (Supp. 2): 161–174.

Lent, John A. 1990. *The Asian Film Industry*. Austin: University of Texas Press.

Leong, Pauline, and Siau Yen Yap. 2007. 'Malaysia.' *Media Asia* 34 (3/4): 156–170.

Lerner, Neil. 2010. 'Listening to Fear/Listening with Fear.' In *Music in the Horror Film: Listening to Fear*, edited by N. Lerner, viii–xi. New York: Routledge.

Levine, Michael. 2004. 'A Fun Night Out: Horror and Other Pleasures of Cinema.' In *Horror Film and Psychoanalysis: Freud's Worst Nightmare*, edited by S. J. Schneider, 35–54. Cambridge: Cambridge University Press.

Levy, Emanuel. 1999. *Cinema of Outsiders: The Rise of American Independent Film*. New York: New York University Press.

Lim, Bliss Cua. 2009. *Translating Time: Cinema, the Fantastic, and Temporal Critique*. Durham, NC: Duke University Press.

Lim, Catherine G. S. 2003. *Gateway to Peranakan Culture*. Singapore: Asiapac Books.

Lim, David C. L. 2008. 'Introduction.' In *Overcoming Passion for Race in Malaysia Cultural Studies*, edited by D. C. L. Lim, 1–12. Leiden: Brill.

Lim, Teck Ghee. 2009. 'Malaysia's Prospects: Rising to or in Denial of Challenges?' In *Multiethnic Malaysia: Past, Present and Future*, edited by T. G. Lim, A. Gomes, and R. Azly, 1–4. Petaling Jaya, Malaysia: SIRD.

Lin, Xiaoping. 2002. 'New Chinese Cinema of the "Sixth Generation": A Distant Cry of Forsaken Children.' *Third Text* 16 (3): 261–284.

Lincoln, Edward J. 2004. *East Asian Economic Regionalism*. New York: Council on Foreign Relations.

Lindenberg, Jolanda. 2009. 'Interethnic Marriages and Conversion to Islam in Kota Bahru.' In *Muslim-non-Muslim Marriage: Political and Cultural Contestations in Southeast Asia*, edited by G. W. Jones, H. L. Chee, and M. Maznah, 219–252. Singapore: Institute of Southeast Asian Studies.

Lionnet, Françoise, and Shu-mei Shih. 2005. 'Introduction: Thinking through the Minor, Transnationally.' In *Minor Transnationalism*, edited by F. Lionnet and S.-m. Shih, 1–27. Durham, NC: Duke University Press.

Lionnet, Françoise, and Shu-mei Shih. 2005. *Minor Transnationalism*. Durham, NC: Duke University Press.

Logeswary, Subramaniam. 2009. *Interview with Pete Teo*. Accessed 9 April 2010. http://entertainment.malaysia.msn.com/movies/features/article.aspx?cp-documentid=3733455&page=0.

Loh, Francis Kok Wah. 2002. 'Developmentalism and the Limits of Democratic Discourse.' In *Democracy in Malaysia: Discourses and Practices*, edited by F. Loh Kok Wah and Khoo Boo Teik, 19–50. Richmond, Surrey: Curzon.

Loh, Francis Kok Wah, and Boo Teik Khoo, eds. 2002. *Democracy in Malaysia: Discourses and Practices*. Richmond, Surrey: Curzon.

Looi, Elizabeth. 2011. 'Malay Horror Films? Bring Them On!' *The Straits Times*, 5 February.

Lu, Catherine. 2000. 'The One and Many Faces of Cosmopolitanism.' *Journal of Political Philosophy* 2: 244–267.

Lu, Sheldon Hsiao-peng. 1997. 'Historical Introduction: Chinese Cinemas (1896–1996) and Transnational Film Studies'. In *Transnational Chinese Cinemas: Identity, Nationhood, Gender*, edited by S. H.-p. Lu, 1–31. Honolulu: University of Hawai'i Press.

Lu, Sheldon Hsiao-peng. 2010. 'Emerging from Underground and the Periphery: Chinese Independent Cinema at the Turn of the Twenty-First Century'. In *Cinema at the Periphery*, edited by D. Iordanova, D. Martin-Jones, and B. E. Vidal, 104–118. Detroit, MI: Wayne State University Press.

Maberry, Jonathan, and David F. Kramer. 2009. *They Bite! Endless Cravings of Supernatural Predators*. New York: Kensington Publishing Corp.

Magistrale, Tony. 2005. *Abject Terrors: Surveying the Modern and Postmodern Horror Film*. New York: Peter Lang.

Mahathir, Mohamad. 1970. *The Malay Dilemma*. Singapore: Asia Pacific.

Mahathir, Mohamad. 1991. 'Malaysia: The Way Forward'. In *Malaysian Business Council*. Kuala Lumpur: Centre for Economic Research & Services, Malaysian Business Council.

Mahyuddin, Ahmad. 2008. 'Theorising the "Indies": The Market Place, Ideology and the New Malaysian Cinema'. *Jurnal Skrin Malaysia* 5 (1): 151–168.

Mahyuddin, Ahmad, and Lee Yuen Beng. 2015. 'Negotiating Class, Ethnicity and Modernity: The "Malaynisation" of P. Ramlee and his Films'. *Asian Journal of Communication* 25 (4): 408–421.

Manchel, Frank. 1990. *Film Study: An Analytical Bibliography*. London: Associated University Presses.

Mazur, Eric Michael, ed. 2011. *Encyclopaedia of Religion and Film*. Santa Barbara, CA: ABC-CLIO.

McAmis, Robert Day. 2002. *Malay Muslims: The History and Challenge of Resurgent Islam in Southeast Asia*. Cambridge: William B. Eerdmans Publishing Company.

McDaniel, Drew O. 1994. *Broadcasting in the Malay World: Radio, Television, and Video in Brunei, Indonesia, Malaysia, and Singapore*. Norwood, NJ: Ablex Publishing.

McKay, Benjamin. 2006. *The Last Communist: A Documentary about Chin Peng without Chin Peng*. Accessed 19 March 2010. http://www.criticine.com/review_article.php?id=19.

Meor, Shariman. 2010. 'Licence to Scare'. *New Straits Times*, 6 January.

Miller, Joshua L. 2003. 'The Transamerican Trail to Cerca del Cielo: John Sayles and the Aesthetics of Multilingual Cinema'. In *Bilingual Games: Some Literary Investigations*, edited by D. Sommer, 121–145. New York: Palgrave Macmillan.

Milne, R. S., and Diane K Mauzy. 1999. *Malaysian Politics Under Mahathir*. London: Routledge.

Mo, Chen, and Zhiwei Xiao. 2006. 'Chinese Underground Films: Critical View from China'. In *From Underground to Independent: Alternative Film Culture in Contemporary China*, edited by P. Pickowicz and Y. Zhang, 143–160. Lanham, MD: Rowman and Littlefield Publishers.

Mohd Arif Nizam, Abdullah. 2006. 'Fenomena Seni Belasah Yasmin Ahmad'. Accessed 14 August 2008. http://ww1.utusan.com.my/utusan/info.asp?y=2006&dt=046&pub=Utusan_Malaysia&sec=Hiburan&pg=hi_01.htm.

Montlake, Simon. 2008. Race Politics Hobbles Malaysia. *Far Eastern Economic Review*, 171(2), 36–39.

Montillo, Roseanne. 2009. *Halloween and Commemorations of the Dead*. New York: Chelsea House.

Morgan, Diane. 2010. *Essential Islam: A Comprehensive Guide to Belief and Practice*. Santa Barbara, CA: Praeger/ABC-CLIO.

Morris, Meaghan. 2004. 'Transnational Imagination in Action Cinema: Hong Kong and the Making of a Global Popular Culture'. *Inter-Asia Cultural Studies* 5 (2): 181–199.

Mumtaj, Begum. 2005. 'Sepet Scores Big'. *The Star*, 19 July, 16.

Munby, Jonathan. 1999. *Public Enemies, Public Heroes: Screening the Gangster from Little Caesar to Touch of Evil*. Chicago, IL: University of Chicago Press.

Mundorf, Norbert, and Joanne Mundorf. 2002. 'Gender Socialization of Horror'. In *Communication and Emotion: Essays in Honor of Dolf Zillmann*, edited by J. Bryant, D. Roskos-Ewoldsen, and J. Cantor, 155–179. Mahwah, NJ: Lawrence Erlbaum.

Mustaza, Masami. 2009. 'Umno Wing Gives Moviemakers the Creeps'. *The Malay Mail*, 15 October.

Naficy, Hamid. 2001. *An Accented Cinema: Exilic and Diasporic Filmmaking*. Princeton, NJ: Princeton University Press.

Nagarajan, S. 2009. 'Marginalisation and Ethnic Relations: The Indian Malaysian Experience'. In *Multiethnic Malaysia: Past, Present and Future*, edited by T. G. Lim, A. Gomes, and R. Azly, 369–390. Petaling Jaya: SIRD.

Nam Ron. 2009. Personal conversation with Yuen Beng Lee. Kuala Lumpur, Malaysia, 27 June.

Narayasamy, Balaraman. 2005. 'The Legislative System to Support Cinema: Instruments and Policies'. In *Seminar on Film Industries in Asia and Europe*, edited by L. Feilberg, 12–15. Singapore: Asia-Europe Foundation.

National Economic Advisory Council. 2010. *New Economic Model for Malaysia, Part 1: Strategic Policy Directions*. Putrajaya: National Economic Advisory Council.

Naughton, John. 2001. 'Contested Space: The Internet and Global Civil Society'. In *Global Civil Society*, edited by H. K. Anheier, M. Glasius, and M. Kaldor, 147–168. New York: Oxford University Press.

Neale, Steven. 1980. *Genre*. London: BFI.

Neale, Steven. 2003. 'Questions of Genre'. In *Film Genre Reader III*, edited by B. K. Grant, 160–184. Austin: University of Texas Press.

Nelson, Andrew Patrick. 2010. 'Traumatic Childhood Now Included: Todorov's Fantastic and the Uncanny Slasher Remake'. In *American Horror Film: The Genre at the Turn of the Millennium*, edited by S. Hantke, 103–118. Jackson: University Press of Mississippi.

Newman, John. 1997. 'Eating and Drinking as Sources of Metaphor in English'. *Cuadernos de Filologia Inglesa* 6 (2): 213–231.

Ng, Andrew Hock Soon. 2009. 'Death and the Maiden: The Pontianak as Excess in Malay Popular Culture'. In *Draculas, Vampires, and other Undead Forms: Essays on Gender, Race and Culture*, edited by J. E. Browning and C. J. K. Picart, 167–185. Lanham, MD: Scarecrow Press.

Nonini, M. Donald. 2002. 'Transnational Migrants, Globalization Processes and Regimes of Power and Knowledge'. *Critical Asian Studies* 34 (1): 3–17.

Noorsila, Abd Majid. 2011. 'Local Horror Movies Spark Controversy'. *The Daily Chili*, 14 October.

References 265

Ochoa, George. 2011. *Deformed and Destructive Beings: The Purpose of Horror Films.* Jefferson, NC: McFarland.

Ong, Aihwa. 1999. *Flexible Citizenship: The Cultural Logics of Transnationality.* Durham: Duke University Press.

Ong, Aihwa. 2006. *Neoliberalism as Exception: Mutations in Citizenship and Sovereignty.* Durham, NC': Duke University Press.

Ong, Kian Ming. 2008. *JPA Quota Revised.* Accessed 15 April 2010. http://educationmalaysia.blogspot.com/2008/06/jpa-quota-revised.html.

Ong, Sor Fern. 2004. Wayang New Wave. Malaysia's Film Industry Is on Fire, Fuelled by the Box-office Bonanza of Puteri Gunung Ledang and the Success of Indie Filmmakers'. *The Straits Times*, p. 3.

Ooi, Kee Beng. 2006. 'Bangsa Malaysia. Vision or Spin?' In *Malaysia: Recent Trends and Challenges*, edited by S. H. Saw and K. Kesavapany, 47–72. Singapore: Institute of Southeast Asian Studies.

O'Pray, Michael 2006. 'American Underground Cinema of the 1960s'. In *Contemporary American Cinema*, edited by L. R. Williams and M. Hammond, 62–72. Maidenhead, UK: Open University Press.

O'Riley, Michael F. 2007. 'Postcolonial Haunting. Anxiety, Affect, and the Situated Encounter'. *Postcolonial Text* 3 (4): 1–15.

Parry, Benita. 2004. *Postcolonial Studies: A Materialist Critique.* London: Routledge.

Penney, Sue. 1999. *Islam (Discovering Religions).* Oxford: Heinemann.

Pickowicz, Paul. 2006. 'Social and Political Dynamics of Underground Filmmaking in China'. In *From Underground to Independent: Alternative Film Culture in Contemporary China*, edited by P. Pickowicz and Y. Zhang, 1–21. Lanham, MD: Rowman and Littlefield Publishers.

Pickowicz, Paul, and Yingjin Zhang. 2006. 'Preface'. In *From Underground to Independent: Alternative Film Culture in Contemporary China*, edited by P. Pickowicz and Y. Zhang, vii–xii. Lanham, MD: Rowman and Littlefield Publishers.

Pinedo, Isabel Cristina. 2004. 'Postmodern Elements of the Contemporary Horror Film'. In *The Horror Film*, edited by S. Prince, 85–117. New Brunswick, NJ: Rutgers University Press.

Portes, Alejandro, Luis E. Guarnizo, and Patricia Landolt. 1999. 'The Study of Transnationalism: Pitfalls and Promise of an Emergent Research Field'. *Ethnic and Racial Studies* 22 (2): 217–237.

Pramaggiore, Maria, and Tom Wallis. 2005. *Film: A Critical Introduction.* London: Laurence King.

Prince, Stephen. 2004. 'Introduction: The Dark Genre and its Paradoxes'. In *The Horror Film*, edited by S. Prince, 1–11. New Brunswick, NJ: Rutgers University Press.

Radcliffe, Ann. 1826. 'On the Supernatural in Poetry'. *New Monthly Magazine*, 145–152.

Rafferty, Terrence. 2008. 'Screams in Asia Echo in Hollywood'. *New York Times*, 27 January.

Raju, Hossain Zakir. 2008. 'Filmic Imaginations of the Malaysian Chinese: "Mahua Cinema" as a Transnational Chinese Cinema'. *Journal of Chinese Cinemas* 2 (1): 67–79.

Ratanachaya, Kitti. 1996. *The Communist Party of Malaya, Malaysia and Thailand: Truce Talks Ending the Armed Struggle of the Communist Party.* Bangkok: Dungkaew.

Rawle, Steven. 2010. 'Video Killed the Movie: Cultural Translation in *Ringu* and *The Ring*'. In *The Scary Screen: Media Anxiety in* The Ring, edited by K. Lacefield. Farnham, Surrey: Ashgate.

Reid, Anthony, and Michael Gilsenan. 2007. *Islamic Legitimacy in a Plural Asia*. London: Routledge.

Rich, Ruby B. 2004. 'To Read or not to Read: Subtitles, Trailers, and Monolingualism'. In *MIT Press*, edited by A. Egoyan and I. Balfour, 97–114. Cambridge, MA: MIT Press.

Riddell, Peter G. 2005. 'Islamization, Civil Society and Religious Minorities in Malaysia'. In *Islam in Southeast Asia: Political, Social and Strategic Challenges for the 21st Century*, edited by K. S. Nathan and Mohammad Hashim Kamali, 162–190. Singapore: Institute of Southeast Asian Studies.

Robbins, Bruce. 1998. 'Actually Existing Cosmopolitanism'. In *Cosmopolitics: Thinking and Feeling Beyond the Nation*, edited by P. Cheah, 1–19. Minneapolis: University of Minnesota Press.

Rodowick, David Norman. 1988. *The Crisis of Political Modernism: Criticism and Pedagogy in Contemporary Film Theory*. Chicago: University of Illinois Press.

Rumford, Chris. 2007. 'Introduction: Cosmopolitanism and Europe'. In *Cosmopolitanism and Europe*, edited by C. Rumford, 1–19. Liverpool, UK: Liverpool University Press.

Russell, David J. 1998. 'Monster Roundup: Reintegrating the Horror Genre'. In *Refiguring American Film Genres: History and Theory*, edited by N. Browne, 233–254. Berkeley: University of California Press.

Ruzita, Alias. 2008. *An Interview with Aida Fitri Buyong*. Accessed 31 October 2008. http://www.sinemamalaysia.com.my/main/index.php?mod=article&id=345.

Saat, Norshahril. 2010. 'The State, Ulama and Religiosity: Rethinking Islamization of Contemporary Malaysia'. In *Secularization, Religion and the State*, edited by M. Haneda, 131–141. Tokyo: UTCP (The University of Tokyo Center for Philosophy).

Said, Edward W. 1978. *Orientalism: Western Concepts of the Orient*. New York: Pantheon Books.

Santhi, Ganesan. 2004. 'Local Pix Draw Kudos Abroad'. Accessed 31 August 2009. https://variety.com/2004/film/news/local-pix-draw-kudos-abroad-1117912053/.

Sarris, Andrew. 1968. *The American Cinema: Directors and Directions, 1929–1968*. New York: Dutton.

Sarris, Andrew. 2005. 'Auteur Theory and Film Evaluation'. In *The Philosophy of Film: Introductory Text and Readings*, edited by T. E. Wartenberg and A. Curran, 99–107. Malden, MA: Blackwell.

Saw, Swee-Hock, and K. Kesavapany. 2006. *Singapore-Malaysia Relations Under Abdullah Badawi*. Singapore: Institute of Southeast Asian Studies.

Schiller, Nina Glick, Linda Basch, and Cristina Szanton Blanc. 1995. 'From Immigrant to Transmigrant. Theorizing Transnation Migration'. *Anthropological Quarterly* 68 (1): 48–63.

Schneider, Steven Jay. 2004. 'Introduction: Psychoanalysis In/And/Of the Horror Film'. In *Horror Film and Psychoanalysis: Freud's Worst Nightmare*, edited by S. J. S. Schneider, 1–14. Cambridge: Cambridge University Press.

Schwartz, Vanessa R. 2007. *It's So French! Hollywood, Paris, and the Making of Cosmopolitan Film Culture*. Chicago, IL: University of Chicago Press.

Shamsul, Amri Baharuddin. 1995. 'Inventing Certainties: The Dakwah Persona in Malaysia'. In *The Pursuit of Certainty: Religious and Cultural Formulations*, edited by W. James, 112–133. London: Routledge.

Shamsul, Amri Baharuddin. 1996. 'Nations-of-intent in Malaysia'. In *Asian Forms of the Nation*, edited by S. Tønnesson and H. Antlöv, 323–347. Surrey, Richmond: Curzon.

Shamsul, Amri Baharuddin. 1997. 'The Economic Dimension of Malay Nationalism: The Socio-historical Roots of the New Economic Policy'. *The Developing Economies* 3 (September): 240–261.

Shamsul, Amri Baharuddin. 1998. 'Debating about Identity in Malaysia: A Discourse Analysis'. In *Cultural Contestations: Mediating Identities in a Changing Malaysian Society*, edited by I. Zawawi, 17–50. London: ASEAN Academic Press.

Shamsul, Amri Baharuddin. 2001. 'The Redefinition of Politics and the Transformation of Malaysian Pluralism'. In *The Politics of Multiculturalism: Pluralism and Citizenship in Malaysia, Singapore and Indonesia*, edited by R. W. Hefner, 204–226. Honolulu: University of Hawai'i Press.

Shamsul, Amri Baharuddin. 2005. 'Islam Embedded: "Moderate" Political Islam and Governance in the Malay World'. In *Islam in Southeast Asia: Political, Social and Strategic Challenges for the 21st Century*, edited by K. S. Nathan and Mohammad Hashim Kamali, 103–120. Singapore: Institute of Southeast Asian Studies.

Sharifah Aleysha, Syed Zainal Rashid. 2009. Personal conversation with Yuen Beng Lee. Melbourne, Australia, 7 October.

Sharifah Zaleha, Syed Hassan. 2002. 'Strategies for Public Participation: Women and Islamic Fundamentalism in Malaysia'. In *The Freedom to do God's Will: Religious Fundamentalism and Social Change*, edited by G. ter Haar and J. J. Busuttil, 49–74. London: Routledge.

Shih, Shu-mei. 2007. *Visuality and Identity: Sinophone Articulations across the Pacific*. Berkeley: University of California Press.

Sin Chew Daily. 2011. 独立电影赚不回本 • 大荒电影喊停业 [Da Huang Pictures closes citing failure to recuperate costs]. *Sin Chew Daily*, 10 August. Accessed 14 August 2011. https://www.sinchew.com.my/20110810/%E7%8B%AC%E7%AB%8B%E7%94%B5%E5%BD%B1%E8%B5%9A%E4%B8%8D%E5%9B%9E%E6%9C%AC%EF%BC%8E%E5%A4%A7%E8%8D%92%E7%94%B5%E5%BD%B1%E5%96%8A%E5%81%9C%E4%B8%9A/

Sipos, Thomas M. 2010. *Horror Film Aesthetics: Creating the Visual Language of Fear*. London: McFarland & Company.

Siti Suhada, Ahmad Fauzi. 2011. Personal conversation with Yuen Beng Lee. Kuala Lumpur, Malaysia, 22 June.

Sittamparam, R. 2004. 'Eye-opening "Sepet"'. *The New Straits Times*, 2 October.

Skal, David J. 1993. *The Monster Show: A Cultural History of Horror*. New York: Norton.

Skeat, Walter William. 1965. *Malay Magic: An Introduction to the Folklore and Popular Religion of the Malay Peninsular*. 2nd ed. West Germany: Frank Cass & Co.

Smith, Anthony D. 1991. *National Identity*. London: Penguin.

Solanas, Fernando, and Octavio Getino. 1976. 'Towards a Third Cinema'. In *Movies and Methods: An Anthology*, edited by B. Nichols, 44–64. Berkeley: University of California Press.

Sta Maria, Stephanie. 2010. *NEM a Fresh Gloss on Old Idea, Says Prof*. Accessed 20 May 2010. http://freemalaysiatoday.com/fmt-english/news/general/4010-nem-a-fresh-gloss-on-old-ideas-says-prof.

Stavropoulos, Peter, and Richard Phillips. 2000. *An Interview with Bernice Chauly—Malaysian Filmmaker*. Accessed 1 March 2010. http://www.wsws.org/articles/2000/may2000/sff9-m10.shtml.

Stephens, Chuck. 2011. *Fleurs de Malaysia*. Accessed 1 August 2011. http://www.sfbg.com/39/29/cover_filmfest_malaysia.html.

Subhadra, Devan. 2009. 'From Shorts to Cannes'. *New Straits Times*, 3 May, 22.

Surin, Jacqueline Ann. 2005. 'No Business Like Show Business'. *The Sun*, 1 April.

Syed, Husin Ali. 2008. *Ethnic Relations in Malaysia: Harmony and Conflict*. Selangor, Malaysia: SIRD.

Syed Hussein, Alatas. 1977. *The Myth of the Lazy Native: A Study of the Image of the Malays, Filipinos and Javanese from the 16th to the 20th Century and Its Function in the Ideology of Colonial Capitalism*. London: F. Cass.

Tamborini, Ronald C., and James B. Weaver III. 1996. 'Frightening Entertainment: A Historical Perspective of Fictional Horror'. In *Horror Films: Current Research on Audience Preferences and Reactions*, edited by R. C. Tamborini and J. B. Weaver III, 1–15. Mahwah, NJ: Lawrence Erlbaum Associates.

Tamura, Eileen H., Linda K. Menton, Noren W. Lush, Francis K. C. Tsui, and Warren Cohen. 1997. *China: Understanding Its Past. Vol. 1*. Honolulu: University of Hawai'i Press.

Tan, Lee Ooi. 2010. 'The Emergence of a Virtual Civil Society'. In *Building Bridges, Crossing Boundaries: Everyday Forms of Inter-ethnic Peace Building in Malaysia*, edited by F. K. W. Loh, 273–296. Jakarta: The Ford Foundation.

Teh, Yik Koon. 2008. 'Politics and Islam: Factors Determining Identity and the Status of Male-to-Female Transsexuals in Malaysia'. In *AsiaPacifiQueer: Rethinking Genders and Sexualities* edited by F. Martin, P. A. Jackson, M. McLelland, and A. Yue, 85–98. Urbana: University of Illinois Press.

Teusner, Paul. 2005. 'Resident Evil: Horror Film and the Construction of Religious Identity in Contemporary Media Culture'. *Colloquium* 37 (2): 169–180.

The National. 2009. 'The Taboo-Breaker of Malaysian Film'. Accessed 11 May 2010. https://www.thenationalnews.com/uae/the-taboo-breaker-of-malaysian-film-1.601557.

The Star. 2005. 'Self-Taught Filmmaker'. *The Star*, 13 March, 13.

The Star. 2009. 'Puteri Wants Ban on Horror, Fantasy Movies'. *The Star*, 15 October, 14.

The Straits Times. 1957. Advertisement column 1, 1 May, 4.

Thomas, Tommy. 2005. 'Is Malaysia an Islamic State?' Paper read at the *13th Biennial Malaysian Law Conference*, Kuala Lumpur, 18 November.

Thomson-Jones, Katherine. 2008. *Aesthetics and Film*. London: Continuum.

Tioseco, Alexis A. 2006. *Revolutions Happen Like Refrains in a Song*. Accessed 10 April 2010. http://www.criticine.com/feature_article.php?id=36.

Tudor, Andrew. 1989. *Monsters and Mad Scientists: A Cultural History of the Horror Movie*. Oxford: Basil Blackwell.

Tudor, Andrew. 1997. 'Why Horror? The Peculiar Pleasures of a Popular Genre'. *Cultural Studies* 11 (1): 443–463.

Tudor, Andrew. 2004. 'Excerpt from Why Horror? The New Pleasures of a Popular Genre'. In *Horror Film and Psychoanalysis: Freud's Worst Nightmare*, edited by S. J. Schneider, 55–67. Cambridge: Cambridge University Press.

References

Turvey, Malcolm. 2004. 'Philosophical Problems Concerning the Concept of Pleasure in Psychoanalytical Theories of (the Horror) Films'. In *Horror Film and Psychoanalysis: Freud's Worst Nightmare*, edited by S. J. Schneider, 68–83. Cambridge: Cambridge University Press.

Tzioumakis, Yannis. 2006. *American Independent Cinema: An Introduction*. Edinburgh, UK: Edinburgh University Press.

Utusan Malaysia. 2005. 'Pemuda UMNO Bantah Filemkan Aktiviti Chin Peng' [UMNO Youth objects to filming Chin Peng's activities]. *Utusan Malaysia*, 15 April, 27.

van der Heide, William. 2002. *Malaysia Cinema, Asian Film: Border Crossings and National Cultures*. Amsterdam: Amsterdam University Press.

van der Heide, William 2006. 'Malaysia: Melodramatic Drive, Rural Discord, Urban Heartaches'. In *Contemporary Asian Cinema: Popular Culture in a Global Frame*, edited by A. T. Ciecko, 83–95. Oxford: Berg.

van Hooft, Stan. 2009. *Cosmopolitanism: A Philosophy for Global Ethics*. Montreal, QC: McGill-Queen's University Press.

Varma, Devendra P. 1966. *The Gothic Flame: Being a History of the Gothic Novel in England: Its Origin, Efflorescence, Disintegration, and Residuary Influences*. New York: Russell & Russell.

Verma, Vidhu. 2004. *Malaysia. State and Civil Society in Transition*. Boulder, CO: Lynne Rienner.

Vertovec, Steven. 1999. 'Conceiving and Researching Transnationalism'. *Ethnic and Racial Studies* 22 (2): 1–25.

Vertovec, Steven, and Robin Cohen. 2002. 'Introduction: Conceiving Cosmopolitanism'. In *Conceiving Cosmopolitanism: Theory, Context and Practice*, edited by S. Vertovec and R. Cohen, 1–24. New York: Oxford University Press.

Watson, Paul. 1996. 'Critical Approaches to Hollywood Cinema: Authorship, Genre and Stars'. In *An Introduction to Film Studies*, edited by J. Nelmes, 129–183. London: Routledge.

Weightman, Barbara A. 2002. *Dragons and Tigers: A Geography of South, East, and Southeast Asia*. New York: John Wiley.

Weissberg, Jay. 2007. 'Mukhsin'. *Variety*. Accessed 11 May 2008. https://variety.com/2007/film/reviews/mukhsin-1200510385/.

Wells, Paul. 2000. *The Horror Genre: From Beezlebub to Blair Witch*. London: Wallflower.

Werner, Roland Werne. 1986. *Bomoh/Dukun. The Practices and Philosophies of the Traditional Malay Healer*. Berne: The Institute of Ethnology, University of Berne.

White, Patricia. 2000. 'Female Spectator, Lesbian Specter. The Haunting'. In *The Horror Reader*, edited by K. Gelder, 130–150. New York: Routledge.

White, Timothy R. 2005. 'Japan Meets Hollywood in the Films of P. Ramlee'. In *P. Ramlee di Cakera Nusantara*, edited by Awang Azman Awang Pawi and Khor Chooi Lian, 196–216. Kota Samarahan: Universiti Malaysia Sarawak.

White, Timothy R. 1996. *Historical Poetics, Malaysian Cinema and the Japanese Occupation*. Accessed 28 January 2009. http://www.kinema.uwaterloo.ca/article.php?id=292&feature.

Wierzbicka, Anna. 1999. *Emotions across Languages and Cultures: Diversity and Universals*. Cambridge: Cambridge University Press.

Willemen, Paul. 1989. 'The Third Cinema Question: Notes and Reflections'. In *Questions of Third Cinema*, edited by J. Pines and P. Willemen, 1–30. London: BFI Publishing.

Williamson, Thomas. 2002. 'Incorporating a Malaysian Nation'. *Cultural Anthropology* 17 (3): 401–430.

Willis, Andrew. 2004. 'From the Margins to the Mainstream: Trends in Recent Spanish Horror Cinema'. In *Spanish Popular Cinema*, edited by A. Lazaro-Reboll and A. Willis, 237–249. Manchester, UK: Manchester University Press.

Willis, Andrew. 2005. 'The Spanish Horror Film as Subversive Text: Eloy de la Iglesia's *La Semana del Asesino*'. In *Horror International*, edited by S. J. Schneider and T. Williams, 163–179. Detroit, MI: Wayne State University Press.

Winstead, Antoinette F. 2011. 'The Devil Made Me Do It! The Devil in 1960s–1970s Horror Film'. In *Vader, Voldemort and Other Villains: Essays on Evil in Popular Media*, edited by J. Heit, 28–45. Jefferson, NC: McFarland.

Wong, Kim Hoh. 2007. 'Chinese Boy, Malay Girl — It's All about Heart'. *The Straits Times*, 1 September.

Wong, Noel. 2020. 'Sarawakian Engineer Makes Film Directorial Debut with "One Day"'. Accessed 1 May 2021. https://www.freemalaysiatoday.com/category/leisure/2020/07/16/sarawakian-engineer-makes-film-directorial-debut-with-one-day/.

Wong, Tuck Cheong. 2010. Personal conversation with Yuen Beng Lee. Kuala Lumpur, Malaysia, 26 July.

Wood, Robin. 1979. 'An Introduction to the American Horror Film'. In *American Nightmare: Essays on the Horror Film*, edited by A. Britton, R. Lippe, T. Williams, and R. Wood, 7–28. Toronto, ON: Festival of Festivals.

Wood, Robin. 1985. 'An Introduction to the American Horror Film'. In *Movies and Methods*, edited by B. Nichols, 195–220. Berkeley: University of California Press.

Wood, Robin. 2004. 'Foreword: What Lies Beneath?'. In *Horror Film and Psychoanalysis: Freud's Worst Nightmare*, edited by S. J. Schneider, xiii–xviii. New York: Cambridge University Press.

Worland, Rick. 2007. *The Horror Film: An Introduction*. Malden, MA: Blackwell.

Xu, Gary G. 2007. *Sinascape: Contemporary Chinese Cinema*. Lanham, MD: Rowman & Littlefield.

Yasmin, Ahmad. 2004. *SEPET-Notes from the Writer/Director*. Accessed 20 January 2011. http://yasminthestoryteller.blogspot.com/2004_08_01_archive.html.

Yasmin, Ahmad. 2006. 'A Drop of Indigo Can Indeed Spoil the Milk'. Accessed 20 January 2011. https://www.nst.com.my/Current_News/nst/Saturday/Columns/20060513081426/Article/index_html.

Yasmin, Ahmad. 2009. Email to Yuen Beng Lee, 6 May.

Yau, Esther C. M., ed. 2001. *At Full Speed: Hong Kong Cinema in a Borderless World*. Minneapolis: University of Minnesota Press.

Ye, Lin-Sheng. 2003. *The Chinese Dilemma*. Kingsford, New South Wales: East-West Publishers.

Yeoh, Brenda, Karen P. Y. Lai, Michael W. Charney, and Chee Kiong Tong. 2003. 'Approaching Transnationalisms. Studies on Transnational Societies, Multicultural Contacts and Imaginings of Home'. In *Approaching Transnationalisms. Studies on Transnational*

References

Societies, Multicultural Contacts and Imaginings of Home, edited by B. S. Yeoh, K. P. Lai, M. W. Charney, and C. K. Tong, 1–12. Boston, MA: Kluwer Academic.

Yoshimoto, Mitsuhiro. 2006. 'National/International/Transnational: The Concept of Trans-Asian Cinema and the Cultural Politics of Film Criticism'. In *Theorising National Cinema*, edited by V. Vitali and P. Willemen, 254–261. London: British Film Institute.

Zaid, Ibrahim. 2008. *Malaysia — A Lost Democracy?* Accessed 14 August 2009. http://www.malaysianbar.org.my/speeches/datuk_zaid_ibrahim_malaysia_a_lost_democracy_.html.

Zakaria, Haji Ahmad, and Kadir Suzaina. 2005. 'Ethnic Conflict, Prevention and Management: The Malaysian Case'. In *Ethnic Conflicts in Southeast Asia*, edited by K. Snitwongse and W. S. Thompson, 42–64. Singapore: ISEAS.

Zawawi, Ibrahim, ed. 1998. *Cultural Contestations: Mediating Identities in a Changing Malaysia Society*. London: ASEAN Academic Press.

Zawawi, Ibrahim. 2003. 'The Search for a "New Cinema" in Post-colonial Malaysia: The Films of U-Wei bin HajiSaari as Counter-narrations of National Identity'. *Inter-Asia Cultural Studies* 4 (1): 145–154.

Zawawi, Ibrahim. 2004. 'Globalization and National Identity: Managing Ethnicity and Cultural Pluralism in Malaysia'. In *Growth and Governance in Asia*, edited by Y. Sato, 115–136. Honolulu, HI: Asia-Pacific Center for Security Studies.

Zawawi, Ibrahim. 2007. 'The Beginning of Neo-realist Imaginings in Malaysian Cinema: A Critical Appraisal of Malay Modernity and Representation of Malayness in Rahim Razali's Films'. *Asian Journal of Social Science* 35 (4): 511–527.

Zhang, Yingjin. 1997. 'From "Minority Film" to "Minority Discourse": Questions of Nationhood and Ethnicity in Chinese Cinema'. *Cinema Journal* 36 (3): 73–90.

Zhang, Zhen. 2007. 'Introduction: Bearing Witness; Chinese Urban Cinema in the Era of "Transformation" (Zhuanxing)'. In *The Urban Generation: Chinese Cinema and Society at the Turn of the Twenty-First Century*, edited by Z. Zhang, 1–45. Durham, NC: Duke University Press.

Index

13 May 1969, 38, 43, 76, 78, 103, 119, 171

15Malaysia, 58, 67

2046, 135

35 mm, 85, 91, 93, 140, 141

abject, 164, 168, 169

accented cinema, 103, 106, 107, 110, 111, 112, 130

Actor-Network Theory, 90

adat (customs and traditions), 50, 54, 175, 176

aesthetics, 1, 5, 7, 15, 18, 21, 24, 25, 65, 74, 90, 101, 109, 112, 115, 116, 137, 145, 146, 147, 148, 167, 177, 180, 190, 192

Ah Beng Returns, 134

Almódovar, Pedro, 137

Amir Muhammad, 18, 35, 36, 60, 61, 69, 71, 75, 78, 80, 83, 85, 86, 87, 88, 94, 96, 119, 120, 134, 138, 141, 176, 177, 191

Amok, 4, 55

Anwar Ibrahim, 13, 18, 36, 37, 38, 54, 80, 88

art-house, 56, 83, 89, 90, 97, 112, 115, 116, 135, 145, 146, 147, 148

Asian Cinematic Imagined Community, 183

A Tree in Tanjung Malim, 138

At the End of Daybreak, 25, 73, 86, 92, 138

Australia, 1, 4, 16, 18, 37, 63, 91, 94, 119, 127, 138

auteur, 42, 64, 66, 68, 97, 112, 116, 132, 133, 134, 140, 146, 155, 156, 157

Avellana, Lamberto V., 46

Back to the Future, 2

Bangsa Malaysia, 14, 30, 31, 32, 55, 100, 101, 121, 122, 191

bangsawan, 45, 46

Barbarian Invasion, 193, 194

Barisan Nasional (BN), 13, 38, 50

Bayer, Rolf, 46

Bazin, Andrè, 133

Beautiful Washing Machine, 18, 25, 90, 92, 112, 116, 135, 136

Before We Fall in Love Again, 87, 134, 135

Beijing Film Academy, 78

Ben Hur, 2

beyond multiculturalism, 1, 7, 8, 20, 21, 56, 75, 100, 101, 103, 104, 105, 107, 109, 111, 113–115, 117, 119, 121, 123, 125, 127, 129, 131, 133–135, 137, 139, 141, 143–145, 147, 149, 151, 153, 155, 157, 191, 197

Bollywood, 2, 4

borders, 22, 23, 25, 27, 28, 33, 36, 39, 40–43, 56, 57, 63, 82, 83, 86, 89, 90, 91, 100, 101, 103, 105, 106, 110, 111, 130, 140, 155, 169, 182, 189

Borneo, 6, 42, 88, 195

British, 27, 42, 44, 84, 105, 114, 120, 152

Bujang Lapok, 43

Bukak Api, 25, 74, 75, 110, 126, 127

Bumiputera, 27, 28, 30–32, 43, 50, 52, 53, 69, 82, 119, 121–123, 161, 174, 196

Bunohan (Return to Murder) 10, 193

Busan International Film Festival, 13, 18, 68, 87, 196

Index

Cahiers, 132, 133
camaraderie, 31, 73, 87, 96, 126
Cannes Film Festival, 55, 61–63, 68, 86, 89, 90
capitalism, 15, 24, 26, 27, 29, 39, 56, 60, 102, 163
Cathay-Keris, 1, 42, 46–48, 50, 52, 53, 55, 92, 171–173
censorship, 15, 16, 18, 27, 33–37, 39, 54, 68, 77, 83, 84, 91, 94, 95, 98, 108, 109, 112, 120, 126, 133, 136, 176, 180, 191
Ceritaku, Ceritamu (Your Story, My Story), 55
Chalanggai (Dancing Bells), 61, 74, 87, 120, 131, 132
Chan, Fruit, 16, 181
Chaplin, Charlie, 137
Chemman Chaalai (The Gravel Road), 17, 25, 74, 85, 120, 132
Chen, Kaige, 97
Chinese-ness, 72, 74, 78, 142, 144, 156
Chinese Sixth Generation Cinema, 16, 64, 65, 77, 89
Chiu, Keng Guan, 73, 193
cigarette, 2, 4, 117–118
cinematic community, 90, 155
cinematography, 145, 159, 162, 163, 177, 188
civil society, 27, 36–39, 41, 119, 191
class, 19, 22, 25–29, 32, 35, 38, 40, 45, 49–50, 55, 60, 71–72, 79–80, 91, 107, 109–110, 112, 114–115, 117, 119, 123, 129, 139, 142, 147, 151, 154, 164, 170, 191
colonial, 27, 44, 50, 174, 184
commercial mainstream cinema, 24, 60, 62, 81, 107, 146, 151
communication, 4, 9, 11, 33, 40, 41, 49, 53, 78, 79, 81, 87, 116, 122
community, 4, 22, 25, 27, 28, 32, 38, 40, 43, 50, 52, 56, 57, 69, 71–74, 76, 79, 81, 88, 90, 100–102, 104–106, 115, 120, 122, 124, 126, 131, 133, 138, 143, 144, 152–155, 170, 179, 183, 197
confrontation, 117, 168

contestation, 5, 25, 26, 33, 38, 40, 72, 100, 123, 129, 137, 139, 149, 152, 155, 156
co-production, 7, 14, 24, 25, 35, 53, 60, 74, 85, 86, 98, 108, 140, 193
cosmopolitan, 8, 15, 16, 20–22, 24, 26, 42, 56, 75, 79, 80, 82, 92, 100–113, 115–116, 119, 123, 125, 127, 129–132, 136, 139, 142, 149–151, 154–157, 177, 179, 182, 190–191, 193, 196–197
COVID-19, 12, 14
crisis, 13, 28, 36–37, 49
critical, 14–15, 18, 23, 25, 30, 35, 37–38, 46, 50, 54–55, 74–75, 77, 79, 82, 101–102, 110, 116, 121, 126, 138, 147, 155, 162, 164, 174, 190
criticism, 24, 35, 37, 43, 50–51, 63, 68, 72–73, 75–77, 88, 104, 112–114, 116, 119, 137, 149, 152, 157
Cultural Revolution, 78
culture, 15–16, 19, 21–22, 24, 26–27, 29–30, 34–35, 39–41, 43–44, 47–51, 58, 60, 65, 67–70, 72, 75–76, 80, 87–90, 94–95, 97, 100–109, 113, 119, 122–123, 139, 141–145, 149–153, 155, 157–159, 161–162, 164–165, 167, 169–170, 173, 175–176, 182–183, 191, 193

Da Huang Pictures, 18, 74, 94–98, 132, 134, 192–193
Dalam Botol (In a Bottle), 126, 127
Danker, Brenda, 84, 109, 119, 121, 202, 225
DAP, 13, 37, 38
Dari Jemapoh ke Manchestee (From Jemapoh ke Manchester), 89, 202
Days of Being Wild, 135
dialect, 7, 72, 73, 75, 88, 110, 113, 115, 135, 140, 144, 145, 152, 251
diaspora, 111
Digital Golden Era of Malaysian Cinema, 10, 14
divide-and-rule policy, 105, 120
Dogme 95, 59
Dukun (Shaman), 7, 175, 186
DV technology, 14, 15, 59, 61, 70, 97, 131
DVD, 64, 86, 90, 132, 192

274 Index

Elephant and the Sea, 17, 94, 123, 125, 131
Estella, Ramon, 46, 173
European cinema, 53, 65, 108
exhibition, 5, 7, 14–16, 18–22, 25, 33,
    41–42, 44, 46, 51–52, 56–58, 63–65,
    68–70, 77, 89–90, 92–97, 99, 106–107,
    109–112, 130–132, 134, 158, 182, 190,
    191, 193

female monstrosity, 161
Femina, 55
feminist, 55, 71, 255
Festival Filem Malaysia (Malaysia Film
    Festival), 71, 76, 142, 150, 159, 162,
    177
Fifth Generation, 77
Filem Seram (Horror Film), 20, 158, 170,
    173
Filipino directors, 46
Film Censorship Act 2002, 34
film festivals, 4, 7–8, 14, 16–18, 22, 24, 46,
    48, 55, 57–58, 61–64, 67–69, 71, 76–77,
    85, 87, 89–92, 94, 97–98, 107, 109, 112,
    127, 130–132, 134, 138, 148, 177, 195
FINAS, 18, 51–52, 59, 82, 84–85, 87–88, 93,
    95, 98, 109, 113, 133, 137, 141, 156,
    161, 177
Flower In the Pocket, 61, 81–82, 87, 113,
    125, 134
folklore, 162, 171
food, 124, 125, 129, 152, 170
Freedom Film Festival, 93, 122, 195, 196
French New Wave, 134
funding, 7, 14, 16, 20–22, 25, 44, 51, 56–57,
    61–65, 67, 69–70, 73, 85–86, 88–89, 94,
    98, 109–111, 130, 132, 134, 138, 141,
    158, 190, 193

Gadoh, 17, 81–82, 84, 91, 93, 95, 109, 121,
    122
general election, 13, 38
Geong Si (Chinese Hopping Vampire), 186
German Expressionism, 66
globalisation, 15, 19, 22, 40, 42–44, 57,
    60–61, 63, 79, 182, 190

global justice, 20–21, 100, 107, 112, 191
Golden Age of Malaysian Cinema, 10, 18,
    42, 48, 161, 171, 176
Golden Harvest, 5
Golden Screen Cinemas, 5, 93
Gubra (Anxiety), 76, 137, 139, 148, 150, 155

Hamzah Hussin, 42
Hantu (Ghost), 6, 127, 135, 159, 161,
    171–173, 176–179, 181, 183–184,
    186–188
Hantu Kak Limah (Ghost of Kak Limah),
    6, 159
Hassan Muthalib, 6, 18, 71, 151
Haunted Changi, 179, 184, 187
hegemony, 20, 37, 56, 60, 72, 83, 90, 101,
    108, 137, 139, 151
Histeria (Hysteria), 25, 96, 135, 177,
    187–189
history of Malaysian Cinema, 20, 39, 42
Ho, Ah Loke, 46
Ho, Yuhang, 60–61, 68–69, 71–74, 78, 82,
    85–87, 93, 109, 119, 124, 134, 138
Hollywood, 1, 4–5, 44, 46, 49, 63–66, 68,
    82, 107–109, 116, 166–167, 182–184,
    187–188, 196
Hong Kong, 2, 4–6, 16, 36, 49, 61, 73–74,
    86, 115, 131, 135, 144, 172, 174, 177,
    181, 184–185, 188, 193
hope, 13, 100–101, 129–130, 146, 155
horror, 6–7, 15, 17, 20–21, 25, 34, 93–94,
    96, 127, 135, 143, 158–159, 161–189,
    191–192, 196–197
Hubert Bals Fund, 67–68, 85–86, 131–132,
    134
Hui, Sam, 144
humanism, 20, 100–101, 106, 129, 139, 143,
    146, 155
Hussein Haniff, 55
hybridity, 37, 46, 54, 107, 114, 115, 145

Ice Kacang Puppy Love, 73, 88
identity, 15, 19–20, 22, 24, 26, 30, 32, 40, 43,
    47, 49, 51–52, 54, 56–57, 60, 70–71, 73,
    75–76, 79, 83, 90–91, 97, 102–105, 111,

Index

118–119, 121, 123, 133, 139, 149–150, 154–156, 173, 176, 191, 196–197

ideology, 5, 17, 19, 46, 70, 90, 101, 133, 169, 174

imagined community, 32, 104, 155, 183

independent cinema, 5, 14–16, 19, 24, 63–65, 67, 69, 78, 101, 135, 137, 177

Indonesia, 19, 37, 49, 50, 88–89, 136, 172, 174, 177, 182–183

instant noodles, 116–117, 124, 136

Internal Security Act (ISA), 25, 35

In the Mood for Love, 135

Ipoh, 7, 140, 195

Italian neo-realism, 24, 109, 115

Jagat, 8, 9, 193

Japanese schoolgirl, 189

J-Horror, 167, 181–182, 189

Jins Shamsuddin, 53, 199, 201, 202, 206, 211

Jogho (The Champion), 43, 133

Ju-On, 167, 182

Kaki Bakar (The Arsonist), 17, 55, 89, 133

Kampong/Kampung (Malay Village), 83–85, 90, 94, 120, 127–130, 161, 185

Kaneshiro, Takeshi, 36, 141, 143–144

Kawaii, 189

KeAdilan, 13, 37–38

Kelab Seni Filem (Malaysian Film Club), 18, 93–94, 195

Kerana Korona (Because of Corona), 12–13

Khoo, Eng Yow, 60, 72, 97, 115

Kitano, Takeshi, 137

Korea, 6, 18, 58, 63, 85–86, 90, 161, 182, 184, 188, 196

Krishnan, L., 45–46, 75–76

Kuala Lumpur, 6, 8, 18, 33, 37, 45, 50, 60, 77–79, 84, 87, 92–93, 96–97, 120, 126, 138, 149, 185, 195

Laila Majnun, 45

Langsuyar/Langsuir, 162

Lang Zi Xing Shen (浪子心聲), 144

Layar Lara (The Sad Screen), 55, 147

Lee, James, 18, 34, 58, 60–61, 69, 72–74, 79, 82, 85–87, 90, 93–94, 96, 98, 116–117, 124, 134–135, 176–178, 181, 191, 192

Lelaki Harapan Dunia (Men Who Save the World), 10–12, 193

Lembaga Penapisan Film (LPF)/Malaysian Film Censorship Board, 18, 34–36, 61, 70, 76, 82–84, 91–93, 95, 109–110, 125–126, 133, 138, 148–149, 153–154, 156, 176–177, 180, 185–186, 192

Liew, Seng Tat, 11–12, 35, 60–62, 81, 85–87, 96, 128–130, 132, 134, 138

Lips to Lips, 61, 69, 71, 75, 87, 96, 124, 134

Li Wo Qian Xiao (梨渦淺笑), 144

Loke, Wan Tho, 46

love, 1, 4, 7–8, 43, 45, 50, 59, 61, 72–73, 76, 79, 85, 87–88, 95, 100–101, 109–110, 116, 123, 125, 129, 134, 139, 141–142, 144, 146, 148–150, 153–156, 185–186, 193, 197

Love Conquers All, 61, 73, 85, 87, 110, 123, 134

Lynas, 127–128

Mahathir Mohamad, 13–14, 18, 30–33, 36–38, 88, 102, 113, 152, 174, 176, 196

Malaya, 42, 44–46, 48–49, 114

Malayan Union, 38

Malay cinema, 47, 49, 70, 72, 101, 257

Malay Film Productions (MFP), 42, 46, 48, 50, 53, 171–173

Malaysia, 1, 5–6, 8–21, 23–26, 30–39, 42, 44, 46, 48–52, 54–57, 60–65, 69–80, 82–93, 95–98, 100–102, 105, 108, 110, 112–115, 117–119, 121–122, 124–128, 131, 133, 135–136, 138, 140–146, 148–150, 152–156, 158–159, 161–163, 170–171, 174, 177–178, 181–182, 184, 191–193, 195–197

Malaysian Cinematic Imagined Community, 32

Malaysian Digital Indies (MDI), 1, 6, 14, 24–25, 27, 29, 31, 33, 35, 37, 39, 41, 43, 45, 47, 49, 51, 53, 55–59, 61, 63, 65, 67,

69, 71, 73, 75, 77, 79, 81, 83, 85, 87, 89, 91, 93, 95, 97, 99, 101, 158
Malaysian Gods, 18, 80, 120
Malaysian Horror Renaissance, 20, 158, 159
Manglish, 113, 114, 140, 142, 145
Mansor Puteh, 43, 53, 69, 209
marginalisation, 19, 28, 38, 43, 55, 103, 112, 119, 123, 126
Mat Kilau: Kebangkitan Pahlawan (Mat Kilau: The Rise of a Warrior), 6
Mekanik (Mechanic), 17, 75
Melbourne, 17, 119, 138
Menado, Maria 172
Menon, Deepak Kumaran, 33, 60, 61, 74, 85, 120, 131, 132
Merdeka, 44, 50–51, 78, 84, 108, 136, 173
Merdeka Studios, 50–51, 78, 173
Metrowealth Films, 95
metteurs-en-scène, 133
MHZ Film, 26, 140–141, 156–157
Min, 17, 74, 138
minimalist, 66, 80, 116, 118, 146
minority, 41, 83, 175
mise-en-scène, 5, 116, 118, 145–146, 188
modernisation, 19, 22, 29–31, 43, 54–55, 64, 80, 102, 184–185, 191
Monday Morning Glory, 62, 96, 110
monster, 20, 158, 161, 168–173, 187, 189
Movement Control Order (MCO), 12–13
Mr. Vampire, 168
Muallaf (The Convert), 86, 137–138, 143, 148
Mukhsin, 87, 137–139, 148, 150–151, 155, 193
multiculturalism, 1, 7–8, 15, 20–21, 26, 30, 56, 72, 75, 82, 100–101, 103–105, 107, 109, 111, 113–115, 117, 119, 121, 123, 125, 127, 129, 131, 133–135, 137, 139, 141, 143–145, 147, 149, 151, 153, 155, 157, 191, 197
multiethnic, 1, 170, 251, 261, 261, 264
Multimedia Super Corridor (MSC), The, 27, 32–33, 37, 39, 191
Munafik (Hyporcite), 6
mythologies, 169, 170, 183

Najib Razak, 29, 30, 38, 88
Namewee, 73, 88
Nam Ron, 18, 84–85, 109, 121, 134, 191
Nang Nak, 182
Nasi Lemak 2.0, 73, 88, 93
national cinema, 22–23, 39, 54, 56–57, 60, 62–63
National Culture Policy (NCP), 27, 191
National Development Policy (NDP), 27, 191
national identity, 15, 20, 22, 26, 30, 32, 47, 49, 51–52, 54, 56–57, 60, 70, 73, 75–76, 79, 83, 97, 119, 150, 173, 191, 197
nationalism, 15, 31–32, 36, 38–40, 50, 54, 60, 79, 114
nation-building, 15, 29–32, 41–43, 51–52, 78–79, 100–101, 119, 124
nationless, 123
negotiation, 40, 65, 119, 144–145
New Economic Policy (NEP), 27, 191
New Wave, 16, 27, 43, 53–56, 64, 66, 68–70, 74, 77, 134, 168, 176, 191
non-Bumiputera, 30, 32, 52, 82, 119
Nusantara, 183

Ola Bola, 8, 193
One Two Jaga, 193
Orang Asal, 179, 196
Orang Minyak (Oily Man), 129, 173
Osman Ali, 69, 74, 93, 126
Other, The, 20, 169
Othman Hafsham, 53, 126, 206, 208, 210, 229, 230, 244
ownership, 22, 27, 33, 46, 50, 51, 52, 190
Ozu, Yasujiro, 137

Pakatan Harapan (PH), 13
pan-Asian, 21, 177, 180–182, 184, 186–189, 192
PAS, 13, 37, 38, 54, 175
Penang, 17, 84, 159, 195
Penarik Becha (Trishaw Puller), 48
Peranakan, 143
Perempuan, Isteri dan . . . ? (Woman, Wife and Whore), 54–55, 133, 153, 162, 176

Index 277

periphery, 5, 62, 64, 124, 192
Petaling Street Warriors, 93, 135
Pinewood-Iskandar Studios, 10
piracy, 27, 33, 36, 191
pluralism, 103–105
political economy, 5, 14–15, 18–19, 25, 27–31, 39, 58, 63, 73–74, 101–102, 184, 190
polylingualism, 112, 142
pontianak, 1, 17, 59, 89, 91, 135, 147, 159, 161–163, 171–174, 177, 181–182, 185–187
Pontianak Harum Sundal Malam (Pontianak Scent of the Tuber Rose), 89, 147, 161–162, 181–182
postcolonial, 15, 23, 48, 57, 153, 159, 183–184
postethnic cosmopolitan cinema, 16, 20, 75, 100–101, 103–104, 106–113, 115, 119, 130, 132, 142, 154, 177, 190, 197
post-2000 Malaysian cinema, 1, 7, 12, 14, 17, 22–23, 25, 56–57, 59, 102, 133–134, 161, 190
P. Ramlee, 1, 4, 8, 42, 45, 47–48, 75, 138, 153, 176
Prebet Sapu (Hail, Driver!), 10
Primeworks Studios, 177
Puteri Gunung Ledang (Princess of Mount Ledang), 71, 89, 150

Rabun (My Failing Eyesight), 82, 137–140, 143, 153, 155
race and ethnicity, 8, 15, 19–22, 25–26, 31–32, 56–57, 60, 71, 75, 77, 79–80, 82–93, 100–102, 107, 119, 128–130, 134, 178, 184, 191–193, 196–197
Rahim Razali, 43, 53, 55, 147
Rain Dogs, 61, 73, 86, 123, 138
Rajhans, B. S., 45, 46
Rao, B. N., 46, 172
Ray, Satyajit, 48, 137
Reformasi, 36–38, 55, 80–81, 119, 120
research, 16–17, 21–22, 33, 67, 85, 89, 98, 108, 159, 193
resistance, 21, 41, 61, 65, 67, 74, 91, 95, 117, 130, 138, 150, 177, 192

Rex cinema, 3
Ringu, 167, 181–183
Roh (Soul), 10, 172, 191, 193
Room To Let, 61, 79, 124, 135–136
Rotterdam International Film Festival, 67, 131

Saadiah, 55
Sabah, 7, 13, 21, 27, 42, 88, 196
sanctuary, 74, 82, 85–87, 111, 123–124, 134, 153
Sarawak, 6, 7, 13, 21, 27, 42, 55, 88, 196
schoolgirl, 187–189
screen, 2, 5, 34–35, 44, 55, 76, 80, 93, 110, 115, 119, 138, 146–147, 150, 164, 195
Sedition Act, 35, 70, 88
Selamat Tinggal Kekasihku (Farewell My Lover), 45, 75, 76, 149
Sell Out!, 114
Sepet (Chinese Eyes), 1, 25–26, 36, 61, 71, 72, 76, 85, 92, 103–104, 122, 136–137, 139, 141–157
Seremban, 3
Sergeant Hassan, 46
Seru (The Calling), 161, 177, 179, 180, 185–187, 189, 191
Shanjey Kumar Perumal, 9–10
Shaw, Astro, 7, 12, 73, 195
Shaw Brothers, 1, 42, 45–46, 50, 52, 69, 171
Sheong Hoi Tan (上海灘), 144
Sheraton Move, 13
Shuhaimi Baba, 43, 55, 75, 89, 114, 133, 146–148, 161–162, 176, 182
Silat, 6, 63
Singapore, 5, 16, 18, 36, 42, 44–46, 49–50, 59, 63, 73, 83, 86, 89, 92–94, 96, 113, 127, 135–136, 140–141, 148, 163, 170–172, 174, 177, 179, 182–184, 187, 193, 196
Sini Ada Hantu (Here Got Ghost), 135, 177–179, 181, 184, 186–187
Sinophone, 74, 98
Siput Sarawak, 55
S'kali (Altogether), 25, 122, 135

Skim Wajib Tayang (Compulsory Screening Scheme), 51, 93
song and dance, 45, 47, 114
SOSMA, 25
Soviet montage, 66
Spinning Gasing, 25, 75–75, 91–92, 113, 120, 124, 126–127, 132
S. Roomai Noor, 48
Sundance Film Festival, 61
surrealism, 66
Survival Guide Untuk Kampong Radioaktif, 127, 129
Susuk, 25, 96, 138, 186–187
Syamsul Yusof, 186

Tagore, Rabindranath, 143–144
Talentime, 137–138, 143, 149, 193
Tan, Chui Mui, 33, 60–61, 72–73, 85–87, 94, 96, 98, 109, 129, 134, 138, 193
Tanjung Golden Village (TGV), 5, 90, 161
Tayangan Unggul, 95, 177
Teck, Tan, 75, 91, 113, 119
Teo, Pete, 58, 67, 88
terror, 89, 165–166, 170
Thailand, 16, 36–37, 84, 135, 174, 182, 185, 188
The Big Durian, 61, 80, 87, 92–93, 120, 132, 134
The Bird House, 93, 96, 110
The Blair Witch Project, 17, 59, 167, 179
The Eye, 184, 187
The Journey, 8, 193
theory, 16, 49, 90, 107
The Pirate and the Emperor's Ship, 93, 115
The Sound of Music, 2
The Terminator, 2
The Year of Living Vicariously, 85
Things We Do When We Fall in Love, 87, 134
Third Cinema, 66, 103, 106–109, 130
Third World cinema, 108
Three . . . Extremes, 181
Tokyo International Film Festival, 61, 71, 92, 96, 131, 134, 148
Tokyo Magic Hour, 85, 134
Tolong! Awek Aku Pontianak, 135, 177, 185–187

transnational cinema, 15, 19–20, 22–23, 26, 42, 44, 46, 56–59, 61, 63, 65, 67, 69, 71, 73, 75, 77, 79, 81, 83, 85, 87, 89, 91–93, 95, 97, 99–100, 190
transnationalism, 24–26, 39–42, 44, 50, 56, 62
Truffaut, François, 133
Tsai, Ming-Liang, 74, 79, 86, 97, 134–136, 145, 196
Two Sisters, 135, 188, 192

UMNO, 13, 28, 38, 50, 53, 83, 175
underprivileged, 107, 124
universalism, 15, 20–21, 100, 107, 191
U-Wei Haji Saari, 55

vampire, 162, 181, 185–186, 189
VCD, 6, 36, 141, 150
verisimilitude, 116
VHS, 2, 36
Vision 2020 (Wawasan 2020), 14, 27, 30–32, 39, 191, 196
Visit: Hungry Ghost Anthology, 6, 93, 96, 135, 176

Waiting for Love, 87, 135
wayang pacak, 1
Woman on Fire Looks for Water, 25, 62
Wong, Kar-Wai, 97, 134–135
Wong, Tuck Cheong, 87, 94, 138
Woo, Ming Jin, 17, 61, 94, 96–97, 119, 129, 131, 160, 176, 179, 191, 193–194
world cinema, 107–108, 112, 130, 132

XX Ray, 55

Yasmin Ahmad, 1, 4, 7–8, 17, 36, 55, 60–61, 69, 73, 76, 82–83, 85–86, 94, 134, 136, 140–144, 146, 148–151, 157
Year Without a Summer, 85
Yip, Francis, 144, 152
Yusof Haslam, 146–147

zombie, 161, 185, 195
Zombie Kampung Pisang, 161

CPSIA information can be obtained
at www.ICGtesting.com
Printed in the USA
JSHW032248181022
31781JS00001B/4